FRONTIERS OF FEMINISM

FRONTIERS OF FEMINISM

Movements and Influences in Québec and Italy, 1960–80

Jacinthe Michaud

UBCPress · Vancouver · Toronto

30 29 28 27 26 25 24 23 22 21   5 4 3 2 1

Printed in Canada on FSC-certified ancient-forest-free paper (100% post-consumer recycled) that is processed chlorine- and acid-free.

Library and Archives Canada Cataloguing in Publication

Title: Frontiers of feminism : movements and influences in Québec and Italy, 1960–80 / Jacinthe Michaud.
Names: Michaud, Jacinthe, author.
Description: Includes bibliographical references and index.
Identifiers: Canadiana (print) 20210117524 | Canadiana (ebook) 20210117834 | ISBN 9780774865265 (hardcover) | ISBN 9780774865272 (softcover) | ISBN 9780774865289 (PDF) | ISBN 9780774865296 (EPUB)
Subjects: LCSH: Feminism – Québec (Province) – History – 20th century. | LCSH: Feminism – Italy – History – 20th century. | LCSH: Feminists – Québec (Province) – History – 20th century. | LCSH: Feminists – Italy – History – 20th century. | LCSH: Women – Québec (Province) – Social conditions – 20th century. | LCSH: Women – Italy – Social conditions – 20th century.
Classification: LCC HQ1154 .M53 2021 | DDC 305.4209/046—dc23

Canada

UBC Press gratefully acknowledges the financial support for our publishing program of the Government of Canada (through the Canada Book Fund), the Canada Council for the Arts, and the British Columbia Arts Council.

This book has been published with the help of a grant from the Canadian Federation for the Humanities and Social Sciences, through the Awards to Scholarly Publications Program, using funds provided by the Social Sciences and Humanities Research Council of Canada.

Printed and bound in Canada by Friesens
Set in Futura and Warnock by Apex CoVantage, LLC
Copy editor: Joanne Richardson
Proofreader: Helen Godolphin
Indexer: Margaret de Boer
Cover designer: Will Brown
Cover image: Taken by the author during Pope John Paul II's visit to Québec City in 1984.

UBC Press
The University of British Columbia
2029 West Mall
Vancouver, BC V6T 1Z2
www.ubcpress.ca

To all non-professional and self-made feminist journalists and media activists around the world

Contents

Preface and Acknowledgments

During the first phase of my research, I met and interviewed several feminist activists who built the women's health centres movement as well as other networks of women's service groups in Québec City, Montréal, and many other regions outside urban centres. Though the Regroupement des centres de santé des femmes du Québec has ceased to exist, some women's health centres continue to offer a range of services on health issues, including abortion services. Many feminists I met during field research offered me a place to stay and food to share. To them, I would like to reiterate my gratitude. Today, most of these feminists have shifted their careers in order to face other challenges, just as I am moving on with my research to explore new dimensions of feminism as a political movement.

In Québec City, where I was a feminist activist before my doctoral years in Toronto, I became an active member of the socialist feminist journal *Marie-Géographie*. Parts of this book rely on moments from exchanges and debates that occurred among members of the collective when the journal's political activism interacted with the leftist politics in the city. I am deeply indebted to Andrée Bérubé, Lorraine Bérubé, Emilia Castro, Claire Deschênes, Denise Genest, Sylvie Jobin, Marie-Thérèse Lacourse, Georgette Lebel, Marie Leclerc, Nicole McClure, and many other feminist contributors who helped to create and produce a small journal with scarce resources. We were not professionals, but we believed in feminist journalism as a space for debates and strategies, a space to refine ideas and to disseminate feminist analyses that matter for the political life of the movement. To all self-made feminist journalists unknown to me – those who created alternative and progressive periodicals as well as those who acted inside and outside the official media sphere – I express my deepest acknowledgment: these media activists acted – and continue to act – during a period when having a voice and feminist communication tools mattered. For those who are acting in the present moment, I sincerely hope you will leave valuable archives containing traces of your activist lives for feminist researchers. The reading of feminist periodicals, even those that were short-lived, was particularly important for this research and composed one of the most important primary sources for this book. A particular thanks to Lyne Kurtzman, who lent me her precious collection of *Pluri-elles/Des luttes et des rires*, a Montréal feminist journal whose complete collection has not been re-edited to this day – unlike *Québécoises deboutte!* and *Les têtes de Pioche*, which have been published by Les éditions du remue-ménage. *Pluri-elles/Des luttes et des rires* has been very helpful in reconstituting part of the genealogy of women's groups in Montréal.

During the course of researching and writing this book, many people asked me why I had chosen Italian feminism for comparison rather than French feminism, which would have made sense in terms of similarity of language. The answer is that the angle of vision from which I wanted to reassess my knowledge of the Québec feminist/women's movement required a certain shift. Québécois and Italian feminisms are subaltern feminisms, shaped by their respective, essentially leftist, political trends and actors (which were themselves deeply transformed by feminism) and by two dominant feminist movements in the Western world, namely, French feminism and American feminism, both of which, to varying degrees, needed to be put under the microscope. In choosing Italy, I wanted to contrast its discourses and practices with a movement evolving along the same scale of importance, knowing perfectly well that, despite many similarities, Québec and Italian feminisms have many differences. For instance, the Italian population is much bigger than Québec's; the number of groups – feminist/women's collectives; leftist groups; progressive, alternative, and political journals; and so forth – are far more numerous on the other side of the Atlantic. The present research reflects this difference of size and volume.

I began learning Italian and travelled the Italian peninsula, from north to south, meeting feminists who had witnessed major political events and had something to say about them. I visited feminist/women's archives and met Italian feminists who generously gave me precious testimonies and a lot of valuable documents, some of which cannot be found in institutional archives and libraries, not even feminist ones. As happened with my previous research on the women's health centres movement, many of these feminists offered me a place to stay and food to share. This book is dedicated to these women and to members of feminist collectives whose genealogy I attempted to retrace. Special thanks go to Paola Melchiori, who was the first to open her personal archives and her address book. She paved the way to fruitful feminist encounters. She also agreed to do a careful reading of the first version of the manuscript and to help me to understand the complexity of Italian feminist politics. Through her, I met Lea Melandri, an author of many books on Italian feminism, and Anita Sonego, who was the president of the Libera Università delle donne at the time. Like Paola in Treviso, Anita generously offered me a place to stay in Milan. I would also like to thank Francesca Dall'Acqua, who gave me precious contacts in Naples. Many of these contacts led me to others in the Italian South – namely, in Palermo and in Sciacca, a small town in the south of Sicily. Eleonora Cirant, a librarian and feminist activist at the Unione femminile nazionale, demonstrated enormous patience and generosity during my two lengthy visits in Milan. I would also like to thank the Fondazione Elvira Badaracco in Milan, the members of Archivio femminista de la Casa delle donne in Rome, the Centro donna in Naples, and the Associazione nazionale Unione donne Italiane in Palermo, whose members agree to be interviewed twice during my stay in Aspra, in the vicinity of Palermo.

As a member of the Feminist Political Economy Collective (York University) I had the opportunity to present the preliminary findings of what is now becoming a book. Over the many years of my research, I had lengthy exchanges with some the collective's members, like Ann Porter and Wendy McKeen: friendship was deeply embedded in these exchanges and I would like to thank them for all the dinners, including Christmas Eves, trips abroad while attending conferences, and many other leisurely times. I cannot thank Meg Luxton enough for her constant words of encouragement and a careful reading of the manuscript. Her comments were very valuable in improving my analysis of feminism as a political movement.

My research also benefited from the work of very enthusiastic graduate assistants, with whom I enjoyed discussing their findings. During this time Sanjukta Banerjee was doing her master's in translation studies at Glendon (York), conducting extensive research on everything that has been published on Italian feminism, in both French and English and, if possible, Italian as well. There were also graduate students in the Master's in Public and International affairs program at Glendon – namely, the late Marie-Laure Baraud, with whom I had many lively exchanges concerning our respective knowledge of the Italian South; Saido Dialo, who thoroughly researched Québécois leftist and countercultural journals; and Jessica Brousseau, Kevin Ladouceur, and Karina Pogosyan, all of whom participated in their respective capacities.

English is my second language, and I would have never dared to send segments of this book for review or even to attend conferences without carefully revising various aspects of my research. For revising the entire manuscript twice, for her precious advice, and for helping me to present the manuscript in book form, Jane Springer has been the most careful and diligent reader I have had in all my years of English writing and publishing in academia. I also thank Caroline Kunzle for the final touches, as well as Cate Bester, one of the most enthusiastic undergraduate students I have had the pleasure to teach. Finally, Jennifer Sypo-Smith should be thanked for the early fragmented versions of chapters and conference papers, as should Elena Basile, who edited the first version of the introduction. Clara Chapdeleine-Feliciati occasionally helped with the translation of Italian quotes.

Over the years in which I conducted this research, I shared with the MA graduate students in my Feminist Theory course a few classic Italian texts on the theory of sexual difference as well as texts on Québécois feminism as it came into contact with post/anti-colonial theories. These readings often sparked interesting debates when contrasted with classical North American feminist approaches to similar issues. It is in such encounters that comparative approaches show their potential for shedding new light on important, often taken-for-granted, theoretical paradigms. I must thank these graduate students and many undergraduates for asking me questions about my research and suggesting new ways of looking at feminism. These interactions left me encouraged about the interest such research is generating in feminism as a political and social movement.

At UBC Press, I owe a special thanks to Darcy Cullen (assistant director, acquisitions) who enthusiastically supported the project from the moment I submitted it to the press to its final stage. I would also like to thank Nadine Pedersen (editor) and Ann Macklem (production editor), who followed the manuscript, step by step, to its publication, and Joanne Richardson (copy editor).

I must also thank Glendon College (my home faculty) and York University for their financial support, research grants, and other types of research support. Even though this support never entirely funded the cost of living abroad, it was essential in covering reading materials, transportation, and the cost of shipping books and documents through the Italian postal service and communicating with people in numerous ways.

I would like to thank friends in my life with whom, in addition to constantly exchanging ideas, I have shared numerous moments of pleasure and many dinners: Elisabeth Abergel, Guillaume Bernardi, Lyse Hebert, Randy Hesp, Franck Jovanovich, Suzanne Langlois, Stephen Lisinski, Marcel Martel, Jean-Michel Montsion, Roberto Perin (who, through his love of Italy, also helped with the translation of Italian quotes), and Richard Van Delft. Finally, my thanks to all members of my family for the efforts they make every year to spend time together and to stay connected, and, most of all, to my daughter Joëlle, whose perseverance in pursuing scholarly research and whose intellectual vivacity gives me strength, support, and comfort.

Abbreviations

AIED	Associazione Italiana per l'educazione demografica
AO	Avanguardia Operaia
AFÉAS	Association féminine d'éducation et d'action sociale
BR	Brigate Rosse
CCCS	Centre of Contemporary Cultural Studies
CEGEP	Collèges d'enseignement général et professionnel
CdF	Centre des femmes
CISA	Centro Italiano sterilizzazione e aborto
CRAC	Comitato romano per la liberazione dell'aborto
CSF	Conseil du Statut de la femme
CLSC	Centre Local de Services Communautaires
DEMAU	Demistificazione autoritarismo patriarcale
DC	Democrazia Cristiana
FFQ	Fédération des femmes du Québec
FLFQ	Front de libération des femmes du Québec
FLQ	Front de libération du Québec
IFC	International Feminist Collective
LC	Lotta Continua
LCMLC	Ligue communiste marxiste-léniniste du Canada
LF	Lotta Femminista
LOR	Ligue ouvrière révolutionnaire
LVR	*La vie en rose*

MLD	Movimento di liberazione delle donne
MSSS	Ministère de la santé et des services sociaux
PCI	Partito Comunista Italiano
PCO	Parti communiste ouvrier
PdUP	Partito di Unità Proletaria
PO	Potere Operaio
PQ	Parti Québécois
PR	Partito Radicale
RAF	Red Army Faction
RAMQ	Régime de l'assurance maladie du Québec
RtW	refusal to work
UDI	Unione donne Italiane
UGEQ	l'Union générale des étudiants du Québec
WfH	wages for housework

FRONTIERS OF FEMINISM

1

Contrasting the Québec and Italian Feminist Movements

Il n'y a pas d'indépendance du Québec sans libération des femmes; il n'y a pas de libération des femmes sans indépendance du Québec.
– Front de libération des femmes du Québec[1]

There is no revolution without the liberation of women; there is no liberation of women without revolution.
– Cerchio Spezzato[2]

Beyond their apparent similarity, these two quotations, written during approximately the same period in Québec and Italy, respectively, reveal what Manuela Fraire and Biancamaria Frabotta have called the "two souls" of feminism: the first is oriented towards the outside in connection with other political struggles, while the second focuses on the development of a separatist movement, away from any political/ideological interference or contamination by masculine thought (Frabotta 1975, 9; Fraire 2002, 27). These statements also reveal a comprehensive political program for the feminist decade that had just started (Calabrò and Grasso 2004, 38; Cerchio Spezzato 1970; Un groupe de femmes de Montréal 1971; Mills 2004, 2010; O'Leary and Toupin 1982, 27; Péloquin 2007; Seroni 1978, 218).

This book explores the evolution of Italian and Québec feminisms from the mid-1960s until the mid-1980s, focusing on their political activism, their attempts at creative theorizing, and their relationship with a diversity of struggles stemming from the existing social and political scenes. It focuses first on moments of intense mobilization during the 1970s, then on the fragmentation of the feminist/women's movement into small women's groups and larger feminist collectives, and finally on their diffusion throughout all layers of Italian and Québec society in the 1980s.[3] As contemporary feminisms of the 1960s and 1970s became an integral part of the historiography of political struggles, this book also addresses the challenge once raised by British socialist feminist Sheila Rowbotham.

Rowbotham (1996, 13) pointed out the major weakness of feminism – and of political movements in general – which is the tendency to forget important elements of history and the absence of mechanisms to transfer memory from one generation of activists to another. She reminds us that, in the Western world, feminist movements of the late 1960s and early 1970s rejected the project of women's emancipation within modernized capitalism. Instead, feminist activists – mainly radicals and socialists – embraced the project of liberating women through a complete transformation of social relations: the radicals placed gender at the core of their discourses, while the socialists held that race and class were as important as gender.

Other critics have identified the lack of collective memory (Bertilotti and Scattigno 2005, ix; de Sève 2005; Delphy 1980) and the tendency to rely on restrictive theoretical frames when assessing feminist struggles – its gains and its losses – leading to the marginalization of important analytical factors and issues (de Sève 2005, 90; Michaud 2009, 86; Sangster 2010). Some criticize the appropriation of feminist political struggles by political movements informed by patriarchal logic, which maintain a multiple invisibilization of gender hierarchies within the many spheres of political activism (Fillieule and Roux 2009, 12–13);[4] some highlight the occultation of important feminist theorization in the 1970s and 1980s (Mac an Ghaill and Haywood 2007, 125–26, 155); and some, while commenting from outside of feminism, suggest that the lack of memory transfer is the consequence of a generation of political activists who were not interested in leaving any trace of their experience (Warren 2007, 209). Whatever the reason, this period – the political years from the 1960s to the 1980s – is remarkable for the sudden emergence of mass political movements followed by an abrupt descent into disillusion.

Over the last twenty-five years, I have been studying the ways in which feminist discourses and practices are constituted, starting with a doctoral project on the network of women's health centres in Québec, the struggle for access to abortions, the creation of feminist self-help clinics, and the practices some of these centres put at the core of their political platforms (Michaud 1995, 1996, 1998). Some of the major debates that divided feminist/women's collectives for decades concerned whether or not they should collaborate with state institutions in an attempt to force the adoption of new policies, reforms, and services adapted to women's needs (Andrew 1984; J. Lamoureux 1994; Masson 1998; Michaud 1992, 1997b, 2000). The other important area that generated significant and conflicting discussion concerns the difficulty of integrating issues of sexuality and race into feminist/women's movements. Initially, such polarizing debates were conducted within the much larger ideological context of the capitalist and patriarchal state and were led by a substantive number of feminists who forcefully argued for the need to intervene in the social. Although the preservation of the independence of feminist collectives was the ultimate goal, the most important interlocutor with whom feminist activists talked and litigated was the left – both the old left and the New Left, embodied by a whole range of political and social movements, unions, parliamentary and extra-parliamentary parties, and political groups (Crispino 1981b, 25; O'Leary and Toupin 1982; Péloquin 2007; Sangster 2010).[5]

As mentioned above, the 1970s concluded with a decline in the mass mobilization of political movements, including feminism, but the women's movement did not stop expanding as more and more small groups began to emerge in all regions of Québec society, initiating work within local and regional communities. Then, debates on the need for feminists to intervene in the social alongside other political actors diminished and were contained within the frontiers of the movement: for feminist activists, the potential interlocutor and negotiating partner shifted from the left, in all its diversity, to the state and its multiple layers of public institutions. No contradiction was seen between continuing to criticize the state and accepting public funding for feminist/women's groups who provided services to larger communities of women in need.[6] Feminism as a political movement was gone; the women's movement as a social movement had arrived.

Important distinctions need to be made between these two denominations. First, when I refer to feminism as a political movement, I focus on a particular moment in history when debates and confrontations concerning Marxist theories and leftist practices were particularly intense within all movements, including feminism. These exchanges occurred, among other ways, through writings in different journals and were attempts to create distinctive identities for particular political groups. Feminist collectives tried to find ways to distinguish themselves, as clearly as possible, from other political movements. It is important to note that feminism was not a movement born out of the left. Nevertheless, feminist activists were in constant synergy with the old left and extra-parliamentary organizations identified as the New Left. Indeed, the number of feminist activists was small, but they were involved in a variety of struggles they shared with leftist activists. As the number of feminist collectives and women's groups grew and expanded outside large urban centres, as the importance of finding immediate solutions to single issues (health, abortion, violence, poverty, women's sense of isolation) occupied the feminist agenda, feminist activists transformed themselves into women's issues experts and began to play an intermediary role between diverse communities of women and public institutions (Ergas 1986, 104).

Second, when I write "feminist/women's groups" I am not using "feminist" or "women" alternatively. There are important distinctions to make between these two words: not all members of a specific women's group claimed their allegiance to feminism even though their practices were informed by feminist consciousness. However, using the slash in writing feminist/women's groups means these distinctions are not clear-cut. I make the same distinction when I refer to the feminist/women's movement, although the shift from being a political movement (feminist) to being a social movement (women's) appears clearer. Despite this qualitative shift being neither defined nor definitive, feminism as a political movement remains at the core of the women's movement. It is still a formidable terrain of political engagement aiming to resolve unfinished struggles led by the feminist/women's movement as well as other struggles happening within political/public spaces shared with other political actors. This is also the main reason I chose not to focus my research on the feminist/women's movement on its relationship with the state or with political parties such as the Québec Liberal Party, the Parti Québécois, or any other parliamentary party. There are already several feminist publications devoted to the subject of "women and the state" or "the women's movement and the state." The list is too long to address here. Furthermore, in Québec in particular, feminist scholarship has paid much less attention to the synergy between feminism and different leftist political schools of thought. Solely studying the feminist/women's movement through its internal dynamics and its contradictory and/or tense relations with public and state institutions is indeed important, but it is too restrictive as it leaves out significant and determining factors in the making of feminist discourses and practices. This book intends to fill this gap.

Thus, the present study enlarges the scope of analysis to the study of synergies and frictions, dialogues and confrontations, between feminism and the old left as well as the New Left. This enables us to shed a different light on what has contributed to shaping contemporary feminism. With the objective being to retrace and highlight the making of the current trends of a movement and its genealogical intricacies, I began to search for comparable feminist movements I could analyze side by side. I found in the Québec and Italian movements two feminisms that have never before been compared and that could shed new light on the past and present theorizations of issues and modes of organizing.

Although they have many similarities, the Québécois and Italian movements must be compared and contrasted in relation to their own specific political contexts. First, both paid significant attention to the American feminist movement, especially its use of consciousness-raising, and to the French feminist movement. Second, both paid attention to these movements' choice of issues, such as: the quest for personal and organizational autonomy (i.e., the separation of feminism from any masculine political interference); the demand for wages for housework; the call for free abortion and the politics of self-help; the liberation of women's bodies and their sexuality; the theorization of sexual difference and the self; and, finally, the constitution of a new autonomous political subject. Third, there are similarities in the ways in which Italian and Québec feminist activists perceived their respective societies as homogeneous in terms of race and in their representation of whiteness. This being the case, it is important to consider their respective approaches to difference and how their processes of racialization created hierarchies among social categories of women.

This enumeration of similarities does not mean that there were not important differences between Italian and Québécois feminisms. Italian feminists, for instance, went deeper into the theoretical elaboration of sexual difference as well as of the mode of inquiry they named *autocoscienza* (consciousness-raising).[7] The place occupied by psychoanalysis – mainly within feminist collectives that resolutely separated their feminist thought and practice from any involvement with male-centred thought and practice – had more depth and resonance in Italy than in Québec. Moreover, the old and the New Left seemed to have a stronger hold on feminist orientations and choices of political strategy in some segments of the Italian movement (Ciuffreda and Frabotta 1975), whereas the demand for autonomy in Québec was the issue that generated most of the tension and controversy between feminists and leftist groups. Marxism, as a grand narrative, imposed many terms of reference on Italian feminists in the early years, and the same ideological influence existed in Québec. Another grand narrative – nationalism – was less significant in Italy: Québec leftist nationalism, mirroring Third World liberation discourses, had an important influence on political movements, including the feminist/women's movement in the 1960s and 1970s. However, Italian feminists developed a narrative that emphasized the importance of *separatism* in relation to masculine thought in much the same way as their Québec counterparts did.

Although I outline the similarities and differences between these two movements, I do not follow a traditional chronological approach. Quite the contrary: I focus on major themes, shedding light on the type of political actors with whom feminists engaged; on feminist theorizations of sexuality and the body; and on the institutional structures they created, such as women-only spaces made up of small groups, larger collectives, and/or networks in all areas of human activities. This thematic approach allows me to show the extent to which feminist theorizing and feminist principles that sustain collective action were very different in the 1960s and 1970s than what had existed within major women's organizations following the Second World War. The genealogical reconstitution proposed here should help to avoid a homogeneous and restrictive interpretation of a period in which, too often, the liberal paradigm is invoked to explain the evolution of feminism up to the present. My approach aims less to analyze women's groups in their intermediary position between communities of women and public institutions than to propose a transversal genealogical analysis; that is, it seeks less to describe the origins of a movement than to highlight relations of proximity, of synergy, and of rupture with other social forces that, like feminism, sought to be at the forefront of political transformations.

Early organizations clearly devoted to feminist issues and feminist/women collectives' action began long before the "'68 years."[8] We have to look back to the end of the Second World War for elements that explain strategies taken by some groups in the 1970s.[9] The period ends in the mid-1980s, with the institutionalization of specialized services for women as well as the partial success of women's groups in disseminating feminist principles (Masson 1998; Michaud 1995, 1997a, 1997b; Pravadelli 2010, 61). The 1980s is a period during which women activists focused less on mass mobilization than on putting their limited resources and personal energies into the development of study groups, documentation centres, and permanent feminist/women's institutions of their own (Calabrò and Grasso 2004).

In the following section, I summarize some of the elements evolving at the frontiers of these two movements. I show how they intermingle in such a way that what seems to be the boundary of one dimension is precisely the point of entry of another.

Exploring the Frontiers of Feminist Discourses and Social Practices

Many feminist activists worked with terms of reference that were not their own before rejecting most, but not necessarily all, of them. Marxist ideology and class struggle analysis, nationalism and Third World liberation discourses, counterculture and the desire to break with old ways of doing politics – all of these political discursive trends shaped feminism and its political orientations. This is why the question of political and ideological influences from the left as well as the impact of Italian and Québec feminisms on leftist organizations and political parties is central to this study. Both feminisms were shaped by this type of synergy.[10] A genealogy of political effervescence from the end of the 1960s and throughout the 1970s should highlight the dialogical dynamic that existed among movements – a dynamic characterized as much by alliances and solidarities as by conflicts and ruptures over old political discourses and ideologies (Dupuis-Déri 2008, 259; Michaud 2010). In this book, the concept of "synergy" is used to highlight the moments of interaction among political movements. This concept also allows us to conceptualize feminism as an independent movement that is not born out of the left (Winter 2000, 107): it existed earlier and is not derivative. However, there are always segments of feminism and moments of its history that interact with the left.[11] Women, LGBTQ people, intersex people, Indigenous people, people who are racialized, people who are living with different ability and capability are not acting in the margins of political struggles: they are in it, bringing complexity to the internal/external relations of any given movement. They are at the crossroads of any debates between specific conditions and their perversions (Rossi-Doria 1978, 14–15).

Returning to the 1960s with this in mind, both feminism and the New Left shared a similar quest for autonomy and experienced divisive debates around its meaning. This quest emerged out of disagreements over how the old left intended to maintain its control over emerging political movements as well as over the expression of new subjectivities and desires (Balestrini and Moroni 2008; Warren 2008).[12] In Italy, as in Québec, the late 1960s witnessed the political outburst of student movements and working-class youth opposed to paternalism and authoritarianism in the family and the education system as well as in unionism and traditional leftist politics (Balestrini and Moroni 2008; Berardi 2007; Donolo 1968; Reid 2009; Warren 2008).

In spite of the originality of these political movements, they were haunted by dominant narratives. While in Québec many actors of the New Left seemed to ambiguously adhere to some sort of nationalism, in Italy the Partito Comunista Italiano (PCI) was incontestably the point of reference as well as of confrontation in the movement's efforts to overturn the capitalist state (Annunziata 2007; Fortin 1993, 211; Warren 2008, 2007).[13]

New Leftist activists – who were sometimes friends or companions with whom feminists shared their lives (Fraire 2002, 24; Raymond 1980, 10) – were often the same people who disagreed with the ways in which women talked about their oppression and their sexuality. On many occasions, they made their opposition known with harsh words and even used physical violence to make their point (L. Capobianco and Minneci 1981; Fraire 2002; D. Lamoureux 1986; Michaud 2010; Miles 1992). Paradoxically, for the separatist segment of Italian feminism, the notion of autonomy is as suspect as is the notion of emancipation itself. For this segment, the fight for autonomy remains associated with attempts to create spaces where women's issues can be discussed both inside and outside the structures of the left, while remaining closely connected to the struggles dominated by male leftist leaders.

Obviously, the distinction between autonomy and separatism is articulated differently in Québec than it is in Italy because the meaning attached to separatism is related to the independence of Québec from the rest of Canada. The word has a negative connotation when appropriated by opponents of the independence project. There are some exceptions, however, such as the *Manifeste des femmes Québécoises* (Manifesto of Québécois women) (1971), where the word "séparatiste" is used with the same meaning as it has in Italian feminism, though only once (Un groupe de femmes de Montréal 1971, 57). Political activists from the left (Vallières 1994 [1968]) rarely used notions such as "separatist" or "separatism": Québec nationalists prefer terms such as "independence" or "sovereignty." Most Québécois feminists used the term "autonomy" to identify the distance their movement should assume vis-à-vis the left.

In the Italian context, the notion of autonomy takes on different connotations when characterizing feminist groups that claim their independence from the PCI and traditional union organizing. Within Italian feminism, invoking autonomy signified invoking freedom of speech and freedom of action for women within the leftist structures of the old and New Left without demanding a complete separation from social struggles, which was the case when feminist separatism was invoked. Within such confrontational contexts, feminist autonomy covers two strategies of self-determination that were sought simultaneously: (1) the autonomy of feminist organizations from any political interference from external forces and (2) personal autonomy for women as political subjects. For a significant portion of the feminist movement (DEMAU 1966a, 1966b; Fraire 2002, 57–65; D. Lamoureux 1986; O'Leary and Toupin 1982), the struggle for autonomy stands against the idea that women should integrate into the masculine sphere to achieve necessary political, social, and cultural transformations; it stands against any attempt to compromise with organizations and/or institutions dominated by masculine thought.

The feminist theorization of the notion of and quest for autonomy ensured that notions such as "the personal is political" overrode the type of autonomy the New Left was willing to give (Fraire 2002).[14] Reading analytical accounts by those who witnessed the political struggles of the 1970s and the ways in which they were confronted with the "woman question," it is obvious that a new generation of feminists rejected any reformist demands. Their goals threw the old as much as the New Left into a profound ideological and theoretical crisis (Bianchi and Caminiti 2004; Lamontagne 1978; Warren 2007). In Italy, however, separatists within feminism were not satisfied by the mere demand for autonomy, and they refused to collaborate with any struggle if there was even the slightest chance that it was informed by masculinist thinking. This separatist segment of feminism was always suspicious of the autonomy segment, which it perceived as too willing to collaborate with the current social order instead of being engaged in its radical transformation, in creating a world informed by an entirely feminine system of thought.

The conflict between the autonomous and the separatist sides, which divide feminism into two souls – or two axes – did not come to pass without personal dramas in women's lives (V. Boccia 1987). Many Italian feminist activists who contributed to the foundation of autonomous women's collectives came from the PCI and the ranks of the Unione donne Italiane (UDI), which operated under the control of the Communist Party.[15] Since the end of the Second World War, the UDI had made demands for day care, labour rights, and pensions for housewives and was the model for women's emancipation. The associations went into a deep crisis over the nature of these emancipatory demands, caught between the authoritarian hold of the socially conservative PCI and the strength of the new feminist collectives. These collectives in fact proposed a radical model for complete liberation from the traditional ways of doing politics and from the existing models of theorizing oppression. The term *doppia militanza* (double activism or double militancy), coined by Italian feminists, best characterizes what Laura Lilli and Chiara Valentini (1979) call the "schizophrenia" of working inside and outside the old and the New Left as well as inside and outside autonomous feminist collectives along with new generations of activists.[16]

On top of provoking tensions and crises within the left, a new generation of Italian feminist activists continually challenged and destabilized traditional and well-structured women's organizations like UDI. Nonetheless, the tradition of Marxism as a theory and as a practice was not easily discarded. This was especially true in the theorizing of relations of production and reproduction as well as the relations between the North and the South in Italy (Guerra 2005, 50; Keucheyan 2010, 33). For activists and theoreticians like Lea Melandri (1977), it was impossible to separate women's sexuality from economy, politics, and culture. Even those who forcefully contested the Marxist tradition had to spend time critiquing the fallacies of the orthodox Marxist emancipation project with regard to women. Italian feminist thinkers like Carla Lonzi, who wrote a groundbreaking text, *Sputiamo su Hegel (Let's Spit on Hegel)* (1970), argued that Marxist analysis must be rejected not only as masculine thought useless for the understanding of women's oppression but also as a practice that contributed to perpetuating such thought.

The history of the dominance of the Communist Party of Canada over affiliated women's associations had similar political resonance in Québec, seen in countless testimonies of female communist activists before and during the Second World War (Lévesque 1973, 1984, 1999). In the 1960s – a period strangely named *Révolution tranquille* (Quiet revolution), when the state introduced economic and social policies that seemingly differed from those of the past – events involving political violence were punctuated by brutal capitalist practices and harsh police repression of independentist groups as well as emerging Marxist organizations inspired by Third World liberation movements. Third Worldism, socialism, nationalism, and counterculturalism were all ideological discourses disseminated by Québec publications such as *Parti pris,* the most influential leftist periodical of the decade (Beaudry 1990; Fortin 1993; Horguelin 2010; Reid 2009).

The problem of double activism faced by so many Italian feminists had its counterpart within the political lives of many Québec feminists. The Front de libération des femmes du Québec (FLFQ), for example, presented a type of activism torn between its allegiances to women's liberation on the one hand, and to the socialist and anti-colonial struggle on the other (Cardon and Granjon 2010, 32–33; Kinsman and Gentile 2010; Lessard 1989; Péloquin 2007; Reid 2009; Warren 2007). Such tension is indicative of the synergy between feminism and the New Left, influenced by the works of Frantz Fanon and Albert Nemmi, among others, which had commenced in the early 1960s with the student movement (Vallières 1994 [1968]; Warren 2008, 70).

In both Italy and Quebec, the fact that many segments of feminism look towards dominant narratives, either to support or to negate their influence over their respective organizations, is nothing new; but perhaps what is less known – or in need of being reassessed – are the personal dilemmas of women who were caught between two loyalties and who were sometimes ostracized for it. Women quit leftist organizations in great numbers, at times provoking the dissolution of political groups like Lotta Continua in Italy (Balestrini and Moroni 2008, 371–72, 488–89) and En Lutte! in Québec (Cleveland 1983; Lessard 1989; Warren 2007). Many of them continued to advocate the importance of remaining connected with political struggles and other social issues. The concept of double activism refers to this dilemma lived by those who remained members of gender-mixed political groups while, at the same time, helping to create women-only autonomous feminist collectives devoted to the practice of consciousness-raising (Balestrini and Moroni 2008, 496–97; Fraire 2002, 117–50; Lilli and Valentini 1979).

American and French feminisms represent the second political influence on Québécois and Italian feminisms. These influences are interrelated and interdependent: American and French feminisms enrich and further complicate the multifaceted representations of women as political subjects distinct from their male counterparts. Nonetheless, American and French systems of feminist thought remained relatively foreign to one another and never fully reconciled important and significant differences. The difficulties associated with mediation and/or translation get in the way of our understanding of fundamental issues,[17] such as the role of class struggle within feminist social practices; the integration of race and other differences among social categories of women; the meaning of the *personal and the political* and the theorization of sexual difference; the practice of consciousness-raising/autocoscienza and the impact of psychoanalysis within the movement;

and gender relations and relations with public/political institutions (Fraire 2002; O'Leary and Toupin 1982; Péloquin 2007).

With American feminism, the issue of race entered the Québécois and Italian movements through the back door. The problem can be summarized in two ways: (1) the way in which feminists in Québec and in Italy acknowledged the presence of or absence of the integration of race in their midst, and (2) the extent to which they compared women's oppression with other oppression, such as the oppression of Blacks in the United States. Feminist/women's movements based their social practices and their political discourses on the perception that their respective societies were deeply divided by social class but were homogeneous in terms of race difference. Most if not all feminist activists in Québec and Italy thought that the problem of race emerged as an issue solely in the 1980s, oblivious to the fact that Black women, women of colour, and Indigenous women operated organizations parallel to theirs both before and during the period under study. Only occasionally did these activists respond to a call for solidarity, as in the case of Indigenous women contesting their loss of status due to section 12 (1) (b) of the Canadian Indian Act (Ricci 2017, 2018).[18]

The terrain of political activism surrounding the issue of race oppression gets more complex when feminist analyses of the social and economic conditions of working-class women are mixed with anti-colonialist discourse from Third World liberation movements. This additional porous frontier of feminism needs an intersectional and transnational analysis to decipher the ways in which Québec and Italian feminist activists thought of and developed their representations of women's movements elsewhere in the world. Although they more or less acknowledged that important feminist issues were being addressed outside the Western world, their representations of women from the Third World were restrictive, and the way they described their oppression militated against the possibility of Third World feminist thought contributing to the understanding of the condition of Western women (Bertilotti and Scattigno 2005, xiv; Michaud 2008).

Sophisticated feminist analyses abound in which the *foreign woman* is represented as a victim rather than as an agent in her own history, or as a simple object of study rather than as a subject participating in the emergence of new forms of politics. American feminism brought to the Italian and Québec feminist movements the possibility of comparing women's condition with other forms of oppression, such as that of African Americans, but it did this mainly through a type of representation that marginalized

Black feminist thought and Black women's experiences even further (Cerchio Spezzato 1970; Ergas 1986, 19; Fraire 2002, 53; Giuliani and Lombardi-Diop 2013; O'Leary and Toupin 1982, 25; Scott 2011; Spagnoletti 1971; Vallières [1968] 1994; Warren 2008, 70). Patricia Hill Collins and Sirma Bilge (2016, 110) remind us that: "During the 1960s and 1970s, black women criticized their erasure from multiple social movements, an exclusion that catalyzed black feminism. Yet this analogical thinking that categorizes people as being only one thing continually resurfaces."[19]

Thus, the question of race – when intersecting with class categories – must be problematized not only because it is more or less part of formal political discourses of the left and of feminism but also because it remains outside the national fabric and is, in some cases, essentialized in biological terms.[20] The process of comparing women's condition with that of African Americans was highly reductive and not without peril, as Fanon (1952, 170–71) recalls in *Peau noire masques blancs,* where he states: "les nègres sont comparaison."[21] Feminists in Québec, as in Italy, made this type of comparison with African Americans – rather than with women and men living on the African continent – fascinated by the strength and visibility of the Black political protest in the United States. This not only allowed them to favourably self-evaluate but also made them wonder who was the most oppressed and which movement represented the most legitimate claim for redress.

Taking into consideration race and class brings us to the operative meaning of the concepts "subaltern" and "subaltern woman." Gramsci (1975, 5–14, 323–43), in *Quaderni del Carcere,* conceived the subaltern as a position preserving the potential for marginalized or oppressed groups to be agents of their own political consciousness.[22] It should be no surprise, then, that many feminist activists, especially those from the Italian South, use this term not as a descriptor of women's condition but as a research and analytical tool in pretty much the same way as does the subaltern studies group within the totally different context of India (Chakrabarty 2002; Guha 2000). That is to say, they research women's history not from the position of those who are members of movements and institutional structures but from where women are located within their daily lives (Libraro, Mercogliano, and Tommaselli 1981). To be reminded of the trajectory of the subaltern as a concept is also to be reminded that the subaltern woman is as much characterized by class as by race: these two positions cannot erase one another.

Marxism then is not exclusively linked to Italian feminism, just as nationalism is not exclusively linked to Québec feminism. Separating these two dominant narratives in order to distinguish between Italy and Québec leaves aside the nationalist narratives entrenched within discourses on the *woman self*. Analytical and theoretical connections between feminism and nationalism have produced a rich body of feminist scholarship in diverse contexts (Bannerji 2000; Dhruvarajan and Vickers 2002; Green 2009; Kaplan, Alarcón, and Moallem 1999; D. Lamoureux 1987, 1989; Moallem 2005; Stasiulis 1999). Nationalist discourse intersects with the political and methodological practices of starting from one's own experience within small consciousness-raising/autocoscienza groups, of creating women-only-spaces, of exploring personal experiences leading to the emergence of a new political subject. In *Culture and Imperialism*, Edward Said (1993, 214–18), while discussing liberation movements and imperialism, characterizes the women's movement as being central to the liberation process, pointing to women's resistance to male practices within emergent forms of nationalist movements. Said's characterization of cultures as seeking to liberate themselves from imperialism and colonization points specifically to contemporary feminism when describing nationalist consciousness. The theorization of sexual difference – like the discovery of one's own history, language, and culture – is aimed at producing an unprecedented liberation of women at the personal level as well as at the collective level, which, in turn, will lead to a radical transformation of society.

Acknowledging the influence of dominant narratives is one thing, but attributing to them a determining influence in shaping feminism and political events is another. The strength and the novelty of Québec nationalism – for instance, the fact that this society was exploring a modern as well as a leftist conception of nationalist liberation – cannot be explained without smaller narratives. It would make no sense to study Québec during this period without taking Third World liberation movements and countercultural discourses into account. This is because it was not solely a desire for the independence of Québec that animated Québec nationalism but also the desire to transform the way people lived, the education system, the role of the family, the ways in which people went to work and/or to the market. For women within this movement, the desire was to do all that and much more – to put an end to patriarchal relations in their lives, to change the way in which they expressed their sexuality and controlled their reproduction, even to change their relationships among themselves.

This is where the notion of "frontiers of feminism" takes on its meaning. I revisit the most important feminist struggles of a period that witnessed the emergence of innovative feminist social practices, structures, and institutions. I explore several types of articulations: between youth and women's movements, which were at the core of the explosion that led to the sudden political visibility of the '68 years; between feminism and politics as a result of the tension caused by feminist separatism; between politics and culture, which resulted in sites of cultural expression such as the films, plays, and publishing houses that proliferated and became major laboratories for theorization, thus contributing to the creation of a large sphere in which various ideas could be circulated and exchanged; between Marxism and psychoanalysis, which gave space to explore the inner self, the subconscious, and the strengths and limits of relationships among women; and, finally, between the individual and the collective, revealing the constant and laborious practice of *partire da sé* (starting from oneself) and the tension the collective caused the self that was seeking recognition.

The Multifaceted Soul of Feminism

The Italian feminist literature refers to the two souls – or axes – of feminism to characterize two opposite trends: one that connects the movement to political struggles within the larger social sphere and one that confines feminism within its own frontiers. The tension caused by this divide cuts across Western feminist movements with greater or lesser intensity. In Italy, for instance, the divide within the movement was intensely lived among protagonists and provoked irreconcilable fractures within small groups and larger collectives. In Québec, the debates were no less intense, but they never partitioned the movement. Such polarization did not mean that discourses and social practices within feminism were limited to a few points of contention. Each soul/axis of the movement was multifaceted. Each soul/axis had to deal with the multiple meanings and interpretations attributed to "sexual difference" and "women's liberation." Each soul created and managed its own structures and institutions within various layers of society: school and university, arts and science, work and family. The inside/outside schizophrenia, to use the concept coined by Lilli and Valentini (1979), enabled a multiplicity of situations, and this precluded a simple, linear understanding of feminism.

A transversal genealogical inquiry, such as is proposed here, takes into account the richness and sophistication of social practices and discourses adopted by many Italian and Québec feminist collectives, their level of theorization, and their strategies for change. Thus, the origin of feminism – the reasons and conditions of its emergence – becomes less important than its development and its ramification for every level of society (Rossi-Doria 2005, 3). Often deeply involved in political parties, unions, and extra-parliamentary movements, a generation of activists created genuine organizational structures and became political actors in their own mass political movement along with other feminists/women activists who did not have a similar double engagement. A diversity of political trajectories and several ideological influences, coming as much from the outside as from the inside of a feminist movement in the making, ran through multiple solidarities and/or conflicts within feminist structures and collectives. Internal fractures over the issue of separating the movement from the social led to complex choices that still affect present-day feminism.

Almost unanimously, feminist activists dreamt of being liberated from the exploitation and colonization of their minds and bodies, rejecting every reformist path towards emancipation promised by the left (Rossi-Doria 1981, 92; Rowbotham 1996, 13). Nevertheless, the inside/outside fracture is also the story of harsh criticisms directed at feminist individuals as well as groups and collectives suspected of looking at short-term solutions and quick gains. Strategies of action designed to intervene in the public/political sphere were denounced by those in favour of separatism because they believed that these measures did not truly liberate women from the roots of their oppression. Such criticisms run through almost every struggle and caught traditional women's organizations, like the UDI in Italy, off guard. Indeed, the emergence on the political scene of a new generation of feminists armed with a rich and sophisticated set of theories pertaining to the body, sexuality, abortion, family, work, politics, and culture not only sidelined such organizations but also introduced crises into the practising of traditional politics, even in areas that were attempting to renew political activism.

Internally, feminist collectives worked on individual private lives and experiences, believing that such work would raise feminist consciousness: a new political subject was supposed to emerge out of the structural, cultural, and social conditions of gender relations. All the feminist theoretical work of exploring the self, of analyzing women's relationships with men, with their mothers, and with other women, and all political attempts to break women's isolation, were aimed at empowering them to see themselves as political subjects and agents of history (Fraire 2002, 76–77; D. Lamoureux 1986; Libreria delle donne 2005b [1987]; O'Leary and Toupin 1982). In Québec, women's groups explored the self and used consciousness-raising to help express differences in terms of class and sexual practices – but not of race – as opposed to different visions of the world or political affinities (Dûchaine 1986–87; O'Leary and Toupin 1982; Ricci 2017, 2018; Ship 1991).

Many Italian activists consider the feminist work on the self to be one of the great discoveries of feminism (Melandri quoted in Fraire 2002, 78). However, in theorizing differences among women through looking at disparities of knowledge and experience, the Libreria delle donne of Milan carved out a unique position for itself within Italian feminism. It is a position that will appear surprising, even shocking, to readers accustomed to analyzing differences in relation to other categories. The Libreria delle donne aimed to establish a renewed social contract not between women and men but between *women who want* and *women who know*. This way of theorizing sexual difference became the hub of the inside/outside divide within Italian feminism as well as of the liberation/emancipation debates. The Libreria's theorization of sexual difference and of difference among women dominated important segments of Italian feminism and made it unique in the Western world, but it also divided Italian feminism profoundly.

The representation of women as political subjects and the theorization of women's condition within the private sphere emphasized the importance of women-only-spaces within the movement. Such spaces were seen as necessary for women to rebuild the links between the personal and the political, especially since feminists were frequently confronted with the impossibility of bringing women's issues to the fore in male-dominated organizations. Paying attention to the processes leading to the creation of women-only-spaces also allows us to evaluate the evolution of feminism and its expansion into all areas of Italian and Québec societies up to the present day.

There are many ways of assessing the importance of women-only-spaces in the development of feminism, specifically when taking into account inside/outside tensions and conflicts. There is, first, the process of creation itself, the setting up of small feminist/women's groups and/or larger collectives according to women's needs. For instance, in Italy, those structures were supposed to create the necessary conditions for the practice of autocoscienza. Most segments of the movement put this practice at the heart of their inquiry and mode of action. At least at first, both feminists who separated their theorizing from any interference from masculine thought and those who remained involved in wider social and political struggles – especially on specific issues such as abortion, health, violence, work, the production and reproduction of family life – refer to autocoscienza as their point of departure. But even though the vast majority of groups and collectives claimed to base their theorizations and practices on autocoscienza, it was practically impossible to create a consensus regarding the multiplicity of definitions surrounding women's liberation.

A second way of assessing the impact of creating women-only-spaces is to look at the adoption and the application of feminist principles in several layers of society as well as at the conditions of their implementation within women's groups and collectives. These are, among other things, the anti-authoritarian, anti-hierarchical, and consensus-based principles governing the movement's decision making. These principles contain factors that can help us understand the shift from feminism – as a political movement – to the women's movement as a social movement, and from feminism as a political discourse to feminist principles of gender equality being disseminated through multiple layers of society (Calabrò and Grasso, 2004; Epstein 2001).

The third mode of evaluation concerns the role that national and international conferences,[23] workshops, and small encounters played in the sharing of ideas and practices. On many occasions, Italian and Québec feminists attempted to give some cohesion to their respective movements: the rapidity with which small groups and collectives spread through their national territories, under the impetus of a genuine mass political movement, brought with it the need to verify and to test theories and political orientations with other activists. Both the Italian and the Québec feminist movements organized and hosted events that had an impact on them. For instance, in 1973 anglophone feminists in Montréal hosted an important conference on the issue of wages for housework, which sparked debates within francophone feminist/women's collectives where the demand had been rejected. Italy was the site of many similar "international" events. Two of these were organized in conjunction with the French group Psychanalyse et politique and had a major impact on the orientation of the separatist branch of the Italian movement (Schiavo 2002).

The fourth mode of assessment pertains to the space occupied by feminist periodicals, feminist documentation centres, feminist publishing houses, women's bookstores, and other cultural sites for the dissemination and preservation of feminist history. These sites of knowledge production are particularly interesting as they constitute specific locations from which feminist activists communicated among themselves. They were open spaces as well as laboratories for debates around major ideas, new theories, and innovative practices. Feminist journals, for instance, were public sites through which collectives communicated with one another (Fortin 1993; Godard 2002; Michaud 2010; Paoli 2010, 2011).

Finally, there is the evaluation of how porous the frontiers of these spaces were and how much women's groups borrowed or shared their resources with other private and public institutions in society. This takes us back to the question of participation/non-participation in wider social movements and structures. The issue pertains not only to the amount of feminist influence on the adoption of policies, social programs, and legislation such as abortion, health, and violence (M.L. Boccia 1983; Michaud 1992, 1997a, 1997b; Tozzi 1987) but also to the presence within formal institutions of women and feminists who could implement change (J. Lamoureux 1994). The tension between participation and non-participation affects not only areas such as health and social services, state institutions and public services, but also relations with private institutions in the areas of culture and cultural production. It affects the academic sphere as well as the press and public information at large. Critics differ in their assessment of the Italian women's movement in terms of the degree of its academic institutionalization (Magaraggia and Leone 2010; Pravadelli 2010, 61, quoting Bono and Kemp 1991). The Québec women's movement, on the other hand, was keen to engage in projects in partnership with government (Guberman et al. 2004; Masson 1998) as well as in some areas of academic research.[24]

The Organization of the Book

This book relies mainly on information gathered from feminist journals and periodicals as well as group documents – some of them with handwritten comments in the margins – found in feminist archives and documentation centres in Québec and Italian cities. Some documents were obtained from the personal collections of feminist informants. These primary sources have allowed me to retrieve important moments and events that shaped and continue to shape Québec and Italian feminisms. This kind of information is not easily found in secondary sources such as monographs, peer-reviewed articles, and other scholarly documents published years after the fact. During my doctoral research in Québec, I interviewed representatives of six women's health centres, including centres that had terminated their activities a few years earlier. I also interviewed representatives of larger women's health networks (e.g., the Regroupement des centres de santé des femmes du Québec) as well as representatives of three major women's services groups: L'R des centres des femmes, the Regroupement des maisons d'hébergement pour femmes victimes de violence conjugale, and the Regroupement québécois des centres d'aide et de lutte contre les agressions à caractère sexuel. Finally, I interviewed two civil servants from the Ministère de la santé et des services sociaux (as it was called back then) because of the regular contact they had with community organizations, including group networks of women's services. In total, I recorded twenty-two interviews with twenty-five women. In Italy, I interviewed representatives of major feminist collectives in Milan, such as Libera università delle donne and the Libreria delle donne of Milan. In Naples, I interviewed feminist activists who were involved in different feminist collectives from the mid-1960s to the mid-1980s, such as the Nemisiache/Tre Ghinee and the Unione donne Italiane. Some women were, at the time of the interviews, very active in the Donne in nero group. I had the chance to meet the group members during one of their meetings. I also conducted interviews with members of the Partito comunista Italiano. In Sicilia, I met UDI's representatives twice as well as a feminist activist from the small town of Siacca in southern Sicily. She gave me documents to prove that feminist activism was not only taking place in major cities in the north but also in the south. In total, fifteen women agreed to be interviewed. I also informally met former activists and informants in the capital of Rome as well as in major cities such as Milan, Naples, and Padua.[25]

This introductory chapter aims to map out the major areas of discourse and struggle of Québécois and Italian feminisms during one of the most crucial periods for political movements following the Second World War. Chapter 2 focuses on the political and cultural context within which there occurred a specific synergy between feminism and other political movements. Women and youth entered the political arena in the 1960s as political actors, introducing an unprecedented range of desires, needs, and struggles to public/political spheres and highlighting the authoritarian aspects of institutions such as the education system and the family. I follow these protagonists as they give rise to different segments of the New Left, particularly the extra-parliamentary left, and interact with traditional political actors such as parties and unions. I discuss women and youth as political actors within the context of increasing violence, including organizations committed to armed struggle and the growing police repression directed towards anyone who opposed the state and its institutions.

Chapter 3 builds on the preceding chapter by exploring two political discourses originating from the same Marxist paradigm: the refusal to work discourse and the wages for housework discourse. The latter provides one of the most comprehensive critiques of the left's refusal to work discourse. It reveals how demanding to work less in exchange for a better salary negatively affects several other categories of unpaid and underpaid workers, including housewives, who do not receive a salary for their work. Part of the wages for housework movement against the leftist discourse takes into consideration racialized workers and workers from Third World countries, and it contains conditions of possibility for an intersectional analysis of race, class, and sexuality. It also highlights interlocking connections among many sectors of society, such as the community, the market (where goods are sold and/or exchanged), and schools. The wages for housework movement was caught between the extra-parliamentary left, from which it originally emerged, and vast segments of its own feminist movement, who were quick to demonize the demand out of fear that it would crystallize women's identity as housewives rather than seeing the role of housewife as a terrain for feminist struggles.

Chapter 4 enters into the subjective territory of double activism. It looks at activists who were crossing back and forth, bringing the terrain of social struggles to feminism and articulating feminist demands and principles within the political movements of the left. The chapter begins with an attempt to define double activism. There is no doubt that the double activist's consciousness is split by being in two sometimes multiple, different worlds of activism at once. The constant pressure and criticism from feminist separatism exacerbate the difficulty of being a double activist. The pressure, however, requires that the articulation between feminism and politics be revisited from the point of view of the double activist who is determined to locate her politics inside feminism and not outside it. Studying the political thought of the double activist helps to shed light on the implications of feminist separatism.

With Chapter 5, the focus turns towards influential forces located outside national boundaries to see how American and French feminisms shaped the emerging political subject of women in the Italian and Québécois feminist movements. This influence came about in several ways, including through Québec and Italian feminists visiting the United States and France and bringing home theories and strategies of action; through the translation of books, articles, and other related documents; and through cross-border meetings between feminist activists. The unavoidable hurdles constituted by issues of difference punctuated these moments. The translation of American documents in particular, received with mixed feelings among francophone feminists in Québec, shaped the tendency to compare women's oppression to the oppression of Blacks, thus erasing Black feminist thought and the theorizing of women of colour in the United States and elsewhere. Although the seed of a theory of sexual difference had taken root in Italy prior to the encounter with the Psychanalyse et politique group, French feminism strengthened this trend in northern Italy and, to some extent, in other major cities in the Italian South. Similar encounters with

Québécois feminism never materialized, despite the fact that feminists had spent time in France, where many of them became aware of the theory of sexual difference.

The creation of a complete infrastructure of women's health centres *(consultori)* when abortion was still part of the criminal code in both countries is the theme of Chapter 6. Revisiting this emblematic feminist struggle shows that it was never just about abortion but, rather, includes a whole range of theorizations about the body and sexuality. Most activists' energies were oriented towards creating spaces and developing feminist expertise on reproduction. In Québec, as in Italy, some feminist practitioners in health centres believed that abortion was the most important struggle. Many others, however, were convinced that the decriminalization of abortion was insufficient, and they demanded the democratization of medical practices as well as the transformation of women's and men's sexuality so that the need to have abortions would be eliminated. Women's health centres/consultori that tried to bridge the gap between these opposing visions of women's reproductive health experienced difficulties in reconciling the struggle for abortion (seen as more immediate and more rewarding) with the feminist vison of self-help (seen as slow to bring positive changes).

Apart from the small group practising consciousness-raising/autocoscienza, Québécois and Italian movements did not write much about their experience of collectives. Chapter 7 attempts to capture different modes of feminist organizing through documents that show how women's groups' ways of doing politics differed from those of unions and political parties. The chapter also studies the evolution and transformation of these movements at the turn of the 1980s. Diverse phases of feminism intersect and shift from being political movements to becoming social movements. Such ruptures are difficult to capture as they are never definitive and are not the same for the Québécois and Italian women's movements. While the Québécois women's movement increasingly fragmented into specialized groups that serviced women's needs and that began dialoguing/negotiating with state institutions, the Italian women's movement persisted in creating women-only-spaces with no institutional links and remained focused on the internal dynamic of the small group experience.

Chapter 8 explores the multifaceted spaces of feminist cultural production, highlighting how political art and culture were still a terrain for feminist struggles towards the end of the 1970s. It exposes two overlapping tensions within the life of political movements at the time: one concerns the power dynamic between politics and culture, which gave birth to numerous countercultural manifestations; the other concerns the political context, which devalued political artistic productions. It looks at the role played by periodicals and journals: how they built an identity of their own based on the theory they espoused; how they created laboratories for debating and exchanging ideas; and how different journals responded to one another with regard to theoretical issues and points of contention. Finally, the chapter presents two subaltern voices in cultural production and theatre performances. The first voice comes from Québécois feminist writer and playwright Jovette Marchessault, highlighting her Indigenous feminist thought – an aspect often forgotten in her work – making visible the invisible in all living beings. For Marchessault, searching for the origins means recovering a world that existed before Christianity, colonialism, and capitalism. The second subaltern voice is that of the theatre group and cultural production cooperative known as the Nemesiache/Tre Ghinee, a collective of women artists working in the city of Naples. The Nemesiache/Tre Ghinee offers a different representation of the theory of sexual difference through its social and political engagements in local and regional politics.

Chapter 9 highlights how early feminist activists realized the importance of researching and documenting the history of their movement. As feminist mass mobilizations waned, many felt an urgent need to make sense of what had happened during these intense moments in their lives and to control the narrative of what would be told about their experience. Several archives and documentation centres were set up in major Italian and Québécois cities to bring together individual and collective memories. In and out of academic circles, a specific feminist historiography emerged through books, anthologies of classical texts, articles, and research projects. Literary production and documentation centres were designed both to correct distorted accounts of feminism and to address feminist activists and women's groups, facilitating exchanges among them while making sure that the past was not lost to a younger generation of activists. These two approaches towards doing feminist historiography mainly addressed the feminist/women's movements and feminism's fellow travellers.

Chapter 10 concludes the book by looking at some emerging issues for the contemporary feminist/women's movement. Returning to the individual and collective lives of the young women – the students, the activists, the companions, and the fellow travellers of the left who were convinced they could change the world in the 1960s and 1970s – this chapter looks at feminist gains, taking into consideration the perspective of a new generation of activists. Feminism continues to disrupt the left but it also continues to learn from it. Feminist analysis, struggles, strategies, and projects constantly oscillate between the *in* and the *out* of the movement; between the need to remain in synergy with other political actors and the refusal to transgress the security of the stand-alone theories of liberation. Within feminism, this wavering reveals as much ambiguity about the direction to take as it provides opportunities for the renewal of feminist narratives and strategies for action. Feminism may not be the comprehensive paradigm some feminists had hoped for – a movement able to provide theories and strategies for human activities worldwide. Yet its overwhelming diversity offers the promise of renewal through the constant challenge from its margins, which are, without a doubt, the dynamic spaces from which feminism secures its most significant gains.

2 Feminist Synergies with the Left

Yet again, with every search and arrest, with every threat, with every layoff, it is they, the women, who have nothing to do with our revolution, who go back to being wives, mothers, sisters, fiancées, daughters. It is they who go to court to apply for permits, who prepare meals, who phone, who write, who send money. It's true: What do we have to do with their liberation? It's true, what does our revolution have to do with them?
– Sergio Bianchi and Lanfranco Caminiti, 1970s: The Revolution Is Coming[1]

Québec and Italy experienced similar social and cultural transformations during the same historical period. Significant demographic changes as well as rapid economic development affected their respective populations after the Second World War. It is often argued that the Roman Catholic Church had a relentless stronghold on the education system, on family life, and on the political sphere. In Québec, the church's control over schools and hospitals was terminated in the 1960s, but the struggle against its power over people's lives and consciousness had begun well before that, and I argue that the hegemony of the Roman Catholic Church was never total. Even if the church attempted to dominate people's consciousness and beliefs, its authority remained, for the most part, limited to a few decades at the turn of the twentieth century.[2] Countercultural artistic trends, either alternative to or transformative of the social order, always animated Québécois life; rapid urbanization contradicts the myth that Québec was almost entirely rural and remained basically unchanged until the 1960s – the 1921 census shows that more people were living in cities than in rural areas (Charpentier et al. 1990, 278–79; Mills 2010, 4).

In Italy, the presence of the Vatican in Rome provoked open conflict with feminists and others who were determined to change women's social conditions. Italy was one of the few Western countries that did not experience a significant change in its fertility rate, which remained practically the same throughout the twentieth century: there was little increase in the number of births and in the number of women bearing children after the Second World War, with women in the South continuing to have more children than women in the urbanized North (Saraceno 2003). The rapid economic development of northern cities like Turin and Milan attracted a massive immigration of young women and men from the South, filling industries and universities and provoking unprecedented societal transformations.

As the social and economic conditions of Québécois and Italians were improving – depending on class, ethnicity, and region – young women's political consciousness was changing significantly. In this chapter, I explore how young women, determined to have a different life than their mothers, enter the 1960s, and how their presence was felt within leftist political organizations, starting with the students' movement. First, I focus on the interactions between two overlapping political actors: women and youth. Both were at the centre of the burst of events surrounding the '68 years, which, in the case of Québec, occurred from 1967 to 1970. In Italy, it is generally understood that the period lasted a decade, up until what is called the Autonomy Movement at the end of the 1970s (Melandri 1977; T. Negri 2004, 90; Warren 2008, 13).[3]

Women and Youth against the Authoritarian Order

In most countries in the Western world, the birth of feminism is associated with civil rights movements, student movements, working-class movements, and nationalist movements, all of which apparently contributed to women's political awakening. Yet feminism did not really need a push to emerge onto the political/public scene. It was already very active (Winter 2000).

From the 1960s until the mid-1980s, women lived their primary political activism in multiple ways. For a young woman, perhaps still an adolescent, who grew up in southern Italy or was from a region of Québec outside the large urban areas, getting involved with the student movement or a leftist political organization was the best way out of her subaltern condition within her family and her community (Crispino in Lilli and Valentini 1979, 273; Giuliani and Lombardi-Diop 2013, 108–9). Their social consciousness was high, and these women were well aware that the society that surrounded them was in the process of a profound transformation. Soon, an entire generation of young women, most of them students, began talking about their lives, their oppression, and, most of all, about the need to organize autonomously (Cerchio Spezzato 1970; Fraire 2002, 24; Lessard 1989, 91). Like young men, young women became members of the student movement and many other leftist organizations. It is true that a significant number came to political activism with their male companions and/or boyfriends (Ergas 1982, 1986, 63–64; Fraire 1977, 44), but certainly not all of them did. The male companion – if there was one – was himself looking to gain political knowledge, training, and confidence. During their time spent within male-controlled leftist political groups, women matured and learned how to use political tools and organizing methods (Zumaglino 1996, 38–39). When, later on, some female students left the student movement, or when young women activists quit extra-parliamentary leftist groups, it wasn't only because the women's question was impossible to address within leftist organizations: a significant number of them had decided to move on, to do something different and resolutely revolutionary; others quit because of the pressure they felt from feminism itself, which challenged them about their loyalties and their political motivations.[4] Yet many of them remained active members of leftist organizations because they wanted a connection with other social issues and were skeptical of what a separate and self-sufficient feminism could achieve, despite being increasingly conscious of the women's movement's potential for mass mobilization (Dassas 1982; Michaud 2012, 161).

Historically, this was not the first time that young women and young men crossed paths, but, in this instance, they disrupted every dimension of the social and political orders. Young women and young men, in their respective ways, were becoming more and more aware of their experiences within patriarchal families, within the education system, or with regard to the ways they were supposed to perform their jobs in the labour market. This interaction of women and youth cut across many political events, in particular those characterized by an anti-authoritarian spirit, creating what Ruth Phillips (2011, 173) calls "places where collisions often occur." These moments and events, even if associated with violent protests – against forms of authority, against American imperialism, and against the subaltern positions of new subjects – were rich in possibilities for close cultural and political interactions among actors (Mangiacapre 1998; Michaud 2007).

Lea Melandri (1977, 83) makes the intersection between women and youth fundamental in her criticism of the so-called experts who dismissed the youth and feminist movements as certain to be short-lived, arguing that they were merely an expression of bourgeois subjectivity animated by false consciousness. She reaffirms, on the contrary, that women and youth were creating movements that provoked exactly the kind of social change political theorists were hoping to achieve. Women and youth were asking for political transformation and the end of exploitation in ways that were not cast in the economic terms of the Marxist tradition. Their interaction was countercultural, encompassing social, political, ideological, and even ecological dimensions (Balestrini and Moroni 2008, 122; Ergas 1981; Lamontagne 1978, 53; Melandri 1977, 73–98).

The interaction of women with other subjects – young students and young workers representative of the interpenetration of worlds of politics and culture – raises questions about the exact location of feminism within the multifaceted sphere of political movements. It has often been stated that feminism is not a political movement like any other and that it cannot be studied in quite the same way within movement theory. This is not just because it brings together private and cultural dimensions – other political movements have done the same – but because it puts forth its own structures, its own questions, its own political practices, and because it demands an entirely different and more profound revolution in just about every aspect of life (Guerra 2005, 45). Feminism not only interacted with other political actors and political movements but also interrupted, "as the thief in the night,"[5] dominant political discourses and practices.

Once Upon a Time ... the Student Movement

In Québec, a series of ruptures took place long before the 1960s that is best illustrated by a group of artistically engaged young women and men known as the *Automatistes*. The Automatistes questioned the traditional artistic establishment and challenged the authority of the Roman Catholic Church within the education system. The existence of this group contradicts the idea that modernity was achieved later in Québec than it was in most of the Western world. Their famous 1948 manifesto *Le refus global,* authored by the painter Paul-Émile Borduas, was signed by seven women and eight men

(Dubois 2017; Gagnon 1998; Smart 1998). The political outburst the manifesto provoked within the artistic and political establishment resonated many decades after its publication, and its legacy is still debated today.[6] Was it a movement or simply an informal group of individuals willing to explore new artistic expressions (Gagnon 1998, 11)? Was it a rebellious and eclectic group of women and men artists, some of whom happened to be politically engaged? Was the manifesto resolutely atheist or simply an anti-clerical document aiming to shake up the stifling conservative domination of the Roman Catholic Church over every aspect of Québec society (Smart 1998, 70)?

In the 1960s, ideological narratives were renewed as more and more layers of society were permeated by Marxism and a modern type of nationalism. Discursive opposition to American imperialism as well as discourses from Third World liberation movements were openly debated in opposition to the right-wing nationalism that, for most of the twentieth century, had been tainted by the religious conservative right (Reid 2009).[7] Major student associations, such as l'Union générale des étudiants du Québec (UGEQ), reached out to student representatives from the Third World and integrated the international context into their political platform and plan of action (Bourque 1967, 51). Students, artists, and politically engaged intellectuals were reading Frantz Fanon, Albert Nemmi, Aimée Césaire, and other writers from Third World liberation movements. They followed from afar the decolonization process, discussing and commenting collectively on events that had inspired the creation of many groups, movements, publications, and even political parties (Mills 2010; Reid 2009).

There was no definitive political, social, or cultural rupture with the past; rather, there was a societal transformation that allowed new systems of thought to emerge. Possibilities are not necessarily born anew but are revealed when they can be fully expressed. In 1965, Michael McAndrew published an article, "Le syndicalisme étudiant Québécois" (Student unionism in Québec), which recalls that student associations had existed throughout the twentieth century and that the first mass student protest took place in 1958 against the Duplessis government. He describes a politicized student movement that began to organize in 1964 and started to conceive of its activism in the same way as the union movement did. Students aimed to democratize the education system in three major areas: by refounding pedagogy, by ensuring access to post-secondary education, and by transforming university structures (McAndrew 1965; Warren 2008). The idea that students are intellectual workers and active citizens began to take shape at the same time as the idea of an independent Québec became an integrative component of the student project (McAndrew 1965; Warren 2008, 34–36).[8] However, major student organizations were mixing short-term demands with a much larger vision for the future of society. Vacillation between limited but rewarding action and political practices that hinted at a deeper and larger social, cultural, and political transformation – the mark of a true political movement, according to McAndrew – characterized the student movement at that time (McAndrew 1965, 27).

McAndrew sought to make sense of growing political debates and mobilizations among students during a period when the education system was being deeply transformed. The Québec government was taking over the management of schools from the church and attempting to equalize a curriculum that, until then, had had different tracks for girls and boys. The state also introduced new structures into the organization of post-secondary education (such as the creation of CEGEPs, or Collèges d'enseignement général et professionnel) and opened new universities throughout Québec to accommodate the growing number of students. The metropolitan city of Montréal had in the 1960s – and still has – the highest number of university students per capita in North America. For the first time in history, both young women and young men had access to post-secondary education in large numbers.

Women entered CEGEPs and universities, knowing full well that their access to post-secondary education had been blocked for years by religious leaders, doctors, and advisory specialists who tended to direct them towards traditional professional activities suited to their "feminine" characteristics (Collectif Clio 1982, 441). They joined the student mobilizations and participated in numerous protests and, to a lesser extent, were leaders of and spokespersons for student organizations (Warren 2008). Although the vast majority of female and male students were not directly involved in the student movement, their new consciousness was enough to provoke a sense of crisis, or at least a certain malaise, concerning the ability of the social order to provide an adequate response to their needs and desires. The fact that the majority of this generation did not occupy their schools, their universities, or the streets of their communities does not diminish the sudden shift within their political consciousness.

In Italy, the industrial renewal of the capitalist economy and demographic growth put pressure on the political system. However, these factors operated unequally within countries and regions. When it comes to demographic changes within the education system, Italy experienced the same transformation as Québec did, as well as the same increase in its degree of industrialization, leading young students and young workers – women and men – to emigrate en masse from the Italian South to major cities of the North. The University of Trento is an interesting case in point. With the creation of the Istituto Superiore di Scienze Sociali (Higher institute of social sciences) in 1962, Trento became the first Italian university to specialize in the social sciences. By opening its doors to all students, regardless of their origins, the institute created a breach within the Italian university system. The immediate flow of students from the racialized Italian South struck the imagination of the entire society. The social transformation that occurred with this unprecedented internal migration made Trento the first Italian city to become truly national.

The Istituto Superiore, taking advantage of an anti-authoritarian environment, was the site of several innovative courses and counter-courses (Balestrini and Moroni 2008, 204–6). Elvio Fachinelli (1968) reports on his experience of a counter-course on psychoanalysis and repressive society during the winter of 1967–68. He describes an intense debate among students over whether or not the course should be opened up to new members as the group evolved. At the heart of the issue was the willingness or the reluctance to expose oneself through psychoanalysis. The article makes visible the articulation between psychoanalysis and Marxism, with Fachinelli establishing a clear connection between the personal, the collective, and political transformation.

Several cohorts of students, either from working-class or rural areas with peasant backgrounds, were most often the first members of their families to set foot in academia: access to schools and a good education for their children was an investment that working-class families dreamt of achieving in spite of all the difficulties and sacrifices. It was a dream linked to the ethic of work and embedded within their class origin (Lazzarato 2004, 276). Nevertheless, an entire generation of male children fought fiercely against their parent's desires, thinking: Why bother to study if I'm going to die at work like my father before me? For female students, however, the future looked more promising, and their migration from the South to the North to pursue a program of study at the university gave them the opportunity to have a different life than their mothers (Giuliani and Lombardi-Diop 2013, 108–9).

Yet female and male students alike invaded universities that were still controlled by conservative forces and sometimes by fascist student associations. In the 1960s, in Italy as in Québec, student organizations fought hard to erase all of the imprints that extreme right-wing traditions had left within the education system (Balestrini and Moroni 2008, 200; Bourque 1967; McAndrew 1965; Warren 2008, 27). From that moment, universities became laboratories for new ideas that challenged the foundations of the humanities and social science disciplines such as political science, sociology, psychology, and anthropology. Students became increasingly intolerant of any form of authoritarianism coming from academic structures, university teachers, or any type of entrenched societal authority.[9]

In most of these historical accounts, the student profile is white and male and the central issue is the class struggle. Carlo Donolo (1968, 98), for instance, presents the individual Italian student and the student movement as essentially anti-authoritarian and anti-institutional, collectively organizing against: (1) the system of power and institutions, (2) the repression of subaltern groups as well as against internalized repression within institutions such as the family, and (3) the societal environment in general. He portrays a movement that is homogeneous in spite of its political divisions and contradictions – a mass movement destined to play a determining role within the revolutionary process of transforming the political system, of going beyond schools and universities and reaching all layers of society. MacAndrew's and Donolo's analyses highlight the extent to which revolutionary student subjects were able to integrate Third World liberation discourses into their own, augmenting its countercultural tendency. Nevertheless, their analyses were not gendered and the "Other" is always located outside of the nation. For women, these social transformations were lived with a sense of transgression, of their being fraudulent when using university spaces, auditorium benches, and other academic resources. They learned at a very young age what the important issues were and what they had to fight against. As more and more of them arrived at an understanding of their capacity to put forward their own analysis, they began to envision a much deeper revolution than what their male counterparts had wanted for them. The interviews reproduced in *E fu la minigonna* (Here comes the miniskirt) (1998) illustrate some of their experiences in the student movement in the southern Italian city of Naples. These personal narratives are explicit not only about the level of excitement women felt at having access to schools and universities but also about the tension they experienced with their families and educational authorities in general. They indicate the women's sense that all distinctions had been eliminated between workers and students, between politics and culture, between intellectual and manual work, between disciplines, between the sane and the insane.[10]

In 1966, the student journal *La Zanzara* (Milan) published the result of a public opinion inquiry conducted by three high school students: one teenaged girl and two teenaged boys. The article was titled "Che cosa pensano le ragazze d'oggi?" (What are young girls thinking today?). The high school where the inquiry took place had a good reputation and provided education for girls from Milan's bourgeoisie. Based on questions that ranged from the teaching of religion in schools to sex education and women's sexuality, the condition of women in Italian society, women's paid work, and their role within the family, the article generated intense controversy throughout Italy. The school authority and the Roman Catholic Church reacted violently to the publication. The three young students were arrested and interrogated. Using the fascist civil code adopted in 1933, the judge requested that the young people be submitted to a medical examination. The two young men accepted, but the teenaged woman refused to comply. This was sufficient to spark another round of violent controversies, this time on the inviolability of individual freedom. Several public protests were organized in support of the student. The young woman's case went to trial and she won.[11] We do not know if she later became a member of a feminist collective, but she certainly gave judicial authorities one of the first experiences of defiance they were to face in the 1970s.

In and Out of the Left

The New Left and Extra-Parliamentary Groups in Québec

In Québec, we can identify at least three overlapping Marxist phases, from the 1960s through the mid-1980s. These phases interrupted the traditional nationalist narrative characteristic of Québec society and replaced it with a new brand of discursive ideology oriented towards national liberation.

During the first Marxist phase, the rise and the decline of the group Front de libération du Québec (FLQ) represented the hope but also the uncertainty of establishing a truly Marxist society within an independent Québec. Early in the 1960s, the political climate was punctuated by the violence perpetrated by the FLQ as well as by state repression of leftist activists regardless of their political affiliation. It was a time when workers and students always seemed on the verge of a strike: never before had Québec been shaken by such a surge of popular revolts (Horguelin 2010; Vallières 1994).

Pierre Vallières's (1994) *Nègres blancs d'Amérique*, written during his time in an American prison, is emblematic of the first phase of Marxism's intermingling with nationalism. In September 1966, Vallières was arrested in New York while protesting in front of the United Nations building alongside another Québec Marxist revolutionary, Charles Gagnon. In the US prison system, he met several African Americans, both workers and activists. The title of his book came to him spontaneously in English before he found the French translation (31). In it Vallières argues that there is a similarity between the racialization of African Americans in the United States and of white francophones in Québec, contrasting Black nationalism with French-Canadian liberation from Anglo-Canadian capitalism (111–12).

From this experience, Vallières adopted a self-made anti-racist perspective that is evident in many of his writings and public appearances. The preface to the second edition of 1994 reaffirms his commitment to the project of Québec independence, but it comes with the warning that such a project cannot be brought to fruition at the expense of the rights of other categories of people (Vallières 1994, 12–13). Nonetheless, his approach of comparing and contrasting two oppressions led him to claim that the problems Blacks were facing in the United States were nonexistent in Québec, at least in the 1960s (61). It is difficult to forgive him for such an oversight, as well as for his silence on the situation of Indigenous peoples, as he was an intellectual of noted and rich historic knowledge (Austin 2007, 527–28; Mills 2010, 73–84).[12] There is something more: his understanding of Engels's *The Origins of the Family* is equally puzzling and may explain the conflicted relationship he had with his mother. His love/hate of her is difficult to take: no doubt he would have loved her much more if she had adopted the world vision of his father, who was the male worker within the family. Not only are women resolutely absent from Vallières's political project but his text is also riddled with misogynist and sexist remarks (Mills 2010,132).

Pierre Vallières's book was first published by the socialist and anticolonialist periodical *Parti pris* (1963–68),[13] a small publishing group and periodical that dreamed of achieving these two overlapping revolutionary projects: the independence of Québec and a socialist society. *Parti pris* was highly influential both politically and intellectually, and it was the point of reference for all debates around the renewal of nationalism in Québec (Beaudry 1990, 260). According to Malcolm Reid (2009, 33), the history of revolutionary writings began with the first issue of *Parti pris* in 1963.[14] In *The Shouting Signpainters*, published only five years after the periodical's last issue, Reid describes the main male protagonists in this intellectual project.[15] He exposes the virtual absence of women as writers and political thinkers and the misogyny of some members of the group. He presents this climate psychoanalytically – as an attempt to liberate oneself from the authoritarian family and from the figure of an oppressive mother.[16] Pierre Vallières's grudge against his mother is implicit as Reid exposes, with a conciliatory tone, how women's condition in Québec society is theorized by male political thinkers of *Parti pris* – like the nation itself, partly colonized and partly glorified. Reid writes that many male activists felt that women would have been better off with a project of emancipation – such as the right to vote in the 1940s – than with constantly criticizing their male colleagues (98–101).

Of course, women activists had many reasons to criticize their exclusion from important political spaces and events (Laurin 2005). A small group of feminists was quick to organize actions of its own as proof of its dedication to this New Left, which was always asking feminists to demonstrate their capacity to mobilize people. Thus, a first public protest organized entirely by and for women took place in Montréal on 28 November 1969. The context was the new repressive measures imposed by the city of Montréal against political street demonstrations. The municipal police repression of this public protest was particularly violent: 165 of 200 women protesters were arrested (Mills 2004, 187; Péloquin 2007, 30). The Front de libération des femmes du Québec (FLFQ) (1971–72) was created immediately afterwards, and impressive events based on direct action soon followed. Several of these women activists were readers of *Parti pris,* sharing its anti-imperialist, socialist, countercultural, and nationalist ideological perspectives (Péloquin 2007, 248–61). In 1971, FLFQ activists disrupted Lise Balcer's trial. Balcer was accused of contempt because she refused to testify against members of the FLQ who were arrested as terrorists during the October Crisis of the year before. Seven women invaded the space occupied by male jurors, shouting slogans against the exclusion of women from the jury. They were all sentenced to prison for contempt of court. Only then, according to Marjolaine Péloquin, did some men begin to take their women comrades seriously.

The second Marxist phase began following the 1970 October Crisis and the apparent defeat of the idea that Québec independence would lead to a socialist revolution. This phase did not entirely wipe out nationalism in the left. On the contrary, some sort of leftist nationalist trend found refuge in the Parti Québécois (PQ) until it was marginalized within the party and, towards the end of the 1970s, gradually forced out (Laurin-Frenette and Léonard 1980, 18). This phase represented a shift towards a particular brand of Marxism and its radicalization within Marxist-Leninist organizations such as En Lutte! (1972–82), the Ligue communiste marxiste-léniniste du

Canada (LCMLC) (1975–79), which, in 1979, became the Parti communiste ouvrier (PCO) (1979–83). The Ligue ouvrière révolutionnaire (LOR) was another New Left or extra-parliamentary organization with some influence among women activists. Unlike En Lutte! and the PCO, the LOR was a Trotskyist organization and supported a semi-autonomous women's movement.[17]

These groups were opposed to the idea of using independence as a strategy to achieve a Marxist revolution in Québec. Although the extra-parliamentary left appeared to dominate politically during that phase, clashes with the residue of the nationalist left were relentless. During the first referendum on Québec independence in 1980, these groups urged their supporters to vote "no," arguing that the Canadian working class should not be divided. This position shook the nationalist trend adopted by many socialists, partly under the influence of the PQ, which proposed instead the conditional "yes." This was based on the desire and the need for the Québécois working class to proclaim its autonomy vis-à-vis Canadian capitalism and, most important, to keep the national question connected with other important political struggles (Beaudry 1990; Désy et al. 1980, 149–50; Laurin-Frenette and Léonard 1980).

Feminists and leftist supporters of Québec independence lost the referendum, which reinforced, at least for a while, the domination of the extra-parliamentary Marxist-Leninist groups (Beaudry 1990, 265; Lessard 1989). The degree of this domination is debatable, but in some cities, like Montréal and Québec City, En Lutte! and the PCO succeeded in taking over many alternative and progressive groups and their instruments of communication, and they were able to shut down small independent community journals and diverse community grassroots organizations (Beaudry 1983, 52; Beaudry 1990, 265; Laurin-Frenette et Léonard 1980, 2021). Feminist collectives were more successful in their resistance to Marxist-Leninist infiltration (Beaudry 1983, 52), but many women members of these Marxist groups operated within groups like the Centre des femmes (CdF) (1972–74), which was created out of the FLFQ's ashes.

The feminist influence was uneven in these extra-parliamentary groups. For instance, many women in the CdF who were also members of a Marxist-Leninist group used a feminist analysis that articulated both patriarchy and capitalism as the double system of oppression against women (Lessard 1989, 77). The Trotskyist LOR supported the creation of a semi-autonomous women's movement, but En Lutte! and the PCO strongly opposed it (Lessard 1989, 17, 72; O'Leary and Toupin 1982). The fight against feminism was more than simply ideological, it was also organizational: En Lutte! and the PCO did not allow members much space to think and speak freely. Those who were trying to develop the Marxist-feminist version of women's roles within the family and the problem of housework always came under suspicion. The same critique about denial of speech and even free thinking is made concerning the space given to lesbians and gays; homosexuality was simply banned from any debate (Milot 1982, 193, 206–7). Furthermore, if, in the first phase, women had to demonstrate their capacity to organize mass demonstrations, during the second phase they had to prove they were capable of theoretical thought in order to hold prestigious positions within the group (Lessard 1989, 91). According to Lessard (27–28), women were not seen as political agents within the revolutionary process, and proletarian masculine thought overwhelmingly dominated female consciousness.

If the FLFQ best represented the alliance between feminism and nationalism during the first Marxist phase, the CdF is a good example of the second phase, highlighting a type of Marxist feminism that no longer put the independence of Québec at the centre of its agenda. These two feminist collectives dominated during the early years of the 1970s: upon discovering the powerful questioning of feminism, many of their members, who were also part of extra-parliamentary groups, experienced a transformation in their lives. Later, their allegiances shifted completely and dramatically – from being fiercely opposed to an autonomous feminist/women's movement to offering their strongest support to feminist theorizations of women's issues (Cyr, Lalande, and Poulin 1982; Cleveland 1983, 1). Those who had in the past criticized the creation of an autonomous feminist movement were by then expressing guilt for having missed the feminist revolt (Lessard 1989, 19).

Finally, the third Marxist phase emerged at the turn of the 1980s. The major paradigmatic elements that characterized this phase were also noticeable during the 1970s, but they became more visible when the idea of democratic centralism was no longer the organizing principle of the Marxist left (Beaudry 1983, 273). En Lutte! and the PCO were still active but rapidly declining.[18] The Montréal journal *Le Temps fou* (1978–83), which claimed to be politically inclusive but remained highly ambiguous towards feminism, occupied an important niche within the Québec alternative press, similar perhaps to that which *Parti pris* occupied during the first phase (Fortin 1993, 227). Some of its most important journalists came from the ranks of Marxist-Leninist organizations, and some of the women who participated in its creation had feminist experience. *Le Temps fou* located itself resolutely within a type of left that was no longer part of the extra-parliamentary Marxist trends, and it professed a socialist project free to criticize unions and the workers' movement. The journal adopted a tone of skepticism and pessimism, but it did not fall completely under the spell of postmodernism (Michaud 2010, 34). Its main goal was characteristic of the 1980s political scene: a socialist political project that integrated all emerging demands. Movements such as ecology and feminism were presented as the solution to the multiple crises that shook Québec society at the time (Lamontagne 1978, 53; Michaud 2010). Yet this emerging new socialist project was rapidly caught between the reminiscence of the extra-parliamentary left and ongoing feminist criticism: the desire to be sensitive to women's issues was strong, but the understanding of major feminist theorizations and their integration into the core socialist project remained a major obstacle. During this third phase, women were destined to navigate the periphery of Marxist and/or socialist discourse (Michaud 2010) as male – as well as female – journalists expressed ongoing dissatisfaction vis-à-vis feminist activism and the capacity of women to mobilize their members (C.L. 1980, 6–8; Sansfaçon 1982, 27).

The New Left and Extra-Parliamentary Groups in Italy

The political context that created the New Left in Italy was substantially different from what created it in Québec; however, as in Québec, Third World struggles such as those in Vietnam and Latin America, and, perhaps most important, China's Cultural Revolution, influenced the '68 years and the subsequent creation of some, but not all, New Leftist groups (Bobbio 1988, 21; Grandi 2003).[19] The country was the scene of relentless acts of terrorism, orchestrated by fascist groups, and counter-terrorist reaction from the revolutionary left, which felt the need to defend itself against fascism and growing state repression.[20] The Italian New Left was labelled revolutionary and/or extra-parliamentary and had the explicit goal of overthrowing capitalism by provoking moments of confrontation. One of the strategies used by segments of the extra-parliamentary left was to build coalitions during national elections and to win seats in Parliament in order to weaken PCI domination. Notorious political divisions and conflicts abounded during the 1960s and the 1970s. PCI leaders accused extra-parliamentary leftist groups such as Lotta Continua (LC) and Potere Operaio (PO) of being politically irresponsible and/or subversive.

For a very long time, major and influential political groups acted as if women's issues did not concern them (Ciuffreda and Frabotta 1975, 8–16;

Petricola 2005, 201). Some feminists suggested that perhaps it was the "woman question" itself that gave their male comrades such a guilty conscience (Gramaglia 1987, 32). Luigi Bobbio's (1988, 194) book on the history of LC contains few references to women's issues, admitting that women had limited access to the highest structures of the organization. Five years later, Aldo Grandi (2003, 77–78) published the history of PO, which is only slightly more expansive regarding the impact of feminism on male consciousness. Yet the encounter between feminism and the extra-parliamentary left must be analyzed according to the specificity of each organization. Let's look at three of them, all founded in the same year: Il Manifesto (1969), Lotta Continua (1969–76), and Potere Operaio (1969–73).[21]

Il Manifesto was both a political movement and a newspaper that is still in circulation today. The movement was founded by former members of the PCI, expelled in 1969 amidst two years of violent student protests and workers' strikes. The founders of Il Manifesto remained attached to the project of a communist society. In 1976, the group merged with the Partito di Unità Proletaria (PdUP), a heterogeneous political party composed of activists of diverse political trends (Frabotta quoted in Lilli and Valentini 1979, 264). The PdUP, which was not a homogenous party, tried but never succeeded in electing representatives to the Italian Parliament. During the '77 movement the party split between its right and left wings: some members later joined the armed struggle (Annunziata 2007, 51).[22]

As a journal, *Il Manifesto* began publishing a series of articles covering feminist events in the United States. The American content gave the journal the opportunity to criticize the idea that women were a caste – a notion to which I return – fearing that such a concept could become central to the theoretical development of Italian feminism. *Il Manifesto* connected in some ways with the Italian feminist movement, but its analytical base remained unclear, and it persisted in the argument that reason (understood as being male) should oppose what is perceived to be mere feelings (understood as being mostly female) (Gramaglia 1987).

Il Manifesto was often used as a terrain for the exchange of ideas and for pursuing debates within the Italian left. Its pages reveal the extent to which male activists used physical and verbal violence to make their points. Gramaglia (1987), who analyzes the content of *Il Manifesto* and the journal *Lotta Continua*, describes a women's panel organized in Rome in 1973 with the British feminist Juliet Mitchell and two French feminist protagonists of the abortion struggle, Gisèle Halimi and Michèle Chevalier. Halimi was a well-known lawyer who was defending Chevalier, who was accused of having facilitated abortions in France. The event ended up being a disaster, with insults going back and forth between the audience and the panel, followed by vicious verbal attacks and even slaps in the face. Some feminists published an open letter criticizing the New Left workers' movement for not being able to accept an autonomous – although not separate – women's movement (34–35).

Violent intrusions into feminist political meetings and disruptions of street demonstrations organized by women punctuated the 1970s in Italy. At the heart of these violent confrontations was the willingness, on the part of extra-parliamentary groups, to control the feminist agenda. It is important to note that women were also frequent targets of extreme-right groups. For instance, in January 1979, a group of four fascist men broke into the studio of Radio Città Futura in the working-class neighbourhood of San Lorenzo in Rome. The attack took place during programming by a feminist collective. The men forced the five women present to sit on the floor before opening fire on them. Two women were seriously wounded. The attack was claimed to be in retaliation for the killing of fascist members by leftist activists the day before. Several other examples of lethal violence against women perpetrated by extreme-right political groups contributed to feminist theorization on the intersection of class, fascism, and masculinism in Italy (Annunziata 2007, 58; Carlini and Ciuffreda 1979).

As the number of feminist collectives grew throughout the country, women members of Il Manifesto began to participate in feminist political events (Fraire 2002, 125). From the conflictual moments reported in *Il Manifesto,* we can sense the duality experienced by some of the women and how the dilemma of double activism affected those who were caught between feminist collectives, political movements, unions, and political parties. Feminist activists who got their political expertise from leftist groups or political parties were more inclined to analyze women's condition, especially within the family, from a social and economic perspective rather than from a psychological perspective that takes into account negative social relations between men and women (Gramaglia 1987, 33; Zumaglino 1996, 199–200).

Among the extra-parliamentary left, LC was unique. It was created following a split in an important student organization and in the midst of major worker mobilizations in the North of Italy (Grandi 2003, 67, 86). The internal migration of low-skilled workers from the South paralleled in intensity and in importance the migration of students to northern cities. An older generation of workers carrying the memory of resistance against fascism remained convinced that the capitalist system would collapse on its own. These older workers were confronted by a new generation of youth motivated by a different political ideal (Balestrini and Moroni 2008, 128–29; Grandi 2003, 65). Balestrini and Moroni (2008, 221–22) underscore how the new movements were "transnational and polycentric" and insist that any attempts to interpret these years should be made case by case, country by country, and town by town through differentiated analyses and contextualization.

LC, as an extra-parliamentary organization, presented a modernist profile that was attractive to young people, many of whom were women and homosexuals. Its eponymous journal – which outlived the organization – was grounded in spontaneity and was an example of the anti-authoritarian trends of the time (Annunziata 2007, 44). Yet the journal's analysis of women failed to impress. One document, "La donna, la famiglia, la rivoluzione" (Women, the family, and the revolution), describes women's oppression using a superficial explanation for male sexist attitudes within the family.[23] Some women from the Commissione femminile di Lotta Continua (Women's commission of Lotta Continua) in Turin responded, issuing two major documents. The first, in 1973, urged the group to put proletarian women's conditions at the core of its political platform and argued that any resistance to addressing women's issues directly and thoroughly meant leaving all the space to radical feminist analysis or to other groups without a class analysis. In contrast, the second document, written only a few months later, makes more use of feminist terminology. Piera Zumaglino (1996, 223–29) was struck by the difference between the two documents seemingly written by the same group. It seemed as if some women in LC were having second thoughts about the Italian feminist movement.

At the end of 1975, many women members of LC openly criticized their male comrades and their use of physical violence during the feminist protest in Rome in December of that year. The protest, organized in support of free abortions, was one of the biggest feminist public demonstrations in Italian history, with more than twenty thousand participants. Feminists came from all regions of Italy and other European countries. Many feminist publications reported on the confrontation with male members of the Rome section of LC.[24] Male sympathizers had been asked to walk at the back of the procession. Unhappy male activists from LC showed up in the midst of the demonstration and clashed violently and physically with women. Adriano Sofri (1978), although condemning male violence, explains the men's action as based on LC's line that a united front was necessary to counter state repression. It would take another year before the majority of women members of LC declared their total dissatisfaction with the group's political orientation and opposed the idea that working-class struggle must remain the essential condition for the unity of the movement. The women quit LC en masse during its Congress at Rimini in the fall of 1976, precipitating its dissolution (Bianchi and Caminiti 2004, 40–41; Bobbio 1988; Gramaglia 1987).[25]

LC positioned itself resolutely on the side of student and young workers' struggles, and used these terrains as a point of departure for mobilizing strategies, in contrast to other extra-parliamentary groups (Bobbio 1988, 17). However, it did not champion *operaismo,*[26] or workerism, which was initiated very early in the 1960s (Balestrini and Moroni 2008, 33–42; Grandi 2003, 7). Conceived as a revolutionary project to be practised outside the historical left, operaismo aimed to analyze workers' living conditions from the point of view of the workers themselves.[27] It was a joint research experience based on a renewed approach to Marxist theory and connecting intellectuals, students, and workers.

A similar atmosphere to that in LC prevailed in PO, but with a difference. PO's opposition to feminism led the group to primarily target Lotta Femminista (LF), the feminist organization behind the movement for wages for housework (WfH). Women members of PO used to disrupt public meetings such as the LF colloquium on sexuality in Padua in 1973. Targeting LF was not incidental. The group was founded in Padua by feminist activists, many of them members of PO (Guerra 2005, 37).[28] The rift therefore took place in the same political family. Chapter 3 goes deeper into LF, the wages for housework movement in the country, and its important critique of the refusal to work (RtW) discourse forged within the extra-parliamentary left. It is important to underline here, however, that incidents of violence, either in the form of sudden interruptions of feminist public meetings or the use of physical force during public protests, forced many Italian feminists to face a heart-breaking dilemma: either leave the political group to which they belonged in order to act autonomously or stay despite the relentless confrontations in the hope of obtaining the right to act autonomously from within the group. Both strategies highlighted the idea that, for leftist women activists, the primary autonomous subject is the female worker (Ciuffreda and Frabotta 1975).

One can only ask what it meant for political groups such as LC or, to a lesser extent, PO to lose most of their female membership in a way similar to what happened in Québec with the extra-parliamentary left. At some point, there were desperate attempts to salvage everything (Melandri in Bianchi and Caminiti 2004, 245). Feminist activists who insisted on remaining connected to leftist political struggles realized that a discussion of women's issues and feminist theories was not only difficult but also impossible to orchestrate within the structures of the extra-parliamentary left (Colotti et al. 2004; Ingargiola and Cucchi 1987; Michaud 2010). Tough arguments, relentless quarrels, constant feelings of love and hate were mixed with episodes of trust and repulsion, desire and rejection. At the heart of several moments of tension and confrontation was the intuition among women activists that there was a feminist world out there that offered much more stimulating and exciting possibilities than their own organizations would ever be able to give them, no matter how hard they tried.[29]

Women activists in the extra-parliamentary left were indeed pressured by the growing presence of feminist collectives that advocated for separation from external political influences. By then the practice of autocoscienza in feminist/women's groups had become dominant throughout Italy, and sexual difference was the theoretical challenge to be reckoned with. Feminist members of leftist groups tried to create their own women's caucuses within their respective political organizations in order to produce a feminist analysis of their own. Their documents show that they never relinquished Marxism, but they also never rejected original theorizations coming from the feminist movement.[30] The content of their analysis goes against a version of sexual difference that they saw as divisive of the movement in spite of its increasing popularity among small feminist collectives.

It should come as no surprise, then, that those who promoted the theory of sexual difference showed no respect for feminists practising double activism, demonstrating overt contempt towards what were perceived to be mere "emancipatory measures" promoted by women who were involved in the left in general and with extra-parliamentary organizations in particular. Most of these tensions and moments of conflict illustrate the complexity of relations between feminism and the New Left (Petricola 2005, 200). This is because the feminist critique of the New Left was, at the same time, a critique of women who had chosen a form of political activism that kept them connected with other struggles. It was a critique of those who had chosen to build autonomous structures but had refused to move a step further to create a parallel but separate culture of thought (Fraire 2002, 123–28).

The Autonomy Movement and Countercultural Moments amidst Political Extremism

New Desires and Subjectivities

The atmosphere of the second part of the 1970s was very different from what had prevailed at the end of the 1960s (Guerra 2005, 27; T. Negri 2004, 90). Apart from the fact that the tone of political discourse had changed, the youth subject had also changed: still a student but not really acting like one, and not a worker in the real sense of the term. Thus, there was a rupture between the two generations, the second being composed of a younger cohort of women and men activists who did not recognize themselves in the needs and desires promoted by the protagonists of the previous decade (Ergas 1981, 44–45).

The Italian Autonomy Movement appeared, bringing together a multiplicity of groups affirming their organizational independence from – and opposition to – the PCI and to traditional union organizing. It also provided – at least at first glance – much space to feminist principles and to the innovative and revolutionary theorizations coming out of the feminist/women's movement (Bobbio 1988, 158). This trend of the multifaceted left no longer organized around class struggle alone, underlining the need for a comprehensive synthesis of all emerging political subjects, including women and their demands – at least some of them. Many Autonomy Movement protagonists recognized its failure to respond adequately to the crisis introduced by feminism.

Starting with a wave of state repression and the criminalization of the student movement at the beginning of 1977, the Autonomy Movement launched a series of actions that mobilized what was seen as the most inclusive coalition of the decade. Political attempts were made to retrieve/integrate every desire, every need, and every subjectivity embedded within the feminist "the personal is political" (Balestrini and Moroni 2008, 506; Bobbio 1988, 159–60; Liberare la vita dal lavoro 2007, 175; Segreteria dei Collettivi Politici di Milano 2007, 189).[31]

Suddenly, feminist/women activists became visible but only as they joined with other subjectivities, workers and youth in particular (Michaud 2010).[32] Most leftist political thinkers, observing and commenting on the multiplicity of political subjects, connected their analysis first and foremost to the ongoing transformations happening within the working class and the possibility of focusing on the demands of working-class women (T. Negri 2004; Piperno 2004). In contrast, feminist activists who were part of the coalition created by the Autonomy Movement and who actively participated in one of its most emblematic moments – the occupation of the University of Rome–La Sapienza – viewed the inclusion of feminist issues as coming too late. Several of their demands from years earlier were reissued by the Autonomy Movement – but they witnessed the same processes of marginalization, seeing feminist issues reduced, once again, to a mere question of emancipation (Tavola Rotonda quoted in Bianchi and Caminiti 2004, 220).

Feminism and the Occupation at the University of Rome–La Sapienza

The Autonomy Movement encompassed several highly diverse organizations, including extra-parliamentary and centralized organizations like LC – which, after its abrupt dissolution during the Congress in Rimini, attempted to resuscitate itself during the 1977 events. It also involved decentralized groups such the Indiani Metropolitani, a countercultural organization that introduced innovative performances using humour and theatrical expression in the midst of political tension and moments of violence (Annunziata 2007, 82; Pifano 2004, 373).

The Autonomy Movement evolved after years of intense organizing among associations of workers who held precarious jobs, and it resonated in workplaces and working-class neighbourhoods. It reached working-class women and spread inside many schools and universities. The main characteristics of these highly diversified regroupings were the defence of specific identities and subjectivities, the occupation of public spaces, and distinctive moments aimed at drawing the frontier between the "here and there," the "us and them," and between movements and the state (Caminiti 2004, 51). The complexity and intersection of such a diversity of subjects created a multiplicity of movements.

The decisive Autonomy Movement protest exploded in February 1977 in cities in the Italian North. It was led by students with the involvement of several political groups. It began with students and an assembly of workers protesting against new regulations issued by the Ministry of Education. For feminists operating outside the separatist way of thinking, the occupation of the University of Rome–La Sapienza represented the ultimate test for the New Left and its potential for inclusiveness. La Sapienza was not the only university to be occupied by a mass of students, but it proved to be the home of the most enduring and the most violent occupation of the year.

Many feminists went into the occupation with the explicit desire to express their demands, knowing that the difficulty would be not only having them adopted as part of the larger political platform but also maintaining the integrity of feminist analysis. The range of issues and the number of women's commissions created during the occupation helped to make the feminist presence visible. These commissions or workshops tackled numerous issues, such as relations with institutions, cultural production, paid and unpaid work, and women and politics. All the themes and theories that the movement had been working on for years – the personal and the political; the politics of autocoscienza; abortion, sexuality, and the body; the exploitation of women's work within the domestic sphere – were central to the occupation. It rapidly became clear, however, that these issues were revised and transformed under the male leadership that dominated the occupation (Anna et al. 1977; Donne e politica, 1978; Fraire 1977).

Manuela Fraire (1977), in her article "Il nostro movimento e il loro" (Our movement and theirs), revisits her experience of the La Sapienza occupation. She describes the ways in which the press negatively portrayed women activists and feminism in relation to the student movement. The feminist movement, she argues, was caught between two realities: the state repression on one side (in which the PCI was actively participating) and the student movement on the other. She expresses deep disillusion with a coalition that was supposed to be against all forms of oppression but that was once again unable to minimally understand women's condition.

Fraire had the impression that two types of women were active on campus as political subjects: the marginalized student and the feminist student. Unfortunately, she says, nothing was said about a third subject: the woman student who struggled side by side with her male companion. It was not clear, she argues, that feminist activists had defined the identity of "women as political subjects" in the context of this third neutral actor (Fraire 1977, 44–45). Fraire's argument adds nothing new to what had already been said about women's need for liberation as opposed to mere emancipation. However, her analysis takes a significant turn when she looks at how the statement "the personal is political" was co-opted by male comrades and placed at the centre of their political platform – but shorn of its original feminist meaning. The student movement, she continues, had no desire to transform its way of practising politics or showing how it could benefit from using the feminist revolutionary politics of autocoscienza. If there is truly a masculine consciousness, she says, it must not come from men's private lives, no matter how well they succeed in copying feminist methods of inquiry. She writes:

> A masculine "consciousness-raising" would be more convincing to me if it was not starting from the frustration of the "private" but from male's

> obstruction from public roles and power, meaning from the historic site from which masculine identity is affirmed or negated. Until the profound roots of power in the lives of male comrades are analyzed, I do not believe that there will be a real renewal in their way of doing politics.[33]

The title, "Il nostro movimento e il loro," seemed to highlight the conflict between feminism and the student movement as much as the ongoing rift between women in different political movements. The interesting aspect of Fraire's article is its presentation of the multifaceted figures of the female subject – the feminist, the activist, the student – who, during the course of the university occupation, seem to have forgotten the difficult position each of them holds. Fraire lays out the political differences between them as well as the differences in their political strategies. She shows how the feminist practice of autocoscienza united some of them in a relation of solidarity that would have been almost impossible to create without this experience. Nevertheless, the use of "us and them" dominates Fraire's assessment of events, a sharp distinction that highlights the profound rift that divided Italian feminism throughout the 1970s – between women who practised autocoscienza and those who did not – an irremediable division leading to an impossible solidarity.

Feminist accounts of the series of events leading to the occupation of the University of Rome–La Sapienza diverged, depending on the political position activists occupied, but almost everyone saw this period as a turning point. Disillusion vis-à-vis a potential coalition ran deep in view of the many times the leftist organizations tried, but failed, to integrate all subjectivities and struggles against all forms of oppression into their platforms. This failure appeared to be the revenge of separatist feminists, who were often criticized for isolating the movement. They were witnessing the defeat of double activism through the marginalization and distortion of feminist issues (Colotti et al. 2004).

Some argued, however, that, during these moments of interaction with political movements, feminists came out as frontrunners on key issues: their political subjectivities were partially recognized by others and, to some extent, taken seriously (Ergas 1981, 45). Although they had been treated as marginal, even as delinquent, women succeeded in some ways in maintaining their synergy with the youth component of the movement and their enduring attempt to create a new culture. They came out of this experience as transformed political subjects, although their changing subjectivities were not enough to counter negative experiences of employment, to enhance their project of liberation, or to hold state authorities, political parties, and unions accountable for the contempt with which women had been treated.

The War between the Communist Party and the New Left

The Old Left-New Left Conflict in Italy

As we have seen, the Italian New Left was critical of the PCI and traditional union organizations. But the conflict reached its peak during the most repressive years of the 1970s. In 1977, Aldo Moro was still in control of the governing system – unaware of what was in store for him – as he manoeuvred to conclude a series of negotiations with the PCI. Called the *Compromesso storico* (Historic compromise), these negotiations were considered by the extra-parliamentary left to be the mother of all betrayals. In negotiating an alliance with the most reactionary segments of the Democrazia Cristiana (DC) (Christian Democrats), the PCI had agreed to participate in the repression of any group resisting the current political order (T. Negri 2004, 95). The Compromesso storico crystallized the atmosphere of violence that had poisoned the political climate of the 1960s and 1970s. By the mid-1970s, groups such the Brigate Rosse (BR) (Red Brigade) intensified their terrorist activities (Glynn 2009, 2). Suspicious and perhaps afraid of the return of a fascist regime in the manner that had occurred in Chile, the PCI accused just about any leftist group opposing its policy and its dominance over the Italian left of being fascist agents themselves (Annunziata 2007, 21; Grandi 2003, 103). The student movement, the workers' movement organizing outside official unions, and extra-parliamentary groups were all targeted as responsible for the climate of violence. By siding with state repression, the PCI leaders declared war on any elements within civil society who opposed them and warned that there was no alternative: either you are with us, the communists, or you are with them, the terrorists (Pesante 1977, 35–36). Feminists were not spared in the repression, and the feminist/women's movement as a whole was asked peremptorily to take sides.

Among the communist/leftist personalities, Rossana Rossanda is worth mentioning. Rossanda can be characterized as a "fellow traveller" of the New Left because of the proximity she maintained with political movements, feminism included, throughout her career as an activist and a journalist. She was expelled from the PCI after two years of agitation in the youth movement in 1969 and was one of the founders of the journal *Il Manifesto*. However, she neither supported the New Left in general nor the Autonomy Movement in particular. She accused the New Left of creating a profound rift between students and workers and of dismissing the significant impact that an entire generation of young workers had had on the making of extra-parliamentary leftist organizations such as the LC and the PO.[34] Rossanda (2004, 158) argues that "L'Italia si è pensata fino al 1976 in termini fondamentalmente marxisti" (Up until 1976, Italy thought of itself in fundamentally Marxist terms). She argues that the choices made by the Autonomy Movement and its culture of violence are the main reasons that, in Italy, the left regressed to a pre-Marxist and anarchist culture (157).

Lucia Annunziata (2007), a journalist at *Il Manifesto* at the time that Rossanda was director of the journal, argues that the Autonomy Movement signalled the end of the relationship between the PCI and the extra-parliamentary left. The moment of rupture resembled the "assassination of the father," after a long cycle of conflict that began at the end of the 1960s. The depth of the rift between those embracing the New Leftist trends of the 1960s and those who shared the traditional communist vision of how to end capitalism seemed irreconcilable. For some, it was important to avoid a return to the fascist regime at all costs, while for others, political strategies involved a mix of Anglo-Saxon individualism and neo-Marxism (16). Yet the deplorable way the Autonomy Movement ended – with a massive demobilization and the defection of several extra-parliamentary activists to armed struggle – signalled, according to Annunziata, the end of politics (53).

The movement never managed to reconnect with the spirit of the '68 years. But the real split might not have been between the PCI and the extra-parliamentary groups after all. The rupture was internal to the New Left movement itself: all channels of communication were broken between the rigid and unmovable segments of the extra-parliamentary left and the most creative elements of the Autonomy Movement (Annunziata 2007, 82). After the defection of feminist activists and other political actors as a result of the increasing violence, the movement basically remained in the hands of radicals (124). A year later, with the kidnapping and assassination of Aldo Moro in May 1978,[35] confrontation intensified between leaders of the Autonomy Movement and many segments of the coalition over the use of violence. The level of violence in the contemporary history of Italy was at its highest in the spring of 1977, and that was when every person who wanted to be part of the movement had to face a choice: to be armed or not, to support those who decided to be armed or those who decided not to be armed (116).

The Old Left-New Left Conflict in Québec

This tension between the old left and the New Left has a much different history in Québec than it does in Italy. The history of the Communist Party of Canada is characterized by the persecution and repression of its members. Because the party was banned in 1941, the only far left seat ever won was that taken by Québécois communist Fred Rose, who ran as a Labour-Progressive (formerly the Communist Party of Canada). He stayed in Parliament for only a short period of time (1943–45) before he was jailed for communicating secrets to a foreign country.[36] Communist influences were felt outside of Parliament within small political groups and groups of immigrants coming from Central and Eastern Europe, bringing with them the spirit of the Soviet Revolution (Kostash 1992; Reiter 2016). The unfolding history of communism in Canada was also shaped by its constant rejection by ultra-leftist groups, which fiercely opposed Bolshevism but remained faithful to the communist project (Marcolini 2012, 10; Sangster 2011, 86).

The presence of strong women leaders in the Communist Party of Canada was noticeable in Québec. Two names in particular, Lea Roback and Madeleine Parent, have been reclaimed by the Québécois feminist movement, less for their connection with communism than for their lifelong political engagement with women's rights (Lacelle 1988). The historic Communist Party had some impact on women's organizations before, during, and after the Second World War (Lévesque 1973, 1984, 1999), but its ideological influence on Québécois feminism differs significantly from that of the Marxism professed by the New Left of the 1960s: many feminist activists in the 1970s were members of the extra-parliamentary organizations or operated on the periphery of the New Left's circle of influence. By and large, however, communism did not have the same political meaning (McKay 2005) and the Communist Party did not have the same stronghold on Québécois feminists/women activists as it did on their Italian feminist/women counterparts.

Yet feminism was successful in introducing an important crisis into the left. The third Marxist phase described above reflects the strength and vigour of feminist discourses and practices. By and large, Québécois feminism at the end of the 1970s was not turning towards a sort of individualistic liberal feminism. In the same way, the New Left remained committed to the fundamental principles of Marxism rather than becoming a mere expression of what might be seen as a "new liberal" (Cleveland 2004).

Armed Struggle, State Repression, and the Impact on Feminism

Why did some young women decide to get involved in the armed struggle? How did they shift from a location of legality into the underground world of violence? Did feminists think that the presence of women in the armed struggle enhanced the women's cause? These questions are still difficult to grasp, even for those who experienced the struggle (Braghetti and Tavella 2008; Glynn 2009). Reading narratives, personal documents, and other academic and non-academic materials, one is struck by the significant number of women in underground armed organizations such as the BR in Italy and the Red Army Faction (RAF) (known as the Baader-Meinhof Group in Germany) (Annunziata 2007, 156–57). Their active presence in terrorism was never about any particular feminist demands, such as abortion or wages for housework: women participating in armed struggle were apparently beyond that, feeling that equality between women and men was either resolved or a non-issue. Mario Moretti (2004, 2007), during his interview with Mosca and Rossanda, argues that the presence of women in the BR and their roles in actions were more important and determinant than what has been recorded by history. He maintains that women's position within the BR was not a subaltern one (59).[37]

In Québec, in contrast, one is led to believe, from a quick look at the Wikipedia website, that the number of women in the Front de libération du Québec during the 1960s was insignificant. Louise Lanctôt is the only woman mentioned on this list in a sea of about fifty masculine names. Members of the FLQ were divided into small autonomous cells, and there was little interaction between them. Lanctôt's was named simply Libération. This was the cell responsible for the kidnapping of British diplomat James Richard Cross in October 1970, the event that started the October Crisis and that led to Prime Minister Pierre Elliott Trudeau's adoption of the War Measures Act.

In the early 1980s, Lanctôt (1981) wrote a book about her experience. In *Une sorcière comme les autres* (A witch like any other), she revisits her political engagement, how she went down the path of armed struggle, how she was exiled to Cuba and later to France, and how she returned to Québec to face trial. Her narrative is similar to the ones described by Ruth Glynn (2009) in her study of female ex-members of terrorist groups in Italy: when they revisit what happened, they try to reconstruct a new identity in order to distance themselves from their violent past. The fact that Lanctôt is the only woman remembered as a member of the FLQ is highly surprising. These types of terrorist organizations cannot survive long without the active presence of women, and Lanctôt was not the only one arrested for participation and/or complicity in terrorist activities. In 1985, *La vie en rose (LVR)* published a substantive article on the subject entitled "Femmes terroristes: des sorcières comme les autres" (Terrorist women: a witch like any other). Using the phrase Louise Lanctôt chose for the title of her book, *LVR* looks at women's experiences of terrorism in Germany and Italy as well as at Lanctôt's life in exile. The article focuses on the reasons these women chose to be involved in armed struggle, their presence in gender-mixed terrorist groups, their trials, and the conditions of their imprisonment (Sarrazin 1985, 28–32).

Perhaps it is true that women in Québec were less tempted by violence and terrorism than were women in Italy. Another element of difference between the Québec experience and the Italian armed struggle is that in Québec it lasted a relatively short period of time: it was over after the October Crisis of 1970 with the deportation or arrest of its most important members. Furthermore, the FLQ was not involved in self-defence and acts of retaliation against terrorism perpetrated by well-organized fascist groups. Nevertheless, acts of violence and state repression directly affected the evolution of feminism in both places. Indeed, the majority of feminist activists shared the values promoted by the left in general. They had the same desire to end capitalism and imperialism, and pursued the same dream of a socialist society with a different order of justice and power – one that did not resort to violence, armed struggle, kidnapping, and murder. A significant number of feminists felt some affinity with those who used illegal methods and/or were unwilling to unequivocally condemn the motivations behind acts of violence, even though they strongly opposed terrorism that resulted in death. Anna Bravo (2004), in "Noi e la violenza" (Violence and us), argues that feminist activists experienced difficulty in confronting the violence of those years (Péloquin 2007; Staderini 1979a; Tatafiore 1979).

These sentiments did not prevent accusations from flaring up on all sides of the feminist equation: women engaged in armed struggle accused their feminist counterparts of being bored *bourgeoises* who, in return, accused them of playing the game of the most reactionary elements of society. In some ways, the presence of women in armed struggle aggravated the original fracture within the women's movement – between the political culture that animated women who shared the politics of extra-parliamentary groups and those who advocated feminist separatism and who felt they were being looked at with contempt (Schiavo 2002, 181). There was also the cultural and ideological difference between women of the extra-parliamentary left and those who shifted to armed struggle, as well as the question of how women's issues were lived by those who orchestrated acts of violence (Guerra 2005, 58). Some women members of armed struggle groups later claimed that these issues were resolved and integrated within the political agenda of revolution. They insisted that women participated in the leadership of the groups and were fully integrated into the structures of decision making concerning acts of violence and other strategic issues (Tavola rotonda 2004).

Feminists were well aware that theorizing about the revolution and taking action were two different things, that the lines between licit and illicit activities were somewhat blurred. The special issue published in 1979 in Rome by the feminist journal *Differenze* is a case in point. The editors had initially asked specific feminist activists and writers to express their thoughts on the political repression following Aldo Moro's kidnapping and violent death in 1978. Their objective was to go beyond the mere enunciation of a political declaration on terrorism and violence: it was to understand the context of such violence (Staderini 1979a, 16).

Moreover, those who made the dramatic decision to go underground might have found the experience to be liberating and appealing, a clear rejection of the role society assigns to women (Annunziata 2007, 84; Tavola rotonda 2004, 221). Why did some decide to cross the line when others did not? Why did some decide to pursue their revolutionary dream using arms and to cut all ties with society, including with their friends and family, while others persisted in the path of conventional activism? These are questions that have yet to be answered (Braghetti and Tavella 2008; Bravo 2004; Tatafiore 1979). For certain, women who chose the path of no return rejected women's representation as passive and submissive, but their choice of action was in direct conflict with the dominant feminist discourse, which rejected male violence. Women drawn to the armed struggle were seen by feminists of both autonomous and separatist tendencies as representatives of old male politics (Calabrò and Grasso 2004, 86; Schiavo 2002, 183). Some of the Italian women saw their experience of the armed struggle as an epiphenomenon, oblivious of the fact that acts of violence and terrorism – state repression included – were performed in the midst of a political situation completely blocked by the DC-PCI axis of allegiance (Tavola rotonda 2004, 237).

These years were very difficult for Italian feminism. After a peak of mass mobilization in 1976 and their experiences within the Autonomy

Movement – the last major feminist attempt to intervene in a mixed-gender space – state repression contributed to the movement's downward spiral. Some feminist analysts have suggested that this was when and how the Italian feminist movement, as a political movement, disappeared from the political space (Calabrò and Grasso 2004, 47). What divided the feminist/women's movement to an almost irreconcilable point was not so much personal/political issues –women's sexuality and a woman's body – as how to go about male politics, how to position oneself as a feminist and as a feminist collective according to the political context of the time (Donne e politica 1978, 39–41). The idea that some women, even some feminists, participated in the armed struggle, was for many even more disturbing than participating in mixed-gender organizations. The choice to take up arms had the consequence of blocking any possibility of representing women's subjectivities within leftist coalitions such as the Autonomy Movement (Bravo 2004; Rossi-Doria 1979; Tavola rotonda 2004, 237).

When Aldo Moro was kidnapped and later killed by the BR, a statement from the separatist segment of the feminist movement expressed its unequivocal refusal to take sides with either the BR or the state. This statement was made in conformity with the separatist rejection of any alignment with the politics of men (Schiavo 2002, 179–80). Nonetheless, it was obvious that the strategies to stay away from male politics and masculine thought varied, depending on the segment of the feminist/women's movement. In Turin, on one hand, the leadership of the UDI, a women's organization associated with the PCI, strongly opposed armed struggle, called for street protests, and asked women to side with the state against the BR (Schiavo 2002, 180). On the other hand, many of those behind the statement that supported neither the BR nor the state argued that their declaration had helped to protect feminist collectives from police repression and judicial persecution. A third position, however, argued that the statement – neither with the state nor with the BR – was an indication of the silence that deepened the movement's isolation and that this silence was another way of acceding to the politics of men (Mazzuca 1981, 108–9). This statement did nothing to attenuate the tension and the climate of confrontation within the feminist/women's movement. Those supporting feminist separatism persisted despite the fact that many other feminists had been arrested or had to flee the country.[38] For them, the idea of taking sides either for or against the state, either for or against the armed struggle, ran the risk of annihilating all the work they had done on theorizing sexual difference (Calabrò and Grasso 2004, 44–47; Schiavo 2002, 180).

"As the Thief in the Night"

> *Because of the growing importance of feminist work and the early beginnings of the feminist movement outside in the very early 1970s, many of us in the Centre – mainly, of course, men – thought it was time there was good feminist work in cultural studies. And we indeed tried to buy it in, to import it, to attract good feminist scholars. As you might expect, many of the women in cultural studies weren't terribly interested in this benign project. We were opening the door to feminist studies, being good, transformed men. And yet, when it broke in through the window, every single unsuspected resistance rose to the surface – fully installed patriarchal power, which believed it had disavowed itself.*[39]
>
> – *Stuart Hall, "Cultural Studies and Its Theoretical Legacies"*

"Theoretical work as interruption" is the notion Hall (1996, 268) chooses to describe the coming of feminism to the Centre of Contemporary Cultural Studies (CCCS) in Birmingham in the 1970s. He has no difficulty in characterizing the new developments introduced by feminism as being theoretical, but, as he acknowledges, it was external to what was being researched at the CCCS. Unforeseen feminist interruption forced the reorganization of cultural studies in many different ways: opening up the political to the personal; bringing a radical extension to the concept of power; giving a central position to issues of gender and sexuality; opening up subjectivities, which until then were considered dangerous; using psychoanalysis and reopening the boundaries between social theories and the unconscious (269). However, a theoretical interruption does not necessarily mean subversion. Hall's recognition, even if it appears significant, looks like a trick, based on the words he chooses to describe the moment: "It's not known generally how and where feminism broke in. I use the metaphor deliberately: As the thief in the night, it broke in; interrupted, made an unseemly *noise, seized the time, crapped on the table of cultural studies*."[40]

Hall's description is made in the context of academia, which is different from the political terrain of activism I discuss in this chapter, where scholarly debates and sophisticated analysis mix with the planning of the next strategic move and mass mobilization. Nevertheless, he expresses well the crisis that feminism brought to leftist political movements, with all their diverse political segments and trends. If the young men were up against their fathers – against the paternal authority within the family and within traditional political organizations such as the political parties of the left and unions – then young feminists and women activists rose up against their brothers – and of course against their fathers as well (Rossi-Doria 1979, 28). Perhaps this is why the New Left's crisis happened much sooner than did that of traditional Marxist organizations – because the accumulation of desires and hopes was high and the disillusionment that followed much greater (Rossanda 1979, 25; Trimberger 1979). The crisis of the New Left is the crisis of the male subject, constructed around a working-class analysis. When confronted by the feminist movement, this left was overwhelmed by uncertainties over every aspect of its own project. In spite of all the uncertainties of the present and of the future to come, feminism was a movement resolutely embedded within a project of modernizing the present. It stood in strong contrast to its counterparts on the leftist side of the political spectrum, which was shaken by a series of political crises that had not yet fully developed into postmodernist tendencies (Cirillo 2003, 60–62; Constantino 2004, 250; Michaud 2010, 34).

3 Wages for Housework: Caught between Refusal to Work and Feminism

That day, everything became clear to me: first, it was the men who organized the revolution, leaving women at home to take care of the kids, then they were put away and it was always women who looked after the children, who worked and who took care of their husbands in prison, using all their own savings or selling a small apartment to pay the lawyers. They were the true revolutionaries, the ones who fended off attacks, who kept everything going and who moved forward.
– *Anna Negri,* Con un piede impigliato nella storia[1]

The history of the wages for housework (WfH) movement evolved in parallel with the leftist revolutionary ideal of the refusal to work (RtW) movement, which came out of the operaismo project mentioned in Chapter 2. The RtW – demanding more free time for workers holding a paid job – created a movement that began in the 1950s (Bianchi and Caminiti 2004, 38; Bianchi and Caminiti 2007b, 6; Reyes 2007, 456). The relation between WfH and the RtW is far from harmonious. In a footnote inserted in the collection of essays published during her years of activism, Selma James (2012b, 44) suggests that the groundbreaking document she co-authored with Mariarosa Dalla Costa, *Women and the Subversion of Community,* was, in part, directed against the leftist rhetoric of Italian male-dominated politics (Dalla Costa and James 1997). In other words, Dalla Costa needed a solid analysis to counter the opposition she and her collective had been dealing with while trying to create an autonomous movement – demanding to be paid for a type of work that until then had been considered unproductive – after taking her distance from Potere Operaio, one of the main proponents of the RtW discourse.

Dalla Costa created in Padua the Lotta Femminista (LF) collective, which argued that women, too, needed time away from work: they were exploited in the home just like paid workers were exploited in the factory. Housework, LF maintained, is fundamental to sustaining capitalist exploitation in the workplace and needs to be fought in the same way as does any other working-class struggle. While the capitalists and the state wanted women to perform their domestic duties, they, as feminists, were refusing to play the role required of them: they wanted to be paid for the work they did at home, in the neighbourhood, in and around the school for their children, and in the community. Proponents of the RtW had their own arguments for refusing to do a job for which they got a wage, but these reasons had nothing to do with women's rejection of their feminine role ("Grande è il disordine" 1977; "La 'nuova strategia'" 1977).

There is a paradox in asking to be paid for housework while rejecting it as enslaving women in domesticity. To understand this paradox, we need to look at feminist responses to the RtW discourse. The north of Italy is usually identified as the crucible of the WfH movement, and LF was the collective whose members, for the most part, were also members of extra-parliamentary leftist organizations (Dalla Costa n.d.). LF created new groups throughout Italy, but they fragmented rapidly: some groups adopted different names with different feminist orientations exploring a diversity of aspects of women's work of social reproduction.[2] LF and feminist supporters of WfH had difficulty fending off fierce opposition to their demands, but at least they were able to argue coherently against the RtW rhetoric. Similar coherence was lacking when they needed to argue against criticisms emerging from the feminist/women's movement. For the feminist separatist side, for instance, the fact that LF was engaged in a dialogue with the left was more than suspicious. Indeed, LF's members were practitioners if not advocates of double activism, and their practice of arguing with the male leaders – using the same discourse – was seen as a proof of loyalty to Marxism and a betrayal of feminism.[3]

It is not my intention to write the history of LF and of the international trajectory of the many WfH collectives created in conjunction with people like Selma James, the main leader in England, or the fruitless Québécois efforts to do the same. Nor is it to revisit the conflicts that plagued the movement from the beginning and to determine what might or might not have contributed to its demise. My focus is on how LF and the campaign for WfH were caught between two forces: the extra-parliamentary left and the feminist movement. I start by revisiting the original paradigms of the RtW and follow this with the feminist arguments that were advanced to refuse housework that traps women in a determined feminine role. Then, I focus on two types of criticisms. The first is the comprehensive feminist critique of the implications of leftist discourse and what it means for those who are unemployed and underpaid;[4] the second is the feminist/women's movement critique of WfH. The final section analyzes the shortcomings of the second type of criticism and its tendency to fall back on individualistic, liberal, and productivist arguments when the time comes to decide which strategies the feminist/women's movement should adopt to improve women's social and economic conditions.

The Refusal to Work Discourse

Kathi Weeks (2011, 81–82) demonstrates that the RtW discourse emerged in direct opposition to the older Marxist tradition of the work ethic and productivism. She outlines the two main Marxist paradigms on the issue of work: socialist modernization and socialist humanism. These two paradigms, she says, "are in some ways opposed to one another, but they are based on a similar commitment to labor as a fundamental human value" (86). The first paradigm, the socialist modernization of work, looks like the flip side of the capitalist vision of productivity, with the difference being that it is the communist state that takes over a country's economic production, requesting from the workers "self-sacrifice, perseverance and commitment" to "the proper path of steady and disciplined labour" (Lenin, quoted in Weeks 2011, 83). The socialist modernization paradigm reinforced the leading role of the working class within large coalitions composed of students, young workers, unemployed workers, and, at least for a while, women and feminists (93). It saw these young workers not as mere victims of exploitation but, rather, as political agents who had the capacity to massively mobilize around new forms of organizing – and not as passive witnesses of the ways in which the world was unfolding but as revolutionaries (94).

While worker discipline is the fundamental tenet of socialist modernization, socialist humanism, on the contrary, opposes the economic deterministic trend within Marxism. According to Weeks (2011, 85), the socialist humanism paradigm emerged at about the same time as did the New Left in the 1960s. Socialist humanism also cut across other socialist trends, like the social economy (or solidarity economy) popular among certain Christian leftist groups throughout the twentieth century, and re-emerged with some strength at the turn of the twenty-first century in France, Québec, and Latin America (Guay 1998, 17; Michaud 2006).

From the perspective of socialist humanism, the RtW discourse is opposed to the work ethic, calling for freedom outside the sphere of work. This vision of the working class and its historical role clashed with the socialist modernization tradition advocated by the PCI and unions, and it introduced a fundamental division within Italian Marxism. Signs of rupture with the PCI's traditional work ethic as well as with the ways in which Italian unions protected contractual interests were already visible at the end of the 1960s (Grandi 2003). Very early in the 1970s, LC and PO, among other political groups, proposed rejecting the process of negotiating contracts with capitalists. These two groups believed that traditional unionism was completely out of touch with workers (Bobbio 1988, 56–57; Grandi 2003, 24, 59–61). It is within this context, and in the wake of operaismo, that a new discourse on work emerged and was seen as a bridge between workers' interests and students' interests, between the non-qualified young workers migrating from the South and cohorts of students expecting to become under- or unemployed workers themselves after long years of study. As the 1970s unfolded, critiques of traditional political parties and the union bargaining model dominated the political scene. Members of the extra-parliamentary left were determined to take their distance from this process and to become structurally and politically independent of the PCI.[5]

In his article "Il rifiuto del lavoro" (The refusal to work), Lucio Castellano (2007, 12) recaptures the political meaning of the RtW discourse, suggesting that it was not just an ideology of emancipation but a way of rejecting capitalist society. The movement, he argued, was more than a series of demands for a higher income and a reduced working day or less tiresome and healthier working conditions. It was a proposal for new social structures, for more power over the entire organization of the work process. It claimed that workers have the right to refuse to collaborate in their exploitation, and that they may do so by interrupting the assembly line, by sabotaging production itself in order to have a say in the distribution of wealth and to resist social relations under capitalism (12–13).

The traditional socialist demands, the goals of which were to improve workers' living conditions and wages, were thus rejected by LC, PO, and the extra-parliamentary left as a whole (Berardi 2004, 179). Although young workers and students were linking their political action with the proletariat, they refused to be defined by work under capitalism. They refused to die in factories like their fathers before them (Castellano 2007, 12). Work, they claimed, should be neither a destiny nor a life sentence (Bobbio 1988; Caminiti 2004, 55). Young workers and students demanded more free time to enable them to express their creativity and to produce new wealth to be shared socially and collectively (Bianchi and Caminiti 2004, 55; Piperno 2004, 105). They also accused the PCI of being implicated with the most conservative and repressive political forces in the country.

Not only did the trend towards RtW break with the capitalist work ethic and interrupt the Marxist work ethic, it also signified a rupture with the aspirations of the traditional working-class family, another terrain of struggle shared with various anti-authoritarian trends, with women and youth defying the authority of the school and the family. Political conflicts played out between unions and young workers with the same force as they did between working-class parents and their children, be they students (whose parents dreamed of providing them with a solid postsecondary education and a better future but whose aspirations were shattered) or employed within factories (where the idea of the liberation of free time clashed with idea of work as a liberation) (Dalla Costa and James 1997, 43; Lazzarato 2004, 277–78).[6]

Kathi Weeks (2011, 108) concludes her analysis of the refusal to work discourse by asking this question: "Is it possible to demand both better work and less work without one neutralizing the critical force of the other?" The same question applies to the WfH movement.

The Paradox of Refusing Housework

The WfH campaign in the early 1970s generated the emergence of a variety of feminist groups in England, Italy, English Canada, and the United States, and, at least for a while, WfH was able to secure a niche for itself within the larger feminist/women's movement in these countries. It also put together diverse groups of women to form an international network that was truly intersectional *avant la lettre* (Toupin 2014, 24). Yet, while the WfH campaign was launched with vigour on the national and international scenes, according to most feminists I interviewed, it did not resonate much in feminist collectives or in women's lives. It apparently made little mark in Italy, where the movement was born and where many WfH collectives were created. It succeeded even less in Québec, where it generated discussion up until the 1980s only to be rejected again and again by a majority of feminist collectives and women's groups. Despite the memorable visit of Selma James and Mariarosa Dalla Costa to Montréal in 1973, not a single francophone collective was created. Nationally and internationally, the WfH movement experienced moments of tension, in part based on its inability to control its rapid development and to integrate differences among women despite its inclusive discourse on race and sexuality.

In 1987, the feminist journal *Memoria* published a special double issue on the Italian feminist movement of the 1970s: none of the articles collected discussed the WfH movement in Italy.[7] Few of the books and articles on the history of Italian feminism of the 1970s that I have consulted during the course of this research mention WfH. When they do, the references are short. For instance, Anna Rita Calabrò and Laura Grasso's (2004) *Dal Movimento femminista al femminismo diffuso,* which focuses on the northern city of Milan, does not mention WfH, despite the presence of a collective in that city. In "Una nuova soggettività: femminismo e femminismi nel passagio degli anni settanta" (A new subjectivity: feminism and feminisms in the 1970s journey), Elda Guerra (2005) speaks only briefly about LF, mentioning that its members were also members of the extra-parliamentary left, shared a Marxist framework, and had an international connection – namely, in England. All this scattered information is lost in the midst of mentions of other feminist collectives that made their marks in Italy and abroad (37).[8]

Some books, however, are more expansive on the history of LF. The first example is Manuela Fraire's (2002) *Lessico politico delle donne,* a reference book for the study of the Italian feminist movement in the 1970s. Fraire highlights the serious work done on housework, which led to international recognition, but she points out that attempts to theorize women's work in the home were inadequate (34, 111). Another such book is a collection of essays on the Italian Autonomy Movement edited by Sergio Bianchi and Lanfranco Caminiti (2007a), *Gli autonomi: le storie, le lotte, le teorie* (The autonomous: the stories, the struggles, the theories),[9] which reproduces four documents written by LF and the WfH movement, including one by Silvia Federici (2007), "Salario contro il lavoro domestico" (Wages against housework).[10]

Silvia Federici is a leading figure of the WfH movement. She grew up in Italy and studied in the United States, where she created a collective in New York. Federici adopts the same line of thought as Dalla Costa and James, adding some key arguments of her own that underline her stand against accepting the doing of housework: (1) having more money will never be enough if relations of power are not transformed at the same time and (2) accepting wages for housework would mean that women would continue to prostitute their bodies and minds. Therefore, the nature of the work must change. Federici, like Dalla Costa and James, claims that a change of perspective within family relations would not just signal a feminist revolution but a revolution of the working class as a whole, insisting that the male worker's wage hides all the unpaid work that capitalists use for their own profit. The salary paid to male workers obscures the social relations embedded in housework, which is not the natural duty of women, as is often implied. We forget, she says, all those years of hard conditioning and brainwashing that go into getting people to accept the idea that women make marriages for love. Yet it concerns all married and unmarried women for whom housework has become a sexual and natural thing, a women's attribute. Federici concludes that the struggle against housework is the struggle against the social role imposed on all women and that facilitating housewives' entry into capitalist production will make no difference because they have never been outside of it. Thus, the demand for a wage is a demand against performing housework and is, consequently, the first and necessary step towards refusing this compulsory feminine role.

The Feminist Critique of the Refusal to Work Perspective

The two words *lotta* (struggle) and *femminista* (feminist) were meant to signify women's connection with the struggle of the left and to entrench the political connotation of feminism in opposition to the *femminile* (feminine), which was emphasized by the Roman Catholic Church and women of the bourgeoisie (Zumaglino 1996, 102, 105). In 1972, PO defiantly declared itself to be a feminist political organization and proposed that women's exploitation stemmed from paid work outside the home. LF (Lotta Femminista and Collettivo Internazionale Femminista 1972, 18–21) responded by arguing that PO's analysis of men's wages did not properly address women-specific oppression ("Grande è il disordine" 1977; Grandi 2003, 92; Pompei 1975).[11] The collective indicated that the major difference between the feminist analysis of WfH and PO's approach did not have to do with asking for an increase in overall income for working-class families but in asking for a wage that would guarantee women's autonomy. The left, LF (1972, 19) argued, saw a salary as the best way to increase the wealth of the family, but feminist activists aimed to abolish the very structure of that institution, including housework, in the same way that people who were out of work in the Italian South aimed to abolish the class structure – because it represented the basis of their exploitation ("Grande è il disordine" 1977).

For feminists and women activists, the tension between their demands and those of their male companions/comrades was multidimensional. While male leaders theorized against the work ethic and against the process of negotiating labour contracts between unions and the capitalist bosses, the generation of women who grew up immediately after the war mobilized to have access to the job market, to have the right to hold professional occupations, to have their expertise recognized, and to receive good wages. From the 1960s, feminist strategies for making gains on the issue of work followed two separate and opposite paths. The first strategy was to secure women's entry into post-secondary education, to have access to better professional training, and to eliminate gender discrimination in the job market; the second strategy was to ensure that the work of caring for others was recognized as part of women's contribution to society. These two paths have been travelling side by side ever since. Both strategies have deep implications for income security for women who having difficulty finding work, especially when the forces of capitalism are reorganizing paid work within the national and the global economies.[12]

Despite the commonality of discourses, the fundamental element in understanding the political conflict between LF and members of the extra-parliamentary left relies on the meanings attributed to the notion of productive/non-productive work and on the question of whose work is exploited by capitalism and whose is not. No male comrades, according to LF, displayed even a minimal understanding of the complex mode of exploitation within the home, which capitalism needs in order to survive (Bollettino del Comitato per il salario al lavoro domestico [Bulletin of the Committee for wages for housework] of Trieste 2007, 153–44). Furthermore, the Italian version of the WfH movement linked its demand to all workers who did not receive a wage: women and underpaid male workers and the unemployed as well as certain social categories of people living in Third World countries.

In 1977, the LF journal *Operaie della casa* published a special issue on the refusal to work campaign. According to LF, the campaign, which asked for reduced working hours and more free time for workers, would benefit only some men. For all others, such measures would mean the intensification of the working day without proper pay. In other words, it was a demand that served the interest of capital, which is always looking for a way of intensifying labour to further exploit (non)workers. According to this special issue, proponents of the RtW were asking for the redistribution of work, but their strategies would have increased women's work and the work of those in Third World countries ("Grande è il disordine" 1977, 7; James 2012a, 97; Toupin 2014, 128).

How could feminists who shared the same Marxist discourse as male activists be opposed to the reduction of working hours in factories? The feminist critique of the left goes beyond a simple question of envy: women are exploited through their unpaid work as much as workers are through their meagre wages. Indeed, the absence of pay for housework hides productive activities taking place in the home, and the RtW demand to reduce work in the factories conceals the negative impact such a demand would have on other sectors of the capitalist economy at both national and international levels.[13] Yet, in relation to Third World liberation struggles, many PO leaders were not supportive, believing that solutions were to be found at the heart of capitalism, not at the periphery (Grandi 2003, 267).

LF, however, had a very different analysis and connected racism in the working class – against the Italian South as well as immigrants from the Third World – with the sexism of the capitalist class. The collective pointed out that these divisions in the working class should make male leaders more understanding of the issues at stake: the victory of white workers does not mean a victory for all workers; rather, it has the potential to lead to the defeat of all women and paid and unpaid male workers. Feminist attempts to engage in a dialogue with political leftist groups like PO reveal the depth of the conflict between female and male activists on work, exploitation, class issues, and a whole range of political struggles (Lotta Femminista and Collettivo Internazionale Femminista 1972, 18–21) as well as on issues dear to feminism, such as sexuality and the body and children's education. For the left, these questions were part of bourgeois rhetoric, while for feminists they signified a profound transformation of social, cultural, and political relations (Busatta, Staffieri, and Lanzi 1973, 35).[14]

These feminist critiques should be seen as an attempt to interrupt the perception that the extra-parliamentary left was the workers' only voice. What is rarely acknowledged or understood is that they represent the perspective of female and male non-waged workers from a diversity of classes and races as well as from Third World countries. The process of racialization includes the population in the Italian South as well as racialized groups in the rest of the Italy. Feminist activists' use of the notion of "Third World" is problematic because it refers to categories of people living outside the nation (Giuliani and Lombardi-Diop 2013). However, this notion is specific to the political period and was also regularly used by African American and other racialized people in the United States (Moraga and Anzaldúa 1981).

That being said, few of the usual observers highlight that the WfH was also interested in mixed-gender segments of the non-waged pool of workers. According to Louise Toupin (2014, 24), the WfH movement should be remembered for connecting a variety of feminist struggles across social categories as well as across different sectors of the economy. One of the fundamental aims of the WfH movement was to address the false separation between the public sector of waged work and the private sector and other sectors in which a large amount of unpaid work was carried out.

The Québécois Feminist Position on Housework

In Québec, the principles of the RtW discourse were less well known than in Italy, and the long tradition of operaismo was practically nonexistent. If there is a comparison to make between the two countries in terms of alternatives to the work ethic and the process of collective bargaining, we have to look at coalitions of *hors-travail* (out-of-work), which had some visibility in the early 1980s. In major cities, these out-of-work coalitions provoked divisions within unions, which were unaccustomed to dealing with new types of activism.[15]

Union leaders witnessed the multiplication of small community groups, feminist collectives, and solidarity coalitions loosely formed around issues that apparently mattered very little to the working class. Union leaders persisted in demanding that these constellations of small groups be mobilized to create a second front, all united around their leadership, to fight capital in the absence of a truly leftist political party in Québec. But this strategy failed – not because of the rift between women of different classes but because unions did not see the conditions against which working-class women were struggling; they did not understand that feminist theorizations of issues such as social reproduction, feminist political consciousness, sexuality, and the body were offering new perspectives that could lead to a deeper social transformation. Thus, these feminist issues were not adequately integrated – never mind understood – by the union movement and by the Québécois old and the New Left as a whole (D. Lamoureux 1986, 109; Michaud 1987, 53; Michaud 2010, 36–39).

It was obvious from the start that these loose coalitions composed of young workers, feminist activists, unemployed women, and men living on the margins of prosperity could not be integrated into unions as a mere appendix or even labelled under the rubric "new social movements" (Michaud 1987). The proliferation of movements outside unions and traditional political parties points to Québec's version of RtW activism. We find the same defiance towards the domination of unions; the same refusal to lose one's creativity doing monotonous, painful, and arduous work in factories; the same refusal to see one's identity and political demands marginalized by the traditional workers' movement (Lesage 1986; Michaud 1987, 59–60). Yet coalitions of groups contesting the traditional perspective on work failed to find a harmonious relationship with feminists, some of whom wanted to create a movement of their own and demand WfH (Toupin 2014).

The divide between feminists and extra-parliamentary organizations (first En Lutte!, then the PCO) supporting the demand for RtW became apparent in the early 1970s.[16] A short chronology of events should help us to understand why the WfH movement never took hold in Québec (Toupin 2014, 141–45). It began with Selma James and Mariarosa Dalla Costa's North American tour, to which Silvia Federici contributed by launching, at American universities, a campaign to finance organizations interested in the subject of housework. A series of encounters during their visit to Montréal led to the creation of an anglophone collective in the city. There was, first, a feminist symposium in 1973 at McGill University, which brought some tension to an already complex relationship between the two major linguistic communities.[17] Then, in February 1975, two years after James and Dalla Costa's visit, the International Feminist Collective (IFC) organized a series of international conferences, one of which took place in Montréal and was hosted by the Montreal Power of Women Collective, an anglophone women's group founded a few months earlier, in December 1974.[18]

When James and Dalla Costa were in the city in 1973, they were interviewed at length by representatives of the Centre des femmes (CdF), the feminist collective that emerged out of the Front de libération des femmes du Québec and that owned the journal *Québécoises deboutte!* Louise Toupin (2014, 142) reported that the CdF was not entirely supportive of James and Dalla Costa's analysis of housework. The interview (Centre des femmes 1983c, 190–203), reproduced in *Québécoises deboutte!,* reveals why the whole wage idea was rejected by the CdF.[19] In 1982, Véronique O'Leary and Louise Toupin published the anthology *Québécoises deboutte!* In their introduction (O'Leary and Toupin 1982, 18; O'Leary and Toupin 1983, 12), they highlight how the Dalla Costa and James tour had shaken the Montréal feminist community. They deplore the censorship – a gag order coming from outside the feminist/women's movement – that had been imposed on discussion of WfH. In the second volume of the anthology, they expose the full extent of the CdF opposition to WtH. The authors (O'Leary and Toupin 1983, 12, quoting Centre des femmes 1983d, 132) denounce its reductionist vision and the ambiguity of titles such as "Salaire à la ménagère" (Wages to the housewife) instead of the usual "Salaire au travail domestique" (Wages for housework).[20] On the issue of housework, the CdF proposed the socialization of domestic tasks as a remedy to the conditions imposed on working-class women. In "Introduction to the Power of Women and the Subversion of Community," Selma James (1997) states that such a solution may resolve the problem of women's work within the domestic sphere but that it does not contribute to the understanding of social reproduction itself or of how housework is fundamental to the capitalist system of exploitation. "For these women [those proposing the socialization of domestic tasks] capital is the main enemy but because it is *backward* not because it *exists*. They don't aim to destroy the capitalist social relation but only to organize it more rationally" (James 1997, 34; emphasis in original).[21]

Returning to the content of the interview, James and Dalla Costa addressed the Montréal feminist public – or at least the part they believed were sympathetic to their cause – with a series of feminist demands: to work less, to secure a guaranteed income for both women and men, to ensure women's control of their bodies and the right to not have children, to enact price controls, and to increase services for women and children. The interview also includes a central analytical dimension of their campaign, and one that is constantly overlooked – namely, the interconnection between various sectors of society: the household, the school, the neighbourhood, the community, and the market where goods are bought and sold. Although the questions asked by the CdF representatives reflect their bias in favour of working-class struggles in factories and workplaces, the feminist visitors' analysis comes through:

> Thus, houses and neighbourhoods are not spaces of leisure and of freedom connected to the factory where, coincidentally, women are working as men's servants. On the contrary, the neighbourhood is the other half of capitalist organization, the other sector of capitalist exploitation, the other hidden source of surplus value. The central point of this social factory that is the neighbourhood is that it is the housewife who produces a commodity: the labour force.[22]

Transposed into the Montréal and Québécois context, this quote unveils another dimension of unpaid women's work in the form of all the hours spent in providing community services, assistance to other women living in the vicinity, and, I should add, performing activist work in feminist collectives, women's groups, and community organizing. From this perspective, the feminist and non-feminist scholarship on what is commonly called the "social economy" sector or, since the 1990s, the "solidarity economy" sector, needs to be revisited and critically analyzed with a feminist materialist lens focused on the area of social reproduction. All the unpaid and underpaid work performed in this sector – which found its niche in the interstices of the market economy and the public and para-public state institutions – must be included in this analysis.

Moreover, the WfH movement presented an original perspective on the school system, which is placed in synergy with the neighbourhood and the factory. In *Women and the Subversion of Community,* Dalla Costa and James (1997, 42–44) argue that schools are part of an ideological structure in which children are set up against their parents: "Working-class children then are the first who instinctively rebel against schools and the education provided in schools." The document highlights the strong and clear connection between the women's movement and the student movement. As some Italian feminists (Maria Pia Turri, quoted in Toupin 2014, 116) pointed out, all working activities and hours spent outside the home should count as a strategy "à l'intérieur, à l'extérieur et autour de l'école" (inside, outside and around the school).

Perhaps it is the differences between the Italian and Québécois left on work-related issues that made the historic encounter between the CdF and Dalla Costa and James an impossible dialogue. The documents that have surfaced from the two Montréal international events – the symposium in 1973 and the international conference in 1975 as well as articles in the pages of *Québécoises deboutte!* – mirrored the multiple divides within the WfH movement both nationally and internationally. Some of these divides are related to the form of the organization – centralized or non-centralized – while others highlight conflicts over texts published by feminist leaders of the movement. Others point to important disagreements on the issues of race and/or sexuality.[23] Depending on to whom one is talking/reading, these conflicts may have had the same point of origin (James 2012a; Toupin 2014). In all, these divides and tensions did not help the movement.[24]

Feminist Critiques against Wages for Housework

Large segments of the feminist/women's movement refused to see the WfH demand as truly feminist. This rejection remains clear and unrelenting today, despite the resurgence of feminist scholarship on the issue and the recognition that all the work performed in and around the domestic sphere is invisible, not only because no wage is attached to it but also because theoretical analysis has not yet been able to unveil the fundamental importance it has for the preservation of capitalism.

The response to Selma James's (2012b) document "Women, the Unions and Work" was the prelude to the fierce opposition still to come during the 1970s. It was presented at a national conference on the Women's Liberation Movement held in Manchester in 1972. It contains six demands, one of which was wages for housework. The document was published and distributed widely as a pamphlet and then discussed a second time at the National Women's Conference in London later the same year. James's recollection of this political moment notes the excitement as well as the profound disagreement and rejection that her perspective generated among women, and the ferocious leftist opposition to the demand for a wage. Indeed, "Women, Unions and Work" contains harsh criticisms of the unions' attitudes towards women, their meagre efforts to unionize women, the (un)equal wage distribution among women and men, and working-class women's poor working conditions. Yet the bulk of the opposition to the document was directed at the demand for wages for housework. Most of the opponents were feminists and women activists. Regardless of whether they were affiliated with the left or not, their opposition was simple. James (2012b, 60–61) argues that many participants at the National Conference in London "refused to recognize housework as work." "Women, Unions and Work" was overwhelmingly rejected, along with its six-point proposal.

The London conference was meant to be a national event, though several feminists from European and North American countries participated in the discussion. In Italy, the LF delegation echoed James's assessment but attributed the failure to adopt the document to the heavy presence of women members of leftist organizations and, thus, to the indirect masculine influence on the conference (Lotta Femminista 1973, 5–7). Decades later, Louise Toupin (2104, 138–40) expressed similar views, adding that "Women, Unions and Work" must be seen as complementary to Dalla Costa's *Women and the Subversion of Community*. Nevertheless, in the midst of a massive campaign against the elimination of family allowances, James went on and created the Power of Women collective, composed mainly of single mothers on welfare.

The year 1972 marked the beginning of the International Feminist Collective on wages for housework. The network was small since the movement took root in a very limited number of countries in Europe, the United States, and English Canada. Yet in most of these countries, the campaign for wages for housework generated a significant number of collectives with leaders and members coming from a wide variety of backgrounds in terms of race, class, and sexuality. These collectives helped shape the transnational characteristics of the network, making visible an analysis in line with James's approach to bring race within same frame as gender and class. Yet the intersection with race remained unequal from one country to another and from one collective to another. The main consensual paradigm supporting the movement was that housework is essential to capitalism and that as long as this work is unpaid it has no market value and is therefore judged unproductive.

When we look at the issue of race and sexuality in this discourse, the content of the WfH campaign offered a truly intersectional perspective. Some Italian collectives that arose in the wake of LF always talked about the conditions of the unemployed in the Italian South and/or in Third World countries but rarely mentioned that racialization was also happening in the Italian North.[25] Issues of sexuality, contraception, abortion, and prostitution dominated most feminist discourses (Zumaglino 1996, 109), while in the United States, race and sexuality intersected within the collective known as Black Women for Wages for Housework.[26] In Canada, the issue of sexuality gained visibility with the group Wages Due Lesbians. These are only a few examples. During the lifetime of the IFC, the number of WfH groups grew steadily, and the number of documents produced by the network addressed a wide variety of social categories of women, including Black women, lesbians, prostitutes, working mothers, and single mothers on welfare. All these sociological categories were portrayed within the mainstream media as either outside the norm or deviant – particularly Black single mothers, lesbians, and prostitutes.

In the feminist literature of the 1970s, two key ideas appeared regularly. The first idea claimed that women's condition was comparable to the oppression of Black people, mainly in the United States, and, to some extent, to the oppression of peasants in Third World countries. The second idea claimed that women were a "caste" as opposed to a "class." On this issue, Selma James argues that women should "confront and reject" their condition as part of a caste:

> The Black movement in the United States (and elsewhere) also began by adopting what appeared to be only a caste position in opposition to the racism of the white male-dominated groups. Intellectuals in Harlem and Malcolm X, that great revolutionary, were both nationalists, and both

> appeared to place color above class when the white left were still chanting variations of "Black and white unite and fight" or "Negroes and Labor must join together." The Black working class was able through this nationalism to redefine class: overwhelmingly Black and Labor were synonymous (with no other group was Labor as synonymous – except perhaps with women), the demands of Blacks and the forms of struggle created by Blacks were the most comprehensive working-class demands and the most advanced working-class struggle.[27]

In this quote, women as a group are compared to Black people as a group, a comparison that subsumes all women of colour within one racial category; and, as a group, all are invited to go beyond their claim of being a single "caste." This is a position that many Italian feminists were tempted to take. However, there is no way to disentangle "black working-class" men from "black working-class" women, their demands, and their strategies.

James's (1997, 35) argument appears fragile in the face of feminist criticism that saw the WfH movement as being only interested in engaging with the left and as an attempt to rescue Marxism from its limitations (Mies 1986, 33). Yet James urges women to adopt a strategic use of the notion of caste in order to go beyond it. The notion of caste, with its nationalistic overtones, encompasses women within a working-class regrouping more efficiently than does the category of class itself. In *Women and the Subversion of Community,* these key ideas – women as a group are like Blacks as a group, and women are a caste – are used simultaneously: the working-class housewife becomes "the determinant for the position of all women. Every analysis of women as a caste, then, must proceed from the analysis of the position of working-class housewives" (Dalla Costa and James 1997, 40).

There is a lot to say about the tendency to compare women with Black people as a political tool as well as about the strategic use of caste to get beyond the notion of class. The idea was to conflate all women into a single category, sometimes into the working-class category, other times into a generic oppressed category. Yet, according to Maria Mies (1986, 33), even the wages for housework discourse on Third World peasant society did not transcend the Eurocentric view of capitalism.[28] To this day, the most often-heard critique of WfH is that it tends to crystallize women's role within the family. For Manuela Fraire (2002, 111), for instance:

> The political implications of such a discourse are hard to accept, however, because it definitively sanctions the role of the woman in the family and

> institutionalizes her exclusion from the productive world of men. That would mean to socially recognize the woman as the "negative" side of man, to pay her for this work without really challenging patriarchy, seen as the power of men as a sex to appropriate women's working capacity. Moreover, the political project of the salary is guilty of economism in the sense that it does not recognize that being a housewife is not solely a job but above all a role which at the deepest levels has implications that cannot be reduced to or analyzed as the fair socio-economic treatment of women.[29]

But considering all the societal layers the WfH movement targeted, concluding that it worked only on the terrain of women's economic needs does not do it justice. Some criticized the WfH movement for not clarifying how a salary for domestic activities would uncover the mechanism that makes domestic work so essential to capitalist exploitation. Others pointed out that, beyond improving women's social and economic conditions, a salary would not bring about women's liberation or significantly transform their lives. Most of these criticisms argued – and still do – that liberation will be realized only when women transcend their reproductive roles and stop reproducing the social order that contributes to their exploitation and that prevents them from reappropriating their bodies, their sexuality, and the control of their maternity.

We are back to the paradox of WfH: how to demand a salary for housework while refusing to perform it, how to present one dimension of the demand without neutralizing the strength of the other. Opponents of WfH choose not to consider the paradox as a challenge for feminism, believing that women must enter collectively and en masse into the sphere of production (Fraire 2002, 112). This aspect of feminist strategy is almost identical to what the traditional left wants for women. It is like an "emancipation plus" – equal access to employment plus public services for mothers, adding some feminist demands regarding the body and sexuality. While the WfH movement was turning its attention outward – pointing to women's unpaid work in multiple sectors as essential to capitalist exploitation – the attention of most of the feminist counter-critiques was turning inward, focusing on women's role in the domestic sphere, sparing little thought to the mechanisms inside and outside paid work, inside and outside the home. The fact that LF had already severely criticized the RfW discourse for its shortcomings is disregarded; that the WfH movement had enlarged the scope of its analysis to the school, the neighbourhood, the city, the village markets, and the unpaid productive work of women in these sectors is ignored; that the

WfH collectives in Italy and many Anglo-Saxon countries had built a multilayered analysis of race, sexuality, and the body disappears from feminist analysis. It is true that the WfH documents mainly described women's condition rather than theorizing a better understanding of the field of work. But the feminist critiques failed to propose a better theoretical framework and were oblivious to the fact that, in retrospect, they proposed a reductionist vision of the work of social reproduction.

Furthermore, feminist arguments against WfH highlight tendencies within the feminist/women's movement to privilege productivist solutions that prevent further theorization of the issue of work. They do not provide the necessary critical analysis to assess strategies to alleviate women's precarious economic living conditions (Michaud 2005, 164–71; Weeks 2011, 12–13). The tension between the WfH movement and the feminist/women's movement was not simply a disagreement over the demand for wages in and of itself. The critique against WfH suffered from an oversight and, to put it mildly, a kind of feminist indifference to the analytical paradigm unveiled by WfH with regard to social reproduction. As the discrediting of WfH gained ground within the feminist/women's movement, the narrowness of this opposing view was revealed to be embedded within the quasi-hegemonic vision of work prevalent in capitalist society and the liberal economy.

Wages for Housework: A Movement Poorly Understood

Lotta Femminista's main critiques and political divergences with the refusal to work movement were addressed through the Padua journal *Operaie della casa* as well as other feminist journals, such as *Sottosopra*. From time to time, open letters appeared in leftist publications that enjoyed a broader distribution, such as *Il Manifesto*. At its debut, LF adopted an assertive tone characteristic of the feminist avant-garde, presenting itself as the unique organizing force in a constellation of Italian women's groups and feminist collectives. That is the way *Sottosopra* perceived LF, and many complained that the Padua collective overwhelmed the Milanese journal in 1973 and 1974 with endless unedited articles and documents (Colombo and Giuffreda 1978, 3; Libreria delle donne 2005b, 37).[30] The collective's aim to unify the feminist/women's movement behind the WfH campaign was not popular among feminists and was situated on the opposite side of a variety of feminist collectives, most of which saw the political platform as too extreme. Geographically isolated and practically alone within the feminist camp, LF generated similar groups throughout the country but never succeeded in attracting feminist activists who focused on a multiplicity of issues related to women's needs (Zumaglino 1996, 137). In Québec, there were many political moments when the WfH issue emerged, and, less than a decade after the James and Dalla Costa visit to Montréal, the journal *La vie en rose* attempted to bring WfH back to the centre of the feminist agenda. But again and again the feminist/women's movement rejected the demand: the problem of women's unpaid work remained unsolved, and sometimes the demand itself was distorted.

Finally, in 1983, some women's groups in Turin held an important international conference called *Produre/riprodure* (Produce/reproduce). The conference hosted several workshops on a broad range of issues: the economic crisis, the use of new technologies in the workplace, the development of independent labour, self-management and cooperatives, and, of course, housework. From the authors of the article "Nuovi antichi lavori" (New old work), who signed their names simply as Jessica, Ines, and Marcella, we learn that the discussion on the issue of work addressed non-paid activities: from the reproduction of the species and caring for children to the activities necessary to maintain individuals' vital functions to the physical and psychological well-being of families (Jessica, Ines, and Marcella 1983, 6–7). The workshop's primary focus was the unequal sexual division of labour in the domestic sphere and the recognition that women's work required an equitable redistribution of housework in *respect of sexual difference.* The public policy of tax credits that favoured men within the family was denounced, but what was of real interest was that workshop participants supported some sort of a salary for all women's activities in society, including housework, as the necessary condition for social and cultural value and recognition. The article also argues that the recognition of men's involvement in activities of social reproduction could lead to alternative forms of family, which would no longer be a space exclusive to women. This is as far as it gets. The part that analyzed the exploitation of women's work in the family as the necessary condition for the exploitation of the working class as a whole, including the exploitation of under- or unpaid male workers, has disappeared. The idea that wages for housework could reveal that unpaid women's work is necessary for capitalism is gone; the rejection of housework as a natural condition that entraps women within the so-called feminine role is not discussed. All of these issues once put forth by the WfH movement were put to sleep; fortunately, however, they were not completely wiped from the history books.

4 Double Activism and Feminist Separatism

But do we have to save Mrs. Agnelli as well?
– Piera Zumaglino

Women as a Caste or as a Class?

The question, "Ma dobbiamo salvare anche la Signora Agnelli?" (But do we have to save Mrs. Agnelli as well?), quoted in Zumaglino (1996, 126), emerged at a feminist public event during a discussion of women's shared oppression. Mrs. Agnelli was the wife of the owner of the FIAT automobile company in Turin, who was one of the richest men in Italy. Not everyone at the meeting was convinced that the women's question should have priority over the class struggle. The fact that Mrs. Agnelli was presented as "the wife of" meant little to feminists who defended women's issues by using Marxist principles. Nevertheless, the "Signora Agnelli syndrome," as it was called then, haunted the feminist mindset in Turin and in many other Italian cities for years (Zumaglino 1996, 126–27).

A similar interrogation, "Should women's struggles have priority over class struggle?," was tackled early on by a small women's collective in Trento called Cerchio Spezzato (Broken circle) (1970) in the document "Non c'è rivoluzione senza liberazione della donna" (There is no revolution without the liberation of women). Beyond the document's title – which is often written in reverse and used as a slogan – the core argument urges women to work on a political agenda separate from that of their male comrades. Members of Cerchio Spezzato claimed lengthy experiences in political activism within the student movement and other leftist organizations. They explained their decision to exclude men from their meetings as political, based on their no longer having the illusion that class oppression is similar for men and women. Working-class women are subjected to a double exploitation that transcends class. Women are part of a "caste" based on the fact that their sex is assigned by birth,[1] just like skin colour. A caste cuts across all social classes and it is impossible to escape. "Beyond the fact of being divided by class, our society also presents a caste situation within which some people are forced to live because of easily identifiable physical characteristics, like sex and skin colour. Caste is assigned at birth and no individual action can make it possible to leave it behind."[2]

Cerchio Spezzato's analysis of women's condition in the family and in paid work puts this small Trento collective among the forerunners of several debates: autonomy versus separatism, equality between women and men and the validity of emancipation versus liberation, and the articulation of politics and feminism. The authors' attempt to define women as a caste in biological terms is meant to be a warning against two types of mistakes that feminists should avoid. The first mistake is not to see that women's condition as a caste is the foundation of their revolutionary potential: such a mistake risks invalidating an autonomous movement of struggle. The second mistake is to accept male terms for parity within current societal structures (Cerchio Spezzato 1970, 128).

In 1971, a year after the Cerchio Spezzato document was made public, a small women's group with an indeterminate name, Un groupe de femmes de Montréal (A Montréal women's group), published the *Manifeste des femmes Québécoises* (Manifesto of Québécois women). One of the document's main concerns was the presence of women in mixed-gender national liberation groups. The manifesto was made public within a particular context in Québec judicial history: the Montréal criminal court had just begun to prosecute members of the Front de libération du Québec for terrorism in the aftermath of what is known as the *Crise d'octobre* (October crisis) of 1970. One of the witnesses at the trial, Lise Balcer, refused to testify because the Québécois legislation forbade women to be members of a jury.[3] The *Manifeste* set the tone for a feminist materialist analysis of women's condition, pointing to a double oppression: capitalist and patriarchal. It is also one of the few Québécois feminist documents to refer to the notion of "separatism" as a necessary organizational strategy for developing a feminist analysis as a counterpoint to Marxist schemas (Un groupe de femmes de Montréal 1971, 57).

Groups like Cerchio Spezzato and Un groupe de femmes de Montréal were among the first women's collectives to proclaim the autonomy of the women's movement in relation to the class struggle. Cerchio chastised women activists who chose to pursue their political activities in mixed-gender political groups and to seek equality in workplaces. "Non c'è rivoluzione senza liberazione della donna" echoed the disappointment of young women who had experienced extra-parliamentary left politics, which had always rejected women's autonomy of speech and of action.[4]

Yet in the early 1970s in Québec, as in Italy, many feminists were convinced of the need to organize an autonomous feminist/women's movement while maintaining a connection with the left. This chapter is about this category of activists, those who were willing to cross the frontiers between feminism and the left in both directions and had more than one site of political engagement. My aim is to answer the question: What is double activism? How can we distinguish the desire for autonomy from the constitutive elements that compose feminist separatism? Is it double activism when differentiated social categories such as lesbians and racialized groups of women try to reconcile their engagement in feminist collectives with their active participation in newly formed gay and lesbian groups or people of colour organizations? Or does this term speak only of the situation between feminists and other leftist political actors? Is double activism just a way of connecting more than one terrain of one's political intervention or is it a way of being in the world? This chapter confronts the arguments and counter-arguments of both double activism and feminist separatism.

At the end of the discussion, I come to the conclusion that feminism in Québec during most of the 1970s was not truly separatist but autonomous in comparison with the separatist type of feminism found in Italy, and I explain why. Throughout the chapter, I also explore feminism's articulation with politics, considering whether the emerging "new political subject" of the 1970s was ready for the political terrain she was about to invade.

Allegiances, Loyalties, and Consciousness

Double Activism/Double Subjectivities

Double activism is often presented as an Italian phenomenon, based on the overwhelming presence of the Partito Comunista Italiano (Italian communist party) within the political/public spaces as well as in the life of communist members and fellow travellers (Lilli 1979,10). Determining the moment of emergence of double activism in the political experience of Italian women is as difficult as trying to define the terrain of its practices. Double activism was a fact of life long before the 1960s, at least for members of the national organization Unione donne Italiane (Union of Italian women), for whom the question of its members' allegiance to their respective political parties did not seem to conflict with their dedication to the cause of improving women's conditions.[5] Double activism was the way communist women perceived their primary role: bringing Italian women's conditions on par with that of their male counterparts. It was not unusual in the PCI to describe the average Italian woman's social, economic, and political conditions as backward, while putting the blame on the unwillingness of the state and its institutions to address their problems. Communist women in particular believed it was their mission to save the average woman from poverty, from her lack of education and her subaltern position within the family and Italian society. They believed in the power of emancipation and wanted to bring others to the same level they had been able to achieve as members of the Communist Party. Their representation of women living in the South was particularly negative compared to working-class women in the North. Needless to say, they did not pay attention to their own subaltern condition within the PCI (Zuffa 1987, 39). This became visible with the PCI's refusal to accept divorce legislation in 1974 and its role in negotiating a compromise on abortion, resulting in more restrictive legislation (Gramaglia 1975a). The PCI's stand on these issues was based on the idea that Italian working-class families were conservative and that the role of women within them remained very traditional and not prepared for social change (45–46).

The members of the new generation of feminists were not interested in waiting for mediocre changes, and they were even less interested in wasting their time educating leftist men about feminism. Yet there was an all-new generation of double activists still willing to cross back and forth between movements: from the outside into feminism with the motive of bringing political struggles to feminist collectives and from the inside out to take feminist principles and feminist struggles into the discursive platform of the left. The act of crossing the frontiers of movements and political parties was not new, but it became a problem from the moment some segments of the feminist movement saw double activists as pernicious and dangerous. They were accused by feminist separatists of playing a double game. Communist women were still the target of criticism, but women's activists in the New Left were also targeted, perhaps even more than the previous generation of communist women, because they believed in changing traditional ways of doing politics – of transforming the subjectivity of the revolutionary male subject (Fraire 2002, 119–21).

The student movement and extra-parliamentary leftist groups have a different history of dealing with double activism, and there are many reasons it should be studied differently than the traditional left. One reason relates to the short amount of time an activist spent in emerging political groups compared to the average number of years spent in traditional political parties or unions. The status of being a student is usually short-lived, and most of the political groups composing the New Left in the 1970s lasted a limited number of years (Pasquali quoted in Petricola 2005, 207). Furthermore, a different type of autonomy was granted to women in the New Left than to those in the PCI. Interviews I conducted in Palermo and Naples highlight the difficulties and the lack of autonomy that Communist Party members experienced, particularly during national debates surrounding the adoption of legislation around abortion. Interviewees expressed fear of entering into open conflict with the PCI leadership and the risk of being isolated, especially if they were expelled or decided to leave the party, and the fear of losing friends and comrades.[6]

Practising double activism – and some lived this experience as a political identity – was full of ambiguities, marked by conflicting itineraries and dramatic situations for women who refused to quit their political groups when they decided to join a feminist collective (Fraire 1977, 50; Petricola 2005, 206). At first, some double activists claimed that class struggle was more important than feminist principles. Many of them recognized the awkwardness of their position but had never imagined that it would be so difficult to overcome.

Manuela Fraire (2002) and Gracia Zuffa (1987), respectively, argue that the experience of double activism is key to understanding women's experience in the left. Fraire focuses on three moments: (1) *when* feminist activists raised the women's question within political organizations; (2) *how* they raised that question; and (3) what *results*, modifications, and ruptures they got. Zuffa, in "Le doppie militanze: donna comunista, donna femminista" (Double activism: communist women, feminist women), looks at the issue from a different angle and is more interested in the evolution of the UDI than of individual feminists. The *when* was the moment the UDI was confronted by feminism and discovered the politics of autocoscienza, which it had at first rejected, having viewed it as an elitist practice: some UDI members later adopted a transformed version of autocoscienza. The *how* was an attempt to bring some feminist principles back into the PCI, but this had poor results.

The extra-parliamentary left, despite its conflict with feminism, tried many different tactics. Il Manifesto addressed women's issues early on but refused to create a women's commission, a decision that cut short feminist activism within the group (Fraire 2002, 126; Gramaglia 1987, 30). Other extra-parliamentary groups, such as LC, treated specific conditions, such as that of being women and that of being students, as mere terrains of intervention. The group set up a women's commission – open to men – adopting a very traditional way of functioning and privileging the membership of working-class women in order to criticize what it perceived to be the cultural dimension of bourgeois feminism. Leaders of LC treated the Italian feminist/women's movement as an unrelated constellation of groups, created under the pressure of public opinion, rather than as a mass movement devoted to political struggles (Fraire 2002, 127–28). The fact that some of these women's commissions were mixed-gender fed the perception that women members of the extra-parliamentary left were not free to think for themselves and that their ideas needed to be legitimized by their male comrades. Internally, however, there was tension around the status and role of these women's commissions as well as around the extent of their autonomy.[7] Fierce struggles emerged outside leftist groups as well.[8] The history of LF, which promoted WfH, is an example of the difficulties that haunted double activists, and it is also emblematic of the two axes/souls of feminism: one always trying to win over the other (Fraire 2002; Zumaglino 1996, 207–10).

The specific consciousness of a double activist remains difficult to capture. Women who lived the experience were criticized for not devoting their energies entirely to women, for believing in emancipation, for not thinking freely, and for taking direction from somewhere outside of feminism. This is a state of mind that Lilli and Valentini (1979) characterize as a sort of schizophrenia. They describe the feelings of individuals who have a split consciousness – of being engaged in two worlds at the same time but not feeling whole in either. Lilli and Valentini's field research presents double activism as a political engagement that goes beyond the frontiers of the period. Lilli (1979, 27), for instance, argues that double activism is existential:

> It is the way of being oneself – of facing the world and oneself – of all women being "self-aware": through a life project they take the difficult road of emancipation having in mind the utopia of liberation. For the woman

> unionist, to be a true double activist does not mean staying in the union and in the feminist collective at the same time. It is about "how" to stay in the union. For the woman Communist it does not mean reconciling the party with the group. It is about "how" to live within the party.[9]

Lilli and Valentini's choice of the term "schizophrenia" suggests that one's consciousness is torn apart, that there is a risk of exhausting the double activist's political will regardless of the level of enthusiasm she puts into her political involvement. In *Lessico politico delle donne,* Fraire (2002, 125–26) goes further, describing the excruciating situation women experience while trying to be themselves in both the party and the feminist collective:

> What does *double activism* mean? First of all it means being part of the party's life (starting with section meetings, intervening in the neighbourhood, in the union, in the school, etc.) and being part of the life of the feminist movement (composed of small consciousness-raising groups, of collective meetings, often intervening in the social). Two, three meetings every day, which means having exhausted all the new ways of doing politics women had acquired. It means being a full-time activist in a way that suffocates and contradicts, crushes and upsets the life of feminist women in the PdUP beyond their new consciousness. On the other hand, for several years double activism appeared to be the sole way of being that secured women's autonomy as well as the autonomy of the movement against the risk of recreating a women's ghetto, like the women's commissions on the one side, and on the other side, the external avant-garde that brings the "party line" within the movement.[10]

Several women's narratives appeared in feminist journals such as *Effe, Differenze, Sottosopra,* and *Bollettino donne di Torino.* Stories of double activists indicate that their itineraries were multiple rather than linear. If our understanding of double activism creates the impression that women discovered feminism from their political organizations, like the PCI, the extra-parliamentary group, or the union, many others began within feminist collectives – sometimes separatist collectives – before joining a leftist group or a party. If, at the end, some chose feminism as a sole point of reference for their activism, many others refused to see any contradiction in being both a feminist and a Marxist (Bravo, Del Boca, and Scaraffia 1977; Crispino 1979; G. Francescato 1976, 12; Rowbotham 1981, 74–75). As such, they resisted the most pressing accusation made by feminist separatists, who saw their double involvement as solely benefiting the leftist party or organization, in which women were seen merely as one social problem among others.[11]

The extra-parliamentary left pretended to have integrated the spirit of the "personal is political" during the peak of the Autonomy Movement and stated that this time their organization was taking women's issues seriously. There were at least two categories of feminist activists who were not convinced, though for different reasons: the feminist separatists and those who joined the armed struggle. The former saw the '77 Movement as the defeat of double activism and a moment of vindication, while the latter did not care about any attempt to transform a political system they hoped to eliminate through violence (Fraire 1977; Tavola rotonda 2004).

The Québec Experience of Double Activism

The concept of double activism is virtually absent in the Québécois feminist literature, although a significant number of women were involved in mixed-gender groups as well as in feminist collectives. Yet there were suspicions and accusations of infiltration on the part of extra-parliamentary leftist organizations. For instance, the feminist journal *Les têtes de Pioche* claimed to have been the target of infiltration, and one article accused some women activists of putting the journal's autonomy at risk (Jean 1979, 2). If there were attempts to infiltrate feminist collectives, they were not successful, and they never overcame feminist aspirations to create an autonomous women's movement free from external interference (O'Leary and Toupin 1983, 338; Péloquin 2007, 247–68).

The Front de libération des femmes du Québec, known for its spectacular direct actions, knew from the start that it had to operate from an autonomous feminist perspective (Péloquin 2007, 248). The collective was made up of small cells whose activities were conducted independently from one another. One of these cells organized direct actions in order to provoke changes in public opinion. A second cell worked on decriminalizing abortion in addition to operating a phone line and a reference centre. A third cell focused its operation on daycare centres in working-class neighbourhoods. The FLFQ ceased its activities at the end of 1971, and two ex-members decided to create the Centre des femmes in January 1972. The CdF's connection with extra-parliamentary groups was more explicit, although the new collective still argued that the women's movement must be entirely autonomous.

Both the FLFQ and the CdF engaged in a kind of double activism. Marjolaine Péloquin 2007, 248–57), in *En prison pour la cause des femmes,* attempts to clarify the distinction between these two early feminist collectives that so strongly affected the theoretical and political development of Montréal and Québécois feminism. She echoes O'Leary and Toupin's (1982, 23) warning against confusing the two collectives and contends that feminist historians have repeated many historical errors by amalgamating the two.[12]

The difference between the two feminist collectives indicates that, in Québec, the movement evolved differently than in Italy. With the dissolution of the FLFQ in 1971, feminism shifted from a sort of materialist feminism – tainted by a countercultural discourse, anti-colonial socialism, and a Third World version of Québécois independence – to a version of Marxism dominated by extra-parliamentary groups. It is within this context that a specific double activist consciousness developed among significant numbers of women – a consciousness that differed from one collective to another. Being an active member of a union or being a community organizer within a popular group in a working-class neighbourhood was not the same as being a woman activist of En Lutte! or the PCO. Activism took many different forms during the early years of Québécois feminism, and there was a clear overlap of allegiances: the above-mentioned *Manifeste des femmes Québécoises,* which counts as the first contemporary feminist document, was apparently written by women members of extra-parliamentary organizations. The FLFQ did not lean towards this leftist trend per se, but some of its members were part of leftist mixed-gender groups (Péloquin 2007, 249–55).

Péloquin (2007, 252, 255) is adamant in her argument that the FLFQ did not collaborate with extra-parliamentary organizations and insists on this point of difference between it and the CdF. Yet the left, with all its variances, was a reference for women's groups, including the FLFQ, during most of the 1970s. It would take a major decline of leftist mobilization as well as increasing pressure from feminism before women's groups shifted away from Marxism and Marxist terms of reference. In the 1980s, a series of articles in *La vie en rose* highlights the rupture between feminism and the left as the political vitality that characterized the previous decade began to evaporate.

Dimensions of an Autonomous Feminist/ Women's Movement

At the heart of the problem of double activism, in Québec as in Italy, lie the roles and the spaces occupied by politics and social struggles within feminism. Primary sources show that some activists saw an urgent need to address the problem.[13] Some feminists wanted to reject anything that came close to male politics, to orient feminism outside of the world of masculine thought. The objective was to clearly define the role and the place of the feminist movement apart from other political movements – to move the terrain of action away from the traditional structures of parties, unions, and movements: there was no hesitation to describe feminism as a political movement, something the vast majority of women's male counterparts refused to do.

Double activists were convinced that feminist discourses, feminist practices, and feminist modes of organizing helped to enlarge the sphere of traditional politics through feminist collective action and struggles, contributing to the democratization of public/political practices. They advocated the urgent need to be part of the social, but they also felt a certain alienation due to operating in two worlds that were so far apart. For the double activist, then, being a feminist in spaces that denied her subjectivity, being a member of a feminist collective that expressed doubts about her loyalty to feminism and to women, it was a challenge to overcome the splitting of her consciousness. It meant becoming a political subject according to her own rules, accepting her own gaze on her own actions, both against and beyond the gaze of others, be they male comrades or feminist allies. If she refused the canon of feminist separatism, then she could at least claim autonomy of speech and autonomy of action within whatever terrain she chose to speak or act.

Here, there are two dimensions to the meaning of autonomy, both of which intervene simultaneously in the construction of a political subject based on the position of the double activist: (1) there is the autonomy in relation to masculine interventions in structures and organizations that the double activist seeks to create inside and outside male-dominated organizations such as the party, the extra-parliamentary left, and the union; and (2) there is the autonomy that connects the double activist affirmatively and defensively with other feminist activists – affirmatively, because it creates conditions for solidarity among women, and defensively, because the affirmation of her autonomy is how she defends herself against attacks concerning her loyalties and against the temptation of separation.

Such constructions of a double activist's political consciousness are less a concern for traditional figures, such as the communist women and/or members of the UDI, even though they are the ones who, more than anyone else, dealt with accusations of being unable to face the challenge set by contemporary feminism and its sophisticated and complex discourse on women's liberation.[14] However, the issue of autonomy is above all the concern of the feminist double activist who criss-crossed the frontiers of New Left politics because of its promise of practising politics differently. It concerned the double activist who claimed to act for the total liberation of women and who argued that this liberation could not ignore struggles taking place within public/political spaces. Thus, the double activist was a woman who felt the pressure but refused to choose between two equally attractive terrains: feminism and the left.

The trajectory of feminism as a political movement shows that even separatist collectives were not exempt from the temptation to engage in more than one terrain, particularly the terrain of public/political institutions. The most striking example of such a split within feminist discourses emerged when small and/or large collectives were confronted with efforts to autonomously manage women's service groups, most notably feminist health centres/consultori,[15] in both Italy and Québec.

The tension double activism brought to the lives of those who experienced it, as well as the lives of those who witnessed it in feminist collectives, did not fade with the decline of the mass mobilizations of the 1980s. The phenomenon continued to raise the question of the involvement of feminist activists within political parties and unions. Furthermore, the multifaceted dimensions of double activism refracted into gender-mixed groups organizing around gay and lesbian sexual practices and political visibility.[16] This added another layer of complexity, bringing feminist principles into gay male control structures and making it difficult for lesbians to express themselves in feminist collectives and the women's movement. In the 1970s, newly formed gay and lesbian collectives found some sort of inspiration from feminism: some even suggested that the explosion of feminist subjectivities inspired the emergence of their movements in the United States, Canada, Italy, and in many other countries (Michaud 2010; Schiavo 2002, 26; Wilson and Rény 1978). Yet recreating the origins of a movement, whatever it is, is futile since memory is a disputed terrain where all sorts of narratives and counter-narratives confront one another, gaining their legitimacy from their ability to decide which should be transferred to the next generation and which should not.

Like most mixed-gender organizations, the structures and functioning of the 1960s and 1970s gay and lesbian groups were male-oriented. In Turin, the group Fuori! (Out!), also known as Fronte unitario omosessuale italiano (Italian homosexual united front), dedicated its energies to defending homosexual rights and to maintaining close relationships with the extra-parliamentary left. The presence of lesbians was small, and their practices were modelled on the consciousness of gay men: many lesbians left and joined new groups, initiating a phase of lesbian separatism (Code 2000; Pomeranzi 1984, 73; Schiavo 2002, 192–93; Turcotte 2013).

Within feminism, if the profile of a double activist is that of a heterosexual woman suspected of false consciousness and of living with divided loyalties, the profile of a lesbian double activist is that of someone who is trying to reconcile being in a mixed-gender homosexual group and in a feminist collective. Neither the gay collective nor the feminist collective gives these women space (Laura 1978, 40). The invisibility of lesbians within feminist historiography is still hard to explain (Petricola 2005, 208–9; Schiavo 2002, 25). Some argue that in the 1970s advocating lesbian politics was risky, and it took time before lesbians succeeded in putting the issue on the feminist agenda (Schiavo 2002, 35–36).[17] Yet sexual visibility was not enough to claim a sense of belonging to a movement that lesbians had built side by side with heterosexuals, especially if it meant the silencing of their demands and subjectivities (O'Leary and Toupin 1983, 344; Pomeranzi 1984, 73; Tremblay 1978, 8). A critical analysis of oppression of and discrimination against lesbians was virtually nonexistent in feminist theories (Schiavo 2002, 26). Having exhausted their potential for activism within mixed-gender groups and feminist collectives, lesbians began to organize outside the presence of men and outside feminism as well. The erasure of lesbianism within the movement must be contrasted with the core arguments and statements of feminist separatism and its politics, which was evolving at the symbolic level, creating a dichotomy between itself and the world of man, his culture, his language, and his consciousness. Yet the creation of a separate women's world whose purpose was the institutionalization of a feminine culture remained fundamentally based on heterosexuality and heteronormativity (de Lauretis 1990, 4).[18]

The profile of a racialized double activist – one who participates actively in the creation of collectives composed of racialized members while engaged in the development of a feminist collective, or perhaps a newly created lesbian collective, or a collective devoted to intersectional practice – is still to be imagined. Hill and Bilge (2016, 64) remind us that the practice of intersectionality began at the level of social movement practices long before 1989, when the concept was coined by Kimberly Crenshaw. The concept is not just a buzzword (Davis 2008): it embraces a whole set of discourses and related practices in the terrain of feminist and community activism that shaped feminism (even though it may not have been recorded). The double activism of an Aboriginal woman or of a woman of colour in

Québec or in Italy is hidden in the interstices of movement practices, participating at the margins, perhaps scarcely visible but there nonetheless.

Speaking of the experience of racialized women at the turn of the 1980s, Dûchaine (1986–87), Ship (1991), St-Denis (2007), and Ricci (2017) demonstrate their absence within the Québécois historiography of the feminist/women's movement. But they confirm their activism within spaces where the word "feminism" was not necessarily mentioned. Apart from a few articles found in feminist journals like *Pluri-elles/Des luttes et des rires* and *Marie-Géographie,* feminist literature rarely addresses Indigenous women's struggles and even less their presence within feminist collectives. However, Amanda Ricci (2017, 2018) reminds us that early organizations of Indigenous women in Québec ran in parallel with the core feminist/women's movement. The groups crossed paths on several occasions, interrupting the mainstream feminist narrative. One of the problems of reconciling Indigenous feminist activism with the Québec feminist/women's movement arose from the Québécois feminist conviction that Québec society, too, had been colonized (Green 2009; Stasiulis 1999).

Critiques of Double Activism

Double activists accepted and promoted the idea of an autonomous feminist/women's movement, but their actions clashed with the force of feminist separatism, which rejected their claims for autonomy as limited and counterproductive. I have isolated two types of criticism against double activism in Italy. The first type was aimed at organizations like the feminist journal *Effe.* According to its critics, the journal was the work of women from extra-parliamentary organizations and, to some extent, from the PCI's rank and file (Libreria delle donne 2005b, 8). *Effe* began publishing in Rome in 1973, proposing feminist counter-information at the national level and attempting to expand its audience beyond women's groups. Its goal was to communicate all points of view circulating within the larger movement and not to be limited to a few feminist currents. Nonetheless, it received negative criticisms from separatist segments of the movement and was accused of being paternalistic towards the women's groups it wanted to represent. *Effe*'s pages were supposed to be a site for feminist encounters between groups and activists eager to share and discuss their practices, but this did not happen (Paoli 2008, 258). Moreover, the journal's objectives placed the collective in an awkward position vis-à-vis other feminist journals, like the Milanese *Sottosopra* and its Roman competitor *Differenze,* both of which conceived their mandates as being circumscribed within the limits of the movement. Clashes between *Effe* and these and other feminist journals occurred frequently. A recurrent critique of *Effe* points to the double activism of those who created the journal, accusing them of not originating from within feminist collectives. In other words, they were not considered to be *part* of the movement so much as reporting *on* the movement (250, 258).

A second type of criticism targeted political figures like Rossana Rossanda, who personified the old-fashioned communist woman who kept class struggles at the centre of her politics and who appeared reluctant to acknowledge the principle of an autonomous women's movement (Libreria delle donne 2005b, 64–65). As a long-time member of the PCI, Rossanda remained devoted to communism even after her expulsion from the party in 1969. Rossanda's (1979, 23–24; 1983) position on the theory of sexual difference and of feminist separatism highlights her political trajectory. Her national profile gave her an audible and persuasive voice and allowed her to alter and subvert the meaning of sexual difference so as to make it more palatable to her party (de Lauretis 1990, 14). Yet Rossanda is not the perfect prototype of a double activist because she did not identify back then as a feminist but, rather, as a fellow traveller of the movement.

Rossanda's objections to feminist separatism show her difficulty understanding the autonomous expression of the women's question. In an interview with the feminist journal *Differenze,* she explained that her dissociation from the PCI in 1969 and her role in the creation of Il Manifesto were the result of a crisis between herself and others (Rossanda 1979). Activism, she said, meant working with others towards a common goal. Her comments about the crisis of political activism show that she dissociated feminism from politics and placed the feminist movement clearly and irremediably apart from projects initiated by the left. Ultimately, Rossanda's attachment to equality measures and to the idea of women's emancipation, as well as her interest in working inside public/political institutions in order to change them and make them work for women, positioned her apart from feminism in the eyes of the new generation of activists.

The presence of double activists within feminist collectives raised not only criticism but also fears: the fear of having one's political consciousness contaminated by a masculine system of thought – namely, Marxism –and the fear of a residual attachment to the traditional discourse on women's emancipation from an earlier generation of activists who never succeeded in transforming the social order. It did not suffice to create women-only spaces – although these small groups became fashionable even in the eyes of Marxists who persisted in giving class struggle an advantage over feminist struggle (O'Leary and Toupin 1983). The opposition to double activism was such that one wonders if the idea of woman as "political subject" was itself losing ground. For the feminist separatist, such a concept is necessarily attached to the practice of double activism: it explicitly represents the interference of masculine thought and an attempt to colonize women's consciousness (Collettivo femminista di via Cherubini 1975a, 3). The core argument against the practice of double activism was the refusal to use the same discourse – the language of the left – and the refusal to practise the same politics as other political actors, be they youth, students, or workers.

These arguments reached a peak in Italy during the abortion struggle. The political climate increased the attitude of defiance against the so-called discourse of the left and leftist men who proclaimed their support for abortion. Sharing public spaces with men was perceived as too risky for the integrity of the struggle itself. For example, in 1975, *Sottosopra* published a four-page document "La perdita del nostro corpo" (The loss of our body) that presented these arguments in the context of the abortion struggle. The authors, who self-identified as a small group of women from Turin, charged double activists with having a negative impact on the movement and with preventing the possibility of theorizing about women's bodies and sexualities in a language that was entirely feminist. Women's issues and struggles, the authors argued, were lost in the discourse of the left, and marching the streets and shouting slogans alongside sympathetic men tainted the political content of the feminist message. Even if the discourse of the left adopted feminist slogans, the goal of achieving the complete liberation of all women would be diminished and the good intentions of double activists would be swallowed up by leftist organizations and political parties (Alcuni donne di Torino 1975; Schiavo 2002, 138).

In Québec, Diane Lamoureux (1986, 32) makes similar arguments about the Comité pour l'avortement libre et gratuit, which tried to create a large coalition on abortion but saw its original wording amended by the union movement, which substituted its own slogan, "Nous aurons les enfants que nous voulons" (We will have the children we want), changing the demand for free abortion upon request. Thus, Québécois feminists who wanted to create an autonomous movement feared political interference and control over their collectives. As mentioned, the FLFQ and the CdF had different connections with the extra-parliamentary left, though they shared a similar fate in terms of dissolving and fragmenting into smaller groups.

Returning years later to discuss their experience, members of the two early feminist collectives recalled how accusations of conducting a bourgeois feminist agenda often dominated their meetings. In 1982, a round table reunited some of these women, bringing back the memory of criticisms against those who defended the complete autonomy of the women's movement but who were accused of dividing the working class and of not being truly feminist. Those who were not part of the extra-parliamentary left felt they had lost control of their collective's agenda and the group structures they wanted to run autonomously. The round table of remembrance provided details regarding how everything seemed to go smoothly at first, as if there were a clear consensus among members on group objectives and the same desire to share feminist principles. Then, suddenly, there was the sense that the collective had lost its homogeneity of thought, with one segment accusing the other of questioning whether the movement was prioritizing autonomy. The Québec experience is significantly different from the Italian experience, and yet the similarity is obvious. When the two feminist axes enter into conflict with one another, one attempts to gain ground over the other (O'Leary and Toupin 1983, 356).

The women expressed hard feelings mixed with a sort of friendship, based on all their joint work in regularly publishing *Québécoises deboutte!*, running referral services for abortions, and answering the letters and demands for information coming from everywhere in Québec. Ultimately, a question remained: How could those who were crossing the frontiers of this leftist trend into the terrain of autonomous feminist activism think that what was done in feminist collectives was against the working class (O'Leary and Toupin 1983, 367)? In the end, there was an acute sense that too much time had been lost trying to justify feminism within the left (35).

There are of course other reasons the FLFQ and CdF disappeared so suddenly after having enjoyed so much popularity inside and outside Montréal. The desire to be at the avant-garde of feminism, proposing a genuine feminist theory of women's oppression, clashed with the impossibility of responding to all the Québec-wide requests. By the time the protagonists saw each other again at the round table in 1982, women had left the extra-parliamentary groups en masse and were ready to admit that their attacks on autonomous feminism had been wrong. However, they also justified themselves by speaking of the need for a strong party with a clear political platform and unity of action – something that the feminist/women's movement, as it appeared to them at the time, could not provide (O'Leary and Toupin 1983, 365).

Rejecting the Enemy Within

First, by presenting the genealogy of early feminist collectives in Italy and Québec, I would like to offer a brief introduction to how the idea of feminist autonomy/separatism emerged in the 1970s. The possibility of an Italian feminist separatism was first evoked with the group Demistificazione autoritarismo patriarcale (DEMAU) (Demystification of patriarchal authoritarianism) (Melandri 2000, 18). Its name indicates that the group sought to demystify all forms of patriarchal authority upon which a sexual division of roles was based. It promoted women's autonomy but opposed any attempt at societal integration if it meant that women would have to work and behave under the same conditions and terms that applied to men. Created in 1966, DEMAU was initially mixed-gender and used Marxist terms of reference, even when it aimed to initiate a frank discussion on sexuality and sexual difference. DEMAU founders, like Lia Cigarini and Luisa Muraro, went on to create other groups and became important actors in the development of the feminist theory of sexual difference.[19]

DEMAU's first manifesto (1966) denounced any strategies of emancipation promoted by political parties like the PCI and its national women's organization satellite, the UDI. DEMAU members criticized suggestions that social change for women would come with such things as legislation that addressed inequalities in paid work, in post-secondary education, and in access to professions. For DEMAU, integrating women into the realm of paid work under the same terms and conditions as those applied to men would not transform women into producers – women have always produced wealth and have always had excellent attendance records in the workplace – it would only serve to make them better consumers. Thus emancipation is not a victory but a confirmation of women's secondary status within the family and society. What women need is to be liberated from being men's sexual slaves. The DEMAU document, "Il maschile come valore" (The masculine as value) (Cigarini, Pellegrini, and Rasi 1969), proposed a critical analysis of the sexual division of labour and of the idea that nature was the destiny of women. The document revisits the false promise of women's integration into society and critiques anti-authoritarian movements for not addressing women's roles and places in society as central to their struggles. Paradoxically, "Il maschile come valore" concludes by demanding a return to Marxist principles in order to gain a better understanding of a Marxist conception of the human condition.

DEMAU aimed to develop research projects that focused on women's sexuality and the process of human procreation. "Schema di ipotesi della ricerca sulla procreazione" (Outline of hypothesis for procreation research) contains twelve points for further investigation on human reproduction (DEMAU 1970). The document argues that human reproductive technologies are not neutral and should be seen as elements of an imposed ideology. It suggests that the following themes need further research: the causes of pain in childbirth; ideological discourses on pregnancy; the idea of nature in human reproduction; the distinction between reproduction and sexuality; men's desire to have children; women's rejection of motherhood; contraception as a women's issue only; women and men's roles; and the sexual division of labour; family structures and private property. DEMAU became the first Italian feminist group to propose a theory of liberation that goes against – not beyond – women's integration into society. It is also the first to move towards the theory of sexual difference, although this project was formulated in accordance with the struggle against capitalism. Members of DEMAU (1966b) were not yet proposing a complete separation or even a move away from involvement with contemporary social struggles.

The idea of feminist separatism was clearly expressed in documents from the two subsequent feminist Milanese collectives. Anabasi, created in 1970 by Serena Castaldi, was the first group to bar men from group meetings. The second, Rivolta femminile, founded in 1970 by Carla Lonzi, actively sought the creation of a female culture operating alongside the male world. Both Castaldi and Lonzi had spent time in the United States. In their own separate ways they imported feminist ideas into Italy, particularly the politics of consciousness-raising, but it is Lonzi who coined the term "autocoscienza." Lonzi's group, Rivolta femminile, marked its difference from other feminist organizations (Melandri 2000, 20): from a chronological perspective, Rivolta femminile may well be the first real feminist separatist group and the origin of other such collectives outside Milan.

One central element in the development of the Italian version of sexual difference was present in Lonzi's approach and was revealed in her diary. It concerns the tension caused when an individual woman is recognized by other women. For members of the Rivolta femminile collective, mutual recognition can only come through the practice of autocoscienza (Lonzi in Guerra 2005, 38–39). This mutual recognition is not identical to the more hierarchical model proposed by the Libreria delle donne of Milan. Nonetheless, Rivolta femminile's approach contained the premises for the institutionalization of a hierarchy of dependence among women, a kind of *affidamento* avant la lettre (the term *affidamento* was coined by Gruppo 4 and the Libreria delle donne of Milan more than a decade later [Melandri 2000, 26, 105]).[20] Overall, Rivolta femminile remained apart from the rest of the movement, a feminist group whose activities, in spite of its important ideological influence throughout the country and abroad, were organized for the "happy few" (Zumaglino 1996, 79).

In Québec, the FLFQ understood the need to organize autonomously very early on, but there was also the feeling that a feminist theory of women's oppression was lacking. Members of the collective read contemporary feminist texts, such as the special issue of the journal *Partisans* (1970) and major feminist texts from France, the United States, and other European countries (O'Leary and Toupin 1982, 40–41). These texts were discussed collectively, but the feeling of theoretical deprivation persisted, along with a sense of tension between the need to remain engaged in social economic struggles and the desire to address women's specific issues more deeply, including the theoretical exploration of the conditions within which women lived their sexuality. The tension underlined the difficult cohabitation of politics and culture, and it paved the way for the subsequent marginalization of cultural productions within feminist and political movements in general (Michaud 2007; Péloquin 2007, 230–31).

There was no consensus within the FLFQ on how to manage this tension. The collective was an autonomous organization attempting to keep its activities outside the control of the left. Its major committees on specific issues like abortion and daycare demanded enormous amounts of energy and counted on the participation of women from working-class neighbourhoods in Montréal. The dissolution of the FLFQ was ultimately caused by its inability to maintain cohesion amidst so many ideas and demands generated by its activities – while the ideology of the time required political homogeneity. The FLFQ got its strength, as well as its weaknesses, from being the site of large influxes of new members eager to act on urgent issues like abortion. When the FLFQ ceased to exist, it inspired the creation of other collectives that were themselves at the centre of political and ideological feminist debates.[21]

Constitutive Elements of Feminist Separatism

There are at least four elements of Italian feminist separatism that are rarely found in Québécois feminism.[22] First, as the idea of emancipation was gradually replaced by the notion of liberation, separatism was presented as being more effective than autonomy at achieving the project of women's liberation. When feminist activists started to distance themselves from the authoritarian leadership of the extra-parliamentary left, not all joined the ranks of the separatists. Indeed, the FLFQ and the CdF were autonomous but not separatist in the same way that some Italian collectives wanted to be. Similarly, the Italian group LF and the feminist journal *Effe* were autonomous but not separatist (like Lonzi's Rivolta femminile and later on the Libreria delle donne of Milan). I use these examples among many other possibilities in order to highlight that, for many feminist activists, being autonomous from the left did not mean abandoning important connections with its political ideologies and its struggles. Indeed, several members of the CdF practised double activism and had close ties to the extra-parliamentary left, whose dominance was such during the second phase of Québécois Marxism that most feminist activists were pressured to travel its ideological terrain. However, in the eyes of feminist separatists, there was no way to redeem an autonomous feminist who suffered from a false consciousness contaminated by masculine thought.

The second element constituting feminist separatism was the desire to circumscribe all activism and struggles within the frontiers of the feminist movement alone. Two feminist journals among others, *Sottosopra* in Milan and *La vie en rose* in Montréal, were exemplary of the tendency to privilege the inner life of the movement, even though many of their contributors were leading a double activist's life. *Sottosopra*'s content was directed towards a feminist audience and to feminist/women's groups as opposed to a larger readership; its objectives were to share feminist information internally and to create space for feminist debates and practices. These objectives differed from those of journals like *Effe*, which directed its content to Italian women in order to inform them about feminism regardless of their connection with the movement. In contrast, *La vie en rose* defended clear feminist objectives but refused, almost until the end, to speak on behalf of women's groups or even to represent the women's movement (Dupont et al. 1979–80). Nonetheless, and unlike the Italian *Sottosopra*, *La vie en rose* wanted to be a popular journal and to reach a vast readership. One editorial stated that it wanted to be "original, drôle, humain, diversifié, international et multiracial, qui 'rendrait visibles toutes les luttes, recherches et réalisations des femmes d'ici et d'ailleurs' et qui enfin 'provoquerait de nécessaires débats à l'intérieur même du féminisme.'"[23] *La vie en rose* wanted to defend a single project – feminism – which was presented as much larger than the Québécois women's movement (Guénette 1985a, 15). An autonomous women's movement has the capacity to create and to manage its own structures without external political interferences. Separatism, however, and its various trends, is much more than a simple rejection of political interference: it is the desire to recognize oneself as being part of a single movement. It is the desire to feel the collective force, allowing any small group to be part of the whole; it is the desire to create a mass movement capable of addressing any single issue, any complicated question – like capitalism, for example – from within, developing one's own analyses and one's own theoretical terms of reference, without reference to any other ideology, such as Marxism. Women who are consciously part of such a movement usually claim that the so-called issue of the inside/outside of feminism is a false problem. Everyone is consciously entering into dialogue/confrontation with one another and, as such, there is no need to self-identify with a specific feminist ideology (Alcuni gruppi di donne di Milano 1972).

The third element of feminist separatism hints at the politics of consciousness-raising/autocoscienza as the privileged method of self-inquiry. Yet this approach was soon thought to be *dépassée* by segments of feminist separatism that shifted gears towards psychoanalysis. From the moment small groups claimed to practise one form or another of autocoscienza, this practice became the mark of an autonomous movement and crystallized discussions and practices within any given women's group. Consequently, separatist groups quickly learned to move to another phase, declaring that simply discussing daily life in small groups was repetitive and boring. Using the method of analysis/psychoanalysis to reach women's unconscious to look at the roots of women's oppression was more demanding but much more rewarding. In Italy, the articulation of feminism with psychoanalysis did not come automatically or without conflict: just because it originated in women's lived experience in small groups was not a guarantee that it was exempt from the mediation of a masculine culture and society. In addition, not all groups using the method of the unconscious were separatists. For instance, Lea Melandri's approach remained in close synergy with political struggles and connected the original practice of autocoscienza with a feminist exploration of the unconscious. In contrast, the Libreria delle donne of Milan shifted away from autocoscienza and initiated a search for the feminine essence through the use of psychoanalysis. It aimed to begin from oneself *(partire da sé)* in order to find a genuine women's culture, enabling women to be themselves without the fear of reproducing aspects of social relations determined by masculine rules and norms. Originally, many feminists rejected psychoanalysis because it was a masculine institution of power and prestige par excellence, one that victimized women and used its instruments against them (Schiavo 2002, 113–14). Yet psychoanalysis was brought to feminist separatism with the promise of rediscovering the lost feminine/female world. Its protagonists argued that, as long as feminism remained outside circles of power, there was nothing to fear. Individually and collectively, psychoanalysis was the means by which women's original essence would become accessible.[24]

The fourth constitutive element of feminist separatism sees the mother-daughter relationship as central to the process of institutionalizing relationships among women.[25] However, the figure of the mother contains the seeds of hierarchy among women and the abuse of power. Within a movement structured around small women's groups, shaping women's relationships based on the mother-daughter model mapped the road to dependency. The Libreria delle donne of Milan proclaimed that this type of dependency was necessary because a woman needs to recognize the supremacy of another woman if she wants to be acknowledged in return and to achieve self-worth. Such a model denies any legitimacy to the notion of equality, although this time it is equality among women that is rejected. A feminist movement that is ideologically and discursively based on the commonality of women's oppression needed to address this contradiction. The Libreria delle donne of Milan sought to resolve the problem by introducing the notion of *affidamento,* first promoted in its groundbreaking text "Più donne che uomini" (1983)[26] and later in *Non credere di avere dei diritti*. *Affidamento* is a form of dependence or tutelage structured around the differences between women, and it contains all the constitutive elements for a feminist contract among them while creating a sort of hierarchy based on the recognition that some women know more than others (de Lauretis 1990, 12). According to one of my interviewees, the notion of *affidamento* deeply divided the Italian movement for decades: its adoption was daunting and fascinating, but the concept crystallized the idea that there were acceptable inequalities within the movement based on experience and knowledge.

Members of the Libreria delle donne did not see it that way. They were confident in their capacity to influence groups to shift towards feminist separatism. They did not see that such a move was splitting the movement, and they rejected the vision that feminism was divided along two conflicting axes/souls (Frabotta 1975; Fraire 2002).[27] For instance, women who created the feminist journal *Sottosopra,* which became an important vehicle for several of Libreria's publications in the 1980s, adopted a rule of not discriminating between feminist points of view (Alcuni gruppi di donne di Milano 1972). Nonetheless, the pressure to create a feminist movement away from political and social struggles – and one that denied race as an important dimension in women's oppression – was strong. Almost every small group and collective had to take a position vis-à-vis feminist separatism, even if the end result was to reject it. Many lesbians, at odds with feminism, created their own collectives using a separatist narrative, while others remained caught between feminism and the mixed-gender homosexual movement. Again, in the context of lesbianism, the separatist approach points to a different dual process (Pomeranzi 1984, 73–74).[28]

Positioning oneself individually or collectively within a political movement such as feminism was a declaration of faith. At the time, women were defined in relation to men. Taking personal distance from male politics and masculine thought meant adopting a form of separatism that found its best expression either in the practice of the unconscious or in the search for the symbolic. Women's only choice was either to silence their own desires and needs or to find new ways of expressing them outside the traditional ways of doing politics (Fraire 2002, 24). The criticism of all leftist organizations was perfectly comprehensible, given that the left – both the old and the extra-parliamentary – was at war with the women's movement (O'Leary and Toupin 1983, 364–67). But the harsh accusation feminist separatists directed at double activists – that they were bringing the enemy within, implanting masculine values and ways of thinking that colonized women's minds – was difficult to understand.

How do we make sense of the attempts to develop a racialized feminist theory as well as to include other questions traditionally marginalized by the core feminist/women's movement? What about the difference brought by race and anti-racism, lesbianism and struggles against homophobia, as well as other ways of thinking about feminism? Do these requests to be present, to count at the core of the movement – rather than push at its periphery – represent the enemy within?

Critiques of Feminist Separatism

Using the four constitutive elements of feminist separatism outlined above, it appears that Québécois feminism was autonomous but not separatist. The Québécois movement engaged with other political struggles and attempted to analyze human activities from a feminist perspective. Québécois feminist collectives adopted their own version of consciousness-raising, but few engaged with psychoanalysis or the practice of the unconscious or even with the mother/daughter relationship found in the feminist theory of sexual difference. Their problems arose from the impossibility of achieving unity and continuity from within as well as from external pressure from the extra-parliamentary left. The Québécois women's movement's partial achievement of the separatist experience marks its most important contrast with Italian feminism.

Critics of feminist separatism in Italy, epitomized by groups such as the Libreria delle donne of Milan, aimed to defend a specific type of feminist organizing in a country dominated by the politics of the PCI. Italy was shaken by the radicalism of youth movements and of the Autonomy Movement, and by numerous acts of violence perpetrated by fascists and extreme-leftist groups, not to mention police repression and state terrorism. There was a common belief that the movement should not avoid social issues and political struggles. Double activists were often accused of weakening feminist principles. But feminist critiques of separatism responded that staying away from leftist politics and "the social" marginalized feminism and women's voices. They argued that those who did not have power were condemning themselves to remain powerless and depriving themselves of any possibility of political transformation. Sexual difference, they said, cannot be celebrated as a value (Bocchetti 1987; Cirillo 2003, 37).

Some of these responses were addressed to separatist groups who refused to walk the streets with male allies during public demonstrations, particularly when the struggle for free abortions reached its peak. Feminist critics argued against idealizing feminine solidarity – as if joy and pleasure could be found simply by remaining together, as if the solution to violence was to stay away from all men, as if challenging the roots of oppression meant separating from the rest of society (Lea et al. 1975). Why, when feminists need to develop ideas, arguments, analyses, should they refuse to engage in dialogue with others (Fraire 1979)? Why, when everyone agrees that the feminist project is much more than just the reverse side of the masculine vision of the world – after centuries of being denied a place in history – should feminists choose to remain outside of it?

Terrains of Feminist Activism

> *This [consciousness-raising] is important as a first step (although women have always gathered in small groups, at the market, "at the fountain"). It must be clear however, that it is only a first step: because neurotic elements circulate solely within this small, tight circle, and if it is not open to the outside, they stay there.*[29]
>
> – *Laura Lilli and Chiara Valentini,* Cara compagne: il femminismo nel PCI e nelle organizzazioni di massa

The observation that autocoscienza is only a first step came from a woman member of the PCI. Yet, from the perspective of the PCI and the extra-parliamentary left, feminism could become a political movement only insofar as it limited itself to the expression of working-class women, whose social malaise must be taken into account in order for political groups to remain in touch with emerging societal forces (Zuffa 1987). Not surprisingly, most women members of leftist organizations chose to see things differently. At first, some double activists saw the practice of consciousness-raising/autocoscienza as elitist and as unable to take social disparities into account. Soon, however, they acknowledged that the simple act of starting from one's own experience was neither pre-political nor a mere symptom of social malaise. It was one instrument among others to raise consciousness, including the consciousness of some male comrades during one of the most heated moments of the Autonomy Movement.

Consciously or unconsciously, a certain dualism was constantly at work between the terrain of women's organizing and the terrain delimited by public/political spheres. Grazia Zuffa's critical analysis of double activism within the PCI shows how the discourse of the left was linear and optimistic about the capacity to integrate women's issues and to make them its own while continuing its ongoing celebration of women's emancipation. When the left finally grasped the full force of feminism, issues such as sexuality, abortion, and the personal as political were suddenly presented as though the left had theorized them first within the context of its struggle against capitalism. In a desperate attempt to rescue its hegemony without adopting the transformative potential of feminism, the left orchestrated a forced integration of certain selected issues (Michaud 2010; Zuffa 1987). By the end of the 1970s, in Québec as in Italy, many feminist activists refused to play the game, but they nonetheless clashed with other segments of feminism in their persistent crossing of the multiple frontiers of movements. Those who advocated feminism as the only actor able to address any problem or issue attempted to demonstrate that feminism was *the* movement and that double activism was a form of false consciousness. On the other hand, double activists believed that a separatist feminist movement was a utopian vision, an overly optimistic view full of contradictions and sapped by power relations.

5 The Illusion of Unity and Homogeneity: The Emergence of a Fragmented Political Subject

In the early 1970s, a variety of women's groups and collectives spread throughout Québec. Most of the groups were providing services to women in the areas of reproductive health, cultural production, education, domestic violence, employment, and income security. The number of women's groups varied from one city to another, but in many regions there were enough to create networks pertaining to each of these specialized issues. In Italy, as in Québec, the cumulative effect of the growth of feminism both structurally and mentally supported the creation of women's-only spaces and the need to protect these spaces against external political interference. In both places, feminists knew it would be hard to change traditional ways of thinking and hard for women to avoid defining themselves solely in relation to the men in their lives. Also, their respective feminisms were animated by a desire for homogeneity and political unity despite the ongoing tension between the two axes within the movement. In the process of building their movements, Italian and Québécois feminists got their inspiration from several sources, most notably from American and French feminisms (Fraire 2002; Un groupe de femmes de Montréal 1971; Martucci 2008; O'Leary and Toupin 1982, 1983; Passerini 2005; Péloquin 2007; Schiavo 2002; Zumaglino 1996). Both movements encompassed a collective sense of solidarity and commonality and prepared the conditions of being for women to be seen as political subjects. This chapter initiates an inquiry into the conditions that made the creation of such a political subject possible. This line of thought occurred simultaneously at the level of the individual and at the level of the movement. At the turn of the 1970s, women were almost exclusively defined in relation to men, while feminism was defined in relation to the left and/or the world of political/public spaces. These two levels, the individual and the collective, take their full meaning when they are placed in confrontation/tension with one another.

Multiple Ways of Conceiving the Personal as Political

Acknowledging Difference but Not Differences

This statement – "the personal is political" – offers the reason feminists have never been comfortable simply demanding equality with men (Rowbotham 1981, 125). It aims at transcending disparities among women: the new promised revolution was about much more than simply demanding inclusion in politics. Feminists wanted to remove the frontiers of what counted and what did not count as political. Much more than a simple request, this prompted an investigation into how women are treated at all levels of society. The statement demanded that all human activities – how women and men worked and consumed, lived and loved – be completely integrated into the public/political spheres (Rowbotham 1981, 124–25). Finally, the personal is political demanded the creation of a feminist knowledge that got at the root of men's domination to reveal the mechanism behind the systemic oppression that dismissed women as agents in history while exalting them through imagined myths (Melandri 2002, 210).

A significant portion of the feminist movement wanted the recognition of women's specific identity to be formed under the terms of sexual difference as an overwhelming majority of feminists had already agreed to create a movement they could call their own. At the same time, many others, such as Carla Lonzi (1970a, 1970b), believed that sexual difference transcended all other types of difference. Lonzi's writings marked a definitive rupture with Marxism and with class struggle discourses, with feminist materialism and with all other feminist trends that connected feminism with social issues.[1] The idea that women were political subjects just like men was rapidly confronted with a range of conflicting views. But the theory of sexual difference provoked a deep division within Italian feminism. Many women, and not only those practising double activism, opposed the idea that in order to find women's liberation one needed to create a new identity.

There was, however, a consensus that the notion of equality was no longer enough to change women's conditions. What counted most in feminist struggles was the creation of a sense of solidarity and the recognition of a commonality of oppression. The act of coming together under one movement meant that each woman recognized that the woman next to her had the same lived experience and the same desire for full liberation. Having successfully given legitimacy to the idea of an autonomous movement, feminists had the sense of participating in a revolution that was more revolutionary than anyone had seen before. They belonged to a movement that proposed an identity, positive values, and new codes of identification as well as its own symbolism (Ergas 1986, 20–21; Groppi and Pelaja 1983). Such consensus was sufficiently large to bridge the gap between the two axes of the movement, but for those supporting feminist separatism it was still not sufficient (Libreria delle donne 2005b; Lonzi 1970a, 1970b, 1978; Muraro 1991), and they demanded that the commonality of oppression, so much talked about within the movement, be based first and foremost on the duality of sexual difference. A separate world was more than necessary to recover the roots of women's own selves.

Such a definition of commonality required the simultaneous silencing of differences, whatever they might be: political beliefs, class, race, ethnicity, region, culture, profession, sexuality, and/or age (M.L. Boccia 1981; Groppi and Pelaja 1983). The construction of a unified subjectivity has its counterpart in the exclusion of differences perceived to endanger the cohesion of small groups and feminist collectives. Women-only-spaces were built on the idea that all women shared the same oppression and the same interests in the process of liberation. Not surprisingly, clashes over differences emerged rapidly in many feminist/women's groups and shook the foundations of the entire movement.

Some differences were easier to acknowledge: differences of education, occupation, culture, class origin, generation, and political orientation. Other differences, however, were inexpressible, concealed, or believed to be nonexistent – such as race or the possibility that a different type of feminism could develop. For instance, in the Italian South (or Mezzogiorno), issues such as the violence of the mafia and social and economic development were not recognized as truly feminist issues. Furthermore, these differences point to the process of a racialization in Italy that was interrelated with (but different from) the colonization of African countries during the fascist regime (Giuliani and Lombardi-Diop 2013). The invisibility/silencing of the racialization of the Italian South shaped all political discourses, feminist discourses included. It contradicted the common idea that the word "race" had entered the lexicon only in the 1980s, when foreign immigration began to challenge the homogeneous vision of Italian society.

In Québec, an identical process was at work: feminism in the Montréal metropole snubbed the feminist analysis and practices in smaller cities and regions. Efforts were made only when the strength of a regional feminism was impossible to ignore. Furthermore, there was – and still is – the silencing of certain social categories of women. New immigrants and refugees; women of colour who had arrived on the continent several generations before; Indigenous women occupying the geographical space still colonized by white settlers; and women from rural and semi-rural areas were not included in the core of the feminist movement (Dûchaine 1986–87; Green 2009; Ricci 2017, 2018; Ship 1991; Stasiulis 1999). Lesbians, although acutely visible, were nonetheless pushed into the margins of feminism; they were politically powerful in theorizing women's bodies and sexuality but undesirable because they threatened the unity as well as the respectability of the movement vis-à-vis the outside world. Lesbians were persistent in their request to resolve the heterosexual contradiction that underlined a partial integration of sexuality in feminist politics (Amazones d'hier, lesbiennes d'aujourd'hui 1987; Baeri 2005, 149; M.-H. Bourcier 2013; L. Chamberland 1996; Durocher 1990; Emilia 1981; Laura 1978, 40; Martin 1976, 6; O'Leary and Toupin 1983, 14, 344; Pomeranzi 1984; Turcotte 2013).[2]

In the feminist/women's movement literature, we can observe two strategies unfolding on the issue of differences. The first strategy tried to analyze the problem as though it did not really exist, fearing that differences would negatively affect women's solidarity and the movement's determination to fight a common oppression. A second strategy, more common in Italy, substituted all sorts of differences with the institutionalized model of *affidamento* based on some sort of tutelage between women placed in a hierarchical relationship with one another: "In all meanings of the term, there is a need for a woman higher than oneself."[3] In other words, women who do not have experience, knowledge, and/or personal fame should defer to women who enjoy influence and prestige in society and in history. This approach to difference was meant to help a woman who, having the desire to succeed in the world, gains legitimacy not from men but from recognition by a more powerful woman/women (Libreria delle donne 2005b; Paolucci 1991). It goes without saying that the system of tutelage ignores racialized differences.

The maternal figure is at the core of *affidamento* as well as of the theory of sexual difference. The mother is reified and highlights tensions that are alternatively creative and destructive. The gaze of this other woman so close, so familiar, became an essential component in the constitution of women's subjectivity. And the life of one's own mother was often the object of analytical/psychoanalytical narratives. Practices of self-inquiry within feminist collectives were based on devotion and dependency, but they were not always accepted by every women's group. The collective interaction among women who attempted to use introspective methods – starting with consciousness-raising/autocoscienza in the earlier stage of the movement before shifting to the exploration of the unconscious with the introduction of psychoanalysis – were confronted with a complex set of relations constantly oscillating between sorority and competition, between dependency and defiance. Moreover, narrating one's own experiences modelled on the mother-daughter relationship might have caused guilt: the guilt of not being like one's mother, of being dependent on her love, and of not showing her enough love in return. Such guilt became an obstacle when transposed onto other women members of the same collective. In addition, it created a conflict of consciousness when the maternal figure was very negative in the lived experiences of the individual subject, especially when the mother was despised because of her submission to the patriarchal order. Not surprisingly, many women found that analyzing their relationships with men – instead of with other women/mothers – was much more straightforward and generated far less guilt (Melandri 2000, 63).

The American Influence and the Problem of Race

The ways in which the feminist movements were confronted with differences among women leads us to explore an element often neglected when we look at the American influence on Italian and Québécois feminisms: race and the tendency to compare women's oppression with the oppression of Blacks. Recreating the genealogy of external influences within the Québécois and Italian feminist consciousness allows us to focus on the core of their respective movements as well as on the issues pushed to the peripheries of their main struggles. Québécois and Italian feminists took from other feminisms – namely, American feminism and French feminism – what they needed to develop their own sense of self and their own mode of being in small women's groups. In early feminist publications, the notion of race was used as an element of comparison to add weight to the assertion of women's oppression.

In Italy, there was a fascination with the American way of life and American popular culture, consumer goods, wealth, freedom, and the democratic system. This attraction transformed people's attitudes within public spaces as well as the meanings attached to the cultural and democratic self (Giuliani and Lombardi-Diop 2013, 102). The context of this influence was reinforced by the long history of Italian immigration overseas and by the cultural capital of those who came back after spending some years in the United States.[4] Apart from the overwhelming references to the origins of autocoscienza, the impact of American influences remains difficult to measure. It was certainly important during the early years of the 1970s, given the number of translated documents appearing regularly within a few feminist journals such as *Donne è bello* (Women are beautiful) as well as the work of the collective Anabasi (Guerra 2004, 95–97; Guerra 2005, 31; Passerini 2005, 183–84; Piccirillo 1996, 354–56; Zumaglino 1996, 61–62).[5]

The numerous translations indicate at least three dynamics at work in the process of transferring information from one national context to another. The first highlights the importance of Europe and North America as most of the documents came from the United States, while some came from Germany, France, and England: only a few came from Latin America (e.g., Argentina). In Gramaglia (1975b) we find a few references to Canadian feminism, pointing to intersectional national characteristics, with a specific mention of the case of Québec, but these references do not mention women of colour or Indigenous feminism, probably because these issues were absent in Canadian and Québécois feminist literature.

During the early 1970s, American feminism was evoked as a referent and a model more often than French feminism, whose influence would come later in the decade and would have a heavy impact on the emerging Italian version of sexual difference. The second dynamic suggests that American feminism was important mainly as far as the northern Italian cities were concerned. The third dynamic points to the tendency to select only documents judged useful for one's own movement (Zumaglino 1996, 61). By selecting certain texts that refer to consciousness-raising as a feminist mode of inquiry, by translating emblematic documents such *Our Bodies, Ourselves* on women's health and sexuality, and by showing interest in the issue of race as a significant political struggle in the United States, Italian activists were consolidating their understanding of the United States as well as the kind of feminist movement that American women were building. This provides us with an idea of how a hierarchy of differences among regions in the world is crystallized: of all articles published in Italian feminist journals, only a few highlighted the issue of class and race diversity within the American women's movement. An exception appeared in *Effe*, where Jèwell and Tagliaferri

(1976) identify three components of American feminism: (1) institutional demands, (2) the struggle against institutions, and (3) the development of a complex analysis of society that integrates Marxist analysis. Although the article points to the reformist character of the US movement, it shows the active presence of socialist feminist collectives in the United States, with discourses and practices in constant interrelation with issues of race. Another article, "Qual'è la via da seguire?" (What is the road to take?) (B.L. 1970) presents American feminism using Marxist terms of reference. The significance of these few examples, however, is lost among the number of other translated American documents.

In Québec, these three dynamics were present, but the process of translation was different due, in part, to its geographical proximity with the United States. First, it is important to note that gaining access to original documents mediated by translation provoked a rift between Québécois francophone and anglophone feminists (Mills 2004, 192–93; Mills 2010, 134–35; O'Leary and Toupin 1982, 27, 74). Montréal, where historical feminist collectives were created, was the city where linguistic tensions between French and English were most felt. Québécois francophones were the linguistic majority in Montréal but were a minority on the North American continent, and, as such, there was – and still is – a sense of anxiety over their potential disappearance. In the early 1970s, Québec had a population of slightly over 6 million people, who were surrounded by an English-speaking population of more than 226 million people in the rest of Canada[6] and the United States.[7] Outside the Montréal metropolitan area, the majority of the population was able to strengthen the French character of its social, economic, cultural, and political institutions. However, the English language was – and continues to be – present and active within the individual and collective mindset, continuously working at the level of the unconscious. As in Italy, there is a history of Québécois women and men immigrating to the United States. Almost all French-speaking families had one or two members who had been drawn south by the prospects of a better life and employment, especially in the textile industry in the New England states (Takai 2008). Like their Italian counterparts, Québécois feminists were fascinated by American society and were especially attracted to its multifaceted countercultural lives (O'Leary and Toupin 1982, 25–26). The majority of these women did not need to travel to the United States to get an idea of American feminist politics, although many did go for other reasons, such as vacations, to visit family members, or to get an abortion.

In spite of being in competing linguistic groups, francophone and anglophone feminists in Québec met regularly around politics and feminist organizing. Together, they created the FLFQ in 1969. The texts and documents that came from the United States were translated by anglophone members of that collective who were, for the most part, supportive of Québécois independence (Mills 2004, 2010; O'Leary and Toupin 1982, 72; O'Leary and Toupin 1983, 328; Péloquin 2007). The politics of translation within Québécois feminism had a different meaning than it had for their Italian counterparts. In Quebec, the issue of language was politically loaded and created a conflict when anglophone activists were criticized for controlling the political message and for bringing too much of an American influence to the collective. Only some francophone members were able to read, or agreed to read, documents in English or to rely on translations of English feminist literature. Consequently, the majority of francophone members decided to exclude anglophone feminists from the FLFQ in the fall of 1970 in the midst of the October Crisis (Centre des femmes 1983a, 94; Mills 2004, 192–93; Mills 2010, 134–35; O'Leary and Toupin 1982, 79–80; Péloquin 2007).[8] Relations between francophones and anglophones were conflicted to say the least, but it is erroneous to argue that francophones remained sealed off from Anglo-American feminist theories and oblivious of the evolution of the women's movement in North America. Even if many activists travelled south of the border and met with some women's groups, their knowledge remained dependent on translation.[9]

Yet there is another reason for francophone resentment besides that provided by the linguistic divide, and it is related to the class composition of the FLFQ: francophone activists, when employed, had low-paying jobs, often as community organizers in working-class neighbourhoods. Some women were unionized as teachers and social workers, but overall their class composition and levels of education in the early 1970s were slightly lower than those of anglophone members in the collective, who were often university students at McGill, where they enjoyed easy access to American literature and an academic environment that supported new theoretical discoveries and political debate. It is not surprising, then, that francophones felt they were being force-fed American feminist literature and that they resented this position of imposed subalternity. Given the political context of the time and the sense of political proximity they felt with other liberation movements in other parts of the world – where subaltern groups claimed freedom, self-determination, and autonomy – it is apparent that the francophone exclusion of anglophone feminists was motivated by the desire to find a feminist voice that they could claim as their own (O'Leary and Toupin 1982, 75–77).

The Italian and the Québécois selection/rejection of documents resonated in the project of creating a twofold unity of representation: a representation of woman as "victim of" and a representation of woman as "agent of history." The first representation recalls Cerchio Spezzato's document, in which a comparison of oppression is made between women and Blacks. In this document, Black oppression is evoked twice but never presented in any detail. The members of Cerchio's collective claimed that the history of Black liberation made them conscious of their own condition. Being a woman is like being Black in that it is a biological fact. Too often, Cerchio argued, women rely on two false alternatives in attempting to resolve their oppression: either they accept their private roles as being determined by men or they enter into competition with them in search of equality. Choosing the second alternative is to "accept the competition with the male and to focus all efforts on 'being equal to men' with the result of becoming 'the black with the white head,' discriminated against by whites and detested by blacks."[10]

In Québec, similar comparisons were made from time to time in feminist literature and journals. In 1976, Nicole Brossard wrote: "Une femme autonome et qui n'a pas de conscience féministe est un homme en puissance, c'est-à-dire quelqu'un susceptible de ne rien comprendre des oppressions les plus subtiles qui se jouent en elle mais capable de les faire agir sur quelqu'un d'autre."[11]

In the above sequence, Cerchio Spezzato hints at, although not explicitly and perhaps unknowingly, Fanon's (1952, 170–71) reference to Black consciousness when he states: "Les nègres sont comparaison" (The negroes are comparison). Fanon's approach to comparison has nothing to do with that of the feminists of the 1970s who compare women to African Americans. Yet his thinking provides some answers as to why African Americans were the group that was used to describe the oppression of women. One reason is the above-mentioned fascination with the United States, which appeared to deal with a brand of diversity/discrimination that placed race at the core of liberation discourse (Jèwell and Tagliaferri 1976). Yet it was only the male voices coming from the Black movement that fascinated Western Europeans and Québécois feminists. The feminist anti-racist movement and Black feminism, among other subaltern feminisms, were not included in their gaze, even though they represented a fundamental challenge coming from multiple locations.[12]

If women's oppression was comparable to race oppression, why was little to no attention given to African American feminist thought or the feminist theories developed by other racialized categories of women, such as Chicanas and Indigenous women (Green 2009; Hull, Scott, and Smith 1982; Ricci 2017, 2018; Smith 2005; Stasiulis 1999)? Feminism in the 1970s needed to remove the notion of race from the notion of "woman" before reintroducing her as a subject inside the movement. The most important task of the moment was to build solidarity without the threat of divisiveness. In Québec, for instance, there was already a significant divide between francophones and anglophones both inside and outside the movement. The Québécois and Canadian women's movements were two nationalistic competitive feminisms that prevailed at the expense of other feminisms (Stasiulis 1999). The divide was so strong that it blocked all other debates on difference and prevented any other questions from emerging concerning the racialization of other social categories of women. It displaced the possibility of an Indigenous feminism or any other feminist thought that did not fall under the core of a white feminist discourse. The emergence of autonomous Québécois Black women's groups, women of colour, and immigrant women's organizations resulted from the rejection of their struggles against racism (Ship 1991, 9).

Indeed, most feminist journals in Québec published articles on immigrant and Indigenous women. *Des luttes et des rires*, for instance, provided significant information on women from the Tobique reserve in New Brunswick, who had initiated an important struggle against the Canadian Indian Act.[13] The same feminist journal did not hesitate to publish criticisms of racism against the women's movement itself when Québécois women's groups, with a taint of superiority, pretended to show their solidarity with women living in Third World countries. In Italy, serious debates and research related to connecting women's groups from different parts of the world emerged in the early 1990s. In 1993, the Associazione per una Libera Università delle donne (Women's free university association) of Milan organized a conference to discuss the politics of the relations between women's groups in different countries (Percovich, Petronio, and Damiani 1994). The fact remains, however, that most of the content of these initiatives was descriptive rather than analytical or theoretical. Moreover, much of the feminist research on Indigenous women and on women living in countries from the South was coming from Western feminists, and it brought with it all the negative consequences of this type of research (Mohanty 1988, 52–53).

This brings me to another point, which explains why the process of comparing oppressions was influenced primarily by what was happening in the United States and rarely by what was happening in other countries in the southern hemisphere where many women's organizations – sometimes autonomously, other times in collaboration with political parties, movements, and unions – were advocating and mobilizing on women's rights with a feminist consciousness (Motapanyane 2009). When Fanon wrote, "Les nègres sont comparaison," he meant that Black men always want to compare themselves to someone higher; they are always wondering if the Other is better or worse than they are. Race is the terrain for comparison, and it opens the space for connection; however, in this process, racism becomes the add-on to gender in the same way that, in class analysis, gender becomes an extension of the Marxist revolutionary project. Thus, defining women as a caste meant that their oppression could be presented as the ultimate oppression – an oppression that took precedence over all others, even slavery. By making such a statement feminist activists found solid ground from which to demand autonomy/separation for their organizations (Cerchio Spezzato 1970; Fraire 2002, 53, 75; Gramaglia 1987, 31; Un groupe de femmes 1971; Perilli 2006; Spagnoletti 1971).

Another point concerns the desire for unity of representation. Comparing women's oppression to race oppression is one way of proclaiming the value of women's struggles. Comparing women to Blacks – whose legitimate claims are obviously not in question – was the crucial element in the construction of the woman as agent of history and it was fundamental for political self-representation. Women are endowed with a political consciousness equal to that of other oppressed peoples in search of liberation, at the level of both the societal world and the symbolic world. However, because there was little desire to investigate differences within the movement, and because of the difficulty of facing a diversity of political beliefs, activists of the 1970s presented feminist political consciousness as undivided, allowing no space to bridge the gap between the consciousness of the oppressed and the position of the politically conscious. Using the process of comparing women to Black people, coupled with the hierarchy between "women who know" and "women who don't know just yet" (such as in the practice of *affidamento*), reveals the irreconcilable division between "us" and "them." Such comparison justifies the location of those who see themselves as deserving privilege and as having a high level of feminist consciousness in relation to those who remain animated by a false consciousness for as long as they waver between movements, allowing themselves to be brainwashed by the politics of men (Rowbotham 1981, 104–5).

The act of comparing categories at the societal level – instead of confronting the dynamics of differentiation and discrimination within the movement – broke the circle of innocence. Italian and Québécois feminists who thought they formed a cohesive core, based on a presumed homogeneity, were forced to recognize the racializing, marginalizing, and discrimination within their ranks. Questioning white privilege originated in part from the United States, but the internal dynamics of confronting this privilege was delayed for years. In Europe, as in Italy, the delay was based on the refusal to even use the term "race" for fear of reviving the mass killings of large segments of the population through the racial laws of the Second World War. As Gaia Giuliani and Cristina Lombardi-Diop (2013) so clearly demonstrate in the introduction to their book *Bianco e Nero:*

> This has prevented a coherent approach in investigating the relation between the racial construction of the Self and the construction of gender ... [T]he interrelation between sexual norms and racial norms highlights the coherence between discursive mechanisms which allow the self-representation of the subject in terms of whiteness and the nationalization phenomenon of Italian women as well as their progressive introduction into the symbolic and political sphere of the nation in defence of racial purity.[14]

These two authors studied the genealogy of the racialization of social categories of Italians during two specific periods: one that began at the time of the unification of Italy and that covers the pre-fascist era as well as the Italian colonial wars; and one that began at the end of the Second World War and continues to the present day. As well, the issue of race was split between Nordic countries and the rest of the southern continent. Italians living in the Mezzogiorno were poor and underprivileged politically, economically, and culturally, and they were treated as the darker race. This process of racialization evolved significantly during the Italian colonization of parts of the African continent, and the representation of the Italian "self" was modified in order to integrate all Italians, regardless of where they lived in the country. During this time, a unified Italian whiteness was contrasted with the people living in East Africa, where Italy was waging its colonial wars. After the Second World War, the process of racialization changed its focus once again when thousands of migrants, composed mostly of young women and men, workers and students, moved to the North. With them the mechanism of racial discrimination returned, along with the reinvention of a symbolic whiteness located within the economically and culturally clean North (Giuliani and Lombardi-Diop 2013, 107–12). Giuliani and Lombardi-Diop argue that women were central to the construction of a pure race, inside and outside the country, during both periods of Italian history. These internal migrations benefited women who grew up in traditional families and communities dominated by the Roman Catholic Church in the South (108–9).

What is most significant in comparing women's oppression with Black American oppression is what is absent from the comparison. Black feminist critiques of mainstream feminism were left out of the translations of American texts (Passerini 2005, 192). For a long time, feminist theory kept hidden the triple oppression and exploitation of Black women via capitalism, patriarchy, and racism. When race entered the discursive scene, the partial intersection of gender and class was substituted by the partial intersection of race and gender: the first generation of contemporary feminist intellectuals still had to learn how to handle several layers of analysis. The fact remains that, consciously or unconsciously, foreign texts were selected on the basis of their correspondence with domestic feminism and served as reflections of familiar political and ideological discourse.[15] Yet the American influence over Italian feminism remained unequal throughout the country. In an interview I conducted in Naples during the summer of 2010, my informant – who had been introduced to feminism during her years of stay in the United States – suggested that American feminism did not have more influence than French feminism, considering the importance of French intellectuals like Simone de Beauvoir and Luce Irigaray, whose works were very much discussed among Italian women. As a country, she stated, the United States was very different from Italy, where Marxism had impregnated all layers of political life. I argue that the same can be said about feminism in Québec, which was caught between geographical proximity and linguistic tension. Québécois feminism remained for a long time torn apart by its fascination with American countercultural currents, and it shared with the Québécois left an attraction for liberation movements in the rest of the world. And yet a significant portion of its feminist literature was shipped to it across the Atlantic from France.

The Encounter with French Feminism

Québec

The theoretical attraction to French feminism felt by Québécois feminists was facilitated by language despite the geographical distance. France was engaged in its own production of feminist theory, starting with Simone de Beauvoir, whose work continued to attract young women who thought that biology was not/should not be their destiny. In addition, the aftermath of *Mai 68* brought new writing from a variety of political horizons. One of the titles much read among Québécois feminists was the special issue of *Partisans*, "Libération des femmes, Année zéro" (Women's liberation, year zero) (*Partisans* 1972). Edited by François Maspéro, *Partisans* was a leftist and anti-colonialist journal that dealt with a variety of political themes, ranging from the political thought of Rosa Luxemburg and Frantz Fanon to critiques of the postcolonial war in Algeria, the Chinese Cultural Revolution, the national question, Third World liberation movements, women's liberation, sexuality and sexual repression, and the student movement and the left in the West.

This particular issue of *Partisans* was the work of a group of women and was re-edited in 1972 in book format. The first edition contains texts from the United States, England, and Cuba. The second edition enlarged the collection and was more diversified in its political orientation (Un groupe de femmes 1972, 5; O'Leary and Toupin 1982, 40). Both editions clearly indicated the kind of political issues with which women's groups in France were struggling. Debates focused on feminist activists involved in mixed-gender/non-mixed groups, women wishing to bring feminist principles to the revolutionary left, and the problem of finding a feminist theory able to articulate capitalism and women's oppression. The two axes of the movement cut across French feminism, as they did the feminisms of many other countries, and the movement's autonomy was now declared the new priority for French feminism (Un groupe de femmes 1972, 9). The principle of autonomy is accentuated in the second edition of *Partisans*, with the rejection of a hierarchy of positions and of bureaucracy within feminist structures – a clear rejection of power relations within feminism as new themes are brought in – namely, sexuality and homosexuality, psychoanalysis and the unconscious, and the potential for the creation of a mass women's liberation movement (2).

This issue of *Partisans* was welcomed by Québécoise feminists, who were already familiar with socialist, anti-colonialist, and the countercultural literature promoted by the journal *Parti pris*. They were thrilled by its content, and collective readings created memorable moments in the process of theorizing their own movement, which was still to come (O'Leary and Toupin 1982, 40). One text in particular, "L'ennemi principal" (The main enemy),[16] laid the groundwork for a feminist materialist analysis of patriarchy based on twofold evidence: that the overthrow of capitalism would not suffice to liberate women and that an autonomous political force needed to be created (Delphy 1972, 113). The text appeared to deal with two struggles judged incompatible at that time – capitalism and patriarchy – and it certainly comforted feminist double activists in Québec (Péloquin 2007, 230).

The idea that women's liberation was at year zero, as the title of *Partisan*'s special issue suggested, underlined the need to free feminism from the Marxist analysis that had dominated the political scene: the year zero is the year of an emerging movement no longer controlled by ideologies fabricated by others (K.J. 1972, 90), a movement that is not the work of feminist theoreticians or feminist professionals but of feminists who want to change their living conditions (96–97). Québécois feminists were not just consumers of the French texts: they contributed with their own writings, which were exchanged back and forth across the Atlantic. From Paris and Brussels there arrived feminist journals like *Le torchon brûle* (1971–73), *Les cahiers du Grif* (1973–78), *Le quotidien des femmes* (1974–76),[17] and *Questions féministes* (1977–78). The FLFQ and (later) the CdF contributed with their iconic title *Québécoises deboutte!* In the 1980s, it was the turn of *La vie en rose* to be the most widely read feminist journal in Québec, and it made its way through feminist circles in France. The Québécois women's movement published many other titles that enjoyed a respectable readership outside Québec.[18] Besides the exchange of feminist literatures, some Québécoises spent months or years in France and in Europe and came back with an expertise they adapted to the needs of Québécois feminism: discourses on patriarchy and the exploitation of women under capitalism, analyses of sexuality and the body, contraceptive practices, and the setting up of abortion clinics run by women outside the public health care system. The evolution of the movement in Québec paralleled its counterpart in Italy, except for one major difference: there were almost no traces of the theory of sexual difference.

At some point in the mid-1970s, Québécois feminists adopted consciousness-raising – or a version of it – to orient their discussions and their analyses. They began their regular meetings talking about personal experiences. The gesture of starting from one's self created memorable moments and structured their discussions. It took time before consciousness-raising became an important method of self-inquiry. It proliferated with the newly emerged radical feminism of the second half of the 1970s, but, even then, sexual difference was not adopted as the movement's core theoretical approach. The interrelation between feminism and psychoanalysis as well as the exploration of the unconscious never really infiltrated most groups and collectives. The influence of the French group Psychanalyse et politique, if ever mentioned during feminist meetings, was limited to intellectual/academic or literary circles. These circles included feminist writers like Louky Bersianik, Nicole Brossard, and others who, in the 1970s, created a body of feminist literature that focused on the commonalities among women making strong connections with a feminine world.

Italy

The history of the theory of sexual difference entered Italy before significant encounters with French feminists early in the 1970s, when the influence of American feminism was declining. Then a new phase in the movement was triggered by two meetings during the summer months of 1972.[19] These encounters were led by Antoinette Fouque, the leader of Psychanalyse et politique (Passerini 2005, 189–91). At the time, the notion of leadership was highly contested within feminist collectives, whose principles were based precisely on the elimination of all drives for power and hierarchy within organizational structures, but no one in Psychanalyse et politique ever tried to hide the fact that Fouque was the group's uncontested leader (Libreria delle donne 2005b, 45; Schiavo 2002, 61, 65; Zumaglino 1996, 233–36).

Maria Schiavo's (2002) personal narrative offers insights into the meaning French feminism had for the Italians, who had already begun to develop an approach to sexual difference at the end of the 1960s (Perilli 2006). The meetings initiated a series of confrontations during the height of the abortion struggle when some women refused to engage with the rest of the movement. Antoinette Fouque wanted to get away from feminism as it was commonly understood, rejecting the ideology behind it.[20] According to Fouque, the feminist dedication to equality between women and men negates the difference embedded in the feminine body. She considered emancipation to be an attempt to introduce women into the world of men as *fallicamente mascherato* (phalluses in disguise) (Schiavo 2002, 63). For her, sexual difference is an incontestable fact that should come before and above all other differences (91). There is nothing new here: Carla Lonzi and her collective Rivolta femminile had already rejected emancipation and were among the first to lay the foundation for a theory of sexual difference in Italy (Guerra 2005, 51).[21] Yet Fouque rejected feminism and everything that Simone de Beauvoir – the icon of women's emancipation and an enemy of psychoanalysis – stood for (Schiavo 2002, 63). To de Beauvoir's most famous slogan "On ne naît pas femme, on le devient" (One is not born a woman, one becomes one) Fouque proposed a counter slogan: "Donna non si diventa, si è" (A woman does not become, she is) (quoted in Schiavo 2002, 91).

Fouque was radical in promoting a particular type of relationship among women with a conception of homosexuality that was the opposite of what lesbians, like Schiavo, were looking for. In Psychanalyse et politique the lesbian does not exist on her own account: she is just another woman wanting to be male. The love for another woman, the love between women, is the quest for a specific use of psychoanalysis where men are no longer at the centre of women's lives. Fouque conferred on psychoanalysis a particular meaning that denied any merit to consciousness-raising/autocoscienza because it placed men at the centre of feminist discussions in women-only spaces. Fouque's primary goal was to find the mother before the coming of the father – to find the *original woman* before patriarchy, before the law of the father had eradicated the original essence of women. But the precise nature of her project remained vague:

> In that long distant present, "the mother before the father" revealed herself to be in fact more than a woman we could already call by that name, a pre-oedipal mother, a heavy legacy of all we wanted to name. That is what I think today, but at that time we did not give her that attribute, we simply called her "mother," and felt that she was for us a new figure.[22]

Fouque's version of psychoanalysis proposes a model of relationships among women that excludes homosexuality. Lesbianism loses its political relevance in the context of the homosexual movement of the 1970s (Libreria delle donne 2005b, 43; Schiavo 2002, 87). Furthermore, lesbianism is a competitive notion that stands in opposition to the mother: it represents the impossibility of finding the mother who existed before the law of the father and therefore it must be rejected (Schiavo 2002, 89). Fouque would probably have approved of Joan W. Scott's (2011, 59) statement that "woman as mother is the antithesis of the female public speaker" but probably not for the same reason. Indeed, there is too much of the masculine way of doing politics for women to think they can master political speeches within public/

political scenes: Italian feminists who promoted the mother-daughter relationship as embedded within the theory of sexual difference did so as a counter-model to the notion of political subjects.[23]

Carla Lonzi saw a contradiction in the desire to reconcile multiple scenes: the scene of the unconscious with the scene of the political/ideological;[24] the scene of the interior – the inner soul – with the scene of the external public/political realm (Guerra 2005, 52; Schiavo 2002, 90). In contrast, Psychanalyse et politique insisted on confronting Marxism with psychoanalysis, tracking down any trace of the masculine way of thinking, and then pointing out that these theories were not meant to represent women's groups but to be a feminist philosophical trend within the women's movement (Libreria delle donne 2005b, 41–42). This was not the sole contradiction within Fouque's thought. Almost all women's collectives were confronted with these divisive axes/souls within feminism. Back in Paris, Psychanalyse et politique was dissolved after a long series of conflicts with other feminist collectives, and Schiavo observed an abrupt change in Fouque's orientation. She retreated behind her new creation, La maison des femmes (The women's house), a publishing enterprise devoted mainly but not entirely to women's literature and other cultural productions. Later on, the Libreria delle donne of Milan modelled its bookstore on La maison des femmes (Libreria delle donne 2005b, 102; Schiavo 2002, 94, 96).

Returning to the idea of the mother figure and the idealization of the relationship with the mother, Lea Melandri (2002, 61) casts doubt on the possibility of recovering this imagined ancient world that supposedly existed before the law of the father (Libreria delle donne 2005b, 44–45). For women who desire men, the search for the original mother undoubtedly represents a regression. Referring to the powerful figure of the leader of Psychanalyse et politique, what we get, Melandri (2000, 61) argues, is the reverse of the masculine models. Even if men are excluded from women's groups, gender roles created by men persist, especially within heterosexual couples: "The woman-mother-lover can provoke a regressive anxiety – a person who negates you – when one is beginning to see the traces of a men's culture" (La donna-madre-amante può produrre angosce regressive – un essere che ti annulla – anche quando si comincia a vederci l'impronta della cultura dell'uomo).[25] Whatever was previously instilled in the thought of feminists willing to search for the original mother, it signified the end of autocoscienza as a practice and provoked the shift towards a search deeper into the feminine unconscious (Guerra 2004, 105; Guerra 2005, 52). The Libreria delle donne of Milan pointed out that autocoscienza was never used within

Psychanalyse et politique and that the search for a female symbolic world required the adoption of different instruments than those found in small women's groups (Libreria delle donne 2005b, 41–42).

Not all Italian feminists were mesmerized by Antoinette Fouque's preaching. Women from the Collettivo di via Lombroso (Turin) revisited their first encounter with the French group in France and commented on some disconcerting moments: the overwhelming focus on women's bodies and the erotic tensions expressed during meetings; French women's dependency on the authoritarian Fouque, who was their psychoanalyst in real life;[26] the Lacanian discursive framework and the ways in which Psychanalyse et politique denied legitimacy to the feminist struggle for abortion. There was also a permanent climate of tension: the weird feeling that, in the eyes of the French group, Italian women were politically and culturally backward (Collettivo di via Lombroso n.d., 19–20). For Maria Schiavo (2002, 92), however, these criticisms came from a city (Turin) deeply embedded in its history and culture of class struggle. Psychanalyse et politique was openly against the left and, in particular, the extra-parliamentary left as well as against anything that supported an alliance between feminism and other political actors. For Schiavo, it is not surprising that Psychanalyse et politique raised so much hostility. In spite of her own reservations vis-à-vis Fouque, she takes the time to address these criticisms point by point: the fierce opposition to psychoanalysis within feminism, the authoritarianism of Psychanalyse et politique's leader, and the danger of instituting an unhealthy dynamic of power (Schiavo 2002, 113–14, 206). She disagrees overall with the general statement that the French group had a negative impact on feminist mobilization and pushed women away from feminism rather than towards it (115).

Exploring the Unconscious and the Attempt to Connect Feminism with Politics

> *Unlike the English phrase "consciousness-raising," the term* autocoscienza *stresses the self-determined and self-directed quality of the process of achieving a new consciousness/awareness. It is a process of discovery and (re-) construction of the self, both the self of the individual woman and a collective sense of the self: the search for the subject-woman.*
>
> – *Paola Bono and Sandra Kemp,* Italian Feminist Thought[27]

This is the way Paola Bono and Sandra Kemp define the Italian version of autocoscienza in contrast to the American version of consciousness-raising. Their definition does more than highlight the articulation between the individual and the collective: it describes a method that gives space to a subject who is no longer a victim of oppression but an agent transforming her own history and the history of other women with whom she acts/interacts – as well as transforming the social, cultural, and political environments. Italian feminists owe to Carla Lonzi the coining of the term autocoscienza, which differs in meaning from *presa di coscienza* (awareness), which is closer to a literal translation of consciousness-raising but does not convey its deep meaning.

Autocoscienza became the feminist way to reach commonality among women; to reappropriate women's bodies, women's sexuality, and control over one's own life. The politics and practice of autocoscienza allowed women to collectively scrutinize their living conditions; to analyze and to discuss the mechanisms of their oppression; and to connect feminism with the materialist approach as a way of transforming reality (Fraire 2002, 171; Meringolo 1978; Zumaglino 1996, 35–36).

As in many other countries, autocoscienza spread rapidly, and soon almost all Italian women's groups claimed to use it for analyzing a variety of issues. At first, most women did not doubt that autocoscienza was a great feminist method. Many women's groups working on specific issues – such as wages for housework, women's health, contraception, sexuality, abortion, feminist organizing within working-class neighbourhoods or in cultural production such as feminist publishing or in professions such as teaching and social work – spoke and wrote about their use of this method of feminist inquiry. Journals devoted special issues to small groups' experiences of the dynamics during their meetings.[28] These testimonies were often more descriptive than analytical, but they had the effect of exposing interpersonal tensions and showing how autocoscienza reached a critical point, almost an impasse. At first, the method was said to have the explosive potential to unveil the causes of women's sense of inferiority (Piccirillo 1996, 351, 358–60). But it was precisely during these moments of tension, sometimes provoking a group to explode, that problems with autocoscienza emerged in full, defeating the myth of women's commonality and exposing the potential for an abuse of power (Bicchiere and Roditi 1974; "Femminismo oggi: esperienza di gruppo" 1975, 25–26; Rowbotham 1981, 133–34).

The Libreria delle donne of Milan qualified autocoscienza as the first invention of women's politics and declared the death of the method at the same time. The simple fact that autocoscienza was supposed to make you feel good was no longer enough. The Libreria based its assessment on the accumulation of women's testimonies of boredom and repetition, of feeling of powerlessness vis-à-vis the collection of experiences about which nothing was done or could be done. Autocoscienza gave women a sense of empowerment with self-knowledge, but it also gave them a feeling of rage at not being able to use it as an instrument to impose a new contract in the process of social transformation (Libreria delle donne 2005b, 32–39).

"By its very nature, it was a political practice that had reached its completion; it could not go beyond the accomplishment of providing women with the knowledge of being another sex that could not be subordinated or absorbed within the masculine sex."[29] Thus, after only few years of experience, autocoscienza was pronounced ready for the *archeologia del femminismo* (archeology of feminism) (Fraire 2002, 176). For some, the impasse was partly due to the fact that women's groups focused almost exclusively on the relationship between women and men. It was a disappointing method, unable to move feminism forward, towards something more theoretical, something that connected with the need for personal transformation in women's private lives (Melandri 2000, 51; Melchiori 2015). Other instruments of political investigation of the self were called in, attempting this time to make the link between psychoanalysis and politics; however, for many feminists, the practice of autocoscienza was abandoned too soon (Fraire 2002, 179; Melandri 2000, 71–89; Melchiori 2015).

Two major theoretical currents dealing with the unconscious dominated Italian feminism. The first current was created by Lea Melandri and her *gruppo analisi* (analysis group), within which she experienced the liberating power of women's writing. The second current, the *pratica dell'inconscio* (practice of the unconscious), was initiated by the Gruppo 4 (Group 4) in Milan, whose members were authors of the well-known text "Più donne che uomini" (More women than men) (1983)[30] and founders of the Libreria delle donne of Milan (Melandri 2000, 72; Melandri 2005, 93). These two currents influenced the feminist articulation of politics with psychoanalysis during the 1980s and after. The exploration of the unconscious shifted the focus towards the inner self and its transformation and maintained the connection between the individual and the collective. Despite the traditional feminist reluctance to accept psychoanalysis as an instrument of liberation, the practice slowly made its way into the movement ("Rapporto analitico e movimento delle donne" 1974). Efforts were devoted to analyzing women's oppression with a focus that was not solely oriented towards the world of men and the institutions they controlled.

Lea Melandri and the Power of Women's Writing

Lea Melandri argues that, for centuries, women have been instrumental in their own oppression and have learned how to reproduce it (Fraire 2002,

78–79). She situates herself on the opposite spectrum of Lonzi's approach to sexual difference (Melandri 2000, 26), seeing in her work the kind of feminism that excludes politics, and critiquing the idea that women are entirely constituted by men's vision of the world and culture: "As if women were completely outside this model, as if being 'property' or 'part of' did not have roots even in women's unconscious and ambiguous values of love and violence in each."[31] Melandri engages in a long and sophisticated analysis of Lonzi's works on women's sexuality, in particular "La donna clitoridea e la donna vaginale" (The clitoral woman and the vaginal woman). She declares her writing too abstract: "abstract, for instance, is seeing vaginal sexuality as an act of colonization, and the clitoris as the sole 'specific' and 'authentic' female organ."[32] Melandri implies that the consequence of a clear-cut distinction between the two sexes is to establish a rigid and fixed duality in human sexuality.

In order to recover the richness in women's lives and rethink women's subjectivities, Melandri structured her approach to the unconscious around collective writing in small workshops. She asked women to write about their own experiences. The work that autocoscienza was already doing was thus renewed in the form of multifaceted and interrelated narratives (Melandri 2000, 30). Melandri claims that collective writing – in the process of recovering the unconscious – goes much farther than just starting from oneself *(partire da sé)* (210). It is a way of thinking that maintains a discontinuous line between the conscious and the unconscious; between lucidity and dreaming; between speech and silence; between the individual and the collective; and between autobiography and documentation. Melandri does not attempt to establish a doctrine and she is not interested in an all-women discourse on sexuality at the level of the symbolic. Rather, she wants to work directly on women's unconscious in a way that enables them to use what they have recovered as tools for the transformation of their sexuality (79, 82).

Melandri organized writing workshops first at the Cooperativa Gervasia Broxon and then at the Associazione per una Libera Università delle donne (Free women's university association) in Milan, mainly with working-class women enrolled in the "150 hours programs,"[33] an innovative measure negotiated between unions and employers in the 1970s (Melchiori 1987, 2006, 2015). Women's social and economic conditions were not necessarily at the centre of her workshops. The women wrote on topics that touched their bodies, their sexualities, and their experiences of motherhood. The short film *Scuola senza fine* by Adriana Monti (1980) features a writing workshop on women's personal narratives. An important difference between Melandri's approach to the unconscious and the theory of sexual difference is the recognition that there are differences among women. She acknowledges that, in writing groups, it is difficult to accept these differences (Melandri 2000, 85). However, Melandri's discussion of differences overlooks the race issue. Many women coming from the racialized South, who very likely participated in Melandri's writing workshops, escape her analysis.[34]

Melandri admits that recovering experiences from the unconscious is not an easy task: writing about women's sexuality creates a problem when one is trying to write the history of feminism and of the anti-authoritarian movement at the same time. She also argues that, today, very little is remembered about the analytical experiences that took place during the 1970s, and she laments that the theory of sexual difference dominated not only the feminist scene but also how feminist historiography is carried out. For instance, she severely criticizes the ways in which the work of the Libreria delle donne of Milan is placed at the core of Italian feminist thought, altering how Italian feminism is perceived abroad, especially in the United States. According to Melandri, feminist historiographers tend to associate the journal *Sottosopra* solely with the Libreria. She insists that the Milanese journal was originally conceived to work for the movement as a whole. It was only in the 1980s that *Sottosopra* was appropriated by the Milanese feminist bookstore.

The Trajectory of Sexual Difference

I believe that Melandri is correct when she argues that sexual difference dominated the movement in the 1980s. I also agree with her and others that this theory does not capture everything there is to say about Italian feminism. Indeed, sexual difference in feminist thought began to spread during the decade before the groundbreaking publication of "Più donne che uomini" and before *Sottosopra* was taken over by the Libreria delle donne of Milan. But why, in the 1980s, did it suddenly begin to be seen as the sole theory with which to reckon? Why did the authors of "Più donne che uomini" choose to publish their text in *Sottosopra* after a silence of seven years? Why did the text spread so rapidly, provoking endless debate across all segments of the movement and within the mainstream press? The authors, the Gruppo 4 – which represents the second trend in the approach to the unconscious – revealed no personal identification other than simply mentioning that they were women with a certain number of years of feminist activism.[35] It was the only issue *Sottosopra verde* published in 1980 before once again falling into silence.[36] By choosing *Sottosopra*, Vincenza Perilli argues, the group wanted to indicate some sort of continuity of experience with the past, with a content that marks a rupture with the theoretical tradition of feminism (Perilli 2006, 108–9).

"Più donne che uomini" begins with a critical review of feminist struggles and the gains made by women over the previous decade. It argues that women's experiences, knowledge, and values are not well represented in society, that the best of who women really are remains unseen. There is a huge discrepancy between what women desire to achieve and their failure to succeed in the world of men. Thus, the simple fact of being a woman has no real significance. On the contrary, it diminishes women's intelligence and women's pleasure, and, as a result, it weakens feminist struggles (Gruppo 4 1983, 2). The authors attempt to answer why women are failing and urges them to recognize that they are exhausting themselves in trying to succeed. They declare that sexist discrimination can no longer be claimed as an excuse and that, since women share the same problem, it cannot be said that it is simply coming from the outside world.

> What is stopping us is not coming from the outside. To think of ourselves or to present ourselves as victims of discrimination against women is not the essence of our condition anymore. This argument risks becoming a mask. Above all, we know that when material conditions are tough, discrimination can come back again. However, this is a problem that is easy to identify, that we know how to fight and that does not succeed in making a woman feel inferior, nor does it succeed in making her feel inadequate. On the contrary, experience of inadequacy contributes greatly to reinforcing the residue or the return of discrimination.[37]

Gruppo 4 (1983, 2) continues that, paradoxically, women's desire for success parallels their fear of succeeding, based on the absence of reciprocity vis-à-vis all possibilities offered to them. This omnipresent sense of failure – this sense of being inadequate in a world of men – should be placed at the centre of women's knowledge about society. The authors argue that the sole solution is to re-sexualize all social relations in order to get rid of any appearance of sexual neutrality.

"Più donne che uomini" does not ignite feminist imagination by adding something new. It is true that women have improved their conditions and that they have access to more professions and more wealth than ever before, that they enjoy some public visibility, even some political influence. The document's originality rests on its two critiques of feminism. It complains that separatism has been conceptualized as fixed and static, placing all attention on the difficulty of being with men and on challenging discrimination. The authors remind feminists that separatism is only a strategy and should never be grounded in the social relations between women and men (Gruppo 4 1983, 3).

The second criticism is more surprising because it focuses on women's commonality, which the authors say is still lacking. A world of mutual reciprocity is needed, they argue, to counter what strips women of their essence. Yet the reciprocity and solidarity sought by Gruppo 4 comes at the cost of ignoring differences based on class, wealth, race, or other socio-economic markers. The authors' conception of difference is based on knowledge and experience: some women know more than others and, this being the case, they should lead and they should be accepted as leaders. Only then will it be possible to conquer the external forces that oppose women's success.

> The fact that among women who are meeting together there is recognition of this type of value and this type of *entrustment,* sets a precedent of strength, a point of reference that confirms her womanhood in full, which is what she is looking for. Moreover, by recognizing such disparity [among women] as far as it's possible, they find a rule, a dynamism and therefore fecundity: the basic emotions connect with the antique relationship with the mother. With the recognition that another woman can have an advantage, these ancient emotions succeed in being expressed positively, in being freed from ambiguity, liberating us from discrimination.[38]

The model of *affidamento,* basically a replica of some sort of mother-daughter relationship, is presented as necessary to defeat the malaise women are experiencing in their social relations. However, for this model to succeed, any desire for parity among women must be abandoned.[39] Women should derive their legitimacy from other women who have more strength and knowledge. This is the only way for women, the authors conclude, to have access to their own value and their own sense of success. Among all the arguments presented in "Più donne che uomini," this one was by far the most controversial within the Italian women's movement. Several feminist critics presented the model of *affidamento* as having nothing to do with the principles of starting from one's own experience (partire da sé) (Martucci 2008, 19–20). The statement that women should accept inequality among them in order to be who they truly are was at the centre of intense discussions within women's groups and larger feminist collectives. A vast range of diverse opinions was expressed throughout the country, even many years after the text's publication.

Thus, feminist responses to Gruppo 4 were as complex as the original arguments: most of the controversy was over the gains and losses of the movement (Guerra 2005, 60). In "Il disagio della civiltà e l'agio delle donne" (The malaise of civilization and the ease of women), Chiara Risoldi (1983) answers one of the most frequently asked questions: Why did the text spread so quickly and receive so many reviews both from the feminist press and the mainstream media? She retraces the genealogy of the text and connects it with other similar writings that had been made public more than a decade earlier. She points out the centrality of the city of Milan within Italian feminism, a city that had focused primarily on themes surrounding the body and sexuality, and a site where the politics of autocoscienza was rapidly replaced by the practice of the unconscious and psychoanalysis. Over the years, sexual difference came to override a specific segment of feminism that was still concerned with social and economic issues in Milan, a segment that continued to be central to feminist discourses and practices in other cities (like Rome and Turin) as well as in the Italian South. There was nothing new in "Più donne che uomini," Risoldi explains. It was the time of its publication – a moment of crisis and decline in the mass mobilization of political movements, feminism included – that brought it to attention.

Sottosopra continued to appear irregularly. The next issue was printed four years later in 1987 and contained a number of articles in response to the one of 1983, appearing to create a dialogue on the theory of sexual difference. Lia Cigarini, a member of Gruppo 4, wrote "Sulla representanza politica femminile, sull'arte di polemizzare tra donne e sulla rivoluzione scientifica in corso" (On female political representation, the art of arguing among women and on the current scientific revolution). In it she maintains that it is necessary to recognize sexual difference as a reasonable discourse that draws strength from the notion of a contractual agreement among women as opposed to a so-called legitimacy gained by women from institutions (Cigarini 1987, 1). Luisa Muraro, another co-signatory of "Più donne che uomini," wrote "È in corso una rivoluzione scientifica" (A scientific revolution is coming). She warns that, although sexual difference enjoys some social visibility, as long as it is interpreted solely in terms of a male-female polarity it simply establishes a metaphoric comparison between the liberation of symbolic representations of women and their actual liberation. After all, women's thought is not made out of what men are unable to think or what men are unable to achieve.

Among the counter-arguments to "Più donne che uomini" is the article "Per sé/per me" (For herself/for me) by Alessandra Bocchetti, a fellow traveller on the issue of sexual difference. She states in the opening sentence that women are not better subjects than others (Bocchetti 1987, 2).[40] The authors of "Più donne che uomini" would not object to this, but Bocchetti also emphasizes that women's bodies do not guarantee specificity of women's thought. She sheds light on the ways women have been raised and how their social and economic conditions prevent them from performing major personal transformations. Although she recognizes that a woman's sense of identity comes from other women, she stresses that a pure essence in women's ways of thinking is only temporary. She agrees that a large number of women within political parties and within structures of power will not be enough and that even having authorization from other women to speak and act may not change the ways women live their lives.

A number of groups and collectives that adopted sexual difference were created after the publication of "Più donne che uomini." Diotima was perhaps the most important of these initiatives, founded by feminist philosophers from the University of Verona between 1983 and 1984.[41] Luisa Muraro was a member of Diotima, which published a collection of essays, *Il pensiero della differenza sessuale* (Sexual difference thought), in 1987. The group had some influence in the South, particularly in Naples, where a feminist philosophers' collective, Transizione (Transition), was set up. Laura Capobianco (n.d., 41) organized at least three seminars on feminist philosophy during the 1980s with the active presence and collaboration of Diotima.[42] As elsewhere, the notion of *affidamento* provoked dissension among participants, and important members of Transizione quit during the second seminar. Even though *affidamento* was not a practice within the collective, Capobianco believed it was useful to diffuse its knowledge to others.[43]

At the time when "Più donne che uomini" was published, the Libreria was leading the trend of conducting research on the "symbolic revolution" in a variety of disciplines: pedagogy, philosophy, law, science, medicine, and politics. The most important point was – and is – to demonstrate that women were not a mere appendix in society but part of a distinctive order, moving in parallel with the patriarchal order with the explicit objective of achieving a feminist symbolic revolution, the only path to women's liberation (Martucci 2008, 41–43; Muraro 1985). However, beyond simply highlighting two parallel ways of being and thinking, the impact of working at the level of the symbolic deepened the divisions within the movement, even among feminists who tried to articulate feminism with psychoanalysis.

Feminists practising along the lines of sexual difference were simply not interested in class, race, or any other issue at the heart of the existing system of oppression. Little or no consideration was given to social and economic issues, and feminists who adopted sexual difference were also practising a philosophical approach that implicitly rejected history (Perilli 2006, 26; Rossi-Doria 2005, 2–3). As for the issue of race, neither "Più donne che uomini" nor *Non credere di avere dei diritti* ever mentioned the term, even when comparing oppressions.[44]

In 1989, *Sottosopra* published another issue that pursued the theoretical discussion on sexual difference. The Libreria's book *Non credere di avere dei diritti* was about to be translated in the United States by Teresa de Lauretis (1990). Her introduction to the English version of the book compares the Libreria's theorization with feminist theories produced in the United States. She finds some irony in the Italian approach, which "draws as much on the philosophical and conceptual categories of post-structuralism and the critique of humanism as it does on the classic texts of Anglo-American feminism" (3–4). Yet de Lauretis does not explain either the specific political context or the rationale behind the efforts of early feminist collectives to introduce a definitive rupture with class struggle and Marxism. In following the long and difficult journey of Italian feminism – from the introduction of autocoscienza and its subsequent marginalization to the influence of French feminism and the experience of small women's groups in re-enacting the mother-daughter relationship – de Lauretis presents a critical analysis of her own, ultimately displacing major controversies surrounding the theory of sexual difference.[45] Her presentation and translation of the book solidified in the minds of foreign readers the idea that the theory of sexual difference was hegemonic in Italy and that feminists at the Libreria delle donne of Milan were the avant-garde of their movement. But, in reality, Italian feminism was – and still is – one of the most diverse movements worldwide and is capable of generating mass mobilizations, perhaps greater than those occurring in other Western countries (Rossi-Doria 2005, 3).

The final note on the theory of sexual difference comes from a women's group in Naples. From the content of interviews conducted in 2010 in that city, I reached the conclusion that sexual difference was only one among many moments of rupture between the North and the South of the country. For feminists who worked regularly with feminist groups in the North – the Libreria delle donne of Milan, Diotima in Verona – feminism in the Mezzogiorno did not really exist. Feminists living in the South of Italy felt this rejection bitterly as their major theoretical works were ignored. Important feminist thinkers and philosophers, such as Angela Putino, Lucia Mastrodomenico, Lina Mangiacapre,[46] and others, had developed a differentiated and genuine feminist thought that was – and still is – not well understood or fully incorporated into Italian feminist scholarship or exported abroad.

Women as a Subject and Object of Theorization

The pressure to create a movement able to theorize women's oppression and to find a commonality of needs and desires necessitated, according to feminists in the 1970s, the silencing and marginalizing of any types of difference that could destroy solidarity. Québécois and Italian feminists carefully selected their terms of reference from American and French feminisms and adapted them to their respective political contexts. What Italian and Québécois feminisms had in common was an adapted version of the American practice of consciousness-raising, which, for a while, dominated small women's groups almost everywhere in Italy (Bono and Kemp 1991, 9; Passerini 2005, 185). The practice was shared by the two axes of the movement (Fraire 2002, 171), with the exception perhaps of the trend supporting feminist separatism.

In the case of Québec, the influence of American and French feminisms was simultaneous. The feminist/women's movement is located at the crossroads of these two major influences, and, despite the linguistic difference, translated American texts were brought in. In contrast, despite the linguistic proximity with France, sexual difference in Québec remained limited to a few academic circles. For Italian feminists, American influence came first and was unevenly felt throughout the country. French feminism followed with modes of enforcing the theorizing of sexual difference that were already being implemented in Italy. Teresa de Lauretis's translation of *Non credere di avere dei diritti* (1990) as *Sexual Difference: A Theory of Social-Symbolic Practice* may have contributed to the impression that sexual difference was dominant in Italy. While it is true that sexual difference is not hegemonic in the history of Italian feminism, it is also true that it is not merely parenthetical. Nevertheless, many European feminists aspired to move beyond this theory to explore the multifaceted terrain of gender (S. Bourcier 2018).

Rossi-Doria (1984, 153) warns that the claim of difference has always advantaged the political right, old and new, especially since the left has done nothing to take women's specificities into consideration. Women's issues, she argues, have been rediscovered by reactionary forces, placing sexual difference at the core of political platforms. Acknowledging that this notion dominated the feminism of the 1970s and beyond, Rossi-Doria proposes using this approach historically to see women as political subjects and as the main actors in the transformation of their own lives, in contrast to the Libreria delle donne, which uses it to locate sexual difference outside the historical process in order to entrench it in the realm of the symbolic.[47] The difference between the feminist approach to history and the feminist approach to the symbolic is apparent in the ways in which the political subject is conceived. In the end, feminist thinkers at the Libreria delle donne discarded the idea of woman becoming a political subject because this was representative of the masculine order. Instead, the practice of *affidamento* was proposed as a counter-discourse, at the centre of which lay the reinvention of the mother-daughter relationship (Martucci 2008, 17–23) deprived of affect and empathy.

6 Angel Makers or Troublemakers? Abortion, Self-Help Politics, and the Management of Feminist Clinics

Tremble, tremble, the witches are back.[1]

– Italian slogan heard during the abortion struggle of the 1970s

The hardship of paid work, its impact on workers' bodies and longevity, meant that physical and mental health occupied an important space on the agendas of unions and political movements. In many European countries, the student movement and the extra-parliamentary left were in contact with members of anti-psychiatry organizations. In the 1960s, these organizations were highly political and well known for their radicalism and their direct action strategies against science and medicine, which they accused of being at the service of power. Early feminist groups held similar views regarding the subordination of medicine to the diktat of capitalism, although their analysis went far beyond the boundaries set by political actors of the left as they extended their theorization outside the area of paid work into dimensions of life never examined before (Percovich 2005, 43–45). They demanded that women have complete control over their reproductive rights. Their strategies resulted in bringing feminist underground abortion practices into full view, forcing political actors to debate possible solutions to the problem within the political/public spheres (Laforce and Saillant 1993, 17–18; Libreria delle donne 2005b, 61; Michaud 1995).

The history of the abortion struggle and of contemporary feminist theorizations of reproductive rights in Québec and in Italy is far from linear. Long before the abortion struggle reached its peak, long before heated feminist debates on the best strategies tore the movement apart, there was a history of women acting to control their pregnancies. Moreover, feminist narratives advocating reproductive rights were interrupted by various counter-narratives coming from the frontiers of the movement from social categories of women to whom the right to reproduce was denied. Histories of poor single mothers, of racialized women, of Indigenous women throughout the Americas recount numerous cases of forced sterilization and medical experiments (Smith 2005). The diversity of Québécois and Italian populations, with their deep economic and political divisions, invites attention to the racialization of groups of women as well as to the stigmatization of poor women. Furthermore, a closer look at the history of Italian and Québécois feminist campaigns in favour of women's reproductive rights show that the well-known political struggle of the 1970s was never about abortion alone. This chapter revisits the political context surrounding the abortion struggle, feminist self-help discourses, and the creation of feminist infrastructures pertaining to women's health. We discover that the perspectives coming from race and (dis)abled bodies are absent from feminist narratives on reproductive rights, although other micro-narratives emerged from the margins and were inserted between the lines of feminism to challenge the predominance of the core on issues such as the democratization of medical practices and the meaning of the right to choose.

First, I review different discourses on abortion and the respective Québécois and Italian political contexts within which a diversity of feminist strategies were used as well as the challenge posed by the politics of self-help, which evolved alongside the practice of abortion within autonomous feminist clinics. Then I look at how women's health centres/consultori discussed their involvement – or their refusal to collaborate – with their respective health care systems. Throughout the chapter, we see how the political contexts shaped feminist strategies regarding women's reproductive health. One of the differences between the two feminisms concerns the role of the Roman Catholic Church and of political parties that intervened on the side of the Italian government to regulate women's access to birth control services, including abortion. A second difference touches upon the conditions of possibility for the creation of feminist networks as well as the circumstances surrounding the partial successes of feminist activism in the area of self-help. In Québec, the original concept of self-help served as an alternative to traditional medicine with the aim of transforming medical practices in the long run. However, the drive to be health professionals delivering good services won over the radicalism of feminist criticism against the medical model and the women's health movement's original goal of a radical transformation of the entire health care system.

Abortion Struggles and Feminist Self-Help Politics

Both women's health movements began organizing referral services to abortion clinics abroad. In Montréal, most of the referrals were organized by the Centre des femmes and were directed towards the United States.[2] London, England, was the destination of choice for most Italian referral groups. They provided detailed information on how to travel to London, how to find the clinic and where to live, along with a description of the medical procedure. This information was meant to be useful for those who did not speak English and who did not have much money to spend (Movimento Femminista Romano 1975).

While they covered the same themes – sexuality, health, and women's right to free abortion on demand – feminist debates in Québec and Italy unfolded quite differently. The issue of decriminalizing the practice of abortion did not reach the Canadian House of Commons before the Supreme Court judged the law unconstitutional in 1988. In Italy, the Parliament debated several versions before voting for a law in 1978 that took abortion out of the criminal code. Some aspects of Italian feminist demands for abortion rights were supported by political parties such as the Partito Radicale, but the law – which was finally implemented in 1981 after being contested by referenda – was mainly the result of a compromise forged between two parties: the Partito Comunista d'Italia and the Democrazia Cristiana. Not surprisingly, many feminists felt that their expectations had been betrayed.

Women's Health Centres and Their Network in Québec

After a brief preliminary period, feminists in Québec were faced with two challenges: (1) to provide abortions themselves from a feminist perspective that would radically transform the practice rather than having good doctors – like Henry Morgentaler – performing them; and (2) to set up a series of autonomous women's health centres that would introduce a process to democratize the entire health care system. And they succeeded. This generation of activists created a small number of women's health centres in six major cities. They decided to import the American self-help discourse that had crossed the border at the turn of the 1970s with the publication of *Our Bodies, Ourselves*. Their enthusiasm was great and they never doubted their success, but they didn't anticipate the difficulty they would face in attempting to pursue three strategies simultaneously: (1) developing a feminist discourse on women's body, health, and sexuality; (2) finding a feminist alternative to the hegemonic medical model or at least democratizing its approach to women's health; and (3) balancing the first two strategies with organizing the struggle for free abortion on demand.

If the discourse on self-help was inspired by the American women's health movement, the idea of setting up their own abortion clinics was inspired by the experience of French feminists who had dared to do so, despite the risk of being arrested and criminally charged. Some Québécois activists who had spent time in France brought back the famous account of a feminist clinic in Aix-en-Provence, where those who had performed illegal abortions were sent to trial. Based on these reports, many activists claimed that, when a law is consistently broken, it becomes illegitimate and unenforceable. Some of these Québécoises were present at the 1977 International Feminist Conference in Rome, which facilitated the exchange of perspectives and approaches on the politics of self-help and abortions. The conference gave considerable support to the French feminists and all of those who, in Italy and elsewhere, had adopted the strategy of defying the law (Dossier de lutte pour l'avortement et la contraception libre 1975; Gruppo femminista per la salute delle donne di Roma 1977; D. Lamoureux 1983; Michaud 1995, 76, 92).[3]

Québec, as a province, does not have the right to legislate on matters of abortion and medical practices: only the federal government of Canada has the constitutional power to do so. During the entire struggle leading to the Supreme Court decision in 1988, the government stubbornly refused to reconsider the restrictive legislation of 1969, which criminalized abortions unless a woman's health and/or life was in danger. Of course, the most famous case against those who defied the criminal code involved the Henry Morgentaler clinic in Montréal, which opened in 1969. In 1974, he was charged a first time and acquitted by a jury. But Morgentaler's clinic was not the only one: four women's health centres practised abortions. The first to practise abortions, ten years before the Supreme Court ruling, was the Québec City Women's Health Centre in 1978. The last of the four centres to practise abortions started to do so in 1982. After the Supreme Court ruling in favour of Morgentaler in 1988, the federal government never succeeded in adopting a law restricting and/or (re)criminalizing abortion, in spite of a serious but unsuccessful attempt in the House of Commons in 1988 (Brodie, Gavigan, and Jenson 1992; D. Lamoureux 1993).

Despite Québec's limited provincial power to legislate, feminist activists launched a successful campaign that forced the more progressive Parti

Québécois to abandon the prosecution of doctors performing abortions when the party formed the government in 1976. The PQ chose to set up its own therapeutic clinics, the Lazure clinics, named after the health minister of the time. However, the measure fell short of what feminist activists were demanding. The so-called Lazure clinics were simply forcing francophone hospitals to set up therapeutic abortion committees while respecting the limits of the federal law.[4] Nevertheless, the health minister's initiative gave feminist activists enough space to create a certain number of autonomous women's health centres with medical clinics that performed abortions and developed self-help practices as well.

Between 1978 and 1983 six women's health centres were autonomously created mainly in working-class neighbourhoods. Four of them practised abortions illegally and all six had the objective of completely transforming the traditional medical and scientific representations of women's bodies, their reproductive roles, and their sexuality. In 1985, after years of intense discussion, they created a network called Regroupement des Centres de santé des femmes du Québec (Québec women's health centres network) in order to increase their visibility within the community sector and, more generally, within the terrain of social movements. This small network, like other Québécois feminist networks of women's services groups, created a space in which to share feminist experiences on the issues of reproductive rights and the politics of self-help, with the goal of challenging, politically and ideologically, the traditional meaning of reproductive health.[5]

The struggle in favour of abortion was important, but soon many feminists began to focus their energies on developing a perspective on health and sexuality as well. Self-help was becoming the equivalent of consciousness-raising, allowing women to explore their own bodies – their anatomy and physiology – collectively, without the interference of a medical expert. It also meant taking control of their sexuality by learning how to claim sexual freedom (Michaud 1995, 59; Rowbotham 1981, 136–37). Despite significant differences in women's health centres, most of them, at least in some important moments of their history, organized self-help courses based on scholarly research.

The women's health centres aimed to implement five principles. First, each centre had to subscribe to a collective self-help approach and to facilitating an atmosphere in which women could share their experiences. Second, a feminist discourse and practice required the personal involvement of all women, regardless of their status within the group: providers had to share their lived experience on the same level as the women consumers of their expertise. Third, feminism – as the political discourse that analyzes and theorizes women's specific social relations – required naming the cause of illnesses as social, political, and environmental. Fourth, the feminist approach to health was a holistic, all-encompassing vision of physical and mental women's health. Finally, health centres aimed to have women take charge of their own health in order to eliminate dependency on the medical profession (O'Leary 1987, 118–21). By focusing on self-help discourse rather than solely on abortion, most women's health centres attempted to develop a radical critique of the institutional health care system and the ways in which medicine perceived women. The American influence was clear in the emphasis on individual autonomy, coupled with the collective moments of sharing feminist research on women's bodies and sexuality.

The second principle was quite challenging and time-consuming in terms of developing meaningful interpersonal relationships between users and providers of services: all information and expertise pertaining to women's anatomy and physiology, including strategies on how to face doctors, health care professionals, and the health care system as a whole, had to be shared collectively. This implied that all women were engaged in the collective management of feminist clinics, which meant the abolition of hierarchical functions and positions within these clinics (Michaud 1995, 102). Initially, professionals were not banned from women's health centres, but they were asked to put their scientific knowledge at the same level as the knowledge of non-professionals, even when it came to performing medical procedures. Getting rid of hierarchies between those "who know" and those "who don't" was a critique of the medical profession and the power of the male expert over the female body (Michaud 1995, 103).

These five principles sustained the meaning of being part of a feminist collective and outlined how to share the production of knowledge and the management of the daily operation of women's health centres. They are perhaps one of the best demonstrations – although their application was partial and their duration brief – that non-specialists can/must infiltrate the protected world of medicine; that they can/must challenge its orientations, its limitations, and its practices; that they can/must demystify medical power over bodies and lives. In order to give more depth to these five principles, Québécois feminists proposed three additional concepts – *démédicalisation* (de-medicalization), *déprofessionalisation* (de-professionalization) and *désexisation* (de-sexing) – which they called the three Ds and which they placed at the core of their practice (Michaud 1995, 96).

The presence of doctors in women's health centres was not universally supported. Some centres limited doctors' activities to the strict performance of medical acts that were, after all, their prerogative under federal law. In other centres, however, doctors were accepted. In Québec City, an informant explained that the objective was to give women access to abortion, not to give feminist activists without medical expertise the opportunity to perform them. Indeed, most doctors resisted subordinating their knowledge and their practices to feminist control. Many centres faced the difficult task of recruiting doctors willing to give up their privileges. Some health centres demanded that doctors give back the surplus income they received from the Régime de l'assurance maladie du Québec (RAMQ) (Québec health insurance system) (quote from interviews in Michaud 1995, 128). It also became clear that the feminists' desire to demonstrate that they were as professional as any other clinic or hospital was at odds with the request that medical experts relinquish their position of power (Michaud 1995, 109).

In the end, the fact that self-help was declared an important terrain of struggle provoked divisions and even schisms between those who wanted to put their energies into abortion and those who saw self-help as the only feminist strategy capable of transforming the health care system and its medical practices (Michaud 1995, 101). However, all the efforts surrounding the daily activities of self-help did not prevent the practice of abortion from consuming most of the energy: little by little, the feminist struggle for abortion threatened the development of the more sophisticated analysis of women's sexuality and reproductive health. There was an obvious conflict between the necessity to transform the ways in which women lived their sexualities and looked at their bodies and the necessity to provide abortions to women in need. The ideological and political divide among the six centres eventually eroded the strength of their feminist network.

Tensions and Political Divisions among Women's Health Centres

Feminist activists wrote extensively about their objective to create a genuine alternative to the institutional health care system, about their analysis of women's health and reproductive rights, and about their expertise in representing women's needs in numerous public/political spheres. They wanted to radically change medical practices, and they defiantly attacked the sexism within the medical profession and the health care system. Above all, they wanted to transform the perceptions women had about themselves, to give them confidence vis-à-vis medical experts and health services providers, and to persuade them to see themselves as political subjects rather than as victims of medical practices (Michaud 1992, 1995). However, they were never unified with regard to their strategies on how to transform the health care system and the medical model. There were two main tensions among these centres: (1) the inability to resolve the conflict between the practice of abortion and the politics of self-help and (2) the difference in ideological discourses that affected some centres' connection with segments of the left and/or the rest of the women's movement, on the one hand, and their relationship with public institutions, on the other.

If we look at each women's health centre separately, the two interlocking tensions emerge more clearly. The Centre de santé des femme in Québec City, the first autonomous feminist abortion clinic in Canada, was created with the help of the union movement and was inspired by socialist feminism and working-class struggles. It remained faithful to this political orientation until the end. It critiqued the Centre de santé des femmes du Quartier in Montréal for betraying its original goal and shifting from Marxist feminism to radical feminism (Michaud 1995, 65). Yet the political context within which the Québec City and Montréal centres were set up shows a strong solidarity with the political struggles of their time. The link with unions in Québec City was organic and was prioritized over relations with women's groups because the centre responded primarily to the need to perform abortions. Only later did the Québec City centre develop a series of self-help courses in an attempt to appeal to the larger community and to improve its chances of survival.

In Montréal, the Centre de santé des femmes du Quartier went in the opposite direction, being solidly anchored in the women's movement while still maintaining a connection with leftist political struggles (Michaud 1995, 144). The Montréal centre provided a significant space for the practice of abortion, but its most creative energies were in the area of self-help. It developed an original approach to service, introducing the *para-médicale* (paramedic), whose role was to inform women of their rights. The presence of these people was meant to reassure women and to help them ask the right questions when meeting with the doctor. Why are you prescribing this drug or this treatment? What kind of health problem do I have? What can I do to help solve it? The aim was to empower women and not just let the doctor decide. In addition, a group of lesbians at the Montréal centre contested the heteronormativity of feminist health discourse and practices. They introduced a protocol stating that service providers should not assume the sexual orientation of women users. All of these innovative practices were part of intensive research into how to change the way in which medical practices were carried out. However, when I conducted my research in the early 1990s, the fear that the Montréal health centre would become just another abortion clinic haunted practitioners as well as members.

In the Eastern Townships, southeast of Montréal, the Centre de santé des femmes de Sherbrooke had contact with women's groups in the area, and there, too, feminist enthusiasm around health issues helped to spark the collective. The Sherbrooke centre set up a very creative organization devoted entirely to the politics of self-help, and it rejected the option of performing abortions. The Sherbrooke centre never went through the tensions generated by the practice of abortion, though it claimed to have been inspired by the many innovative practices of the Centre de santé des femmes du Quartier in Montréal (Michaud 1995, 145).

The trajectory is rather different for the Centre de santé des femmes de Trois-Rivières and Clinique des femmes de l'Outaouais in Hull. These two centres had a different beginning from the other three because they did not originally connect with other political movements or maintain close contact with women's groups in their respective communities. Both had the objective of filling a void for women who were in need of an abortion (Michaud 1995, 145). It is possible that the rare contact these two centres had with other women's groups contributed to their high level of institutionalization and collaboration with the public health care system in comparison to other centres. Yet there are fundamental differences between the two. For instance, the Clinique des femmes de l'Outaouais was created with the help of the local Centre Local de Services Communautaires (CLSC), and it kept up a close relationship with the regional health care system (Michaud 1995, 146). Of the six centres, the Outaouais centre experienced the most divisive and traumatizing internal conflict over the politics of self-help: the small group of feminists who wanted to implement the feminist approach to self-help was met by a wall of opposition from a second group determined to focus solely on abortion. After months of harsh debate, the latter group won and the former had to leave the centre. Nothing of that sort happened with the Centres de santé des femmes de Trois-Rivières, which managed to balance the practice of abortions while developing courses on women's mental health, teenage sexuality, and women's aging. Feminists in Trois-Rivières were quite isolated, its being almost the only women's group in the region, and the only way to break their isolation was to maintain contact with other centres – mainly with the one in Québec City for the time it remained open – and with the provincial network for as long it existed.

Finally, the political differences among the health centres are highlighted by the position each of them took over the issue of public funding and their relationship with the Québécois health care system. The women's health centre in Québec City, for instance, refused any direct funding from governmental sources, while the Clinique des femmes de l'Outaouais received most of its funds from institutional connections such as the CLSC, thus running the risk of being totally integrated within the public health care system. The latter mode of funding was seen as unacceptable by other members of the women's health centre network.

In the early 1990s, the issue of acknowledging diversities among women – as opposed to acknowledging only differences between women and men – was partially debated within women's health centres. Compulsory heterosexuality and the need for contraception were contested by lesbians regarding issues of sexuality and reproduction. In some centres, due to the Marxist terms of reference left over from previous decades, issues of class and the health of low-income women predominated. Race and racism were hardly spoken of except to claim that centres were open to all. The necessity to meet the needs of women of colour was not seen as important for it was perceived to be the responsibility of racialized women to make their presence known and their claim understandable. Consequently, different approaches to "women's right to choose" were not heard, and very few protagonists of the women's health movement saw a problem in the fact that almost no racialized women used their services.

In the end, the lack of cohesion between the women's health centres in terms of organizing strategies and the political message they wanted to send out was not their main shortcoming. They can, after all, claim to be the first in Canada to open abortion and self-help clinics that took a feminist view of health and sexuality and that challenged the medical model's hegemonic representation of women's bodies and women's roles. Rather, as the years went by, it was their ambiguity towards the health care system that made them look more and more like any other health clinic, leaving their radical theorizing on women's health and medicine behind.

With the Supreme Court decision in 1988, abortion and the feminist discourse on self-help became more and more estranged from one another, and the practice of federally regulated medical acts that surround women's reproduction got more space and visibility at the expense of other feminist services seen as, politically speaking, less rewarding. Some clinics (Outaouais) went so far as to erase any trace of self-help discourse after experiencing their dramatic split. When this erasure occurred it became obvious that abortion had stopped being a feminist struggle. Elsewhere the idea of self-help had become fashionable but was slowly fading away into the archives of the movement. Without the support of the best feminist analysis and theories this movement was able to produce, women's health centres shifted from being political actors to being places where women could get the same services that were offered in other clinics and hospitals. They changed from being autonomously managed by feminist activists to being simply humanist providers of good-quality services to women in need, from being a political struggle based on women's rights to being another terrain where scientific medicine maintains its hegemony (Jenson 1992; Michaud 1995, 124; O'Leary 1987, 123).

Feminist Strategies towards Decriminalizing Abortion in Italy

In Italy, the violent opposition of the Roman Catholic Church to decriminalizing abortion put enormous pressure on the Italian political arena. According to Percovich (2005), the church hit hard at the heart of the political scene as the two major parties, the DC and the PCI, were both conservative forces. The DC acted in symbiosis with the church while the PCI feared being rebuked by Catholic voters (9–10). Consequently, when the struggle for abortion emerged, the collision between the church and feminists could not have been more brutal: the feminist theorization of sexuality became the terrain of fundamental confrontation (Comitato Triveneto per il salario al lavoro domestico 1976, 2).[6] However, a greater conflict was to come between feminists who believed in the need to have an abortion law and those who did not want women's reproductive rights to be regulated by the state.

Debating Abortion Rights Inside and Outside Parliament

The earliest feminist document to present an analysis on reproductive rights came from Demistificazione autoritarismo patriarcale (Demystification of patriarchal authoritarianism) of Milan. "Schema di ipotesi della ricerca sulla procreazione" (Sketches of a hypothesis for research on procreation) (DEMAU 1970), published a few years before the struggle for abortion had begun, is the first indication of the centrality of issues of reproductive rights and sexuality for the coming generation of Italian feminists. Other feminist analyses soon followed: some remained in manuscript format but others found their way into the young feminist press. In 1973, *Sottosopra* published regularly on abortion, women's bodies and sexuality, and the politics of sexual difference.[7] The journal also published statistics indicating that 1.5 to 3 million women had illegal abortions every year in Italy, often under horrific conditions. A Lotta Femminista group in Ferrara published a document, *Basta Tacere* (n.d.), that argues that, in Italy, "ci sono due milioni e mezzo di aborti l'anno e ogni 1000 donne che aborticono ne muoiono 15" (there are 2.5 million abortions a year and for every 1000 women who abort, 15 die) (quoted in Percovich 2005, 90).

It was not the first time that feminists made public the situation under which women decided to end their pregnancies (Di Lello 1975, 33; Percovich 2005, 90). Throughout Italy, it was becoming the social problem of the moment: witch hunts and reports of illegal abortions appeared in graphic detail in the mainstream media. The feminist press reported identical events from a different perspective, focusing on police arrests, seizures of medical files belonging to women who had had abortions in the past, as well as court trials against these women, their doctors, their nurses, and activists who supported the practice of illegal abortions. In Trento, 263 women were accused of having had an abortion. In Florence, 40 women were denounced by a fascist organization and were arrested in the clinic along with the head doctor and were threatened with forced uterine medical exams as proof of their "crimes." The Florence events sparked major debates on the legality of such exams as well as on the length of time a uterus shows traces of an abortion (Collettivo femminista Trentino 1975, 34; Frabotta 1978; "Il Corpo politico" 1975). The feminist press also drew attention to the fact that many of those prosecuted had declared themselves as having had an abortion, as abortionists, and/or as supporters of those who had received or performed abortions in order to bring the problem into public view. Numerous street demonstrations in Italian cities such as Florence and Trento were organized in support of the accused, reminding the public that the criminal code still contained sections dating back to the Mussolini regime. Abortion carried a sentence of up to twenty years imprisonment (Collettivo femminista Trentino 1975, 34; Di Lello 1975, 33; Foletti 1975, 1b; Frabotta 1975). Feminist activists succeeded in bringing women's rights to abortion to the top of the public/political scene, and, from that moment, the issue could no longer be ignored.

Many male comrades from different parts of the left were in favour of abortion, but many feminists highlighted the differences in their political views. For men, some feminists argued, the meaning of abortion was a matter of science, of law, and of morality – a method of birth control tainted with a Malthusian approach to the problems of poverty and of overpopulation (Percovich 2005, 98; Turone Lantin 1975, 15).[8] The masculine analysis of capitalism and its forced discipline of the proletariat brought male comrades to see birth control methods, including abortion, as a question of necessity (Collettivo femminista di Bologna 1974, 74–75; Fraire 2002, 109), while for many women abortion remained an instrument of violence and suffering (Collettivo femminista di Milano 1973, 93). The idea that abortion is a form of violence in women's lives is recurrent in the Italian feminist press. During the interviews I conducted in the South, some participants told me they had had an abortion, others that they had helped young women to abort. They talked about the difficulty and the suffering related to the conditions under which women were forced to have abortions during the time of secrecy imposed by underground practices, especially in the Italian South. This is part of the context explaining why a significant portion of the Italian feminist movement became suspicious of leftist and progressive politicians supporting their cause (Percovich 2005, 101–8).

Nevertheless, another important segment of the women's movement was not so reluctant to connect the abortion struggle with institutional politics – namely, with the Partito Radicale (PR), which advocated for abortion in the Italian legislature as well as in civil society. When the law on abortion was finally adopted, the PR immediately announced it would contest it, hoping to eliminate all major restrictions imposed on women in need of abortions. Only one of two referenda proposed by the PR was accepted by the Constitutional Court.

Feminist activists unanimously supported the demand for decriminalizing abortion but were deeply divided on the strategy surrounding the adoption of a new law, and many refused to devote their efforts beyond decriminalization of the act. In addition, the movement was deeply polarized between feminists who wanted to reposition abortion within the much broader issue of sexuality, and feminists who wanted to focus their energies on the development of services for women in need. It is a mistake, the first group argued, to focus on an emancipatory solution typical of what the old and New Left always proposed as a solution to women's issues. What women needed was a complete transformation of the ways in which they live their sexuality. As long as nothing changed, too many women would have to go through the difficult experience of abortion. In accordance with this position, many activists created feminist research groups on medicine, analyzing and theorizing women's health and sexuality. For other activists, however, it was urgent to stop the persecution against women having abortions and against the doctors, nurses, and those supporting them. Accordingly, they set up feminist consultori, some of which forged alliances with political parties like the PR. The struggle for abortion, they argued, was not a mere problem of emancipation but a necessary step that would pave the way to women's liberation.

After years of prosecuting women seeking abortions and their doctors, after years of painful and frustrating negotiations among political parties within the Italian legislature, the government adopted two laws. The first, in 1975, created public consultori (law 405) and, for the first time in the country's history, provided birth control and abortion services. The second law (194) was adopted in 1978, legalizing the practice of abortion. This second piece of legislation was immediately contested in national referenda, one organized by the PR mentioned above, the other by the Roman Catholic Church and pro-life organizations. These referenda were unsuccessful, but it took years before 194 finally became law in 1981.

Law 194 is still in force today. Almost all of the feminists I met during the course of this research acknowledge that it is a good law, knowing too well the Roman Catholic Church's continual campaign to repeal it. However, in the 1970s, many activists criticized the restrictions contained in the text of the law, such as the clause allowing doctors to be conscientious objectors and the impossibility of minors getting an abortion without parental consent. Many also contested the fact that law 405 requested existing feminist consultori – those that provided birth control services and, in many cases, abortions – to integrate newly created public structures. In fact, many of these feminist consultori refused, preferring to dissolve. The difference between feminist consultori and public consultori is significant: the former structures are, in principle, self-managed and are supposed to operate outside the state health care system. According to an informant in Palermo, the law on consultori does not allow the operation of private clinics such as autonomous feminist clinics. In addition, a woman cannot ask her personal doctor for reproductive health services if that doctor is not part of a public consultorio. These aspects of law 194 on abortion resemble the Canadian law that existed from 1969 until 1988: abortions were only allowed within accredited hospitals under the guidance of a therapeutic committee. Contrary to Italian consultori, however, where abortions are accessible, the therapeutic committees in Canada had the power to decide whether or not a woman was worthy of having an abortion and/or of being sterilized.

During the entire period, the PCI maintained that working-class women were too close to the Roman Catholic Church, going so far as to depict them as socially, politically, and culturally backward. In line with this representation, the party defended traditional family values (Gramaglia in Frabotta

1975, 195). According to Manuela Fraire (2002), to understand the PCI's position in respect to issues such as abortion and sexuality, one must look at the attitude of defiance the party maintained towards feminism. For years, the PCI gave little political legitimacy to small women's groups, and, consequently, the family became the terrain of confrontation and conflict between the communists and feminist activists (133–36). Nearly all segments of the autonomous Italian feminist/women's movement criticized the PCI's attitude during the referendum on abortion as the party relentlessly defended "responsible" and traditional motherhood (Percovich 2005, 106). A feminist and long-time member of the PCI from the city of Naples told me that the PCI hierarchy warned her not to talk about abortion during party meetings with women because the issue was considered to be too controversial to be discussed in public. These meetings, she said, were often supervised and controlled by party officials. What communist leaders feared most was division among their members, many of whom were Catholics.

Autonomous as well as separatist feminist criticisms targeted women members of the PCI, but the party's influence over its members was so strong that many communist women were unable to act freely. On the terrain of so many struggles affecting women's lives, communist women and Catholic women were constantly litigating on social policies and services, and very often their collaborations and/or confrontations took place within the same women's organizations, such as the UDI.[9] On some issues, like the family and motherhood, it was possible to reach an agreement as long as they remained on the terrain of women's rights and emancipatory reforms. But on issues such as abortion, the rupture between communist and Catholic women was unavoidable: women's right to decide and feminist views on women's sexuality were too divisive (Ripetto 1981).[10]

Ergas and Sassaroli (1976) identify three main feminist positions on the perspective of adopting a law on abortion. The first position supported the proposed law on the creation of public consultori (405) controlled by the state. Such a law was seen as giving women the opportunity to get experience in the management of abortion and reproductive health services. The second position was also in favour of supporting such a law, but it insisted on consultori independence from political parties and state institutions. The third position, however, was opposed to having abortion regulated by law. According to feminists who held this position, a much broader mobilization of women would be necessary for them to have any political influence (37–38).

It is important to note that Ergas and Sassaroli wrote from the position of the Comitato romano per la liberazione dell'aborto (CRAC) (the Roman committee for free abortion), a network whose objective was to bring together all feminist consultori in the country. Taking into consideration the complex synergy of political forces, this network demonstrates the heterogeneity among feminist protagonists, even among those supporting a new law on abortion, all of whom criticized the constraints imposed by the legislation. Feminist supporters of the law were trying to adjust their practices in anticipation of what was to come. Many women were members of CRAC – some were also members of extra-parliamentary groups – or members of UDI affiliated to the PCI, or members of the Movimento di liberazione delle donne (MLD), which was associated with the PR. In this web of memberships and party affiliations, it is important to keep in mind the distinction between the old left and the extra-parliamentary left. The old left occupied many seats in Parliament and was able to influence the legislative process in which negotiations and compromises played a large part, an advantage the extra-parliamentary left never had.

The PR was atypical within the political spectrum. Its constitution was innovative, with several federative initiatives involving all kinds of social movements (Ingargiola and Cucchi 1987, 52–53). For a significant portion of the Italian feminist movement, be it separatist or autonomous, the idea that MLD had a federative link was inconceivable, despite the PR's claim to fight against all oppressions, to enhance individual freedom, and to build a society based on equality (MLD 1975, n.d.). Ingargiola and Cucchi stress that the presence of men in MLD activities was highly contentious, and many women quit over the impossibility of holding women-only events. The political meaning of these defections was scarcely understood. Despite this problem, MLD used its federative connection with the party to create other affiliated groups across Italy. Interestingly, this atypical federative structure allowed some men to have their own experience of double activism (54–56).

Many women members of both the PR and the MLD were in an uncomfortable position. There was relentless pressure from women and men members of the extra-parliamentary left to analyze women's oppression within the national and international context of capitalism and imperialism. However, for feminists in MLD, capitalism was not the only system of oppression: it was one among many other modes of exploitation (Ingargiola and Cucchi 1987, 60). Finally, MLD's relations with the rest of the autonomous/separatist feminist movement – and at times with the UDI as well – were fraught with contradictions and conflicts intermingling with moments of solidarity and collaboration. In its document "Congressi a confronto"

(MLD 1975), MLD explains how PR's federative model structured its work and noted that the party was devoted to secularism, socialism, and libertarianism. MLD took pains to explain its affiliation, reaffirming why the PR's proposed referendum on the abortion law was necessary – that is, to denounce and abrogate the fascist segments of the criminal code regarding abortion; to highlight and support self-denunciations of those who were involved in the practice of illegal abortions; and to make the struggle over the referendum a non-violent weapon for civil rights. In spite of these explanations, many feminists accused the MLD of imposing a referendum on the rest of the women's movement for the sake of becoming the hegemonic force on the issue (Ergas and Sassaroli 1976). Several feminist groups ultimately rallied in defence of law 194: the repeal of the law was rejected by 67 percent of voters in the 1978 referendum (Libreria delle donne 2005a; Ombra 2005). With the victory of the "no" vote coupled with the slow but steady opening of public consultori, the bulk of women's activism was reoriented towards making sure that these two pieces of legislation – law 405 and law 194 – would be implemented everywhere.

The Rationale against a Law Regulating Abortion

Segments of the Italian feminist movement that supported the new law found their relationship with the multifaceted left difficult, but they were also confronted and challenged by other feminists opposed to any legislation regulating abortion. As mentioned, some feminists refused to walk the street alongside men supporting the decriminalization of abortion, even though the proposed law was coming from a popular initiative.[11] The first time some feminists opposed a law regulating abortion was in 1971, it came from Rivolta femminile (quoted in Libreria delle donne 2005b, 62–63). In February 1973, *Sottosopra* published a text denouncing the first versions of legislation brought to Parliament because the proposed law required that women had to rely on the support of doctors to receive an abortion. In 1975, *Sottosopra* came out with two groundbreaking texts. The first, "Noi non vogliamo più abortire" (We do not want to abort anymore) was the work of feminist groups in Florence and Turin, and it called for the complete transformation of the dominant social and sexual structures of Italian society. Feminist members of these groups reaffirmed the importance of working first and foremost on issues of women's sexuality and women's bodies. The main objective of the legislation, according to them, was to continue the same repression and control of women's sexuality but in different ways: even if written by women and for women, the legislation could only negatively affect female sexuality (Collettivo 'Santa Croce' 1975; Libreria delle donne 2005b, 65–69; Percovich 2005, 71).

"Noi non vogliamo più abortire" suggests that the responsibility for the violence generated by an abortion must remain on the side of institutions and that women must refuse to be complicit with any type of American Malthusianism (Collettivo femminista di via Cherubini 1975b, 35; Percovich 2005, 100–4). If feminists want to be involved in political struggles alongside men, these groups argued, they should reorient their energies towards improving social services. Fighting for abortion alone, they maintained, was a mistake: abortion is only an emancipatory measure that does not lead to full liberation (Collettivo femminista di via Cherubini 1975b, 35).[12] A second text, "Noi sull'aborto facciamo un lavoro politico diverso" (On abortion we are doing different political work), made identical arguments and explained why members of the via Cherubini collective did not want to participate in street demonstrations that included men (Guerra 2005, 48–49; Libreria delle donne 2005b, 65; Percovich 2005, 71).[13] Theoretically and politically women's health groups were divided and polarized (Rossi-Doria 2005, 15). Several feminists in favour of decriminalizing abortion said that ending pregnancy was a painful experience. The movement was supporting women's choice, but a handful of women thought abortion should not be considered at the same level as other civic rights demands, opposing MLD's position (Guerra 2005, 46–47).[14]

Research on Women's Health and the Feminist Critique of Medicine

By the mid-1970s, women's groups in several Italian cities were promoting feminist research on and intervention in medicine and/or women's health (Percovich 2005, 37). In the North, women's health collectives offered an array of health practices, ranging from the politics of self-help to the management of a complete feminist consultori providing clandestine abortions.[15] In the South, however, the situation was generally described as abnormally deprived of resources. After failing to open a feminist consultorio in Naples, a group of women appealed to the municipal administration to respect law 194, but the opening of a consultorio was constantly delayed (Senatore 1981). Throughout the country women's health and the related issues of women's bodies and sexuality mobilized women more effectively than autocoscienza and/or the politics of the unconscious – which were considered complex and slow to bring results, if any (Percovich 2005, 38–39). This does not mean that all women's groups working in the area of health rejected autocoscienza. Nevertheless, the early 1970s were years that saw the rapid growth of research groups: Milan had a collective whose orientation was devoted entirely to research on medicine; Rome witnessed the creation of groups daring to practise clandestine and illegal abortions; Padua set up a women's health group that had ties with the New Left, in particular Lotta Continua and Potere Operaio; Turin created a "150 hours" course on women's health. While the particular emphasis in each of these northern cities was different (Percovich 2005, 57), during the earlier years at least, there was a consensus about taking the issue of women's health and women's bodies away from doctors and hospitals.[16]

According to Percovich, regional differences resulted in part because few women's health groups wanted to follow the path taken by the Gruppo femminista per una medicina delle donne (Feminist group for women's medicine) of Milan. The Milanese group took seriously the challenge of doing research on alternative health, of analyzing and theorizing medical practices and their negative discursive representation of women. The first document of the Gruppo, also a member of the larger collective of via Cherubini, claims to be completely separated from the medical system, political parties, and the public health care system as a whole. The spirit that animated the collective is in many ways exemplary of the type of feminism later promoted by the Libreria delle donne of Milan: the group refused to go beyond the mere decriminalization of abortion.

The feminist divide on health looked like this: one side of the movement wanted to set up research groups on medicine and take the issue completely outside medical institutions; the other side wanted to obtain enough resources regionally in order to provide direct health services to women, including abortion. For the latter, the feminist management of autonomous consultori was at the centre of the agenda during the entire period of the abortion struggle (Percovich, 2005, 14–15). These differences illustrate the tension between the organization of direct services and the development of a feminist analysis of women's health and sexuality. The reasoning behind the refusal to develop direct services had to do with the desire to avoid dealing with doctors and the health care system. The opposite reasoning, however, maintained that feminist struggle was not just about medical discourse but also about the state and its control of women's lives. Of course, this reasoning included the need to remain connected with other social struggles (Percovich 2005, 61–62).

In 1974, the Gruppo published a widely circulated pamphlet about different types of contraception. The pamphlet was reprinted several times and reached a large audience of women throughout the country. Its message warned that women's liberation was not going to be an easy process, that contraception alone could not resolve all problems, that a radical change of women's living conditions was necessary to bring about positive results. The pamphlet was distributed by the Associazione Italiana per l'educazione demografica (AIED) (Italian association for demographical pedagogy), an organization created in 1950 and the first to disseminate information on contraception despite its prohibition by the criminal code.[17] However, the Gruppo femminista in Milan was isolated from the rest of the women's health movement. It severely criticized other collectives for being ambiguous about adopting self-help politics.[18] In 1975, members of the Gruppo refused to obey law 405, which compelled them to become a section of the local consultorio. The Gruppo preferred to end its feminist research activities rather than for its members to become experts and professionals at the service of public institutions (Percovich 2005, 63).

Padua was the second city after Milan to initiate a feminist research group on women's health, in the summer of 1974. Some of its members wanted to remain in contact with the extra-parliamentary left and one of the most important feminist groups in the city, Lotta Femminista. Others, however, wanted to focus on women's health, and, consequently, the research group split into two. One segment moved away from political struggles while the core group remained connected with the demand for wages for housework, thinking that the primary struggle was not medicine per se but the state and the public health care system that attempted to appropriate and to subordinate women's bodies (Percovich 2005, 62). In 1977, the core group had to end its activities, apparently due to state repression and the arrests of several members of leftist groups. The health centre continued, however, and obtained funding arising from the new legislation on public consultori (Franzinetti 1987).

Additionally, 1974 was the year when the feminist clinic of San Lorenzo opened in one of the poorest neighbourhoods in Rome, with Simonetta Tosi as its leader.[19] This feminist consultorio adopted self-help politics, using popular education on issues of reproductive health, contraception, and sexuality, but its relations with working-class women in the neighbourhood of San Lorenzo were not always smooth (Damiani 1978).[20] Again, after intense debates about whether or not feminists should work with public institutions, the San Lorenzo consultorio decided to refuse government subsidies and to remain autonomous.

Simonetta Tosi's work is perhaps the best example of someone living the stress of negotiating between two worlds (Farrington 1978; Leonelli 1975, 18; Tozzi 1984),[21] and San Lorenzo is the perfect example of a feminist consultorio that tried to resolve the contradiction between practising the politics of self-help in a working-class neighbourhood and making sure that abortions would be accessible in local hospitals. In 1979, the collective occupied the Policlinico, taking over the supervision of the ward where abortions were supposed to be performed but, up until the occupation, had not been. The action lasted four months and was initially supported by sympathetic doctors and leftist health professionals, but it ended with the intervention of the police.[22]

San Lorenzo was not the only feminist consultorio to organize direct action. In 1978, feminists occupied Santa Anna's hospital in Turin. The hospital was late implementing services following the adoption of law 405. The struggle to obtain services for women, in the absence of autonomous feminist consultori, led members of UDI to occupy the public consultorio in 1979. Such spectacular actions, which revealed poor implementation of the law, went beyond simply demanding services to make clear the urgent need for large-scale mobilization around women's health and to force public services to collaborate with feminist activists (Nolli 1981). In addition, the fact that the South of Italy was deprived of services and that public consultori took more time to open there than elsewhere does not indicate the absence of feminist consciousness and activism: in almost every region there were small groups of women dedicated to issues of women's reproductive rights and self-determination (Ambrosino 1978). Most of the time, however, their voices and the meaning they gave to their struggles were not understood because they differed from the feminist terms of reference voiced in the North.[23] Regardless of their feminist orientation, most feminist consultori that remained autonomous from public services, in both the North and the South, were short-lived (Franzinetti 1987; Gobetti, Graffigna, and Tappi 1979, 28–29; Percovich 2005, 144).

Overall, the history of the abortion struggle and feminist attempts to develop contemporary feminist theorizations on medicine and women's health is not linear and is often interrupted by micro-narratives coming from the margins of feminist discourse. I would like to consider the specific case of the environmental catastrophe in the northern town of Seveso, which represents a rupture in feminist narratives on abortion. In 1976, at the height of heated debates over the issue, an industrial chemical plant leaked a toxic gas (dioxin) into the atmosphere of Seveso. The leak had catastrophic consequences for people's health, particularly that of pregnant women. A special clinic opened, apparently for those seeking therapeutic abortions. Yet many feminist observers thought that the event highlighted public institutions' failure to respond adequately to women's worst nightmares (Bracciali 1976, 27–28). Housewives and working-class women expressing their rage at public meetings were confronted by public officials who attempted to depersonalize them. As always, the Roman Catholic Church refused to consider any possibility of interrupting a pregnancy, even proposing that children born with a disability be given up for adoption.

The feminist journal *Effe* published two articles on Seveso. Yasmine Ergas (1976, 28–30) wrote the first one and the Gruppo femminista per una medicina delle donne di Milano (1976, 38–39) wrote the second. These articles argue that the conditions under which women aborted in Seveso had nothing to do with women's rights to end their pregnancy. Ergas severely criticizes the officials of the corporation responsible for the toxic leak. On the one hand, some pregnant women did not wish to abort but were encouraged to by health authorities; on the other hand, some wanted to abort but were prevented by the church, whose members visited women in their homes bringing images of foetuses. Accepting – or refusing – to have an abortion in these conditions was not normal. Ergas says that these women were asked to choose without having been provided proper information on the effects of dioxin on their health and on the health of the foetus.

This story shows the limits of what a new law – still waiting to be adopted – could do: the version then before Parliament required the approval of three physicians before a woman could have an abortion. The entire process was hypocritical, based on the public authority's request that women obtain a diagnosis of mental illness before getting an abortion. In total thirty-three women obtained an abortion following the Seveso catastrophe.[24] Women have the right to abort or not to abort, and no one can take this choice away from them. They also have the right to a different motherhood. Feminist/women's movements around the world challenged the conditions under which women lived their sexuality. While forcing political actors to take a stand, core feminist discourses were criticized for not paying attention to racialized and subaltern categories of women subjected to forced sterilizations and abortions (Smith 2005). The feminist movement showed its heterogeneity and its internal conflict from the beginning of the campaign. On the issue of abortion in Italy, this movement was able to reach only a minimal consensus on the decriminalization of abortion. Beyond this consensus, activists were divided on the best strategies for securing reproductive rights, improving women's health, and dealing with public institutions.

Participation/Non-Participation in the Health Care System

Québec

In 1978, when feminist activists created the Coordination nationale pour l'avortement libre et gratuit (National coordination for free abortion on demand) its objective was to ensure women's right to have abortions on demand. It also wanted abortions to be performed in women's health centres, outside the institutional health care system, which, at the time, kept very rigid control over access (Michaud 1995, 75). This national coalition was conceived as a means to empower the abortion struggle, to bring political support to the women's health movement, and to encompass all feminist collectives participating in the struggle. The coalition disbanded in 1981. The six women's health centres were still active, and a few years later set up a network called Regroupement des Centres de santé des femmes du Québec, whose purpose was to ensure their visibility within the public/political scene and to strengthen their influence on Québec government policy (141).

Interacting with the state, its bureaucracy, and its services brought major tensions to the daily routine of women's service groups, including women's health centres. At some point, the feminist activists who ran these groups had to shift the positions they had taken in the early 1970s. When the CdF dissolved into several specialized groups, many of them chose to focus on providing immediate services. They saw no contradiction between groups' ongoing criticism of the state and the public funding they received for organizing services, nor did they see any problem in asking for policy reforms, presenting themselves as the only actors with the expertise and knowledge to enable respectful intervention in women's lives.

Officially,[25] the political orientation of the Regroupement differed significantly from that of other networks of women's services groups, most of which had adjusted their positions in order to have a voice in the orientation of public policies.[26] One document written in defiance of the position taken by other networks summarized Regroupement's opposition in five points.[27] First, it considered it impossible to develop political activities and feminist discourses and services while pursuing negotiations with the state. Second, in the case of possible collaboration, there was a fear that feminist and alternative services would be co-opted by the health care system without any recognition of the expertise of women's health centres. Third, feminist activists wanting to promote a feminist ideology within the welfare state system ran the risk of being subsumed by it and of being forced into a position of subservience. Fourth, the women's health centre network contested the discourse of the rest of the women's movement on issues of health and reproductive rights, which did not integrate the radical dimension of the original feminist demands. Finally, the Regroupement challenged the standpoint of the overall women's movement vis-à-vis the state and asked for some reflection on the institutionalization of women's issues within state apparatuses like the Conseil du Statut de la femme (CSF). Institutionalization, the Regroupement argued, establishes a dynamic of negotiation and participation with the state through the benevolent support of the CSF and state feminists while placing women's groups in a very problematic position (Michaud 1992; Michaud 1995, 152–53). The substance of these five points can be contrasted with the rationale presented by the Gruppo femminista per la medicina delle donne in Milan, which accused the Italian feminist movement of not being serious enough about the adoption of self-help politics.

Some voices in the Regroupement make it appear that most women's health centres had claimed complete autonomy from the health care system and had opposed any collaboration with public institutions. It seemed to be the most radical network among women's services groups on the issue of government funding.[28] In reality, however, each centre, particularly those practising abortions, worked in synergy with the health care system (Michaud 1992, 1995, 1997a). Although the Regroupement can claim never to have received public funding from the Ministère de la santé et des services sociaux (MSSS) (Ministry of health and social services), each centre received minor funding for its operational budget. In addition, the four centres that operated like medical clinics got most of their funding through the Régime de l'assurance maladie du Québec (RAMQ) (Michaud 1995, 15), even when abortion was still illegal. All they had to do was to claim a refund for other medical services, even those related to abortion, which were covered by the system, and/or change the labelling associated with the act itself. While their interactions with the state administration were unique among women's services groups and networks, none of these centres was completely separate from involvement with public institutions (Michaud 1992).

Moreover, each centre felt the pressure to demonstrate that it could provide services as good as those available in any hospital or CLSC: contacts with labs for tests and referring women to specialists in the public system when needed meant that these connections had to be established and maintained. Links between feminist services and the publicly funded institutions were not just instrumental: there was circulation of knowledge as well – although difficult to measure – between the public health care system and the women's health centres. Several categories of health professionals – nurses, social workers, women's doctors – contributed to create the women's health centres in their neighbourhoods, many of whom had years of experience within the public health care system and who maintained their relationship with the hospital or the CLSC from which they came (Michaud 1995, 167).

Italy

Silvia Tozzi (1987) identifies three phenomena that facilitated the process of the institutionalization of women's health issues in Italy: (1) the centrality of women's body within feminism, although she argues that the question was never analyzed in depth by some women's groups; (2) the translation of health issues into concrete objectives facilitated by the proximity to political parties during a time when frontline struggles – such as the politics of self-help and abortions – were not sufficiently shared by the women's movement as a whole; and (3) the fragmentation of the women's health movement and the isolation of groups from one another (156). Tozzi also identifies three distinct phases in the genealogy of the Italian women's health movement (157–76). The first phase, from 1971 to 1974, happened before the adoption of law 405 on public consultori and before feminist struggles on abortion reached their highest point. It is during this period that women's health groups of all kinds proliferated throughout the country. Some of these groups became feminist research centres while others devoted their energies to providing direct services, particularly to women living in working-class neighbourhoods.

During the second phase, from 1975 to 1976, feminist collectives were becoming more interested in providing direct services to women. This was also the period when the feminist struggle for abortion reached its peak: the first sites of abortion services were opened, mainly in Rome by the Centro Italiano sterilizzazione e aborto (CISA) (Italian centre for sterilization and abortion), an organization also federated with the PR. For its part, CRAC aimed to be the network to bring together all feminist consultori in Italy after the adoption of law 405.[29] This phase was characterized by high tensions within the feminist movement, mainly over which political direction to take on the abortion struggle: either to remove abortion from the criminal code but refuse to have women's reproductive rights limited by a new law or push the government and political parties to vote for legislation that would legally permit the practice.

The third phase, from 1977 to 1978, is perceived by many to be a victory for the women's movement,[30] although it is illustrative of two types of divisions over the management of services to women: (1) those existing within the feminist movement and (2) those existing between feminist/women's groups on one side and political parties of the left and public institutions on the other. Nevertheless, the turn of the 1980s signalled the intensification of feminist surveillance of public institutions to guarantee that public services were developed and accessible to all women. This was when feminists occupied hospitals and clinics in Turin, Rome, and Naples in order to ensure that the state's promised services were available and were provided according to women's needs.

Overall, however, the final phase marked the increasing involvement of feminist activists in institutional structures of the Italian health care system, despite divergent positions taken by many segments of the movement. Criticisms were directed in particular at CISA because of its sole focus on free abortions. CISA, like MLD, supported the PR's effort to push for a law that gave women access to free abortion on demand. Members of the two organizations argued that, even if the new law did not bring anything new for wealthy women, it had the merit of offering all women the possibility of getting an abortion: anyone supporting progress, these organizations argued, could not oppose legislation that would secure access (Ingargiola and Cucchi 1987; Remiddi 1974, 45).

CRAC, on the other hand, promoted a different project. It tried to prevent any move favouring a referendum on abortion, even opposing the one promoted by the PR, for fear of its potential negative results. Feminist activists of CRAC – some of whom were members of the extra-parliamentary left or of the UDI affiliated with the PCI – organized national meetings and, on at least one occasion, went to the South at the invitation of the Collettivo delle donne d'Amantea (Women's collective of Amantea). This encounter revealed the ambiguous behaviour of northern feminists in a region deprived of public services. Yet, in the attempt to bring commonality of conditions to married women, the word "them" shifted towards the word "us." This meeting with women of the South consolidated, in the mind of CRAC activists, the urgency to open feminist consultori everywhere in the country (Constantini and Sassaroli 1976, 35–36).[31]

In pursuing its objective to be the coordinator of autonomously managed feminist consultori, CRAC used the feminist discourse of self-help, which was not based solely on providing information about contraception, reproduction, and sexual practices but that also adopted a strong critique of the unequal relations between medical experts and women (CRAC 1975, 7–8). Yet if we contrast that with what the Gruppo femminista in Milan was proposing, the meaning of the concept of self-help proposed by CRAC appears diluted (Percovich 2005, 103).

The Un/avoidable Process of Professionalization

An important distinction between Italian and Québécois feminisms is how they positioned themselves in relation to the state and its institutions. In Québec, the inventory of feminist analysis on the interaction between women's service groups and the state – its bureaucracy and its public services – is significant. It emerged out of feminist research, much of it executed by activist researchers involved with feminist/women's groups at some point in their community and/or academic lives. The research shows that the evolution of the women's health centres raised several questions. How much of the original feminist principles and feminist knowledge remained as the self-help spirit faded away in a context in which women's centres closed down one by one or shifted towards professionalism? Did the women's health centre movement have the potential to be truly transformative or was it just a voice proposing an alternative to the medical model? When did the paradigm shift from a strategy based on feminist principles to a strategy based on humanism, as Véronique O'Leary (1987) phrases it, occur? Was the feminist counter-hegemonic discourse aimed at radically transforming medicine and the health care system unrealistic (Michaud 1995, 12)?

In Italy, feminist activists were confronted with a different dilemma than simply being managers of consultori. They had to deal with what was happening in the legislature, with the political debates and compromises in which they could scarcely participate unless they accepted having their voices mediated by political parties. Throughout the 1970s, political actors debated different versions of the law on abortion at all levels of the Italian political system and up to the Constitutional Court. In the meantime, they went through a series of elections that affected political alliances inside and outside Parliament. Political compromises were constantly renegotiated: all versions of the law, including the one that was adopted, put limits on women's reproductive rights.[32] Indeed, the attitude of the Catholic Church, of political parties on the right and, to some extent, on the left, differ in many ways from what occurred in the Québécois context, where the issue emerged in the Québec and federal legislatures through two specific events: the highly publicized court trials of Henry Morgentaler from 1973 to 1975 and the creation of the Lazure clinics by the PQ government at the end of the 1970s.

The problem facing the two feminisms also differs regarding the production of feminist knowledge and the provision of services. In Italy, two years after the adoption of law 405, only six regions out of nineteen had complied with the legislation (Bolognese 1977, 22). One year after the adoption of law 194, all sorts of difficulties were observed. The most important obstacle was the interference of doctors who were conscientious objectors: 72 percent of doctors interviewed declared being opposed to practising abortions, leaving several women with no choice but to abort clandestinely. Strangely, one observer stated that some women – namely, in the Lazio region (Rome) – got clandestine abortions from doctors who had claimed to be conscientious objectors (Constantini 1979, 27). The second difficulty was that it was impossible for minors to get an abortion without the consent of at least one parent.

When the law on public consultori was adopted, many Italian feminists had to make a swift decision: either to transform feminist clinics into public services with the hope of democratizing medical practices through feminist principles or to close down their feminist clinics while continuing feminist research on medicine. Many saw continuing the feminist management of consultori as an important field for political action and alternative practices. The setting up of feminist consultori was not circumstantial: they were part of structures in which serious feminist research took place. They contained the potential to become terrains for autonomous organizing featuring direct democracy and challenging the traditional ways of doing medicine and politics (Menapace 1975, 10). However, public consultori dramatically affected feminist practices. Suddenly research was halted and women's health groups and/or consultori were no longer sites for alternative/transformative practices because of closures or integration into the public system.

Can feminist groups researching and theorizing on women's health accept money from a government to which they are opposed? And can feminist principles of self-help operate within the same system as scientific medicine? These were some of the questions that Italian and Québécois feminists debated in their respective ways. Some feminists claimed that the risk of participating in the health care system was worth trying for the simple fact that it brought a feminist perspective into public institutions (D. Francescato 1977). Unfortunately, the partial recognition of feminist principles within the public system offered no guarantees to those who had acquired expertise over their years of feminist activism. In fact, a paradigm shift was operating within the feminist/women's movements themselves: the discourse on health moved from the consciousness of managing women's health centres/consultori – presented as researching the experience of sexuality in women's lives – to the increasing professionalization and medicalization of abortions (Baeri 2005, 123).

7 Feminist Approaches to Organizing

In the 1970s, Québécois and Italian feminisms were structured around mid-size collectives, some of which were subdivided into small cells with a predisposition for direct action aimed at increasing their visibility in the public/political scene. Each collective had a particular mode of organizing. Individual members intermingled their personal lives with activism. They had feminist principles to defend and to integrate into the decision-making process of every small group: the vision of a forthcoming feminist society was based on these principles.

As the women's movement expanded, it became clear that it was not possible to unify feminist discourses. As the movement entered the 1980s, an entirely different decade witnessed the decline of political mobilizations while the number of groups grew rapidly. The fragmentation of large collectives into a constellation of small groups added to the difficulty of ideologically and politically controlling feminist discourses and practices. Larger coalitions of solidarity were welcome as long as the autonomy of each group was respected and its specificity recognized. It became obvious that not all women members of small groups were willing to identify as feminists, at least not unconditionally. The concept of "feminist collectives" shifted to "women's groups," although in Québec both denominations have always been used interchangeably.

The exact moment feminism in Québec shifted from a political movement to a social/women's movement is not easy to capture. Some observers, like

Diane Lamoureux (1986, 138–39), argue that, from the moment feminist collectives began to specialize, to focus on single issues, feminist demands were easily absorbed by state institutions. Lamoureux later states that the political decline of feminism happened when a significant portion of the movement replaced its original political platform with demands reduced to mere equality of rights. At this point, she argues, feminist activists were easily co-opted within governmental administrations (147–49). Perhaps Lamoureux is too judgmental about the political orientation of Québécois feminism. Indeed, women's groups redirected their activities to services targeting specific social categories of women in need. However, the number of women's services groups that obtained some sort of legitimacy from public/political institutions represented a small fraction of the diversity of activities within Québécois feminism. It is true that some women's groups turned to the state in order to get funding for their services to the community, but there was another reason: the sharp decline of the political left. Most extra-parliamentary organizations, like En Lutte!, had dissolved due to a massive desertion of women. Feminism was losing the primary interlocutor with which it had exchanged ideas and against whom it had so fiercely defended its demands, its analysis, and its legitimacy. If feminism survived the difficult period at the end of the 1970s, it was undoubtedly transformed but certainly not tamed.

Feminist historian Rossi-Doria (2007, xi) observes that terrorism – the kidnapping and murder of the head of Democrazia Cristiana's Aldo Moro by the Brigate Rosse in 1978 – signalled the end of political movements. But even in Italy, and despite the state's repression of a certain number of activists, feminism moved on. The shift of meaning between two contiguous expressions, "feminism" and "women's movement," revealed the difference in the collective identity these notions represent (Calabrò and Grasso 2004, 8). Italian sociologists Anna Rita Calabrò and Laura Grasso put forth the concept of *femminismo diffuso* (diffused feminism) to illustrate the change that took place within individual and collective political consciousness: an evolution that is not linear but, rather, is punctuated by interruptions of political moments that were not always orchestrated by the movement itself. For Calabrò and Grasso, the concept of *femminismo diffuso* highlights the eclipse of mobilization and the fading away of the influence of collective actors. Taking into account the different phases of the movement in Milan, the two authors warn that, in other cities, the sequence of events might have evolved differently:

> Diverse waves of feminism were quite clearly distinguishable, when the movement was passing from being a feminist movement to becoming the

> women's movement, and then to becoming a diffused feminism: elsewhere [i.e., outside Milan] the typology would not have been so recognizable, neither in the diversity of discourses nor in the sequencing.[1]

By the mid-1980s, a certain feminist revolution was over, leaving its imprint on all of Italian society, independently of the action of feminist groups and the number of attempts at recuperation orchestrated by diverse political actors (Calabrò and Grasso 2004, 11). Thus, the concept of *femminismo diffuso,* despite its vagueness and ambiguity (Melandri quoted in Calabrò and Grasso 2004, 8), is nonetheless a useful indicator of how, following a decade of political agitation, feminist principles infused women's lives regardless of their affiliation to feminism. Some feminist observers of the Italian scene characterize the turn of the 1980s as a moment of consolidation of gains and of creation of numerous research units, such as women's centres, libraries, and bookstores. The movement, some argue, went from being political to being cultural (Braidotti 1986, 149; Rossi-Doria 2007, xi).

Yet, as the 1980s began, Italian and Québécois feminism/women's movements appeared to have taken different paths: in Québec, the movement is often presented as reorienting its strategy towards servicing women's specific needs, while in Italy the creation of a number of groups that interconnected women and culture is said to be the dominant characteristic. This way of presenting both movements seems to have persisted to this day, even though in Québec there is an abundance of groups devoted more to "cultural activities" than to the provision of services. And, in Italy, there are segments of the movement that cannot be reduced to the cultural dimension and are instead oriented towards the production of services in close connection with state institutions.

This chapter is an overview of the Québécois and Italian feminist evolution and transformation: from feminism to the women's movement to a *diffused feminism.* I show that, in Québec, several protagonists within the movement were preoccupied by the consolidation of organizational structures and by the active implementation of feminist principles. By contrast, Italian feminists focused on resolving the internal/personal dynamic within small women's groups. The objective of this chapter is to provide tools for analyzing the transformation of feminism during this particular moment in history. In the early 1980s, some feminist scholars tried to circumscribe the movement through the labelling of groups and feminist trends. Yet something always fell outside the frame. Tracing the boundaries of such a multifaceted and pluralistic movement as feminism, even transformed into a women's movement, resists any formal exercise in typology.[2] Other feminist scholars tried to dissect the movement according to different phases. Again, these sociological attempts are perhaps useful for those who want to make sense of the recent historical evolution, but they fall into endless definitions and descriptions. Like Lea Melandri (2003, 40), I would like to avoid the usual linear narrative: feminism emerged, then flourished, then declined. Rather, I prefer to approach the movement with a different perspective and suggest that nothing is created, nothing is lost, everything is transformed.[3]

From the Political Movement to the Social Movement

Fragmentation and Specialization in Québec

Feminism achieved legitimacy and respectability from the political experience of activists immersed partly within movements of the left and partly within separatist/autonomous feminist/women's groups. While large collectives fragmented into smaller entities oriented towards specialized issues, many group members had the feeling of belonging to a community of like-minded women from which a *new political subject* was born, distinct from the usual rhetoric of class struggle. In Italy and in Québec, the growth of small groups brought different sorts of tensions as well as its load of obstacles.

Characteristics that highlight similarities and differences between the two collectives that pioneered Québécois feminism – the Front de libération des femmes du Québec and Centre des femmes – sparked a range of political initiatives through a number of smaller and more specialized groups. The CdF's synergy with extreme-left political movements shaped its feminist ideal of being the avant-garde: an advanced form of feminism capable of leading the way to a women's revolution. The CdF adopted the strategy of opposing other women's groups, especially those it considered ill prepared; it attacked any feminist initiative judged as too centred on the defence of individual rights. Nothing equalled the tone set in *Québécoises deboutte!*, with its frequent CdF criticisms of the former FLFQ for having discredited the feminist revolution. The CdF proclaimed it would not make the same mistake and intended to lead – like a respectable New Left organization – and to present a comprehensive feminist theory of women's oppression as well as a global political strategy for all Québécois women to follow (O'Leary and Toupin 1983, 18).[4]

Members of the CdF also thought they could develop a full-fledged theory of women's oppression. Yet the task appeared insurmountable in view of all that was expected from CdF members: from publishing the journal *Québécoises deboutte!* to organizing the struggle for free abortions, from disseminating feminist propaganda inside and outside the Montréal metropolitan area to theorizing an analysis of women's oppression. Indeed, the collective succeeded in raising political and feminist awareness in most regions of Québec. *Québécoises deboutte!* was so popular the CdF was unable to respond to the numerous letters it received. The collective dissolved over the impossibility of being the feminist avant-garde it wanted to be and over its inability to create the unity it believed was necessary for any extra-parliamentary leftist political organization (O'Leary and Toupin 1983, 365).

The end of the CdF opened the space for the emergence of several small groups with specific mandates and for specialized issues such as health, cultural production, physical and sexual violence, and popular education. For a while some of these groups used the same Marxist-feminist platform. Out of the ashes of CdF was created a coalition of four groups called the Intergroupe, composed of the Théâtre des cuisines (Kitchen theatre), the Comité de lutte pour l'avortement et la contraception libres et gratuits (Committee for free abortion and contraception on demand), Les éditions du remue-ménage (Agitation [or commotion] publishing), and the Centre de santé des femmes du Plateau Mont-Royal (Women's health centre of the Plateau Mont-Royal). In 1976, the coalition issued a manifesto for the March 8 celebration, calling for the end of the exploitation of working-class women and housewives.[5]

Despite fierce opposition to using Marxist terms of reference, some trends of radical feminism flirted with a Québécois version of materialist feminism forged in the intersection of the French and American influences. The journal *Les têtes de Pioche* alternated between an attraction to and a tension with working-class analysis. The journal published twenty-three issues between 1976 and 1979. In 1978, Armande Saint-Jean, one of the main figures and ideologues of the group, wrote "Lettre ouverte à toutes mes soeurs *Têtes de Pioche*" (Open letter to all my *Têtes de Pioche* sisters). In it she identifies two types of conflict that plagued the life of the journal: the first was between socialists and radicals, the second was between lesbians and heterosexuals. Saint-Jean argues that the problem with the women's movement lies among feminist *families* and that everyone seems to struggle for the same cause but remains divided by ideological barriers (Saint-Jean 1978, 2). Two years later, in her preface to the complete collection of *Les têtes de Pioche* re-edited by the feminist publishing house Les éditions du remue-ménage, Saint-Jean (1980, 8) revisited the question, adding a third source of conflict: the tension between working-class women's issues and those of women identified as bourgeoises.

For her part, Micheline de Sève (1998) evokes the multiplicity of feminist trends from 1969 until the death of *La vie en rose* in 1987. She highlights the same set of fractures as Saint-Jean but adds the well-known split between anglophone and francophone feminists (158). She points out that members of the CdF followed two ideologically distinct paths when the collective came to an end: one path favoured the creation of women's groups specializing in single issues while the second path was absorbed by the extra-parliamentary left (165–66). De Sève argues that the fragmentation and the renewed plurality within feminism signalled the end of large and comprehensive feminist collectives. Or perhaps what had disappeared is de Sève's idea of what feminism should be.[6] Once again, issues of race are stunningly absent in these analyses, considering the cosmopolitan composition of Montréal and the anti-racist struggles that took place there throughout the 1960s and '70s (Austin 2007; Ricci 2017, 2018).

The structural and organizational weaknesses of small women's groups do not signal a lack of organizing structures. The abundance of organizations the movement was able to create in all sectors demonstrates the vibrancy of feminist creativity and originality (Bellavitis 1990; Braidotti 1986; Michaud 2007; Rowbotham 1981, 40). In addition, feminists have always claimed the existence of core principles in their mode of operating, a claim that goes beyond the description of a secure and cozy atmosphere created by the practice of consciousness-raising/autocoscienza. In accordance with their opposition to masculine ways of doing politics, women declared the end of hierarchy and of power struggles within their organizations as well as the end of a decision-making process whereby the majority rules. Feminists instituted instead a set of consensual practices in which the defence of autonomy appeared front and centre. The next section looks at the Québec City feminist collective Marie-Géographie, which documented its thoughtful conception of feminist organizing.

A Feminist Conception of March 8 Organizing in Québec

In the 1970s and 1980s, I was an activist in Québec City, which is a third the size of Montréal. Québec City was the site of original and groundbreaking initiatives and collective action. Most women's and popular groups were geographically confined within working-class neighbourhoods, which included parts of the old historic neighbourhood of Québec City. All year round, most groups were aware of activities organized by other groups and most activists shared the feeling of living in a small village. There were women's centres, shelters for women victims of violence, citizens' committees, youth centres, community radio stations, alternative journals, groups defending welfare rights, and organizations defending prisoners' rights. The groups often shared the same addresses and enjoyed the same sources of public funding and union funding.

Marie-Géographie, a part of this community, was a small autonomous collective with an executive that never grew beyond seven or eight members. Nonetheless, the group was highly diversified in terms of political orientation, race, ethnicity, sexual orientation, and alternative modes of community living. Despite these diversities, everyone agreed on the same political platform, which promoted rebellious socialist feminist writings. Marie-Géographie began its activities by publishing feminist posters and by gathering and communicating information on women's issues at the local, national, and international levels. Early on, the collective shifted its activities from being an information/communication group to publishing a feminist journal while pursuing the same objectives of political plurality and diversity. The journal was able to count on a certain number of feminist supporters and sympathizers who volunteered in different ways: journalism, research, photography, sketching caricatures, and so forth.

The collective published a journal carrying the same name, *Marie-Géographie*. This journal appeared three times a year, from September 1984 until the fall of 1987, addressing a multiplicity of themes, ranging from mental health institutions, women living with disabilities, health, sexual violence, food and nutrition, Indigenous women's rights, women's groups' relation with public/political institutions, and cultural production. *Marie-Géographie* was above all a journal that focused on the political context of its time, especially in the metropolitan area of Québec City. The content of the journal highlighted its commitment to the autonomy of the women's movement and its support of other political struggles:

> We want to participate in the development and organization of the autonomous women's liberation movement while at the same time working in solidarity with other struggles. We want to de-compartmentalize the struggles and analyses of women's groups and connect feminism with socialism. We want to help create connections among women's groups.[7]

As elsewhere, there were important ideological and political divides among feminist collectives in Québec City. Marie-Géographie as a collective and later as a journal was afflicted with these questions. At the turn of the 1980s, the March 8 event was well embedded within what I call the "ritual feminist calendar." It symbolized one of the highest moments of activism of the year, with a series of activities that spanned an entire weekend and included a street demonstration, intense feminist debates within thematic workshops, as well as dances and festivities of all kinds. It was during these moments that feminist analysis and demands were formulated, along with future strategies of action: those who controlled the organization of events usually attempted to control the discursive content of feminist slogans, press releases, and thematic workshops.

In 1982, Marie-Géographie (1982, 5) published a booklet, *D'un 8 mars à l'autre ...* (From one March 8 to the next ...), which retraces the genealogy of March 8 celebrations in the capital city. The authors investigated why there was so much tension and conflict between feminist activists and union leaders, in particular during the organizing of the March 8 event. In *D'un 8 mars à l'autre,* the divide between autonomous women's groups and women's representatives from these unions was at the forefront. The group interviewed a number of women protagonists from both sides and analyzed their specific feminist approach to organizing. First, *D'un 8 mars à l'autre* focuses on the difference of organizing principles between autonomous women's groups and union organizations. For most women's groups in the city, their approach is conditioned by feminist principles that deeply transform the usual process of decision making within unions: "The way a group operates is not neutral and it influences both the positions taken and the action."[8] The document contrasts feminist organizing with union organizing and describes how women's groups and unions communicate their decisions differently to the outside world. Marie-Géographie does not assert any superiority of feminist principles – such as the adoption of consensual practices, the absence of hierarchical proceedings, or feminist predilection for direct action. The text limits its analysis to the presentation of results of interviews. Marie-Géographie hoped to convey the impact of diverging visions of organizing and modes of functioning on political strategies, especially in the context in which autonomous women's groups were turning to unions for some of their funding and resources. Another issue is the disagreement between unions and women's groups over the root causes of women's oppression. Women's groups wanted to disseminate their analysis to a large audience that included union members, but they were often blocked from doing so. Over the years, the number of workshops exposing feminist rage against unions imposing their views during March 8 increased. On the one hand, union leaders wanted to emphasize women's paid work and refused to move from their traditional position, including during strategic moments like bargaining with employers; on the other hand, autonomous women's groups demanded that their analysis of the body, sexuality, lesbianism, and the feminist critique of heterosexuality be taken into account.

Interviews conducted by Marie-Géographie showed that these aspects mattered even more than the decision-making process. Here again, Marie-Géographie (1982, 8) was not complacent about women's groups and did not try to find excuses for them. However, the research document underlined what ultimately divided autonomous women's groups from their feminist counterparts within unions: the former were accused of focusing too much on the body and sexuality, while the latter were criticized for toeing the line set by union leaders and their demands (15). For this feminist collective, a minimal consensus could be found around important issues and strategies if, and only if, a plurality of analyses were recognized and feminist viewpoints were respected and protected (9, 17). As a socialist feminist group, Marie-Géographie was not interested in creating an avant-garde within the women's movement: the collective had its own reservoir of feminist intellectuals who were able to propose a genuine and sophisticated analysis of women's oppression and women's liberation anchored within the larger political context of Québec society. Its document had a significant impact at the time of its publication, although it was confined to Québec City and the feminist readership in the region. The tone and the analytical content of *D'un 8 mars à l'autre* is a clear indication that, at the start of the 1980s, feminist strategy had evolved into one that not only defended the autonomy of the women's movement vis-à-vis external political interference but also respected the autonomy of each and every feminist collective and feminist trends within the feminist/women's movement.

The Impossible Representation of the Feminist/ Women's Movement

In Montréal, solidarity among women activists and among diverse feminist organizations remained fraught with tension even after the definitive move away from the left. The journal *Pluri-elles,* which later took the name of *Des luttes et des rires,* was once a terrain of confrontation. During the second half of the 1970s, *Pluri-elles/Des luttes et des rires* was what *La vie en rose* would partially be in the 1980s: a space within which multifaceted feminist discourses circulated and were exchanged. Yet the type of feminism these journals portrayed supported some segments of the movement at the expense of others. *Pluri-elles/Des luttes et des rires,* for instance, was devoted to defending the interests of autonomous women's groups, while, in contrast, *La vie en rose* refused to speak on behalf of women's groups almost to the very end.[9]

Pluri-elles began publishing in 1977. Its content described group activities from a wide range of perspectives, including a women's collective in a Montréal prison and Indigenous women living on the Tobique reserve in New Brunswick who were fighting against the Canadian Indian Act (DesOrmeaux 1979, 18–20; Nancy and Danièle 1980, 26). The desire to show a plurality of voices did not prevent the journal from being accused of discrimination and sometimes of racism. For instance, the coalition surrounding the journal occasionally published views and analyses of patriarchal cultures and on violence against women in Third World countries. Anti-racist interruptions loomed during the creation of a coalition of women's groups and activists on what was called *L'affaire Maschino* (The Maschino affair). It refers to the story of a young Algerian woman who had married a French citizen and who was kidnapped after the couple immigrated to Montréal from France. The kidnapping was orchestrated by members of the woman's family, who did not accept her inter-religious and inter-ethnic marriage. In 1978, the journal devoted an entire issue to immigrant women. Editors of *Pluri-elles/Des luttes et des rires* (*Des luttes et des rires* 1978a) admitted having difficulties getting collaborators for the issue. Nevertheless, the journal did not shy away from reporting counter-discourses containing accusations of racism within the Québécois women's movement.

Feminists who had conceived the journal wanted a faithful representation of the women's movement, but this could only be achieved, they thought, with the involvement of autonomous women's groups themselves. The journal had hoped to decide on both content and operation in a general assembly; it expected that meetings would be well attended and full of creative initiatives and strategies that would lead to clear results. That is not what happened. Tensions and dissensions within the women's movement affected the journal's content, and, in the end, its initial mandate had to be modified.[10] There was also the problem of regional representation. The reporting on women's group activities was mainly concentrated in the metropolitan Montréal area despite the desire to report feminist struggles evolving in the rest of Québec and abroad. When *Pluri-elles* changed its name to *Des luttes et des rires,* a new team of activists/reporters toured Québec during the summer of 1978 in the hope that doing so would help the journal better represent the women's movement outside Montréal. In the fall, the journal abandoned the idea of giving the responsibility of its content and production to autonomous women's groups, but it maintained a minimal requirement that its contributors meet certain feminist principles ("Des groupes d'ici ... " 1978). When a small executive took over the responsibility for publishing it, the content of *Des luttes et des* rires changed: feminist analyses deepened, special issues thickened, and regional representation expanded. The desire to defend women's group autonomy mirrored the extent to which the women's movement had grown and, at the same time, had fragmented.

When contrasting Québécois and Italian feminist journals and the ways in which some of them evolved in synergy with feminist/women's groups, we can observe many similarities and differences. For instance, *Differenze* (1976–82) in Rome is comparable to *Pluri-elles/Des luttes et des rires* in relation to the Québécois autonomous women's movement.[11] In its first editorial; *Differenze* presented its view that the Italian women's movement was multifaceted and that the differences existing among women's groups reflected each group's stance on political struggles – either using Marxist concepts or defending the introduction of psychoanalysis into feminism. Aware that there was no unified mode of communicating information, *Differenze* proposed a specific and decentralized approach that would be accessible to every women's group that wanted to participate in the making of the journal ("Secondo noi" 1976).

If one reads Québécois feminists' ways of communicating information, one can detect a genuine desire to represent the Québécois women's movement as faithfully as possible through a series of comprehensive and cohesive feminist principles. By contrast, the Italian feminist approach to organization showed not only a lack of cohesion among small groups but also the absence of consensus within them. For instance, the second editorial of *Differenze* commented on the internal discontent affecting the feminist collective Donne e psicanalisi (Women and psychoanalysis), which was responsible for the publication of that particular issue. The group used the feminist approach to the unconscious. The editorial underlines the group's angst vis-à-vis a possible divide between the personal and the political or the dissociation of the individual from the collective, described as the sudden separation of a daughter from her mother ("Viaggio attraverso un'esperienza" 1976). The article, "Strutture e tipi di lavoro del gruppo" (Structures and type of work in the group) (1980), speaks of the internal dynamics that prevail when the composition of a special issue is entrusted to a women's group like Donne e psicanalisi. The group devoted several pages to explaining how it had initially opened its regular meetings to everyone. This way of operating complicated the continuity of the group's work and analysis. Consequently, the group decided to back down from the original idea.[12] After five years of publishing based essentially on the work of designated women's groups, *Differenze* showed how its boundaries and its specific operating system were particularly permeable to conflicts experienced within small groups. It was a feminist journal, operating in synergy with the movement in Rome, and deeply affected by the difficulties of the specific feminist collective in charge of producing a themed issue. This brings us back to the functioning of women's groups, their interpersonal dynamic, their use of diverse modes of either consciousness-raising/autocoscienza or the practice of the unconscious or, alternatively, the attempt by some groups to introduce a feminist version of psychoanalysis. By looking at the internal dynamic of women-only spaces, we can shed light on the crisis that tore them apart.

The Personal Is Political and the Small-Group Experience in Crisis

Feminist Sites and Meeting Spaces

Feminist debates and theorization of issues take place in all kinds of settings, especially where self-declared feminist principles are proclaimed and defended. Yet principles such as the rejection of any relations of power or hierarchy among members sometimes lead to unexpected results (Fraire 2002, 60–61). Manuela Fraire provides some examples of the internal dynamic within groups. In her book *Lessico politico delle donne* (2002), she evokes the first generation of feminists who felt deeply that the creation of women-only groups was connected with their own needs and desires in opposition to the traditional masculine ways of doing politics (Fraire 2002, 58). Autocoscienza took place within circumscribed communities – the neighbourhood, the market, the school, the workplace – and focused on specific issues, such as abortion, health, and violence. The small group was the place where early feminist theories were conceived and where the American feminist statement, "the personal is political," made sense (57–59). The small group was the place where a woman was paying attention to the presence of other women. This way of operating guaranteed that what emerged out of an intimate and personal exchange did not remain enclosed within the group but was automatically connected with the collective and the political (97).

Weekly meetings and regular gatherings often took place in individuals' houses or apartments, thereby transforming private homes into sites of political activities (Fraire 2002, 58). Many Italian feminist collectives were named after the streets on which their meetings took place. A somewhat similar situation existed in Québec. For instance, the feminist journals *Les têtes de Pioche* and the collective Marie-Géographie never had official addresses, even though their members met regularly, sometimes on a weekly basis, over a period of many years (Saint-Jean 1980, 10). Producing a feminist journal involved a high level of coordination and resources. Some union organizations provided access to meeting spaces for larger gatherings as well as facilities for photocopying and mailings; some women's groups chose to manage on their own with meagre resources; collectives found an intimate atmosphere more fitting for the sharing of personal experiences, with the idea being to transform oneself and the entire society (Fraire 2002, 59). Nonetheless, the intimacy of small quarters rapidly showed its limits. Milan emerged once again with a specific feminist vision of the creation of sites and spaces to be used – not solely as refuges but as places where the fundamental dimension of feminist politics could be developed. Personal/interrelational moments were valued according to the quality of the physical spaces a group occupied: these spaces were dotted with a potential to transform women's lives. It is not surprising, therefore, to find in some documents that sites are depicted as being almost sacred. The document "I luoghi delle femministe e la pratica del movimento" (Feminist sites and movement practices) from the via Cherubini collective highlights the importance for feminist politics of finding a good place to meet. Via Cherubini acknowledged the sometimes difficult interrelations among women, but it emphasized that such difficulties were the reason feminists needed to maximize the political importance of physical feminist spaces: "These are sites and activities that all have a political value and a practicality that goes beyond their functional definitions, they must be understood and strengthened to the maximum. These sites are the core of our practices between women."[13]

One senses that the document also hints at the practice of *affidamento*, which is understandable since the authors of the document, Gruppo 4, were active members of the Via Cherubini collective. "I luoghi delle femministe e la pratica del movimento" argued that its site is:

> a place that is characterless and alive only if there is someone to direct it. Cherubini is *not meant as a meeting place, but as a group* that speaks and

> listens. The place is defined by those who speak: they are permanent historical figures of the movement. This is reproduced in any group in the movement perhaps because inside a social group like women, where speech has never been expressed, speaking becomes important.[14]

The Libreria delle donne (2005b, 102) of Milan offers an idea of what the creation of women-only spaces meant for the women's movement: "The proposed bookstore wants to be a site within which – the new – is gathered and communicated in order to become a rich collective."[15] In *Non credere di avere dei diritti,* the Libreria (2005b, 104) writes: "The bookstore is a political space because women come together publicly and freely. To be among women ... is ... the point of departure of our politics."[16] The act of opening a bookstore and publishing women's literary works were part of the *politica del fare* (politics of doing). One founder of the bookstore, Lia Cigarini, explains during an interview with Chiara Martucci (2008) that the most important thing is to find a way out of being between pure speech and action. The Libreria delle donne was the instrument with which to engage in the management of relationships among several women and to give the theory of sexual difference a living dimension (Cigarini in Martucci 2008). Martucci also interviewed Luisa Muraro, who said that the bookstore allowed the theory of sexual difference to become a truly feminist practice in her life as well as in the life of the women's movement as a whole (Muraro interviewed by Martucci 2008).

In Rome, the feminist approach to physical sites appeared much more grounded in organizing activities. In 1976, several collectives squatted in an unoccupied historical building on a street named Governo Vecchio in order to force the Commune of Rome to provide free space to women's groups. The building had enough room for the regular activities of several groups. The ways in which feminists took over this crumbling and disused *palazzo* (apartment building) was described to unions and parties as a political act and a major victory for feminism in the Italian capital (Ciuffreda and Raspini 1999, 29–31). The building hosted a diversity of groups: feminist consultori, courses under the 150 hours program, feminist journals, and women's radio as well as several other small groups representing a multiplicity of areas of specialization and feminist orientation. At the height of the occupation, some eighty collectives had set up their activities at Governo Vecchio (Ingargiola and Cucchi 1987, 63). As usual, frequent and endless discussions challenged the possibility of having a harmonious women-only politics. But the squatting, which lasted several years, forced the city of Rome, after much negotiation, to convert an old convent for use by all the collectives. Many of these collectives are still located at the *Casa internazionale delle donne* (International women's house), which shelters a feminist archives and documentation centre, a restaurant, and a women-only hotel. The *Casa* has all the facilities to hold conferences, including international conferences using simultaneous interpretation in several languages. For a number of years, the place hosted the Centro culturale "Virginia Woolf," which organized courses and seminars as well as national and international encounters promoting dialogue and exchange among feminist researchers. Founded in 1976, the Centro culturale "Virginia Woolf" promoted the creation of an autonomous feminist university, but the idea was rapidly abandoned. In 1988, the group split over its political orientation: Group A continued to do research on the issue of the "women's subject"; Group B oriented its activities towards sexual difference. Group B moved out of the Casa internazionale delle donne while Group A ceased its activities in 1992 (Masi 1984, 58; Virdis 1979, 28).[17]

Similar cultural spaces in the southern part of Italy lasted a few years with some success, although they were more short-lived than those in the North. The feminist bookstore Incontro in Naples was celebrated as an iconic site for the movement, and its founders tried to explain why feminism was late in creating women's groups and collectives that had the same vitality as those in Milan and in Rome (L. Capobianco and Minneci 1981, 16). In Naples, feminist/women's groups maintained their own specificity while coming together during high moments such as March 8 celebrations or to support free abortion (Crispino 1981b).

The problem of gaining access to material resources increased as women's groups began to focus on specific projects requiring more energy and more complicated logistics than simply organizing street demonstrations. Publishing women's books on a regular basis is an example of feminists deciding to take matters into their own hands when most publishers and booksellers refused to print women's/feminist works. Publishing initiatives included the already mentioned Les éditions du remue-ménage in Montréal. In Milan, the Libreria delle donne, despite its estrangement from the Italian feminist/women's movement, was part of an important constellation of Italian groups that specialized in feminist cultural production.

It is within these contexts that the frontiers of feminism enter into contact with political/public institutions. In Italy in 1983, Maria-Luisa Boccia (1983) outlines six categories of groups that demonstrate the multiplicity that characterized the women's movement at the turn of the 1980s. First, there are groups open to the public and offering services, including bookstores, feminist libraries, documentation centres, and women's centres. Second, there are groups with a cooperative status that operate as cultural and research organizations. This category provides continuity and the diffusion of women's cultural work to the market in order to finance further projects. Third, there are cultural committees directed by women and integrated within official cultural institutions and associations. Fourth, there are groups of services producing research in specific areas, such as courses in the 150 hours programs. Fifth, there are groups that specialize in the organization of specific events, such as cultural exhibitions, public demonstrations, and other publicly funded events. Finally, there are small politically oriented collectives that meet on a regular basis to reflect on particular analytical/theoretical documents or to practise feminist writing without necessarily making their production public.

The Québécois women's movement in the 1980s experienced an identical burgeoning of feminist documentation centres, research groups, bookstores, theatre groups, publishing houses, and cooperatives dedicated to cultural production and feminist journals (Michaud 2007). Yet having a site/space – or lack of one – reveals another dimension in the internal dynamic of a group: a small women's group cannot function on the basis of self-exploration without running the risk of exhausting its potential for renewal. Groups that did not adapt to the rapid contextual change disappeared after a few years, while others succeeded in renewing themselves with different objectives. Let's have a look at the small women's groups as they transition towards creating larger networks, which marks a specific moment in the history of feminism and one that is not always well documented in feminist archives.

The Situation of Small Groups in Feminist Networks

Exploring women's inner experiences in women-only groups of five to ten was the dynamic upon which the entire system of feminist organizing originally rested. Feminist journals were at the forefront of narrating this experience, although there are few oral narratives or written texts that provide a coherent picture of the consciousness-raising/autocoscienza experience. For Rossi-Doria (2005, 6–10), the number of documents and collected materials – from minutes of meetings to articles published in feminist journals, from posters and letters to more personal reflections – are too scarce and fragmented to give us the meaning and the substance of this particular experience or the positive/negative results of the practice itself. The impossibility of sketching a picture of consciousness-raising/autocoscienza – as a practice rather than as a discourse – contrasts with attempts to characterize the movement through its ideological feminist currents. The discursive paradigm surrounding the dynamic of autocoscienza insisted on linking the individual to a collective that would guarantee the political expression of women's experience. However, small groups were too diverse to draw up a coherent and comprehensive prototype (Fraire 2002, 96–97; Melandri 2000, 121; Staderini 1979b, 35). What the few Italian narratives from small groups express, for the most part, are critiques addressed to the feminist movement. The malaise appeared to be so important that it raised doubts about the capacity of autocoscienza to connect the personal with the political or to make sense of the individual experience through the power of the collective. Some groups concluded that autocoscienza had not reached the point at which scientific rigour could be demonstrated (Collettivo femminista Comunista di Via Pomponazzi 1975).

For other feminist observers however, the problem was the practice itself – its scrutiny of women's personal lives and its imposition of a political discussion on intimate matters. The interactive dynamic among group members was one of the main difficulties: some women had more abilities to lead, to talk, and to impose a political orientation, giving themselves the authority to criticize the experiences of other women and provoking aggressive behaviour in the rest of the group. The problem of maintaining the integrity of feminist structures emerged, with debates surrounding the admission of new members and uncertainty about the directions these persons could impose on other members of the collective. Some groups tended to recreate a political, social, and cultural environment characterized by homogeneity in order to avoid long and agonizing conflicts. At the end, however, a negative and unproductive dynamic contaminated the practice of autocoscienza and ricocheted to affect the entire movement (Calabrò and Grasso 2004, 40–41; Fachinelli 1968; Libreria delle donne 2005b, 51–53; Melandri 1977, 15; Melandri 2000, 123).

The 1970s saw the rise and decline of small feminist groups in Italy. Their positive dynamic kept their defenders writing articles – alongside their gravediggers – in journals such as *Effe* or *Sottosopra*. In *Effe*, for instance, one author argued for a political or psychoanalytical dimension to autocoscienza (Sabatini 1974, 1–2), while another, in *Sottosopra*, celebrated the political and revolutionary potential of exploring women's experiences away from the usual Marxist terms of reference (Bicchiere and Roditi 1974). Yet, in 1976, *Sottosopra* published a series of articles critical of autocoscienza.

These articles aimed to show the power dynamic used to silence some members of women-only groups following two national gatherings in Pinarella, in 1974 and in 1975, respectively.[18] There were other important meetings in Italy, including one that took place in 1976 in Paestum, focused on the body and sexuality. These national feminist encounters shed light on the difficult interaction between the individual and the collective, between the personal and the political. The Libreria delle donne of Milan argued that Pinarella was the definitive defeat of autocoscienza; a year later, the same collective announced that Paestum was the defeat of the movement itself (Libreria delle donne 2005b, 51, 117–18).

My research on the women's health centres network as well as my own involvement as part of a feminist collective in Québec City reveal that *partage du vécu* (sharing personal experience), as it was called in the 1970s and 1980s, was unevenly practiced. The shift towards public/political institutions, resulting from the focus on single issues, characterized most of the debates at the turn of the 1980s: several women's services groups and their networks mapped the entire Québec territory. However, it is important to note that their numbers and their capacity to organize around a single issue – health, violence, popular education – did not exhaust the Québécois feminist/women's movement. The desire for service groups to come together to share information on their practices and their strategies was also an attempt to resist the fragmentation of the women's movement and to increase its visibility on the public/political scene. Originally, these women's services groups and their networks proclaimed their respect for feminist principles such as the rejection of hierarchy and all forms of professionalism in their approach to servicing women's needs. This last principle proved to be unsustainable in view of the desire to demonstrate that feminist practitioners were providing services as good as or better than those they could get in hospitals and medical clinics (Michaud 1995). Over the years, women's services groups and their respective networks experienced numerous transformations: the most important was a greater connection with public institutions, which was perceived as necessary in order to obtain official recognition and regular funding (Michaud 1992, 1995, 1996, 1997a, 1997b).[19]

Women's services group networks in Québec remained operative over a number of years because of the respect they had for the autonomy of each of their members. As already noted, the key characteristics of feminist solidarity coalitions were their flexibility and their capacity to function without coercion, even in light of disagreements and occasional rifts. One of these rifts concerned the relationship that women's services groups should establish with state institutions, an irritant that divided all four feminist networks during most of the 1980s.[20] As years passed and resistance subsided, the strategy of absence at regular meetings of government officials was judged counter-productive. At the turn of the 1990s, a consensus was finally reached among women's services groups to obtain the status of legitimate partners with the Ministère de la santé et des services sociaux for the implementation of services to women in need (J. Lamoureux 1994; Michaud 1992, 1995, 1996).

Another indication that Québécois networks of women's services groups were an effective instrument in the development of women's solidarity – sometimes in conjunction with other segments of the women's movement – is their contribution to the transformation of the already active national feminist organization the Fédération des femmes du Québec (FFQ).[21] The FFQ was created in Montréal in 1966 and supported an agenda that can be described as emancipatory if we adopt the Italian feminist definition. Many of the FFQ demands echoed those of the Royal Commission on the Status of Women created by the federal government in 1967. In the 1970s, the FFQ evolved in parallel with early feminist collectives and the autonomous women's movement, with the goal of bringing together all women nationally regardless of their race, class, status, and religion.[22] By the mid-1990s, the FFQ had become one of the most important voices in the Québécois feminist/women's movement and was able to adapt to complex and multifaceted feminism(s) in Québec. In 1995, the FFQ organized the most impressive feminist march in Québec history: Du pain et des roses (Bread and roses). During the two weeks the march lasted between Montréal and Québec City, the FFQ imposed the discussion of a comprehensive political platform through the mainstream media. The success of Du pain et des roses motivated the FFQ to propose an identical feminist march at the international level in 2000, this time around the issues of poverty and violence against women. Ever since, the Marche mondiale des femmes (World march of women) maintains a permanent structure, with its international centre located in Latin America (Beaulieu 2010; Conway 2010)

In Italy, the Unione donne Italiane was, for a long period after the Second World War, the only women's organization on the left and centre left that had the capacity to develop a national network everywhere in the country. This was possible because of the close relationship the UDI maintained with the Communist Party, even though the PCI was only interested in women's issues from a demographic and electoral point of view (Beckwith 1985, 19). Despite the fact that the UDI membership, leadership, and administrative jobs were open to women from other political parties – most notably the Socialist Party – in reality, the organization operated as a transmission belt for the PCI (23), which controlled its financing and its political orientation.[23] Such dependency on a political party known to hold conservative views on women's issues – based on the so-called traditionalism of the working class – signalled the UDI's decline from the moment it was challenged by feminism in the 1960s and 1970s (31–33). Nevertheless, the UDI was the only national women's organization in Italy, and no other feminist group ever filled the gap after its dissolution.

Manuela Fraire gives two examples of groups that could have claimed the status of national network: the Movimento di liberazione delle donne – affiliated with the political party Partito Radicale – and Lotta Femminista. She argues, however, that these organizations failed because of their rigid and traditional modes of controlling how feminist discourses and practices were disseminated throughout the country. According to Fraire (2002, 62–63), both the networks were inflexible and refused to recognize the autonomy of member groups. On this particular point, the Québécois model of flexibility contrasts with the Italian experience. Fraire also suggests that the *maternal* figure, which haunted the movement, contaminated the dynamics in meetings, revealing profound psychological injuries that women have endured for centuries and evincing sentiments of envy and animosity in women's groups (63).

Feminism Transformed

Despite occasional cross-border encounters, such as with Psychanalyse et politique, both feminisms remained resolutely national in their foundations and cultural specificities (Ergas 1987). In less than a decade, the Italian and Québécois feminisms/women's movements were deeply transformed, but their original discourses and practices continued to hold despite the increasing fragmentation into smaller groups. These two movements survived the decline of the left and moved into something different with another generation of activists more or less willing to go along with their predecessors. It was during these moments of transformation that some protagonists decided to pause to look back and to reflect on what had happened to them; to take the time to collect and to record events and personal memories; to conceive ways to beat the odds, which suggested that political movements were incapable of transferring memory from one generation to the next. Chapter 9 looks at why Québécois and Italian feminists decided very early that it was time to document their history and to create research circles, documentation centres, and women's history journals outside academic settings. Along the way, they provoked a series of debates on memories and on the value of writing feminist history. Before examining this documentation process, however, Chapter 8 looks at how feminism revealed its vitality and its capacity to transgress and to dissent in cultural productions.

8 Capturing Feminist Transgressions through Cultural Productions

Culture as a Terrain of Feminist Struggles

Journals, films, radio programming, publishing houses, visual arts, and exhibitions are the traces left behind in history. Culture and politics reinforce each other even when considering all the tensions and contradictions emerging from documents and texts produced by activists and their movements. Balestrini and Moroni's book, *L'orda d'oro,* published for the first time in 1988, includes a significant amount of information on feminism, its trends, and its theoretical achievements. They dedicate an entire chapter, "La comunicazione, la cultura, gli intellettuali" (Communication, culture, and intellectuals), to cultural and countercultural productions, while other parts of the book provide significant examples of the imbrication/overlapping of culture and politics. Balestrini and Moroni give central space to the ways in which groups and movements put arts at the core of a socialist revolution. Without these references to two decades of cultural effervescence and artistic activities, Balestrini and Moroni's book would have been a mere chronology of events and would have diminished its historical significance. As they argue, art and culture are not mere means of expression but, rather, are terrains of struggle in view of the state repression of political movements, which was particularly brutal in Italy during the 1970s: almost all sites, all structures, and all groups working on cultural productions – journals, bookstores, community radios, publishing houses, alternative cinema – were the target of state surveillance, even repression, up to the point at which they either had to cease all activities or were forced into cultural conformity and homogeneity. Balestrini and Moroni claim:

> Therefore, it is comprehensible that such a political movement grew and recognized itself through instruments of cultural communication rather than through instruments of political communication. Culture is not an instrument of struggle anymore (as it was for the previous generation of revolutionaries) but was itself the terrain of struggle.[1]

When looking at the decades under study, two interrelated phases appear clearly in Italy and in Québec: one is characterized by the tension as well as the attraction between politics and the numerous countercultural manifestations created by movements themselves and/or unfolded in parallel with them; the other is the political context characterized by the increasing marginalization of cultural production from politics, a phenomenon from which feminism was not exempt (Balestrini and Moroni 2008, 604; Michaud 2007). To understand the second phase, or how the marginalization of arts and culture took place somewhere towards the end of the 1970s, we have to look at the process of their displacement within feminism, perhaps unconsciously initiated by feminists themselves, by those who longed to bring their movement to the level of expertise required for institutional recognition, by those who dreamed of bringing feminist arts to the level of megaproductions that mainstream cultural institutions would be willing to praise and to subsidize. This shift in feminist thinking about the arts suggests that many aspects of the "collective 1970s" needed to be relegated to the attic of things past because they have become too amateurish to be taken seriously (F. Pelletier 1980).[2] Thus, the marginalization of culture was accompanied by another sort of dissociation: the de-linkage of the individual from the small group structures that had contributed to shaping the individual's identity as a political subject. The turn of the 1980s marked the end of movement politics for feminism, as we can see in the language used. No longer does one speak of large gatherings of feminists/women but only of some moments when women meet other women (Paoli 2010, 32). Finally, the marginalization/dissociation of culture from politics happened with the repositioning of women's struggles away from other political struggles and the re-centring of its short-term objectives to preserve feminist gains while consolidating communication with state institutions (Michaud 2007; Rutter 1990, 567).

The eclipse of culture from politics should make us forget that culture is a formidable critique of society. The story of the *Automatistes* and their manifesto *Le refus global,* and the attached collection of artistic texts, set the tone for the 1950s and 1960s in Québec. Even if many of its signatories were not known for their political activism, the content of their writings and the artistic productions of some of their members carried a political meaning that inspired agents of social transformation for years. In the 1960s, Gaston Miron's (1998) book of poetry *L'homme rapaillé* and Paul Chamberland's poem "L'Afficheur hurle" (1964),[3] although insensitive to "Others" living among them – women, racialized people, Indigenous people, and anyone whose sexuality differed from theirs – are indicative of the type of poetic productions that inspired struggles for social justice and the ideal of national liberation for Québec and even abroad. The involvement of artists animated many socialist, Third World, and nationalist events with politically engaged poetry, music, and plays focused on the political, economic, and social conditions of Québec society.[4]

Indeed, the countercultural movement was not entirely political, but again, social and political events often found their best expression in the arts. Political movements knew how to make good use of cultural productions to encourage social change. Since significant segments of the counterculture evolved and accompanied important political events, it makes sense to consider it as part of any ideological discourse that shaped the phases of Marxism in Québec. There is no single definition of Québécois counterculture, nor are there definitive beginning-to-end dates to mark the era. Often but not always in synergy with leftist trends, the counterculture was an amalgam of movements, a mix of events and of cultural representations, intermingling a return to spirituality and science and environmental experiences that saw individuals adopting counter-models and making alternative choices (Labelle-Hogue 2013; Larose 2013; Jezo-Vannier 2013,1). A significant number of countercultural productions appeared within leftist and alternative journals, and, again, the best place to trace the artistic genealogy of political movements resides in the journals of that period: from the nationalist third-world vision of *Parti pris* to the individualist *Mainmise,*[5] with the loose socialism of *Le Temps fou* located somewhere in between.

Québec

In Québec, the early 1970s saw the creation of several feminist journals, theatre productions, publishing houses, and visual arts groups. Yet, at the turn of the 1980s, the idea of feminist arts as a collective effort somehow vanished. *La vie en rose* began publishing articles on the uneasy cohabitation of arts and politics; some feminist journalists went so far as to downgrade collective productions, judging them as less valuable than an individual mega-creation, even expressing sadness that no famous women were being produced (F. Pelletier 1980). It is worth remembering that, before this process of marginalization, feminist collectives emerged in full force out of solidarity coalitions that were undeniably a mix of cultural, social, and political feminist groups. The Théâtre des cuisines (1973–81), for instance, was a group of women who had no training in theatre and no plan beyond putting into plays what its members considered to be the most pressing issues of the moment.[6] Unexpectedly, this small theatre company continued for several years (Beauchamp and Renaud 1980, 99) and, along with the Théâtre expérimental des femmes (Women's experimental theatre group) (1979), produced several plays on political struggles promoting women's liberation. Productions such as *Môman* (1975), *As-tu vu, les maisons s'emportent?* (Did you see, the houses are losing their temper?) (1980), and Jovette Marchessault's *La saga des poules mouillées* (Saga of the wet hens) (1981) not only inspired many other plays but also illuminated a world of possibilities for an entire generation of activists (Camerlain 1985).

Montréal was not the only city to enjoy important feminist artistic creativity. In Québec City, Les folles alliées produced several humorous and acclaimed plays throughout the province,[7] including *Mademoiselle auto-body* (Miss auto-body) and "Enfin duchesse" (Duchess at last).[8] Feminist theatre groups – like other leftist cultural groups – were often asked by unions and other community organizations to perform during special events, and their presence was not just instrumental. They portrayed women and men and economic and social conditions in ways that other media were not always able or willing to do. They were part of a popular education network used to enhance political consciousness, and their methods were effective and powerful. Feminist cultural groups in particular participated in consciousness-raising practices, contributed to the diffusion of women's anger and feminist rage around major struggles, and enhanced feminist theorization during the same period (Michaud 2007:38).

Italy

Similar to the Québécois counterculture, the Italian political scene witnessed multiple uses of popular arts as well as the creation of an abundance of cultural organizations, including publishing houses, alternative cinema, underground radio programming, and journals. Members of the extra-parliamentary left were great consumers of culture in all its forms, starting with intensive readings of classic revolutionary texts that included revolutionary and popular songs (Annunziata 2007, 134–35; Balestrini and Moroni 2008). Aldo Grandi (2003, 137–38) shows how members of Potere Operaio hated sports but enjoyed going to the cinema together and watching all kinds of movies. Several periodicals, such as *Quaderni Piacentini,* regularly published film critiques linking aesthetics with a critique of the social and the political.

Italian feminist creative spaces, such as journals, radio, theatre groups, publishing houses, free feminist universities, and cooperatives of cultural productions, emerged simultaneously and overlapped one another, provoking debates and moments of confrontation. As always, major cities like Milan and Rome ignored or marginalized what was happening in smaller cities and in the South, and the variety and multiplicity of forms of cultural expression privileged written texts over oral expression. There are exceptions, however. The history of the Comitato per il salario al lavoro domestico (Committee for wages for housework) of Padua is remembered for its theorization of domestic work, manifestos, journals, and other types of publications. The group also created a musical ensemble that performed during public demonstrations.[9]

Every feminist journal reserved a certain number of pages – although these spaces were of unequal length and quality – for reviews of books, films, plays, and TV programming so long as it had feminist content or had some interest for women. In the area of theatre production the work of the well-known feminist writer Dacia Maraini (2003), a regular contributor to *Effe,* is worth mentioning. In the 1970s, Maraini created with other women a theatre group, Teatro la Maddalena (Magdalen theatre), in a working-class neighbourhood in Rome. The group used alternative and anti-hierarchical approaches to theatrical production in order to give women a voice. Teatro la Maddelena produced plays from the early 1970s until the end of the 1980s (Maraini 2003, 77; Rutter 1990, 569). It did not proceed without pain and frustration. During an interview with Branko Gorjup, Dacia Maraini echoed Francine Pelletier's (1980) criticisms of feminist collective works. She says about the Teatro la Maddalena:

> The biggest problem came from the contradiction between democratic politics and professionalism. Professionalism called for competition, selection and artistic rigor. Democratic politics on the other hand, insisted that all be equal, that all have the same opportunities. But art is not democratic. Some have talent and some don't, some have [a] gift for expressing themselves and others don't. This contrast created the most

> difficult conflicts within the group. On one hand, we gave space also to those without talent, without skills, out of pure democratic spirit. On the other hand, we realized that by doing so we were dangerously lowering the level of quality of our theatre. So we decided to be more rigorous but rigor gave birth to frustration and rancor. All in all a difficult cycle to break. Finally professionalism won out. It was a theatrical necessity. But it cost us so much in arguments till three in the morning, fights, insults, hurt feelings, vindictiveness and bad humor![10]

Despite second thoughts about the quality of collective works, Maraini (2003, 78) remains convinced that theatre is a powerful instrument for raising consciousness. Another type of art production may be found in the huge collection of posters that the UDI published over its sixty-year history. This collection contains more than thirteen hundred coloured images of high-quality drawings portraying different themes: from the formation of an anti-fascist culture to equality of women at work and in the family; from the demand for access to social services for mothers and families to abortion and the campaign for divorce; from advertisements for UDI congresses to publicity for the journal itself (Ombra 2005, 11). These posters are a testimony to an important national movement caught between the PCI and the autonomous/separatist feminist collectives during the 1970s. The role each poster played for UDI members as well as for all the women the journal wanted to reach highlights the interconnection between reporting and visual messages; between writing and reading the UDI journal *Noi donne* and the challenge of illiteracy; between visual arts and the problem of gaining access to culture for those to whom it has been denied (Tani 2005).

In Naples, the collective Nemesiache was equally remarkable for its longevity, the range of cultural forms and expressions the group used over the years, as well as its desire to reach inaccessible categories of subaltern women, in particular those imprisoned in psychiatric asylums. The second part of this chapter focuses on feminist theatre productions, offering two examples that connect politics and culture: the Nemesiache/Tre Ghinee in Naples and Jovette Marchesseault's feminist works in Montréal. Let's first revisit the locations of and roles played by journals within the movement: how these journals, in their own ways, attempted to orient feminist issues, debates, and group practices; how they criticized each other over elements of analysis and feminist orientations; and how they expressed their intention to represent feminism and/or women's needs and desires as a whole.

Who Is Our Audience? Conflicting Views on Feminist Journalism

Laboratories for New Ideas and Revolutionary Theories

Periodicals served as laboratories for elaborating new ideas, concepts, and theories that were constantly exchanged, discussed, critiqued, transformed, and/or rejected (Balestrini and Moroni 2008, 587; Fortin 1993, 8; Godard 2002; Michaud 2010, 31; Rutter 1990). Journals and periodicals had a specific identity of their own, produced and reproduced through theorizing about politics, struggles, and daily life. Theoretical writings served as political instruments designed not only to construct this identity for the collective that owned the journal but also to confront and to oppose the identity of other political formations and their leaders (Marcolini 2012, 217). Feminist journals are not neutral and objective, but they are the type of instruments that help to seize the political and the feminist moment of the past: the synergy among feminist titles, acting in conjunction with other feminist titles and with titles from other political movements, gives us valuable information about the specific social context in which small groups and larger collectives were evolving.

In this section, I underline the fundamental importance of feminist journals and what they represented for the movement. Indeed, I look at journals and periodicals not only as primary sources of information but also as a terrain of feminist struggles where new analyses are endorsed or contradicted, where ideas and debates are communicated and exchanged. Journals were vital for their movement and are now essential for the feminist researcher because they give us a picture of the evolution of generations of activists and provide us with the genealogy of feminism at a particular moment of its history. During the period under study, feminist journals were at the core of the feminist/women's movement: the closure of a feminist collective that had given life to a particular journal often signalled the brutal end of the title (Paoli 2011, 51). I do not intend to present all feminist journals created between the end of 1960s and the end of the 1980s. In Canada alone, Barbara Godard (2002, 212) estimates that, "since the late 1960s[,] there have been more than 300 feminist publications." Some titles are dearly remembered years after their disappearance, such as *Québécoises deboutte!*, *La vie en rose*, *Sottosopra*, and *Differenze*. Most of these journals published for a period of more than ten years,[11] while others succeeded in publishing only one or two issues – just enough time to fix a particular event, like, for instance, the occupation of the University of Rome–La Sapienza (Paoli 2011, 40).

Critical analyses of journals and periodicals belonging to political movements and, in particular, to the feminist movement are not abundant. Among these works in Québec there is Andrée Fortin's book (1993) *Passage de la modernité: les intellectuels québécois et leurs revues*. This work is a historical overview of journals and periodicals that begins in 1778 and ends with the twentieth century. Fortin (1993, 12) divides the period into three simple descriptive categories: pre-modernity, modernity, and postmodernity. The presentation is comprehensive and contains a chronological index presenting all periodicals in three large categories: journals of arts, journals of ideas, and scholarly journals. Fortin's analysis focuses on intellectuals and their influence on the social, but she restricts her analysis to the editorial of the first issue (10–11), as if this one text alone could capture the soul of the journal. What is relegated to the shadows is the evolution of a particular title over the years in conjunction with the evolution of the group or the movement to which it was attached as well as the ways in which it was confronted by other ideas and was transformed by societal debates and conflicts. Moreover, the way Fortin depicts the action of intellectual(s) doing her/his/their periodicals gives no indication of the synergy existing among political/intellectual actors. Such a perspective leaves aside the collective dimension of each periodical.[12]

Centred on the Canadian women's movement, Barbara Godard's (2002) "Feminist Periodicals and the Production of Cultural Value" offers a sophisticated analysis of Québécois and Canadian feminist periodicals in the cultural field. Using a feminist political economy approach, informed by Pierre Bourdieu's sociology of cultural production, Godard highlights feminists' insistence on creating periodicals despite their slight or complete lack of market value:

> Feminist periodicals exist outside the dominant mode of capitalist publishing, on the margin and in opposition, both through their borderline position with respect to the marketplace and their commitment to contestatory ideology. These periodicals are developed to further feminist ideologies: they create new circuits for disseminating among women knowledges and practices that seek to transform the feminine condition under which women have been subject to systemic oppression.[13]

Godard (2002, 211) demonstrates how feminists bring a sense of disinterestedness into cultural production that is not cast in economic terms, only to be trapped within the paradox of being dependent on state funding while pursuing their relentless criticism of the state and its public policies (209–10). Regarding feminist strategies of self-financing, Godard noted that: "For the fraught situation, negotiated repeatedly, is that support is needed from the very economy that a feminist project of social transformation contests" (212).

Godard does not directly address the problem of art and culture being increasingly marginalized within the feminist movement, but she points to external mechanisms – one of which is the institutionalization of funding for targeted and narrowly defined topics, forcing feminists to apply for grant after grant – that lead feminist periodicals to discard topics not directly related to their funding requests. For instance, feminists engaged in the conception of a specific issue of a journal were subjected to pressure by state funding agencies to de-link the publication of literary genres from social and political documents (Godard 2002, 221). This process slowly began somewhere near the end of the 1970s, but the divorce between genres was completed in the 1990s. By then, feminist periodicals in Canada were either artistically oriented and marketable or destined for academic or specialized audiences: they were no longer the property of the movement or the group that had contributed to their creation.

Back in Italy, Balestrini and Moroni contextualize decades of national and international tensions as well as the struggle of intellectuals to invest all spheres of knowledge with revolutionary ideas and anti-authoritarian culture, even of counterculture. They argue that journals have a multiplying effect much superior to that of books. While books have the potential to extend thinking over a much longer period of time and are still the best instrument for transmitting knowledge, journals have an immediate impact on cultural ways of living (Balestrini and Moroni 2008, 587–88). They reserve few descriptive pages (501–3) for feminist journals and pay attention only to those they consider to be the most important: *Sottosopra, Differenze, DWF, Quotidiano Donna, Le Operaie della casa, E siamo tante,* and *Lillith.* Surprisingly, *Effe,* perhaps one of the most important feminist titles in the Italian capital and nationally, is not on the list.

Among recent works dedicated specifically to feminist journals of the 1970s, the most noticeable is *Pratiche di scrittura femminista* by Federica Paoli (2011). Paoli did her doctoral dissertation on feminist journals in Rome. Her book focuses specifically on one title, *Differenze,* which appeared regularly between 1976 and 1982. Paoli takes great care to place *Differenze* in the context of its time, describing the controversies surrounding its opposition to *Effe* and its goals. The journal's objective was to communicate internally to create a better exchange of information among feminists and to turn this information outward to reach a much larger audience of women interested in feminist politics and practices. Paoli's (2011, 10) book is an attempt to show how feminist writings and political practices are interconnected. She also indicates why feminist journals were so important for the movement, underlining one of their most significant characteristics as constituting "un luogo di *relazioni* e di *pluralità,* in cui le soggettività di quante vi lavorano si incontrano e si confrontano" (a site of *relations* and of *plurality* where the subjectivities of all of those who work are meeting and are confronting each other). Finally, Paoli brings to the discussion a statement from Ida Dominijiani (Dominijiani quoted in Paoli 2011, 20): "Una rivista non parla infatti solo dei suoi contenuti e attraverso i suoi contenuti ... parla attraverso la chiave di scrittura che sceglie di adottare; e parla soppratutto, io credo, del gruppo e attraverso il gruppo che le dà vita." (In fact, a journal does not only speak about its content and through its content ... a journal speaks through the kind of writing it has chosen to adopt; and it speaks above all, I believe, of the group and through the group which has given birth to it).

Dominijiani highlights the context within which a political movement like feminism represents its own identity by using diverse communicative instruments such as feminist journals. The act of representing covers more than one dimension. The Marxist understanding of representation referred to by scholars such as Godard (2008, 131–32) and Spivak (1988a, 275) has two meanings, which unfold simultaneously: one meaning points to the action of "speaking for" someone or a group of people and the second meaning is the practice of describing as faithfully as possible a person or the category of people one is representing. However, the individual or the collective who is doing the act of representing is also actively engaged in the representation of itself in order to make its action legitimate.[14] This means that a third dimension is embedded within the double dynamic of representation that gives power and visibility to a specific group – one that opens channels of communication for social categories of women that the group intends to represent. The tension over the type of journalism produced by feminist collectives is enmeshed in the interstices of the multiple meanings of representation: On whose behalf are we speaking? In what ways are we speaking about those we intend to represent? Who other than us can represent women's needs?

Journals created their identity and their fame through theoretical experimentation, many times in opposition to other journals and periodicals.

Indeed, ideas and theories were not meant to be marketable, but the number of times an idea was taken up by others; the ways in which a political theory was debated within pages of another publication; the extent to which sexual difference, the wages for housework, the refusal to work movement, travelled largely outside their countries of origin – all of this helped to increase the value of the publications in which these analyses and ideas originally appeared.

"Più donne che uomini" (More women than men) (1983), the groundbreaking document on the theory of sexual difference, is one of the best examples of such phenomena. Here I use Kathi Weeks's terms (2011 128–34), which she utilizes when she speaks of the feminist demand for wages for housework, qualifying the demand as a "perspective" and a "provocation" that generated a flow of reactions, pro and con. I found the concepts of perspective and provocation perfectly suited to "Più donne che uomini." Those who opposed the document accused its authors of authoritatively reordering the direction of a particular feminist perspective that was judged provocative, polemical, and divisive. Yet the point of reference of these criticisms was not solely the document itself but also *Sottosopra,* the journal in which it was published, which, at its debut, was supposed to be at the disposition of all feminist collectives throughout Italy and open to the diversity of the movement's experiences. However, at the turn of the 1980s, the journal changed its orientation to become the voice of a unique tendency: sexual difference. Such a shift in theoretical trends signified a definitive and dramatic move away from a type of feminism imbricated within the political and the social (Zumaglino 1996, 255). From that moment, *Sottosopra* was remembered outside Italy, and in the United States in particular, as an iconic Italian feminist journal, the theoretical voice of sexual difference and of the Libreria delle donne of Milan.

Ways of Conceiving Feminist Journalism

Two categories of journals followed a vision of feminist counter-information – that is, the targeting of mainstream media (daily newspapers, periodicals, TV and radio programming), in which feminist activists and women's movement activities were represented negatively (Bergeron 2011a, 2011b). In the Italian extra-parliamentary left, counter-information initially denounced fascist acts of terror before shifting to another form of communication that spoke positively of armed struggle (Balestrini and Moroni 2008, 592–95). First, there were journals strictly devoted to exchanging information on ideas, practices, and activities among small groups or larger collectives and that remained within the limits of the movement. *Sottosopra, Les têtes de Pioche, Differenze, Des luttes et des rires* were exemplary with regard to this tendency of limiting communication to circles of well-informed activists. The second category was composed of journals that addressed non-specific audiences of readers, mostly women, beyond the frontiers of feminism but with clear feminist content: *Québécoises deboutte!* and *La vie en rose,* both in their own radical and respective ways (Bergeron 2011a; Des Rivières, 1995), along with *Effe, Noi donne,* and a constellation of smaller titles mirroring some practices of double activism but that did not want to be the voice of feminist collectives only.

In the first category, we see that the controversy surrounding *Effe* was based on the belief that it practised a sort of journalism estranged from the movement and therefore not truly informed by feminist principles. The most well remembered and popular Québécois feminist journal, *La vie en rose,* attracted similar frustration for its persistent refusal to speak on behalf of women's groups, from which the journal kept its distance until its last year in 1987, when *LVR* finally appealed to their support (Bergeron, 2011b; D'Amours 1988; Des Rivières 1995; Dupont et al. 1979–80; Michaud 2012).[15]

Apart from the pressure to demonstrate professional journalism generated by the lure of institutional funding (as Barbara Godard argued), there is another reason, at least in Québec, feminist journals and feminist cultural productions more generally were progressively marginalized within the feminist/women's movement. In the beginning, the movement was small, with a very limited number of collectives, although the number of feminist initiatives was impressive. Producing a journal such as *Québécoises deboutte!* and *Pluri-elles/Des luttes et des rires* was essential to the construction of a political and feminist identity for some small women's groups as well as to the movement as a whole. By the mid-1970s, feminist journals became autonomous collectives in their own right, although still created by and for the movement. Women who wrote in their pages were not trained journalists – though many made successful careers in the mainstream media following this experience – but activists who took advantage of this forum to exchange news and practices emerging from their groups or collectives. At the turn of the 1980s, as the movement grew throughout Québec, the space taken by feminist journals within a constellation of feminist/women's collectives diminished; the pressure of professional journalism increased, making it easier for a journal such as *La vie en rose* to take its distance from women's groups, although feminists still looked to the publication hoping it would represent them and speak for them.

Feminists practising counter-information against the mainstream media did not work without risks, including the risk of being highly criticized by other feminists. In Rome, those producing the journal *Effe* were not members of a feminist collective and thus not viewed as true representatives of the movement; the journal's goal was to practise professional journalism; it had a paternalistic and condescending tone; it disseminated misinformation about the movement; and it censored feminist authors and their articles (Paoli 2011, 23–24, 33–34).[16] *Effe* resolutely refused to be a terrain upon which theories were debated, but it wanted to be recognized as a place where information on feminism was exchanged. In addition, the journal did not want to reach a specific audience of individualized, well-educated, and well-informed readers (Tagliaferri 1977). Nevertheless, the accusation of being an elitist journal operating outside the structures of the movement clashed with *Effe*'s statement that its members were true feminists and that making the journal was part of their activism ("Care compagne" 1976). Undoubtedly, the controversy began when *Effe* announced its decision to adopt a self-management model and to become a women's group in its own right. *Effe* wanted to act as a bridge, to cross the divide between feminism and the rest of the world, but the editors split over this issue, leading to the creation of a competing journal on the feminist scene in Rome: *Differenze* ("Autogestione" 1975, 2–3; Paoli 2011, 28).

Less than a year after the split, *Effe* began publishing articles in an attempt to start an exchange with other feminist publications and collectives.[17] One of these articles, "La diversità che c'è tra di noi" (The difference there is among us), highlights the distance between *Effe* and *Sottosopra* ("La diversità che c'è tra di noi" 1976). The January 1976 article refers to a round table organized by *Effe*, with representatives of feminist journals present, to discuss the difficulties and the meaning of feminist journalism.[18] At this meeting, two seemingly opposite visions emerged. For *Effe* the problem of feminist journalism was the absence of a solid self-management infrastructure to secure the independence of feminist journals. *Sottosopra* argued that the most important issues were not material but political, pointing to the fundamental problem of informing versus communicating feminist discourses and practices. Question such as "Why produce a feminist journal and for whom? What kind of experience should feminist journals write about?" underlined the tension between the idea that content matters more than resources. The debate also pointed to the frontiers of the movement, the internal/external lines that separated the world of feminist activism from the world of women not linked to the movement. For *Sottosopra*'s representatives, there was no such division, and informing women about feminist practices was the best way to reflect feminist evolution and to build a stronger movement. This position triggered the criticism that the Milanese journal was interested solely in women with feminist theoretical knowledge ("La diversità che c'è tra di noi" 1976; Paoli 2011, 24–25).

Both *Sottosopra* and *Effe* believed in the autonomy of feminist collectives: *Effe*'s shift towards a self-management model was made to preserve its financial independence. It argued this was the only way to prevent external political interference. For feminists in Milan, however, this concern for resources was the indication that *Effe* gave secondary importance to feminist practices. For *Sottosopra,* it was vital for a journal to write and reflect feminist experience in women's groups, and it set its roots in the same terrain in which feminist struggles were being fought.

Following its split with *Effe, Differenze* sought to emulate *Sottosopra* with the difference that specific feminist collectives – or a gathering of women from different women's groups – would be responsible for producing each issue, with a coverage limited mainly to Rome. *Differenze* concentrated its efforts on attracting a variety of activist experiences through the participation of collectives. Those involved in the process had all the responsibility of producing the journal, which required a tremendous amount of energy and, at times, generated intense debates over what to write when the recollection of experience and events was not shared by everyone. Some collectives imploded over the process (Guerra 2005, 55; Paoli 2011, 18, 56).

Like *Sottosopra, Differenze*'s audience was women who had acquired feminist knowledge and feminist consciousness (Paoli 2011, 50; "Secondo noi" 1976). Like *Sottosopra,* which was well known outside Italy, it was recognized as an important Italian feminist journal. It had its ups and downs, but it published a total of twelve issues over a period of seven years. According to Federica Paoli (2011, 53), "letti uno di seguito all'altro offrono un racconto corale e polifonoci, mosso e participato" (reading one issue after the other offers a narrative that is choral and polyphonic, moving and participative). The voice(s) that was speaking was different from one issue to the next: that voice – or fractured voice(s) if we take into account the fact that these collectives were not homogeneous – may have wanted, at times, to go back to the objective set by the original collective: communicating and mirroring feminist experiences. Soon, however, *Differenze* was no longer in a position to transfer onto the feminist scene a replica of this experience, being aware of the discrepancy between attempting to live feminist principles and to write about them. Those who conceived the journal believed nonetheless that differences among women, among feminist collectives and among feminist ways of apprehending the social, were not impediments to unity of action (Paoli 2011, 54; "Viaggio attraverso un'esperienza" 1976).

Québécois Feminist Journals Mirroring Their Times and Places

In Québec, most feminist journals began at the centre of the feminist/women's movement but moved progressively to its periphery towards the turn of the 1980s. Our inquiry begins with *Québécoises deboutte!* and concludes with *La vie en rose,* the strong feminist voice, independent of any external influence.[19] The move from the centre to the periphery of the movement was accelerated by the multiplication and fragmentation of groups and collectives. It became more and more complicated to offer a good-quality journal accessible to a readership that was becoming increasingly diversified and demanding; the search for professionalism contributed to this dynamic.

The small number of Québécois feminist titles makes it difficult to compare them with their Italian counterparts, but they had the same pugnacity in bringing debates onto the political scene and the same capacity to extend the national borders. For most of the 1970s, the Québécois feminist press had few examples to compare themselves with in terms of theoretical content, new ideas, and debates. *Québécoises deboutte!,* for instance, was one of a kind. The degree of synergy between this feminist title and other alternative and progressive journals, operating within a large ideological spectrum – from the New Left to the individualistic but countercultural avant-garde – is difficult to determine apart from the fact that many feminist activists were also contributing to leftist journals. In contrast, at the turn of the 1980s, *La vie en rose* established a relationship with activists disillusioned by the left and disenchanted, especially with the new kid on the block, *Le Temps fou.* But, by then, *LVR* had already declared that the left was dead and that feminism was the movement within which all struggles must be represented. One should not see a contradiction in *LVR*'s firmly grounding its content within the feminist movement while refusing to be the voice of women's groups.

The trajectory – from *Québécoises deboutte!* to *La vie en rose,* or moving from the metropolis to creative and innovative regional publications – is like a play produced by a fringe theatre group. Each feminist journal presented a succession of acts and intermissions, as if playing its own characters with intensity and determination. *Québécoises deboutte!* reverberated widely and covered the vast Québec territory despite the paucity of its resources. The play the journal put on the scene talked about women's lives in a way that no other playwright/journal had before. The Centre des femmes, to which the journal belonged, had many other problems to deal with, such as the struggle for abortion. Yet the CdF's original goal with *Québécoises deboutte!* was to propose its own feminist theory of women's oppression, just as a respectable avant-garde journal should do if it wanted to lead the Québécois feminist/women's movement (O'Leary and Toupin 1982, 171–73; O'Leary and Toupin 1983, 8). And so, page after page, *Québécoises deboutte!* attempted to present a coherent feminist analysis of the oppression of working-class women that looked almost like a verbatim translation of the orthodox Marxist theory on the capitalist exploitation of the working class. Soon, the journal began to receive an enormous amount of mail from every region of the province with requests impossible to satisfy. In a few months, those publishing *Québécoises deboutte!* had doubts about the journal's tone and message. In September 1973, the journal launched a questionnaire to capture readers' thinking. The results appeared in the March 1974 issue, but they were so roughly presented that it was almost impossible to make sense of them. Nonetheless, some sort of paradigm shift took place as the editorial team made two announcements: one, that fewer theoretical articles would be printed and, two, that the journal was taking a break for a few months. *Québécoises deboutte!* never appeared again ("Le journal, pourquoi" 1982, 3). The journal remains, with *La vie en rose*, one of the most influential Québécois feminist journals (Bergeron 2011a; Des Rivières 1995; Fortin 1993). Although these two titles were widely distributed, they never really shifted their focus outside of Montréal or even, in the case of *LVR*, outside the major influence of American and French feminisms.

Other important feminist titles appeared in the interval between *Québécoises deboutte!* and *LVR*. Two journals in particular were exemplary of what many Italian feminists termed the "two souls" of the movement: *Les têtes de Pioche* (1976–79), with a total of twenty-three issues, and *Pluri-elles* – later renamed *Des luttes et des rires* (1977–81) – which published twenty-one issues. *Les têtes de Pioche* wanted to inform about feminist struggles, to increase awareness about discrimination against women, and to put an end to women's powerlessness ("Éditorial" 1976, 2). The journal claimed to be the voice of radical feminism, but the potential to develop a theory of sexual difference is not part of its content, despite the number of Québécois feminists who travelled to Europe and brought back loads of documents. The second journal, *Pluri-elles/Des luttes et des rires*, was created with the hope that it would fill the void left by *Québécoises deboutte!*, but those involved denied they ever wanted to be a feminist avant-garde like their famous predecessor.[20] The most important feature of this journal was its defence of the autonomy of the women's movement and the creation of a space for feminist exchange on contemporary political struggles ("C'est quoi Pluri-elles" 1977, 10; "Éditorial" 1977, 2). These goals were much more complicated to achieve than first thought: at the end of the first year, it became obvious that *Pluri-elles/Des luttes et des rires* had not succeeded in obtaining the commitment of women's groups. Yet its expectation of feminist collectives was much lower than that of the Italian *Differenze*, which was to take complete responsibility for the planning of an issue.[21] *Pluri-elles/Des luttes et des rires* had no choice but to become an autonomous women's group of its own in order to fulfill its mandate of representing the multiplicity of women's voices and supporting the women's movement demands ("Éditorial: Pluri-elles" 1978). By changing its structures, its objectives, and its modes of operating, this Montréal journal hoped to establish stability and efficiency. The shift gave *Pluri-elles/Des luttes et des rires* the opportunity to reflect critically on the issue of feminist press and media communication, and it dedicated an entire issue to this subject in 1980.[22]

Occasionally, Québécois feminist journals criticized each other's projects, but, at the turn of the 1980s, contrary to the Italian scene, women's groups adopted a tone of serenity and had few political disagreements. If some editorials or articles were polemical they were rarely inimical: there were too few journals to engage in a war of defamation and elimination, but their numbers were sufficient to create a climate of dialogue. Most of these short-lived journals accomplished their mandate of informing their readership about feminist practices and women's group activities as well as theorizing/analyzing the evolution of women's condition. From time to time they reproduced articles and information from the feminist press around the world. They announced the arrival of new titles within the small but vibrant field of feminist counter-information opposed to the mainstream media. *Des luttes et des rires* announced that *La vie en rose* – not yet the most important feminist journal of the 1980s – was being inserted between the pages of the leftist countercultural title *Le Temps fou*. It also announced the release of the lesbian journal *Amazones d'hier, lesbiennes d'aujourd'hui*, inspired by Monique Wittig's political thought, which is publishing to this day.

The Modernity Project of *La vie en rose*

If *Québécoises deboutte!* was the instrument of in/formation and the property of the CdF, and if *Les têtes de Pioche* represented the Québécois voice of radical feminism, and if the bulletin *Pluri-elles/Des luttes et des rires* was confident it was the true representation of women's movement's autonomy, *La vie en rose* claimed to represent no one but its feminist self. When the journal appeared on the scene of feminist publishing, the political landscape had changed completely from what it had been a decade earlier: the shift towards neoliberalism was under way, although no one guessed the devastating impact it would have with the privatization of public services. The newly created *LVR* adopted the tone of a renewed liberal feminism while flirting with some sort of socially conscious feminist radicalism. *LVR* was certainly not going to play the role of "organic intellectual" vis-à-vis any segment of the women's movement.

> We are tired of a certain kind of moralistic, "ghettoistic" and prude feminism; of the type that extolls universal sisterhood and is still searching for goddesses and prophets; tired of speaking only to ourselves and imprisoning ourselves in what we have painstakingly succeeded in making visible as "women's affairs." We are feminists but we are tired of the moaning tone we are forced to use to denounce injustice and oppression; of narrowing our issues to four or five demands in a movement that aspires to freedom; we are tired of letting the power define feminism, making it either a scarecrow or the only path of salvation for humanity and leaving all the work to us as usual; we are tired of being at the beck and call of each and every one, and even of women's groups.[23]

"Les filles" of *LVR* were determined to have fun for a change while creating "the magazine of their dreams" (Godard 2002, 214). For seven years, the journal fiercely defended feminism but insisted on being free of any type of interference, including from the women's movement itself (Bergeron 2011b; D'Amours 1988). Although *LVR* never refrained from criticizing the direction taken by women's groups, it also never let anyone defame the women's movement. The journal introduced a loyalty to another type of feminism, a type of feminism no longer constrained within its local and national boundaries, and this loyalty lasted to the end. *LVR* reported on what was happening outside of Montréal, although it was more interested in what was happening in the rest of the world than in the rest of Québec. In doing this, it brought in a multiplicity of feminist voices and influences from elsewhere without necessarily endorsing everything that was conceived abroad. When it came to criticizing the government and the political party in power, *LVR* journalists never lacked caustic words. But the journal was also representative of the most significant shift that happened in Québécois feminism in the 1980s: feminists were no longer interested in merely criticizing the left for its lack of sensitivity to feminist theorizing. Thus, *LVR* became the voice of those who had been deceived by some sort of activism that had hoped to transform the left.

What is most interesting in this rupture with the left – which seemed to contradict *LVR*'s refusal to be the voice of women's groups – is the journal's call for the renewal of a feminist avant-garde able to capture all struggles within the boundaries of the feminist movement (Guénette 1985b; F. Pelletier 1985). Such a vision was obviously not shared by feminists who were already worried that the journal was adopting liberal and individualistic trends. Articles reporting on the living conditions of women from the Third World, even if substantial, were mainly descriptive and were not devoted to rerouting the well-embedded emphasis on white, heterosexual, middle-class, urban women and their struggles and privileges. *LVR* was famous not only for its interviews with well-known French and American feminist personalities such as Simone de Beauvoir, Benoîte Groulx, Kate Millett, and Marguerite Duras but also for its encounters with businesswomen and politicians like Lise Payette and Pauline Marois. The interview with Marois was not unanimously appreciated by *LVR*'s readership, and the journal was accused of giving too much space to powerful white women who were not devoted to feminism.

The journal was more professionally produced than any Québécois feminist journals that had come before. *LVR* offered its readership a product of outstanding quality, much higher than the mainstream press of the time.[24] The journal had little resemblance to the Milanese *Sottosopra*. In fact, the Italian equivalent of *LVR*, in terms of aspiring to reach a type of professional journalism, was *Effe*, but the comparison stops there as *Effe* was very conventional in the ways in which it reported on the practices and activities of the movement. But both *Sottosopra* and *LVR* were exemplary for their outrageous provocations, highlighting the divisions and conflicts emerging from the movement. The Montréal journal followed the line of heterosexuality rather than that of sexual difference. Both journals represented, in their own ways, a rupture with a certain type of militant feminism that prevailed during the 1970s.

LVR was a journal of many surprises, especially the casualness with which it addressed eroticism, publishing cartoons with a pornographic tone, directing the female gaze towards men, embarrassing them, provoking many controversies. For example, after long and excruciating debates and much ambiguity on the part of the editorial board, *LVR* agreed to publish a short story, "Histoire de Q" ("Tenter l'érotisme" 1985), which detailed the sado-masochistic revenge of a woman against the lover who abandoned her. "*Histoire de Q* n'est pas un texte érotisant, mais bien une fable moralisante. Si *Histoire d'O* est l'histoire d'une femme qui aime trop, *Histoire de Q* montre ce qu'il arrive lorsqu'un homme n'aime pas" (Dandurand 1985). (*Histoire de Q* is not an erotic story but a moralist fable. If *Histoire d'O* is the story of a woman who loves too much, *Histoire de Q* shows what happens to the man who does not love).

The text triggered angry reactions hardly ever seen in Québécois feminist circles: *LVR* received an abundance of letters whose content underlined the absence of unanimity on issues of censorship and on what constitutes pornography.[25] Yet sexuality was not the only theme with which *LVR* was obsessed. The journal sparked debates on the relationship between women and men in a way that no other feminist periodical did. The intended audience was clearly white and heterosexual, urban and middle class: *les filles* of *LVR* knew perfectly well that a significant number of men were passionate readers of their feminist insolence. Several issues displayed provocative titles aimed at responding to some outrageous male accusations against feminists. For instance, "Aimons-nous les hommes?" (Do we love men?)[26] echoed Adrienne Rich's theory on the constraints of heterosexuality ("Éditorial: Aimons-nous les hommes?" 1982), with an editorial that criticized the women's movement for marginalizing lesbians. The question was blunt and intended to reach a variety of audiences outside feminism.

LVR had a caustic sense of humour (Des Rivières 1995). Its cynical way of addressing violence against women in its various forms was to ask: "Quel genre d'hommes au juste demande-t-on aux femmes d'aimer?" (Exactly what kind of men are we asking women to love?). Besides the question of love – of women loving men – the journal in its earlier years provided a significant space for lesbian expression. Nevertheless, lesbianism never entirely diverted *LVR*'s attention from heterosexuality. After a few years, lesbian-related issues were rapidly pushed into the margins, while the focus on men – paternity, the relationship between women and their fathers, the prototype of *pink* masculinity that replaced the leftist male – never subsided.

Overall, *LVR* represented the prototype of the white heterosexual woman, the political subject who stands strong in the face of power, including the power of the left and Marxist ideology; who never apologizes for taking the side of women's rights and who never shies away from demanding the kind of social and political transformation she believes is needed to change women's living conditions. The "girls" of *LVR* were never confused about the type of society they were dealing with, and what they believed in was solidly anchored in a project to achieve modernity for a homogeneous community of women.

Theatre and Performance: Voices of Indigeneity and of Subalternity

The quest for the origins, the desire to rediscover the world as it was before patriarchy, to relive a society where women – mothers and grandmothers – were triumphant and the transfer of memory was governed by matriarchs, dominated feminist narratives of the 1970s. Allegorical representations of ancient, independent feminine figures occupied a significant segment of feminist cultural productions. Film, literature, plays, songs, and poetry evolved in parallel with the representation of the contemporary reality of women struggling against all forms of oppression. This section presents two significant feminist approaches to the origin myth. The first is the work of feminist playwright and novelist Jovette Marchessault. Marchessault benefited from the support of many other feminist writers and creators, although she was not always well understood. The second approach comes from the Nemesiache, named after Nemesis of Greek mythology. This theatre company was founded in 1970 in Naples by Lina Mangiacapre, a feminist philosopher and artist. A few years later, Mangiacapre created another cultural group, the Association of the Tre Ghinee, a feminist cooperative supporting women artists in Naples, some of them subaltern women, such as those interned in a psychiatric hospital in the city.

Uncovering a World before Christianity, Colonialism, and Capitalism

Jovette Marchessault was an autodidact who was born before the Second World War into a poor working-class neighbourhood in Montréal and who quit school in her early adolescence.[27] Linda Gaboriau (1985, 97) wrote of her: "as a self-educated woman with only a grade-eight education, she had to fight to build her vocabulary word by word." Before she became the feminist writer that we know and a playwright solidly implanted within the Montréal theatre scene, Marchessault was a visual artist, creating a variety of masks and colourful paintings as well as sculpting heteroclite structures and sculptures she called *femmes telluriques* (Telluric women). Her paintings in particular were shown and acclaimed in many North American and European cities, but unfortunately very little of her early work seems to have survived (Potvin 2012, 249). We know that some of her paintings were purchased by well-established financial institutions. In an essay she wrote for the literary journal *La nouvelle barre du jour* and that was reproduced in *La vie en rose* in 1981, Marchessault says she discovered some of her paintings hanging on the walls of a Montréal banking firm when she was working there one evening as a cleaner. She cried when she saw her work hanging next to the work of famous painters such as Carr, Riopel, Miro, and Picasso, and she left without completing her evening shift. This incident convinced Marchessault to quit canvas and paintbrushes for the typewriter and let the less expansive white page be the vehicle of her imaginary world (Dufault 2012; Gaboriau 1985; Marchessault 1981; Michaud 2007).

Marchessault's numerous literary creations celebrate women's strength and energies, and she is remembered as one of the leading feminist figures in Québécois literature. Her novels include *Triptique lesbien* (Lesbian triptych), published in 1980, which opened spaces for the expression of lesbian subjectivity but also set the stage for metaphorical figures crossing the frontiers between the real and the mythical. Marchessault staged her plays at the well-established Théâtre du Nouveau Monde (Theatre of the new world) as well as the feminist Théâtre experimental des femmes (Women's experimental theatre group) (Camerlain 1985, 73; Gaboriau 1985; P. Pelletier 2012, 39). Her theatre work is animated by a diversity of living creatures and by the spirituality of Indigenous ancestors, and it is embedded in the gynocentric creation of the world (Lamar 2012, 18). Her plays differ from other feminist theatre productions in her use of images of women outside the ordinary representation of humans. The play *Vaches de nuit* (Night cows) was presented in 1979 for the first time at the Théâtre du Nouveau Monde, with Pol Pelletier playing a cow. Pol Pelletier, a renowned Québécoise actor, recalls the play decades later in a text celebrating Marchessault's imaginary visions and feminist un/consciousness:

> In my culture, to say that a woman is a cow is the most abject and vulgar insult. To use that expression of supreme contempt to narrate women's history, to take the liberty of transforming human females into grandiose and sovereign beasts, celebrating their beauty in the starry night, to make the Milky Way a veritable path of squirting breastmilk, shows a capacity of synthesis and of transformation of multiple elements – of female humans, animals, vegetables, cosmic beings that can only be characterized as visionary.[28]

Not all her female characters are borrowed from the animal or plant or extraterrestrial world. When she depicts humans, Marchessault does not represent women as "victims" or describe the materiality of their living conditions. She stands resolutely on the side of women's achievements and grandiloquence, putting their biographical lives on stage. Her theatrical work stems from the representation of great names (Burgoyne 1991, 113), women and men who are more or less forgotten by her audiences. In "La saga des poules mouillées" (Saga of the wet hens), she presents Québécois contemporary women writers like Germaine Guèvremont, Laure Conan, Anne Hébert, and Gabrielle Roy. Elsewhere, she allegorically illustrates the life and times of Canadian artists in, for example, "Le voyage magnifique d'Emily Carr" (The magnificent voyage of Emily Carr). In "La terre est trop courte Violette Leduc" (The earth is too short Violette Leduc), Simone de Beauvoir is brought onto the scene showing her true imaginary self. In "Alice & Gertrude, Natalie & Renée et ce cher Ernest" Marchessault creates strange dialogues between famous lesbian couples like Gertrude Stein and Alice Toklas, Renée Vivien and Nathalie Barney, the last name of the title referring to Ernest Hemingway. These characters and many others are often mixed with invented ones: "appartenant à la fois au Ciel et à la terre" (belonging to heaven and the earth at the same time) (Lamar 2012, 20). Because most of her theatrical production differed significantly from other contemporary feminist plays that denounced women's living conditions and oppression, Marchessault was judged by many contemporary critics as being elitist, oblivious of the social and economic factors that plague women's lives (Gaboriau 1985, 97–98). Indeed, Marchessault was interested in staging an alternative vision of politics, one more inclined to celebrate than to decry. She illustrates the power of women and makes visible all the traces they have left behind in history, "in the comet's wake."[29] Her female characters are triumphant, which could potentially make Marchessault an ally of the theory of sexual difference, but she did not share the same world vision as her feminist contemporaries.

According to Lamar, representing women allegorically through living creatures or through reinventing the biography of real people was Marchessault's way of making *visible the invisible*. In the 1970s and 1980s, she was recognized for her celebration of lesbian existence in a series of autobiographical works (Ricouart 2012). Yet lesbianism was not the only dimension of her artistic production. Her Indigenous ancestry as Montagnaise-Cree, and tracing the history of her people – which was not considered central in the eyes of her public and her critics, perhaps because she did not appear to address it directly – was at the core of her quest (Dufault 2012, 77; Michaud 2007, 36). In reconnecting herself with her Indigenous subjectivity,

Marchessault succeeds in making Indigenous spiritual ancestors a part of every one of us. Her literary life carried the history of the Americas, from the North to the South, as well as the conquest that preceded the genocide that decimated the continent (Blais 2012, 29–30). Marchessault had the certitude that such violence was the evil work of *male divinities,* that neither appeasement nor collaboration would bring back what had been lost unless there was a revolution of myths (Feman Orenstein 2012, 65). She resolutely took up the direction of the revolution to come by foregrounding all the living creatures, all the spirits living in the sky or descending to earth, the Indigenous vision of the world that once dominated the land. Pol Pelletier (2012, 42) suggests that, in history, no other woman has carried such a powerful ethnic unconscious within herself. Understanding what lies at the core of her cultural production helps us see how she became the playwright and the novelist she was, how her relationship with Indigenous ancient spirits helped her to establish a line of communication with past and present creatures of the universe, with the pressing desire to reincarnate them so that they could be seen.

If for the protagonists of the theory of sexual difference the goal was to find the pre-oedipal mother, the original maternal figure existing before the law of the father (Schiavo 2002, 88), for Jovette Marchessault the objective was to recover the way the world was before Christianity, colonialism, and capitalism (Feman Orenstein 2012, 57). When it comes to the position of women in the family, Marchessault does not hesitate to present a series of intergenerational dialogues and conflicts between herself and her mother, between her mother and her grandmother, between her and the grandmother she loved and whom she prefers over her mother, whom she accused of being complicit in patriarchy and its violence. The grandmother connected her granddaughter to a symbolic world of the living spirits and familiar figures in Marchessault's Indigenous origins. The grandmother is also celebrated for defying the patriarchal order, unlike the mother, who provoked anger for obeying the law of the father, who personifies Christianity, colonialism, and capitalism (Bentaous 2012; Feman Orenstein 2012; Vergerau-Dewey 2012). Substituting the grandmother character for the more direct presence of the mother does not contradict the sexual difference paradigm. However, Marchessault is much more complex in replacing the law of the father within colonialism. Her grandmother represents a direct link with Indigenous ways of living as well as an extraordinary example of resistance against the church and civil law (Bentaous 2012; Vergereau-Dewey 2012, 132).

There are conflicting analyses of Marchessault's fiction, and, perhaps for this reason, her novels are not as well known as her theatre productions (Purdy 1991). On one hand, Gloria Feman Orenstein (2012, 55) calls Marchessault a "nouvelle chaman féministe" (new feminist shaman), a prophet who foresees and replays each phase of the decline of Western civilization:

> Considered from a metaphorical point of view, *Like a Child of the World*[30] replays each phase of the sacred vocation of the shaman during the decline of western civilization as it is perceived by the clairvoyant eye of the seer. Fundamentally, the author becomes the prophetic scribe of her people, and her book is a spiritual guide to relive, in space and time, the shamanic voyage that will redeem the human race from the Fall; that will exorcise Christianism, Capitalism and Colonialism, which will be followed by a new revolutionary era where woman will be restored in her pre-patriarchal role of cosmic magnificence.
>
> For the woman prophet coming from North America, the fall goes hand in hand with the evangelization of the Aboriginal people and the civilization of the New World. Now the evil inherent in the patriarchal myth of the Creation imposed by the colonial oppressor must be exorcized, in order to resuscitate the natural order of the universe symbolized by the mother-of the-herbs, the Great Goddess of Vegetation, and so that life on the planet enters into a cycle of renewal and regeneration.[31]

For Feman Orenstein, Marchessault's work walks along with the theory of sexual difference and a mythical universe derived from her Indigenous origins (Lamar 2012, 17). On the other hand, critics like Anthony Purdy (1991, 270) criticize Feman Orenstein for homogenizing the complexity of Marchessault's entire production into a false harmony, erasing all the conflicts and contradictions that exist among women, including silencing Marchessault's descriptions of violence among lesbians. For Purdy, it is impossible to reduce the complexity of Marchessault's creative works to an essentialist celebration of women.

Making the connection with her Indigenous ancestry – something that her critics were late to discover or to accept as fundamental to her work – brings Marchessault to an irremediable conflict with the theory of sexual difference, its essentialism, and its separatism. Never afraid to explore a variety of universes, to travel the world with a multiplicity of layers, continents, and languages, Marchessault creates a mythical and metaphorical world where she leads not just women – indeed not just women and men but all living creatures – to a revolutionary era that allows the visible to emerge once again out of the invisible (Marchessault 2012, 11). For me, the ways in which Marchessault contextualized the moment and interconnected her life as an artist with her social class, her gender, and her indigeneity are absolutely stunning.

In an interview published in a special issue of *Voix et images* dedicated to her in 1991, Marchessault said she wanted to present human characters in more nuanced ways. After all, she argues, there are things that only a man can say (Marchessault quoted in Potvin 1991, 226). Some of her novels suggest that there are forms of violence that find their expression in women, including in lesbians in love.[32] This desire to have a nuanced approach to her human characters is a partial move away from the feminism of her time. Again, the profound influence of Indigenous history and Indigenous spirit blurs the frontiers between genders of the living. Marchessault's understanding of gender should not be seen as fixed but as constantly shifting between worlds: the world we know here on earth and the world of the galaxy where all kinds of creatures meet, communicate, and are transformed;[33] the world of today's reality and the world that existed before Christianity, colonialism, and capitalism and that is always here in the present. Perhaps in the near future, Marchessault's work and life will be relocated within the intersectional two-spirited approach of sexuality, indigeneity, and gender.

Feminism in Synergy with Subaltern Women in Naples

Jovette Marchessault benefited from the support of the women's movement during the time she produced her plays and novels. She was an independent feminist and was only one among a plethora of artists, although an important one, within the feminist and artistic circles of Montréal. The case was different for Lina Mangiacapre, the founder of the Nemesiache, a feminist theatre group in Naples. Mangiacapre represented a type of feminism particular to the Italian South, and she occupied a position that contrasted with the feminist theorizing that unfolded in the North. She used corporal expressivity to find the path towards the origin myth as it existed before patriarchy. Mangiacapre's intention was not simply to put a play on stage as a mere spectacle to be seen by an undetermined audience.

Born in Naples after the Second World War, Mangiacapre was younger than Marchessault, and her upbringing differs significantly. She graduated in philosophy from the University of Rome–La Sapienza, where she got involved with the student movement during the turbulent period at the end of the 1960s. She described these years as dramatic, a good laugh, and a romantic moment.[34] Regarding the meaning of the '68 years, Mangiacapre disagreed with Lea Melandri (1977), who stated that "Il 68 dava legittimità al non-detto" (the 68 provided legitimacy to the non-saying). Mangiacapre argued, on the contrary, that the period represented a search for authenticity that cannot be reduced to a mere psychologism.[35] In Rome, she connected with Rivolta femminile, the movement created by Carla Lonzi, and was introduced to the politics of autocoscienza. When she returned to Naples, Mangiacapre developed the method of the *psico-favola* (psycho-tale), a sort of autocoscienza specially designed for feminist theatre. She also challenged her philosophical knowledge with a group of fishers in Mergellina in the vicinity of Naples. She talked about this experience as an attempt to start from the particularity of daily life in order to reach the universal while demolishing the barriers between intellectuals and workers. It was, she says, her personal way of living the '68 years.

The story about the fishers of Mergellina highlights how the social and economic reality of Naples and the Italian South shaped Mangiacapre's creative vision. Nonetheless, the idea of returning to the origin myth in order to rediscover the androgynous character who existed before patriarchy and the crystallization of sexual difference cut across all her artistic activities. The name of her first group, Nemesiache, comes from Nemesis, the goddess who, according to the group, represents the femininity of the origin. All members of the Nemesiache adopted names borrowed from ancient Mediterranean classic mythology instead of using the patriarchal names with which they were born. The idea was to reconstitute an ideal genealogy for themselves (Signorelli n.d., 3). Nemesis (Mangiacapra's mythological name), Niobe, and Nausicaa were some of the women who participated in the company's theatrical productions. In Naples, the Nemesiache intervened in political events, conferences, and debates on issues the group considered essential for the well-being of women. Mangiacapre's method was always the same: she and her group interrupted the proceedings by reading their texts and manifesto out loud, as if they were putting on a theatrical performance.

The psico-favola is at the centre of Nemesiache's political interventions and cultural production. As an instrument of feminist self-inquiry, the psico-favola can be portrayed as the twin sister of autocoscienza in the Italian South. Specially adapted for feminist theatre, it was tried out for the first time in 1973 with the play *Cenerella* (Mangiacapre n.d.).[36] The method relies on non-verbal communication, gestures, and rhythms. It allows a sort of psycho-emotional liberation, inviting women to struggle in order to find their way back to the myth of the origin, to return to the root of a historical past, to fight for the recuperation of the origins of life and beauty and to understand why this myth has disappeared.[37] Like autocoscienza, the psicofavola represents a collective and personal instrument leading to women's liberation. It was used in most of the Nemesiache's plays and in her films (Mangiacapre 1979).[38]

In 1977, Mangiacapre created another feminist group, Tre Ghinee, a cultural cooperative, today known as the Associazione culturale Le Tre Ghinee. The cooperative's objectives were to deepen and expand instruments of cultural expression for women in Naples.[39] Throughout the 1970s, the Nemesiache/Tre Ghinee mobilized several women artists and non-artists around projects involving plays, films, visual arts, and, beginning in 1976, the Rassegna femminista di Sorrento (Feminist film festival of Sorrento). Asked why this event was titled "Feminist film festival" and not "Women's film festival," the Nemesiache/Tre Ghinee replied that the notion of "women's cinema" expresses the limitation and ghettoization of women's experience. These two terms – "women's cinema" – when put together signify a split between theory and practice, two dimensions the group wanted to reconcile.[40] Together, the Nemesiache and the Tre Ghinee put forth a new brand of feminism that had not been seen in Italy until then.

The Nemesiache's version of sexual difference cannot be understood outside its southern context. Women's activism in Naples surfaced between leftist organizations and newly created feminist collectives. Accordingly but disturbingly, Mangiacapre's approach to sexual difference is in constant connection with the opposite side of the soul (or axis) of the movement, which is the social and economic reality of women's lives and women's experience. This synergy with the materiality of women's lives is at the core of several of Mangiacapre's artistic activities, and it is the dimension that is ignored by the separatist segment of feminism located in the North. Because Mangiacapre was not indifferent to the political affairs of her city and of the women who lived there, the notion of "political arts" finds its true meaning in her work. She and her group often intervened on the side of the most forgotten social categories of women, such as those confined in psychiatric institutions, the women and children in the poorest neighbourhoods, and the feminist/women's collectives that worked with them.

Nemesiache's political and feminist activism come together in one of her slogans, "tutto deve essere arte" (everything must be art), which she preferred over the feminist "tutto è politica" (everything is political). In "tutto deve essere arte" lies the true spirit of Mangiacapre/Nemesiache's political activism:[41] arts and creativity, the beauty and the myth, become the terrain of feminist struggle. Mangiacapre thought it was dangerous to look for a feminine specificity, which would lead inevitably to the ghettoization of women. Her group counter-posed androgyny as an ideal model (Signorelli n.d., 2–3).[42]

In accordance with its approach to feminist arts, the Nemesiache/Tre Ghinee had its first experience of collaboration with the Mensa bambini proletari (Proletarian children's canteen), a group working with underprivileged children and women in the most impoverished part of the city. The Mensa was founded by young activists and leftist intellectuals in 1972 and served as a laboratory for the development of animation techniques. For years, the Mensa was a point of reference for multiple cultural forces working on the problems of marginalized childhood. It occupied a beautiful site for feminist events and group meetings, and this is how the collaboration with the Nemesiache began (C. Capobianco n.d., 10–11; Mastrodomenico in C. Capobianco n.d., 93). One of the numerous Nemesiache manifestos addressed the question of childhood, denouncing the masculine ideology of protection of women and children. It declared the need for childcare spaces where girls and boys could struggle for their freedom.[43]

The second experience of collaboration was the daring and courageous reaching out to women living at the Frullone, a psychiatric hospital for women and men. Apparently, the presence of men in the project provoked reactions from those who would have liked a women-only event (Reale in C. Capobianco n.d., 139; Riccio in C. Capobianco n.d., 129).The Nemesiache/Tre Ghinee's project involved the Mensa as well as other groups, and it lasted from 1977 to 1979, at which time Mangiacapre produced the film *La follia come poesia* (Madness as poetry). The goal was to show that anxiety is everywhere in daily life and not something that is incomprehensible or unexplainable (Reale in C. Capobianco n.d., 129). The event began with an occupation of the site in the same manner as students take over their universities or squatters seize unoccupied buildings. It was a surprising and disturbing moment for both the health care workers in the hospital and for those participating in the occupation.[44] The experience at the Frullone was the context of the play *Noi siamo tutte prigionere politiche* (We are all women political prisoners), which was put on during the trial of some members of the Brigate Rosse and in reaction to the participation of feminists in public demonstrations supporting their liberation. The play aimed to demonstrate that leftist solidarity with feminism does not exist when it comes to defending imprisoned women such as those confined in psychiatric institutions. After Naples, the play was shown in Venice and Mestre in the North of Italy (C. Capobianco n.d., 6).

Another experience that had a significant impact on the feminist/women's movement in Naples was a two-day conference titled "Vogliamo una città a dimensione donna" (We want a city for women), which looked at the problem of reconstructing the city after the historic centre and the most populated neighbourhoods were devastated by an earthquake in 1980. It was a dramatic moment when everyone seemed to go through a period of madness, accompanied by a massive exodus out of Naples because of a lack of water and electricity and a surge of violence perpetrated by husbands against wives (Improta in C. Capobianco n.d., 81). The Nemesiache/Tre Ghinee took the initiative of organizing the conference, taking a comprehensive approach to the problem of reconstruction and asking for the support and collaboration of several women's groups:

> The women of Naples, in a resistance that is never ending, come together in this very moment, with the utopia of their needs, following the earthquake which, as a natural phenomenon, comes inserted within a series of political phenomena which, since the end of World War II until today, have seen women, in all these moments, struggling to stay in a city, not to go away, not to mediate and not to die. To these struggles today, all other struggles are united and as a Neapolitan feminist group, our struggle as always began with a dose of consciousness concerning the historical expropriation of one dimension: that of our origin ... Not only are [we] not willing to go away and not willing to accept the destruction of alleys and the marginalization of the historical centre. In this moment, [we must] confront the problems of the territory, confronting together and united, the utopia of needs and the need for utopia.[45]

The conference is remembered as the last large feminist gathering in the city. The encounter held the promise of a future for the movement. Unfortunately, the Nemesiache's dream and intuition for reconstruction was lost. The Commune of Naples, with the PCI at its head, had promised that the conference proceedings would be published. But that did not happen. It was a political mistake to let another type of politics take over the feminist solidarity of the time (Cavaliere in C. Capobianco n.d., 48). What remains of this historical event are a few traces lingering in feminist archives, a few articles in the *Quotidiano donna*, the feminist newspaper based in Rome with a Neapolitan branch managed by the Nemesiache – as well as in the memory of participants who did not forget the action of criminal organizations, such as the Camorra, in the aftermath of the earthquake (Riccio in C. Capobianco n.d., 141). In 2010, when I visited Naples thirty years after the earthquake, almost everyone evoked the catastrophe that had cut off the possibility of the development of a very diverse and living feminist/women's movement. Pessimism taints the city, which is still struggling to recover from the spiral of economic decline and political neglect that has been its lot since the Second World War.[46]

Bringing Feminist Cultural Production Back to the Centre of Feminism

Feminist cultural productions were central to the shaping of feminist discourses and practices. What is missing in many feminist historiographies is the recognition that culture plays a fundamental role in the way feminist theories are communicated and portrayed. This role does not concern merely the writing of plays and novels, the drawing of posters and colourful illustrations. Indeed, all the works on the history of feminism in the 1960s and 1970s bring attention to the astonishing number of feminist journals and creative projects, but it is not the quantity that matters. These journals interacted and responded to one another: they created an identity of their own with revolutionary analyses of women's condition. These exchanges did not simply delineate the terrain of a particular *war of positions*. They helped to shape a feminist *we* and sometimes an *us* and a *them*, all within the space of the same movement. The same argument can be made for feminist cultural groups that went out of their way to work with categories of subaltern women (like the Nemesiache/Tre Ghinee, which worked in women's asylums in Naples or set plays that were commissioned by unions) and in a multitude of community organizations (like the Théâtre des cuisines, which operated in a working-class neighbourhood of Montréal). Using political arts and the practice of making visible the culture of ordinary people, the feminist/women's movement aimed to represent itself to the outside world and to demonstrate its capacity to organize feminist exhibitions, publishing houses, and libraries. All of these innovative and creative projects did much more than simply service the movement: they sustained it both structurally and theoretically.

In retrospect, one wonders if feminism, as a political movement, was aware of the central place of culture in its midst. Towards the end of the 1970s, some observers of the Italian scene regretted that feminists did not address the question of culture by proposing a feminist vision of the subject

(Bravo, del Boca, and Scaraffia 1977, 77–79). Occasions to articulate the relation between women and the arts existed: in 1978, an important gathering titled Convegno Donna, Arte, Società (Women's art and society congress) took place in Milan, revealing the tense relationship between women artists and mainstream cultural institutions: many participants would have preferred that the congress restrict itself to a significant exchange on feminist creations ("Convegno donna ante società" 1978; "Convegno Donna – Arte – Società" 1978; Virdis 1978). In Québec, as in Italy, the problem of culture and, more specifically, of political arts is not rejection but misrecognition and marginalization. Activists who were busy building a movement were living the moment of their activism, adopting the path of creation as a form of expression. Cultural productions were at the heart of feminism because collectives and small groups used a variety of creative modes of representation that interconnected with direct political action and practices. Yet, individually and collectively, activists did not pay attention to the danger of disconnecting culture from politics, and they misrecognized the moment of rupture. The marginalization of political arts and culture within feminism occurred due to the institutionalization of the women's movement as well as due to the path taken by a variety of forms of feminist cultural expression: with the increasing fragmentation of the movement, the individual artist became disassociated from the collective and a constellation of groups took up the challenge posed by the state and its institutions. Years later, the delinking of feminist politics and culture became almost a natural state of affairs.

9 Who Should Write Our History?

L'histoire ne doit pas être faite par les historiens des universités mais par les gens qui la vivent.
– Raymonde[1]

Researching, Documenting, and Writing Feminist History

Trying to make sense of what had happened to their movement, women from diverse feminist trends began collecting documents and writing from their memories of events. They questioned their roles and locations within the student movement and political groups until the moment mass mobilizations were replaced by alternative forms of feminist organizing and more focused but fragmented specialized research (Mantini 2000, 175; Zancan 2003, 11). The shift towards documenting and researching feminist history is part of the selective process by which one tries to control which narratives deserve to be told to future generations. A sense of urgency animated the numerous debates on the setting up of feminist archives and documentation centres. It occupied significant time and space within women's groups and in the minds of many founders (Baeri 2002; Bertilotti 2004; Braidotti 1986; Dumont and Toupin 2003; Melandri 2002; O'Leary and Toupin 1983; Péloquin 2007; Pesanti 2002). These discussions about researching and documenting feminist history unveiled the grey area in the interstices between the individual and the collective, among those who had found an identity of their own within small women's groups.

The collective memory/history of a particular group – or what was left of it – could not have existed without the voice and action of its individual members. Yet memory is different from history: researching, (re)collecting, and documenting a movement, such as feminism, relies on individuals as well as on the collective research of those who were once part of social networks of small groups, political parties, unions, and public/political institutions. It has been carried out as much by individual/collective efforts as by feminist academic researchers using the tools of scientific research and supported – although not always – by academic networks and publicly funded research. Inside and outside of academic circles, many articles and books were written; several anthologies of the best feminist texts and conferences were organized; many documentation centres and feminist libraries were created, some with limited scope, others with multiple purposes. Almost all of these projects bore the idea that the most recent history of feminism needed to be properly documented. In order to know where this movement was going, feminists had to break away from negative impressions or fears that they were running the risk of starting all over again (Rossi-Doria 1979, 27).[2]

Doing a history of feminism from the 1960s to the 1980s is a challenge, considering that the terrain of feminist organizing is often disconnected from the type of research conducted in academic circles (Scott 2011, 26–27). There are at least three major categories of feminist historians, often but not always operating outside an academic setting. The first category aims to correct the wrongs and articulate the silences found in formal historical feminist research and subsequent related publications (Dumont and Toupin 2003; O'Leary and Toupin 1983, 368; Péloquin 2007). The second category is designed for an audience of feminist activists and is devoted to facilitating exchanges among groups as well as making sure that past feminist experiences are not lost to the younger generation. The challenge is how to teach the history of contemporary feminism as well as the principles of feminist organizing to undergraduate students majoring in women's studies programs – often renamed either gender and women's studies or gender and feminist studies or gender, sexuality, and women's studies. There are huge differences between learning in academia and learning within the community (Melandri 2003, 42; Michaud 2007). By contrast, a third category of researchers is more concerned with providing information to an audience located outside the movement and trying to bring meaning to particular events. Some argue that this research replicates the constructed dualism that opposes the two axes of feminism, while others point to an understanding of history that tries to balance the necessary communication with the rest of the world with the preservation of the movement's integrity (Crispino 1981a, 6; Ellena 2005, 226).

The desire to redress the wrongs and to articulate what historians, including feminist historians, have kept silent is well illustrated by the type of exchanges that took place during two round tables organized in Montreal in the early 1980s. At the time, participants were trying to make sense of what had happened a decade earlier. During their exchange, they expressed their views on the republication of the complete collection of *Québécoises deboutte!* by Véronique O'Leary and Louise Toupin (1982).[3] It was a moment to tell each other some truths about what had happened and to criticize the misinterpretations of feminist historians who had written about their movement. One participant made the statement that appears at the beginning of this chapter, about the dangers of leaving the history of the movement in the hands of academics, whether they are feminists or not. Such a critique echoes the impression of lost experiences that Joan W. Scott (2011, 27) evokes in *The Fantasy of Feminist History* – a sort of estrangement felt by many activists vis-à-vis feminist historians. Scott explains that there is a disconnect between academia and political movements, including feminism, a movement that had become increasingly fragmented and that was going in different directions.[4] However, Scott speaks about feminist history as if it happens essentially within academic circles. I would like to point out in contrast that researching and writing feminist history and the women's movement's history – and of course the process of its institutionalization – happens not only within academia but within the terrain of feminist organizing.

Some have suggested that, in Italy, contrary to what happened in the United States and to some extent in France, women's history was made completely outside of academic settings (Bellavitis 1990). In "L'io diviso delle storiche" (Disentangling the self in feminist historiography), Angela Groppi and Margherita Pelaja (1983) analyze the gap between feminist historiographical production and the women's movement. They invite us to rethink the relations/interrelations between the feminist researcher and the subject of her study, between the activist and the object of her political-ideological activism. When they wrote the article, Groppi and Pelaja were part of a group of editors of the Italian feminist journal *Memoria*. They evoked the ambiguity of feminist research, constantly shifting between the desire to apply disciplinary methodological instruments and the desire to take into account the most recent experiences in feminist practice (16).[5] They initiate their analysis by arguing that feminist historiography in Italy is composed of two generations of women activists. The first generation acted outside of institutional structures and was strongly motivated by the political context. This first generation gradually gave way to the second one, which had moved closer to academic institutions and disciplinary research (8). Their assessment is somewhat similar to Scott's: they are critical of the type of feminist research performed within academia, arguing that sophisticated research is at the expense of innovative feminist experiences and what is happening on the terrain of collective organizing (17). In their conclusion, Groppi and Pelaja state that the trajectory of feminist research has followed two lines or two moments of feminist historiography. The first one is loaded with ideology and is dedicated to a select audience, which is the women's movement; the second moment dissolves and negates ideology and is dedicated to a community of historians (18).

Whether or not feminist research in academia can be taught without ideology is a misleading question. Perhaps looking at the ways the practice of writing and documenting feminist history – again, whether it happens inside or outside academia, by and/or for women's groups and feminist collectives – should focus on how these bodies of research consolidate particular representations of feminism. As I argue elsewhere (Michaud 2013), there is no such thing as a lonely intellectual: the researcher is always embedded in networks of influence either inside or outside academia. Feminist research on women's organizing always relies on information provided by representatives of women's groups and feminist collectives that, over the years, have developed an important expertise pertaining to multiple aspects of women's conditions. Attributing the status of intellectual to feminist activists should not be surprising since they contribute to the theorization of women's living conditions and develop alternative, progressive, even revolutionary practices. It is precisely for their privileged position that they are sought by feminist academic researchers. Feminist activists propose feminist discourses and principles of organizing that are later co-opted within academic settings. Feminist intellectuals in the community sector feed feminist teaching and research, and, thus, they are active participants in the reproduction of knowledge both inside and outside formal academic institutions (161).

Feminist Archives, Documentation Centres, and Information Networks

Let's briefly evoke an important moment of activism: the documentation of the history/memory of the movement. Joan W. Scott argues that archives are constituted according to what counts and does not count as feminist knowledge worth preserving. She writes:

> The decision to collect and house the papers of a generation and more of feminist scholars is an effort to continue the critical work they (we) engage in by attributing to its value as history. I don't mean history in the sense of something dead and gone, but rather something worth holding onto – a living heritage, if you will, an enduring legacy ... .
>
> And even if these were not objectionable practices, did an attempt to preserve the critical thinking of another era undermine the very purpose of critique, which was to deconstruct the legacies of the past in order to open new ways for thinking the future? Would putting these papers in an archive impose the weight of the past, the burden of tradition, on the possibilities for new thought? Would it confirm the idea that origins – of movements, ideas, and events – can really be found? Was it possible that what was once lively critique would become stultifying orthodoxy? (Scott 2011, 143)

Scott suggests that these "troubling" questions be answered by "philosophers and others who haven't spent much time in archives" (ibid.). The constitution of feminist archives, for Scott, seems to be conceived within the context of institutions, most likely in academic research circles. Nevertheless, her questions/concerns cannot be disputed, especially by feminists who are alternately activists and researchers of their movement and who are resisting the institutionalization of a particular memory of feminism. The first danger is to forget that, before institutionalization and outside the process of creating an archive, there was a moment in which the collection and concentration of materials brought to light something from somebody's garage or basement, belonging to someone who did not intend to become an archivist (Baeri 2002; Cooper 2016) but who one day, alone or with a small group, decided to deal with the documents, photographs, films, and videos that ran the risk of being thrown away or recycled. We have to imagine the possibility that these first acts of preservation come from a social process that occurs long before a feminist/women's collective interested in doing archivist work is confronted by the difficult task of what to do and how to attribute value to handwritten notes taken during countless meetings.

Sometimes the process is organized and the intended outcomes are deliberate: the personal experience of participating in a collective may have sparked the initiative of collecting and documenting crucial moments in the life of a group and its members, becoming, down the road, a priority in making sense of what had happened during crucial moments that had transformed the existence of so many. First, there is the desire to account for the sudden burst in numbers of certain groups motivated by specific demands. Second, there is the willingness to understand how splits and fractures occurred along ideological lines; how conflicting views and power relations among group members came about. The dominant impulse is to find explanations for this feminist phenomenon that ignited the imagination of so many young women and not leave the writing of feminist historiography in the hands of strangers. Attempting to reconstitute a history so close to the present, trying to recover heterogeneous discourses and practices, tracking down the multifaceted dimensions of the life of a movement – all raise more questions when the purpose is to transfer memory to the next generation of activists. Going back to the lack of mechanisms devoted to the transfer and/or preservation of memories within political movements (Bertilotti and Scattigno 2005, ix; de Sève 2005; Fraire et al. 1977, 7; Rowbotham 1981, 33–34; Rowbotham 1996, 13), we can at least say that, at the turn of the 1980s, these attempts took place in the midst of a crisis of the left and its metanarratives, particularly in the midst of the crisis of Marxist historiography (Lamontagne 1978; Rossi-Doria 1981, 89).

In line with the first category of feminist historians mentioned above, the first impulse would be to keep feminist history solely in the hands of those who lived through important moments of feminism rather than risk having it be reinterpreted by a younger generation or by feminist outsiders or professional historians. The rationale behind this resistance lies in the refusal to put foreign interpretations on past experiences, to put judgments on such painfully built feminist strategies and women's organizations. According to this strategy, the members of the first generation of activists must secure the transfer of "their" memories/histories to the next generation in the belief that memory is identical to history and the conviction that the collective *we* is all there is to remember. The Italian concept *memoria possessiva* (possessive memory) characterizes this attitude of a particular generation of the 1970s – the need to control the past. Some argue that, to this point, this phenomenon had not been seen in the Western world (Betta and Capussotti 2004, 117). According to Bertilotti (2004, 227–28) however, the problem lies in the representation of the relationship between generations, in the perception one has about the *other* generation. She argues that tensions among feminist generations lead to an unnecessary hierarchy, and she pleads for the end of generational duality.

Besides the desire to preserve/control the memory of the 1970s, the fear of institutionalization is another motivation when the value – read commercial value – of the materials worth preserving is decided by those who are alien to feminism. The first generation of feminists was absolutely fearful of the risks of institutionalization, and many saw this process as the equivalent of a death and burial of women's voices and experiences (Melandri 2002, 206; Melandri 2003, 39–40).[6] Strangely, it was among the most fearful that decisions to proceed with a sort of self-controlled institutionalization were made: these feminists built archives, specialized libraries, and documentation centres, and they went on to create very sophisticated networks that linked different parts of the country and abroad (Bertilotti 2004; Fondazione Elvira Badaracco 2003; Melandri 2003).

Finally, apart from being a site for preserving the memory/history of the past – remote and current – an archive can also be a place/home where documents, articles, and books are collected and preserved and where research is carried out. However, the initial mandate of a feminist archives or a documentation centre is never permanent. Original objectives are always changing and evolving according to the types of items collected. The space occupied by particular historical moments within a specific archive can be moved from the centre to the periphery of the movement and back again. Furthermore, the argument that the institutionalization of archives dispossesses the movement of one of its features is not entirely erroneous: retrieving the archives from the movement involves retrieving its soul from its multifaceted profile.

The Traces of the Subaltern in Feminist Historiography

Let's imagine that the action of collecting documents was conducted originally through personal and fragmented initiatives. Such a practice could also take place in order to classify feminist trends and to avoid the loss of diversity in the face of an abundance of experiences. Beyond written documents, flyers, buttons, and posters, there is the repertoire of events, sites, struggles, and feminist regional, national, and international gatherings; of clashes with judicial authorities, such as the police; of judicial searches and arrests; of the confiscation of group files, including lists of subscribers; of material evincing the joy and love through difficult moments of organizing a bookstore, a theatre group, a journal, feminist health clinics/consultori; of organizing, in resolute secret, the illegal practice of abortion and underground political activities. Documents are selected according to their importance, the determination of which depends on who is in charge and who decides what counts and does not count as knowledge for a particular historical period.

Not all documents are saved, unfortunately, especially during periods of state persecution and police repression. After the kidnapping and murder of Aldo Moro by the Brigate Rosse, members of Lotta Femminista in Padua decided to bury their documents because of the information they contained on members and the activity of their collective (Rousseau 2016, 35–36). The reasoning in this type of situation is that they could always be recuperated once the danger had passed. That is, if they remembered where the documents were hidden and if the materials had not been damaged or destroyed.[7] Researching, documenting, and writing feminist history found some sort of resolution in the Gramscian notion of the "pessimism of the intellect, optimism of the will."[8]

For feminist historians working outside academia, there was very little indication of how to proceed, but the desire to control which narratives were to be transferred somehow prevailed. Regardless of the location of feminist historians, there is a consensus among them that women's history should not be a mere extension of an official history. Rossi-Doria (1981) suggests three directions to take in order to avoid this. The first direction is to establish a close interrelation between women's history and social history in order to correct the influence of structuralism, which imposes a static vision of women within societal structures such as the family. The second direction is to revisit the link between the social production of ideologies and the level of affect within a feminist collective: the entire tradition of Marxism treated women's work as a necessary step towards their emancipation, but it did not give them much autonomy within the family, within the party, or within society as a whole. The third direction mentioned by Rossi-Doria is the desire to be more theoretical regarding important issues, such as relations of power or the link between nature and culture, as these issues are believed to be central to the history of women (91–93). She recognizes that the risk of making political choices for the sake of the movement can be part of choosing which direction to take (93).

Feminist historiography is also closely related to other interests in the production and reproduction of knowledge, which brings Rossi-Doria

(1981, 91) to argue that the history of women is the history of the social. It aims to be pedagogical, to recreate the genealogy of oppression and of feminist revolts as well as moments of empowerment and victory. Feminist historiography aspires to give a voice to women who have been silenced in the past. So, the first question is: Who is the subject/object in the historiography of feminism as a political movement? Whose voices are we researching (93–94)? When feminist research focuses its attention on the diversity of modes of inquiry – consciousness-raising/autocoscienza, the practice of the unconscious and of psychoanalysis – the focus falls on the individual woman subject/object of that inquiry who is simultaneously and automatically reintroduced into the collective to which she is attached. Nonetheless, the voice of the individual woman who spoke and acted runs the risk of remaining hidden behind the collective that brought her with others to perform political strategies that make the group visible within public/political spheres.

The tension between the inside and the outside of the movement is similar to the tension existing between the rebellious woman and the subaltern woman, who may or may not be the same person. The sustained tension between the individual and the collective informs and enriches them both (Chianese 1981, 63–64). Yet, in some articles in the third section of the collection *I modi e le tematiche del femminismo a Napoli* (1981), we find innovative projects that aimed to reinscribe the history of the subaltern woman – the woman who does not belong to any structures or movements – within the history of organizing and activism in the region. The reconstitution of women's history is not the same as is the reconstitution of the history of movements, even though it sometimes includes important moments of solidarity, resistance, and rebellion with other women (Chianese 1981, 65; Libraro, Mercogliano, and Tommaselli 1981, 70), as we have seen with the Nemesiache/Tre Ghinee in the previous chapter. One is struck by the similarity with the Subaltern Studies Group – or a critique of this type of historiography from the perspective of women's voices – and in particular the desire to do the history "from below" (Bannerji 2001; Chakrabarty 2002; Guha 2000; Spivak 1988a, 1988b).

These approaches to history take place within regions traditionally marginalized in mainstream historiography in general and in feminist historiography in particular. To that effect, Elda Guerra (2004, 87) underlines the importance of pluralizing feminism(s) and suggests developing a historiographical map/geography of women's movements that takes into account differences among regions as well as the relationships of feminist movements to other political movements in any given historical time and space

(88, 91, 96). This notion of "mapping" the women's movement appears in many feminist writings, particularly those that borrow from several disciplines.[9] The notion involves the recognition of the geographic materiality of the women's movement in space and time, that movements are structured around a capillary of networks and espouse particularities of regions. Finding elements for researching and writing feminist history in connection to the subaltern condition is not incidental, considering that feminist discourses and practices in southern Italy remain peripheral to the core of mainstream Italian feminism.

In Italy and in Québec, the attention of feminist historians focuses almost entirely on major urban centres: Milan, Turin, Padua, and Rome; Montréal and, to some extent, Québec City. The type of feminism coming out of big cities was supposed to be easily exportable, and in comparing countries scarce attention was paid to what was happening in the peripheries. Ian Chambers (2008, 95) reminds us that, in the eighteenth century, Naples was the second largest city in Europe after Paris and the second in the Mediterranean after Istanbul. His book presents an interdisciplinary and intercultural interpretation of the culture and history of Naples, a city that has always been open to the Mediterranean and offers a diversity of cultures, languages, and religions. Chambers argues that the region has never been unified and that many elements of its history have been erased (36). Quoting Gramsci, who insisted that struggle or conflict lay not between *tradition* and *modernity* but, rather, between the *subaltern* and *hegemony* (8), he suggests that the concept of the subaltern is everywhere, interpreting the world, "extending the 'Southern Question'" on a planetary scale (17).

Thus, when retracing the history of their movements, feminists living in the Italian South or in marginal Québécois regions often characterize their own organizations and their institutions as being late in comparison to the feminism of major urban centres and/or dominant industrialized and culturally developed countries such as the United States and France. Despite this *inferiority complex,* which some Québécois and some Italian feminists have in common when comparing the birth of their respective movements with feminism(s) of the European North and the Anglo-Saxon world (Bono and Kemp 1991, 1–2), their struggles had similar important and genuine mass mobilizations – ones that favoured free abortion and the setting up of feminist health centres/consultori and the creation of women's groups with the same impulses towards autonomy/separatism. Only later, when the political excitement faded away, did it become obvious to feminist historians – unfortunately, not all – that these marginalized feminisms were quite right in their need to find different ways of theorizing and of mobilizing (L. Capobianco 1993, 54; Ramondino 1993, 88–89).

Producing Feminist Anthologies

The fluidity and hybridity of feminist historiography covers several disciplines, although this does not mean that all historic works are interdisciplinary. For instance, most written recollections of political moments, series of events, and issues that were intensely debated – such as street protests or mass mobilizations demanding reforms and social policies – are not presented as works of history but under specific disciplinary frameworks, such as the sociological approach adopted by Yasmine Ergas (1986) or the political science approach of Diane Lamoureux (1986). Feminist history also comes in the form of personal narratives such as those by Maria Schiavo (2002) and Marjolaine Péloquin (2007). Some are true feminist historians, like Anna Rossi-Doria (2007), Micheline Dumont and Louise Toupin (Dumont and Toupin 2003), and Véronique O'Leary (O'Leary and Toupin 1982), who co-edited the complete collection of the first feminist journal in Québec, *Québécoises deboutte!*

Feminist anthologies are interesting attempts to recuperate major and minor feminist written works and testimonies during specific historic periods, but they are also characterized by the problems of the limitation/delimitation of the specific time frame, by the selection/exclusion of documents, by the interpretation/representation of events and political moments, and by the inclusion/exclusion of race, sexual diversity, ability, and so forth. Let's look at three anthologies that focus on feminism as a political movement. The first anthology is on Québécois feminist thought, edited by Dumont and Toupin (2003). The second anthology, on Italian feminism, is composed of two volumes edited by Frabotta (1975, 1978). Finally, the third anthology is a collection of Italian texts translated into English by Bono and Kemp (1991). These three anthologies aim to reconstitute genuine feminist political thought in Québec and in Italy, and all three are successful to some extent.

Dumont and Toupin's anthology is particularly important for the history of Québécois feminism. Its objective is to reveal the configuration of a movement shaped by women's activism, showing how small protests led to larger networks of activism, ultimately creating a body of feminist ideological and political thought similar to other political ideologies active at any given time in Québec society.[10] Dumont and Toupin cover the entire twentieth century, divided into three periods: "Le féminisme et les droits de la femme, 1900–1945" (Feminism and the rights of woman); "Le féminisme comme groupe de pression, 1945–1985" (Feminism as pressure group); "Le féminisme et la pensée radicale, 1969–1985" (Feminism and radical thought). The last two periods overlap, forming two distinctive but equally influential feminist trends. The documents selected for the second period feature issues such as the right to education, women's right to work, civil and civic rights, issues related to criminal law, and social rights. These issues are all indicative of liberal theoretical paradigms. The third and last period is much more eclectic and covers an extensive list of theoretical questions, such as autonomous feminist thought, women reappropriating their bodies, abortion, contraception, reproductive health, violence, pornography, love and sexuality, heterosexuality and lesbianism, women's invisible work, social categories of marginalized women,[11] feminism and community organizing, and power, politics, and peace. In other words, this section includes all the major themes of 1970s feminist theorizing.

The title chosen by Dumont and Toupin for the third and last period suggests that the 1970s was dominated by radical feminism. Given the diversity of theoretical feminist paradigms in circulation then, this denomination may seem partial and/or reductive. Dumont and Toupin (2003, 31–32) warn that such a trend is impossible to circumscribe, so they prefer to use the notion of *mouvance radicale* (radical influence) to contrast the 1970s with the previous period, which was dominated by the feminism of equality.[12] They highlight how the same type of tension existed in other countries between two categories of feminists: those who manoeuvred in favour of policies for the emancipation of women in general and working-class women in particular, and those who claimed that only complete liberation would bring significant change for the entire community of women. Dumont and Toupin are clearly aware of the ideological diversity within 1970s feminism, but they insist that there was a consensus among activists to preserve the autonomy of the women's movement. They characterize this consensus as "féminisme comme pensée autonome" (feminism as autonomous thought) (459) and go on to propose a definition of radical feminism, explaining why the priority was to look for the roots of women's oppression. In developing this argument, Dumont and Toupin hoped to counter reductive analyses that presented the FLFQ and CdF as infiltrated and entirely dominated by the extreme left. Québécois feminism, they argue, was genuinely autonomous and not the extension of any other political ideology (460).

Nonetheless, the way in which Dumont and Toupin characterize the 1970s contains a glimpse of potentially reductive interpretations of future feminist history. It is one thing to say that a consensus was found on the need to maintain and to preserve the autonomy of the movement and another to suggest that the definition then given to radicalism differs from the definition as it is understood today. As well, it is perilous to argue that all sorts of feminist trends were contained within radical feminist thought (Dumont and Toupin 2003, 461). Leftist male leaders were not members of the FLFQ and CdF collectives, and all the texts of *Québécoises deboutte!* were written by women. Nonetheless, Dumont and Toupin do not pay enough attention to the fact that socialist and radical feminist expressions, even if they shared the same desire for autonomy for their movement and the desire for women's liberation, did not cohabit in theoretical and practical terms. The theoretical approach used by the FLFQ and CdF was materialist feminism, interrelating two major struggles: patriarchy and capitalism. This materialist feminism was, to some extent, transformed under the influence of radicalism, but it cannot be amalgamated into it and it cannot be qualified/disqualified merely on the basis of being emancipatory or being relegated to the realm of other traditional feminist ideologies (456). Thus, in reading this section of the anthology, the problem is not with how Dumont and Toupin critically analyze the leftist discourses of the 1970s period – nationalism, Third World liberation discourse, and socialism are all ideologies dominated by masculine thought (460) – but with the implication that women members of leftist groups were a mere epiphenomenon within feminism as a whole. The fact that one can practise some sort of double activism *à l'italienne* – fiercely defending the autonomy of the movement from the standpoint of feminist collectives like the Théâtre des cuisines and the Comité pour l'avortement libre et gratuit while being a member of a leftist group – is not spoken about. Feminism is, and always has been, a multifaceted movement both ideologically and discursively. Here, I am hoping to highlight a dynamic that has led so many feminist scholars (as well as others) to arrive at interpretations of a historical period that are either partial or reductive. Dumont and Toupin remind us that the idea of independent feminist thinking is present not only during the 1970s but also throughout the twentieth century and that movement autonomy contributes to and influences discourses and practices in any given historical period (462).

The two volumes of the anthology edited by Biancamaria Frabotta take a different orientation. The first volume, *Femminismo e lotta di classe in Italia, 1970–1973,* was published early in the 1970s and was edited a second time in 1975;[13] the second volume, *La politica del femminismo, 1973–1976,* followed in 1978. The anthology is structured around key themes: thus, the works of specific women's groups are given more space than others. Again, I do not want to minimize the difficulty of selecting from an overwhelming abundance of documents. Nonetheless, the selection has important repercussions for the interpretations/representations of a specific historic collection. I give the benefit of the doubt to editors of selected works who must be consciously aware that the type of audiences they hope to reach will not always be the audience they get.

In Frabotta's edited volumes, the place attributed to Marxist feminism and other feminist trends associated with political parties of the left dominates at the expense of feminist separatist segments of the movement. When the first volume was published, critics were quick to point out that it concentrated overwhelmingly on the city of Rome at the expense of other important urban centres and that too many pages had been dedicated to Lotta Femminista, the group promoting wages for housework. Other critics, however, perhaps more in synergy with the New Left, were delighted to have their documents reproduced (Frabotta 1975, 5–6). Frabotta locates her collection in an international context within which feminist movements in the United States, France, Germany, and England predominate, which is indeed the context of *capitalismo avanzato* (advanced capitalism) (8).

In terms of the national scene, Frabotta places feminism in relation to the student movement and the years of strikes that hit many universities throughout Italy, highlighting the synergies of feminism with other political movements, most importantly the extra-parliamentary left. Frabotta's genealogy of feminism is specifically oriented towards certain themes, such as domestic work and feminist activism in working-class neighbourhoods; the struggle against the education system in secondary and postsecondary education; feminist struggles in paid employment and struggles for social services; abortion, contraception, and maternity; and communist women organizing. Her choice of texts marginalizes the influence of feminist separatism, which had a tremendous resonance in Italy and abroad (9–10).

In the second volume, Frabotta's selection of feminist works gives space to small women's groups and the politics of autocoscienza. This volume highlights the huge diversity of feminism, which, she argues, is greater than in any other mass movement (Frabotta 1978, 11). There is a small evocation of the attempt to use psychoanalysis as well as a few works from feminist collectives in Milan but no mention of the theory of sexual difference per se.[14] For Frabotta, the most difficult task is not to distance the specific axis of the feminist movement she knows so well from the other axis of feminist separatism. She avoids responding to feminist critiques of the failed politics of the PCI on women's issues. In the end, feminist relations with political struggles remain at the core of Frabotta's thinking, and she opposes feminist separatism, which leads to social isolation (14).

While Dumont and Toupin and Frabotta dedicate their anthologies to their respective national women's movements, Bono and Kemp (1991) dedicate their selection of translated works of Italian feminism to a completely different audience of British and Anglo-American readers. In an introductory statement they touch on the separation between academia and the terrain of women's organizing. Bono and Kemp are right to point out the ambiguity experienced by feminists, who are coming in and out of both worlds, who are crossing the frontiers of culture and politics, who are living the tension of those who are constantly questioned about their loyalties (Bono and Kemp 1991, 4; Michaud 2013). Another opening statement focuses on how quickly some Western feminist theories have become canonized while others, evolving outside Europe and the United States, have fallen victim to cultural imperialism.[15] This argument allows Bono and Kemp (1991, 1) to differentiate Italian feminism from other national feminisms and to locate it among countries of the European South, in contrast with France, Britain and the United states. This is an important remark only insofar as the canonization of feminist theory has its own internal dynamic. Aware that their selection has left out some important collectives that developed significant Italian feminist theorizations, Bono and Kemp mention some of these in their introduction, including the collective of feminist philosophers (Transizione) and the cultural production group (the Nemesiache), both from Naples (5). Questions remain: Are these groups named only in the editors' introduction because of the feminist trends they represent? How can we connect them with the feminism of the European North when the Italian North has marginalized them?

Nevertheless, Bono and Kemp present Italian feminism with a multifaceted character and with what makes this movement unique in comparison to other Western feminisms: the long Marxist tradition of the country that had shaped the first and the most important national women's organization, UDI; the tension between the traditional left and the New Left, both shaken by the active presence of feminist activists; the tension between the UDI, favouring measures of emancipation, and the autonomous/separatist feminist activism animated by the spirit of liberation; the distinctive Italian version of autocoscienza, feminist discourses of the unconscious, and the introduction of psychoanalysis to feminism; and the importance and plurality of small groups. The editors successfully map out the Italian feminist/

women's movement and pay attention to the two axes that constantly cut across it. Yet they emphasize what probably remained crystallized in the minds of foreign feminist readers when they write:

> Certainly there has always been theorizing; to a greater or lesser extent, we feel that all the writings included here are theoretical, both in their critique of the present and in their revision of the past. What is different is the explicit assumption of the need to go beyond critique and revision, towards a fully original construction, a theory of sexual difference.[16]

Political art and culture is one of the most overlooked of all issues in these three feminist anthologies. None gives much thought to cultural production and how – as feminism entered into the 1980s – this role became more and more marginalized, to the point at which some even suggest that art and cultural production had little impact on shaping the movement. Others prefer to brush the entire subject aside (Rebick 2005). Bono and Kemp mention culture in their substantial introduction, evoking the Nemesiache of Naples, but they do not give us much information about the content of their artistic production, their feminist and political orientation, or the importance the group occupies within the women's movement in the southern region of Italy. Dumont and Toupin make a conscious decision to set aside the influences of art and culture in shaping the Québécois movement: they confess that the choice was very difficult to make in view of the unprecedented abundance of cultural events and productions between 1970 and 1975 (Dumont and Toupin 2003, 25). This type of anthology cannot reproduce lengthy excerpts of groundbreaking feminist novels and plays, nor can it cover all the controversies feminist cultural productions raised in society, including in some feminist circles. As for Frabotta, there is a small section in the second volume called "La cultura al femminile" (Feminine culture), which contains a miscellaneous collection of texts on feminist publishing and women's documentation centres, but there is no attempt to analyze the role and place of culture within the movement, even in the introduction to both volumes.

Preserving Feminist History in the Present

Those who lived through the intense moments of the 1960s and 1970s and years of creative organizing were haunted by how the history of their experience would live on. They began searching for ways to describe and bear witness to their activism while they were still living it. They were concerned that new generations of women were becoming members of their movement. They were concerned that young students were discovering feminism during academic seminars rather than in the street protests or feminist groups in which they themselves had encountered it. Thus, there was a need to explain, to convince young feminists that the earlier feminists' gains had exceeded their losses and that their victories had outlived some of their defeats. Their conviction was not only that something must be done to preserve feminist experiences but also that these efforts of collecting and documenting a movement from the recent past should be controlled by those who lived through those experiences. They believed that the institutionalization of feminist archives had to be avoided at all costs, but they did not know how to go about it on their own. They were working under difficult conditions of police surveillance and state repression. Self-made feminist librarians and archivists were nonetheless concerned about the traces of professionalism they would leave behind. As time passes, all activities constitutive of knowledge production had to adapt – with more or less success – to the political, economic, sociological, cultural, racial, and sexual contexts, as well as the social relations of power, within which these activities were located.

While working on this research, I relied extensively on feminist archives and feminist libraries as well as on documentation centres. The richness of the information I found in these spaces and the enormous help I received from feminist librarians and feminist archivists convinces me that this type of historical work performed outside academia by dedicated people who often lived on meagre wages is of primary importance for feminist scholars. These sites are not deserted spaces. Many researchers, students, and other people are using feminist collections to search for what they cannot find anywhere else: from a simple piece of information to a journal article; a simple newspaper clipping to a full academic journal; a roughly typed and barely readable document, with scribbled comments in the margins, to a recently published book. Many of these original documentation centres and feminist libraries, together with newer ones, have created large feminist networks dedicated to documenting and preserving feminist archives. Some form of institutionalization may have happened along the way, such as connecting archives to municipal or academic libraries, but many of these original documentation centres are still performing the task for which they were created. These spaces are sites where the terrain of feminist research in academia intersects with the terrain of community research. There is a dialogic interaction happening between two categories of feminist intellectuals – the feminist researcher and the feminist activists – who "enter into a dynamic which sets aside, at least temporarily, their specific connections with the 'subaltern woman,' even though it is precisely on her that both want to base their legitimacy" (Michaud 2013, 168). While researching the living conditions of social categories of people from a feminist perspective, the academic researcher cannot ignore the presence of a "native informant" who is, in many ways, producing knowledge to be used, and sometimes reshaped and re-theorized, both inside and outside universities. It is impossible to escape this interaction while doing feminist history.

10 This History Has No End and Offers No Conclusion

Throughout this book, I attempt to present the multifaceted trajectories of young feminists by featuring different aspects of their individual and collective lives. We have seen that the large majority of these women were convinced that the 1960s and 1970s represented the most important moment of their existence, that they were the actors in a new kind of revolution – one that had never been seen before. At the turn of the 1980s, however, they realized that their generation was getting older and that the movement they thought they had control over was escaping them. Small women's groups had emerged and spread but not always in the direction they had hoped. There were too many rifts, too many ideological and political trends within the movement, and, as always, too many wonderful projects abandoned or still defined as works-in-progress. While several feminist principles survived, they were widely diffused (Calabrò and Grasso 2004).

Feminism is a successful movement – one of the most formidable forces of modernization of the twentieth century – but it has shifted, and it has a future that is difficult to predict (Scott 2011, 26–27). The strong presence of Québécois women in the student movement – along with social categories of people who are, among other things, racialized and queer – and two students' mobilizations in 2005 and 2012 seem to indicate a shift in Québécois feminisms towards a renewed platform (with collective actors) that has the potential to again make feminism political and revolutionary (Bonenfant, Anthony, and Lapointe 2013; Dupuis-Déri 2008; Michaud 2016;

Surprenant and Biguaouette 2013). Feminism has never been relegated to the past and the New Left is not dead: their synergy is still at work.

As a political movement, feminism interrupted – but did not destroy – traditional narratives of the left, from the old left of parties and unions to the New Left of extra-parliamentary groups to the underground/clandestine struggle groups. In the introductory chapter, I claim that, by shifting its interlocutor – from engaging in dialogue with other political movements to negotiating with the institutions of the state – the Québécois women's movement ceased to be a political movement and became a social movement. This situation predominated through the 1980s and 1990s. But it never eliminated segments of feminism(s) that remain resolutely anchored in the political project of a profound transformation of society. As such, we should not talk about this movement in the singular, either when looking at the past or when looking at the present.

Italian feminism's experience with institutions differs from that of its Québec counterpart. The Italian government did not invite women's groups – or any community groups, for that matter – to participate in the elaboration of social programs and policy reforms. Channels of communication with the state were available only through a relationship with political parties. Some organizations, like the Movimento di liberazione delle donne, took the challenge to establish an affiliation with the Partito Radicale to push for a law on abortion. Indeed, Italian referenda on divorce and abortion laws can be counted as feminist gains against fascist forces, the Roman Catholic Church, and the PCI, whose position revealed a party more interested in reaching Catholic voters than in seeking changes for working-class women. Yet feminist relative successes during the abortion struggle were overshadowed by a series of negotiations among DC and PCI political leaders in parliament that ended with a compromise that eclipsed the full recognition of feminists' original demands. Thus, the feminist consciousness moving along the two axes (or two souls) of the movement was much more intensively lived in Italy than in Québec. It cut across the tension generated by the dual location of the double activist, who is constantly questioned about her loyalty to feminism and who must prove what she contributes to the movement.

For the historian of Italian feminism Anna Rossi-Doria (1979, 28), feminist activists inherited two elements from the New Left. The first is not so much the refusal of reformism and compromise – when feminist demands are at stake – as it is the ideological and historical tendency to reject any alternative to the revolutionary process. The second element is feminists' tendency to transfer their insecurity to someone else: a group or a collective.

This sense of insecurity within feminism increased when the extra-parliamentary left entered into crisis. Many feminist activists were led to look for new alternatives, as if there were always an elsewhere – a place for the constant renewal of some sort of double activism – while others refused to do it, risking paralysis due to the lack of a political project. This last point also suggests that many feminist activists, especially those who got their political training in the student movement and who believed that feminism should not remain a prisoner within its own borders, felt deprived of a genuine political interlocutor after the decline of the left. This issue raised the theoretical as well as the practical question of relationships among social categories of women and, when it was realized that not all women share the same experience (Staderni 1979b, 34), revealed one of the greatest challenges facing the feminist/women's movement.

Québécois and Italian feminist strategies and projects are constantly challenged by the distinction between the *in* and the *out* of the movement. This tension, however, can also be very productive when the time comes to determine what differentiates feminism from other political/social movements; when the want for transformative changes points to demands that are more revolutionary than any revolution had been dreaming of; when feminisms initiate both provocations and perspectives. The *in* and *out* of the movement is a line always oscillating between the need to remain in synergy with others and the refusal to transgress feminist frontiers and the stand-alone theories of liberation (Paolucci 1987, 130–31). The FLFQ and the CdF in Québec, the Rivolta femminile and the Libreria delle donne in Italy, each in its own way was attempting to create homogeneity– and to some extent a feminist avant-garde – around its feminist project. These feminist collectives tried to create unity in political discourse, to find a commonality of language, of common codes and concepts, that would be recognizable by everyone *in* and *out* of the feminist movement (O'Leary and Toupin 1983, 348–68). Yet, looking in from the margins, this period also generated a multiplicity of discourses and modes of organizing that make classification impossible: too many of these discourses and practices evade predetermined codes of conduct and unities of thinking (M.L. Boccia 1981). Imposing homogeneity of thought, of speech, and of action wasn't sustainable as it created a lot of pain for members of collectives and perhaps even more for activists engaged with the politics of the New Left. Yet the movement survived not only the hostility of leftist politics but also its own destructive politics.

Feminisms are movements that create a multiplicity of theories, modes of inquiry, and political practices, movements that aspire to achieve a paradigm within which no human activity can escape the scope of feminist analysis. However, there is something odd about such a vision: there are too many ideas, too many elements of discourses and practices, too many social categories of people who have been pushed aside to the margins to think that feminism(s) – even written in the plural – can achieve such a comprehensive paradigm. When trying to preserve what has been the most radical roots of feminism – women's bodies, sexual practices, affective lives, and personal narratives – the core discourses and practices become targets of conflict and challenges in constant need of being resolved and renegotiated. What remains silenced are the parts that made possible such radicalism in the 1960s and 1970s – namely, the antiauthoritarian movement within schools, the student movement, the connection with the extra-parliamentary left, the racialized subject who is always hunting the consciousness of the activists at the core of feminist discourses and practices. The margins of feminism are not a void where successes or failures of the past are hiding. The margins must be seen as a dynamic force contesting any hegemony feminism is trying to achieve (Michaud 1992, 2005). The revolutionary and radical elements evolving there are essential and fundamental to the renewal of feminism, allowing it to continue its dissent and to contest both society and itself.

Notes

Chapter 1: Contrasting the Québec and Italian Feminist Movements

Unless otherwise indicated, all translations from French and Italian are by the author, with occasional assistance from the individuals mentioned in the Acknowledgments.

1 There is no independence of Québec without the liberation of women; there is no liberation of women without the independence of Québec.

2 Non c'è rivoluzione senza liberazione delle donne; non c'è liberazione delle donne senza rivoluzione.

3 This process of social diffusion was called *femminismo diffuso* (diffused feminism) by Italian feminist researchers Anna Rita Calabrò and Laura Grasso in their book *Dal Movimento femminista al femminismo diffuso*.

4 According to Fillieule and Roux, the three invisibilizations are: (1) invisibilization of women within political struggles, (2) invisibilization in the ways in which official histories are constructed and written, and (3) invisibilization in the fact that social sciences disciplines were and still are androcentric. See Fillieule and Roux (2009, 13). Analysis informed by an intersectional approach highlights similar hierarchies between race, sexual practices, and other social categories of analysis that pervade political movements.

5 For Razmig Keucheyan (2010, 14), the cycle of the New Left started in 1956 with the Hungarian Uprising and the Suez War. It reached its highest point in 1968 and ended some ten years later, in 1977, with a defeat.

6 Among the feminist specialists of the Québec women's movement aware of this shifting dynamic is Diane Lamoureux, who makes several references to the relationship with the New Left in her first book *Fragments et collage* (1986) only to abandon all reference to this link to focus on the movement's direct relationship with the state

in another study, *L'amère patrie* (2001), published fifteen years later. On the change of negotiating partners in Italy, see Calabrò and Grasso (2004, 43).

7 From now on, the word will appear without italics.

8 I use the expression "'68 years" in reference to the period of important political protests at the end of the 1960s: the most well-known political moment of this kind took place in France, where it is referred to as *Mai 68* (May 68). While many countries in the Western world were affected by similar uprisings, it is important to keep in mind that these events should be analyzed within their own contexts. From now on, I use this expression without quotation marks.

9 This way of presenting the recent history of contemporary feminism looks like a long 1960s decade. We should keep in mind that women's living conditions in the 1950s were very different from those of the 1960s and the 1970s. However, it remains difficult to decide when one decade ends and the other begins.

10 According to Keucheyan (2010, 33), Marxism is the most powerful critical theory and most comprehensive paradigm, and it occupied a hegemonic position from the mid-nineteenth century until the 1970s. I suggest seeing Marxism as dominant but not as hegemonic. As such, it had an influence in shaping aspects of discourses and practices within many segments of feminism, though obviously not all of them.

11 Just as there are segments of feminism that continuously interact with the right.

12 When I speak of the historical or the old left in Italy, I am referring mainly to the Partito Comunista Italiano (PCI) and, to some extent, the union movement. I use the notion of "extra-parliamentary" to refer to organizations outside the parliamentary system. My research focuses mainly on Lotta Continua and Potere Operaio and, to a lesser extent, on Avanguardia Operaia and Il Manifesto. In Québec, the historical left is important but underestimated in the history of political movements. See Lévesque (1973). The Parti Québécois cannot be considered a leftist political party in the same sense as European leftist parties. Extra-parliamentary organizations played an important role in the history of Québécois feminism. My research focuses mainly on the student movement at the end of the 1960s as well as on political groups such as En Lutte! (In struggle!) and the Parti communiste ouvrier (PCO), two major Marxist-Leninist organizations, and the Ligue ouvrière révolutionnaire (LOR), a Trotskyist group that, in contrast to En Lutte! and the PCO, accepted the idea of a semi-autonomous women's movement. I thank Meg Luxton for pointing this distinction out to me.

13 During the period under study, the PCI was the most powerful communist party of its kind in Western Europe, obtaining more votes during legislative elections in the 1970s than any other political party, including the Democrazia Cristiana (DC). Nonetheless, the DC was able to maintain control over the government and its institutions from the end of the Second World War up until the early 1990s.

14 The "personal is political" first appeared as a slogan during feminist street demonstrations in the United States. Ever since she used it for the title of her essay published in the anthology *Notes from the Second Year: Women's Liberation; Major Writings of the Radical Feminists*, Carol Hanisch (1970) has most often been credited for the phrase. On its origin and political meanings, see Napikoski (2017).

15 The UDI is the most important and historical women's association at the national level. Originally, the UDI was supposed to represent all anti-fascist women involved

in the resistance at the end of Second World War. Another parliamentary party, the Partito Radicale (PR), is also mentioned in this research, but only through its federative connections with the Movimento di liberazione delle donne (MLD), which played an important role during the abortion struggle.

16 For the most part I translate *doppia militanza* as "double activism," although I sometimes use "double militancy," depending on the context. From now on, I use these terms without quotation marks.

17 In Québec, for instance, American feminist texts were received later than in the rest of Canada and were most often the product of translations by Anglo-Québécoise feminists. Similar obstacles around mediation and translation were observed in Italy. See Fraire (2002, 53); O'Leary and Toupin (1982, 1:27); and Péloquin (2007, 258).

18 In Québec and in Canada, settler society began with Contact, the first encounter between European settlers and Indigenous peoples, in 1492. In the Americas, excluding differentiated categories of Indigenous peoples, everyone is an immigrant, including French and British white settlers who stole the land through the process of colonialism. See Lawrence (2004) and Smith (2005).

19 See also Hull, Scott, and Smith (1982). The editors challenge the invisibility of African American women in feminist theories and feminist scholarship and reaffirm the importance of Black women's politics and feminism. Scott (2011, 82–83) highlights how we come to think that feminist theory is superior in the West and how translation is more likely to go from the West to the East, with the latter being asked to fill in the blanks with empirical data.

20 See, for instance, Cerchio Spezzato (1970); and L. Capobianco and Minneci (1981, 11–17).

21 "The Negro is comparison," translation from French by Charles Lam Markmann in 1967.

22 Similarly, Gayatri Spivak (1988a, 141–45; 2012, 226) underscores that there is nothing romantic or essentialist about being a subaltern. She adds later during an interview that the subaltern has no identity.

23 Using the term "international" here is excessive. Most of these events were limited to a small number of European and North American countries, with a slim representation from the developing world.

24 The research protocol signed several years ago, through the Institut de recherche en études féministes, between the Université du Québec à Montréal and the umbrella women's group Relais-Femmes is indicative of a close connection between feminists working in academia and feminists working within the community. I have explored the importance of studying this interaction from a feminist epistemological perspective in Michaud (2013). See also Spivak (2012).

25 All interviewees, in Québec and in Italy, signed a consent form. Their names and their affiliations were concealed to preserve their anonymity. I used the open-ended qualitative method of interviewing, with an average time of one hour and thirty minutes. Through these encounters, I collected numerous precious documents that were used as primary sources along with feminist journals, some films, conference proceedings, and so forth.

Chapter 2: Feminist Synergies with the Left

1 Ma di nuovo a ogni perquisizione e arresto, di nuovo a ogni minaccia, di nuovo a ogni licenziamento sono loro, le donne, loro che non c'entrano con la nostra rivoluzione, che tornano a essere le mogli, le mamme, le sorelle, le fidanzate, le figlie. Che vanno in Tribunale a chiedere un permesso, che preparono i pranzi, che telefonano, che scrivono, che mandano dei soldi. È vero: "Che c'entriamo noi con la loro liberazione? È vero, che c'entra con loro la nostra rivoluzione?"

2 See Bradbury (2011) on political parties and political actors active before and during the Act of Union that united Upper and Lower Canada in 1840. Although her study is on the social, political, and economic conditions of women whose status changed from being "wives to widows," her detailed analysis contrasts progressive and conservative discourses and laws – from the Patriotes to the Loyalists – that affected women's rights.

3 The Autonomy Movement was also called the "'77 movement." One is left to wonder what these dates – 1970, 1977 – really signified. Was it the end of mass mobilization or, rather, the intensification of state repression? Warren (2008, 12–13) contests the idea that the vitality of the period was overwhelmingly revolutionary.

4 According to Trimberger (1979), women were involved differently in the New Left than in the old left. The New Left had a stronger impact on the feminist movement of the 1960s and 1970s, while women remained relatively longer within the old left.

5 See Hall (1996, 269).

6 See Gagnon (1998) and Borduas (1987). Concerning the place of women within the group, see Smart (1998); Renaud (2004); and Dubois (2017).

7 In his inspiring and well-written *The Shouting Signpainters* – the French version appeared in 2009 with the title *Notre parti est pris* – Malcolm Reid (1972) compares and contrasts the two versions of nationalism. He convincingly demonstrates that Pierre Elliott Trudeau, a co-founder and director of the influential periodical *Cité libre,* never understood the new political context of Québec and, in fact, saw political movements influenced by nationalism as merely backwards versions of right-wing conservatism. For Trudeau, Québec would get rid of its social problems when it became more open to the idea of individual rights and freedoms, Anglo-Saxon style (20).

8 Warren proposes an analysis of these movements that differs from that offered by Day (2005). While supporting the argument that student organizations were highly critical of paternalism and the authoritarianism of the family and the education system, Warren (2008) describes at great length how youthfulness was affected by boredom. He characterizes the student milieu as lacking fervour (57) and as having difficulty regrouping around a united front and proposing a coherent political program (147). Thus, he suggests that the New Left was more preoccupied with individual happiness (117) than with collective action. Many segments of Warren's book give the impression that students were participating in an infantile burst of activities rather than in a politically conscious movement. Contrary to Warren, Day describes political movements of the 1960s through the 1980s as motivated by the desire to directly confront the power of the state. He contrasts the political mobilization of the 1960s with the generation of political movements of the early twenty-first

century, the latter being more interested in creating alternative forces than in attempting to overthrow the state and take power. Cleveland (2004) also contradicts Warren, arguing that the New Left was – and remains – at the left of the political spectrum and that it never was a new kind of liberalism.

9 In his detailed history of the extra-parliamentary group Potere Operaio (PO), Grandi (2003) shows how students had difficulty gaining workers' trust due to the long tradition of fascism within the student population (Balestrini and Moroni 2008, 198; Grandi 2003, 65). However, throughout the twentieth century, the movement maintained the capacity to organize and mobilize (Falquet 2005; Fillieule, Mathieu, and Roux 2007, 10; Jacquemart 2013; Michaud 2010, 2016; Roux et al. 2005; Surprenant and Biguaouette 2013; Taylor 1998).

10 Most of the interviews were conducted by Nadia Nappo on behalf of the research group Soggettività femminile (Women's subjectivity) and were published with the help of the Biblioteca Nazionale di Napoli.

11 According to Balestrini and Moroni (2008, 186–90), *La Zanzara* was a tremendous catalyst for the separation of the state and the church. This affair is also reported in a document from the Libreria delle donne (2005a). Chapter 6 discusses how women accused of having abortions were threatened with medical exams requested by state prosecutors in the hope they would find traces of their "crime." And, in 1981, two lesbians were arrested for kissing in public. Subjected to a medical exam, they were sentenced to seven months in prison. The sentence was appealed and overturned (Libreria delle donne 2005a).

12 At the end of his life, Vallières began to integrate Indigenous peoples into his writing.

13 Vallières's book had a difficult debut. In January 1967, the American authorities deported Vallières and Gagnon to Canada, where they were arrested for advocating rebellion. It was published during Vallières's trial in Montréal in 1968 and was immediately used as evidence against him. His sentence was overturned a year later by the Court of Appeal for being based solely on Vallières's writing and attitudes. He went to trial a second time on the same charges in 1969 and was sentenced to thirty months in prison. The book was banned by political authorities until 1973, when the Québec Court of Appeal ruled against a second publication ban.

14 See also Major (2013), who reproduces important articles from *Parti pris*.

15 For this book, I used the French translation, *Notre parti est pris*.

16 Micheline Dumont (1998, 32) is much less conciliatory than Reid in her assessment of the misogyny and sexual violence evidenced by many authors of *Parti pris*. On Malcolm Reid's book, see Simon (2004).

17 These Marxist extra-parliamentary groups had strong roots in Québec. The fact that there were branches elsewhere in Canada is, according to Diane Lessard (1989, 5), a mere phenomenon of exportation.

18 In their assessment of the decline of En Lutte!, Cyr, Lalande, and Poulin (1982) minimize the role of feminism in the crisis of the left in general and in the dissolution of extra-parliamentary groups. They put more emphasis on the influence of other movements, such as the gay movement, and the presence of disillusioned workers.

19 The Potere Operaio, unlike other extra-parliamentary organizations, never adopted Third World discourses, considering it opportunistic to place Third World liberation movements at the centre of the revolutionary process (Grandi 2003, 10).

20 There is a difference in the degree of violence between Québec and Italy, but Québec had seen similar moments of violence during the Marxist first phase.

21 Avanguardia Operaia (AO) is another extra-parliamentary group that operated during the same period and that had many active women members. Piera Zumaglino (1996, 93–97) published some testimonies of AO women members. I limit my analytical scope to the above-mentioned groups based on their more frequent appearance in the literature.

22 The PCI monopolized almost all seats on the left of the political spectrum in Parliament and blocked any other voices. In the 1970s, the PCI and the DC initiated negotiations called the *Compromesso storico* (Historic compromise), which would have allowed the communists to enter the government. These negotiations created tension from the extreme right to the extreme left and failed following Aldo Moro's kidnapping and murder in 1978. Extra-parliamentary groups, such as Il Manifesto–PdUP, Lotta Continua, and Potere Operaio tried but never succeeded in creating a coalition that would have given them enough political clout to gain some seats in Parliament (Annunziata 2007, 41–42; Donolo 1968, 96–97; Donolo 1976, 35).

23 This text is reprinted in Frabotta (1975, 177–85).

24 For a detailed account of these events, see Commissione femminile di Lotta Continua (1978, 244); G. Francescato (1975, 9–10); Guerra (2005, 45).

25 LC tried to re-emerge in the spring of 1977 during the occupation at the University of Rome–La Sapienza (see below). However, in the second edition of the history of the group, Luigi Bobbio (1988, vii) states that the group ended definitively at the Rimini Congress in 1976.

26 From now on, operaismo appears without italics.

27 At the centre of this experience was the leftist journal *Quaderni Rossi*, with the participation of Italian intellectuals like Toni Negri. Many later became involved in extra-parliamentary organizations such as Potere Operaio. The refusal to work discourse and movement, which I discuss in Chapter 3, came out of operaismo (Balestrini and Moroni 2008, 33–42; Grandi 2003; Murphey 2012, 68–76).

28 For an account of the origins of the name Lotta Femminista and the group's connection with Potere Operaio, see Zumaglino (1996, 104–7).

29 At the end of 1975, 20 percent of women quit the PdUP, just before its upcoming congress (Fraire 2002, 127; Gramaglia 1987, 36).

30 Some of these feminist documents, reproduced in Frabotta (1975), were printed in *Il Manifesto* and come from the small women's collective at the Istituto Gramsci di Roma (Gruppo Gramsci di Roma, 1973, 222–26) and the Gruppo di compagne del centro romano del *Il Manifesto* (1975, 227–48).

31 Luigi Bobbio (1988, 158) recalls that, during a congress in Naples in 1975, a male comrade opened a speech saying, "Il personale è politico" (The personal is political). He was using feminist discourse on women's sexuality and women's liberation to highlight the fundamental importance of achieving happiness.

32 In Toni Negri's "Quell'intelligente moltitudine" (This intelligent multitude), reprinted in Bianchi and Caminiti (2004), the feminist movement is evoked as a consciousness-affecting behaviour as well as the entirety of daily life (92). Other articles in this collection show how feminism was pertinent only when it was joined with other subjectivities and/or presented as an extension of the revolutionary project without changing the central meaning of leftist discourse.

33 Mi convicerebbe di più un "autocoscienza" maschile che partisse non già dalle frustrazioni del "private," bensi dalle frustrazioni del ruolo pubblico e di potere, dal luogo storico cioè nel quale viene affermata o negata l'identità maschile. Fino a che non verranno analizzate dai compagni le radici profonde che il potere ha nelle loro vite, non credo che vi sarà rinnovamento reale neanche nel loro modo di fare politica (Fraire 1977, 47).

34 Rossanda (2005) suggests in the last section of her memoir that the New Left emerged out of the need to develop a contextual analysis and to adopt strategies that would go beyond mass street demonstrations. She saw Avanguardia Operaia as the most reflective of the extra-parliamentary organizations, Potere Operaio as the most cultivated, and Lotta Continua the most widespread. These groups were opposed to the "here and now" of grassroots organizations, but, she argues, they never succeeded in doing more than a conventional political party (364). According to Anna Negri, Toni Negri's daughter, Rossanda softened her discourse against the extreme left during the 1980s. Anna Negri met Rossanda during her father's trial, and Rossanda offered much support during those difficult moments (A. Negri 2009, 244).

35 On 16 March 1978, Aldo Moro was kidnapped by Brigate Rosse and was in captivity for fifty-five days. His body was discovered in the trunk of a car on a street in Rome halfway between the headquarters of the DC and of the PCI. See the account by Braghetti and Tavella (2008). Braghetti was the only woman member of the cell responsible for kidnapping and killing Moro.

36 For more information about the accusation against Fred Rose, see Reiter (2016, 128–30).

37 See also Tavola rotonda (Round table), "Dissonanze," in Bianchi and Caminiti (2004, 228).

38 The level of state repression reached a high degree of intensity and generated international protests. See Sartre et al., "L'apello degli intellettuali francesi" (Appeal from French intellectuals). This document expressed dismay about the numbers of Italian intellectuals forced to take refuge in France and the level of criminalization of faculty and students of the Istituto di Scienze Politiche di Padova (Institute of political science of Padua), where Alisa del Re, Mariarosa Dalla Costa and Toni Negri were teaching.

39 Hall (1996, 268). Hall's text first appeared in Grossberg, Nelson, and Treichler (1992, 277–86). Hall talks about two types of interruptions at the centre: the second was race.

40 Hall (1996, 268; emphasis added). For an analysis of Hall's comments on feminism and a critical rereading of that period, which was perceived as being particularly tense in the CCCS, see Brunsdon (1996).

Chapter 3: Wages for Housework

1 Quel giorno mi è parso tutto chiaro: gli uomini prima facevano la rivoluzione lasciando le donne a casa ad accudire i figli, poi venivano messi dentro ed erano sempre le donne a crescere i figli, a lavorare, a occuparsi dei mariti in carcere, dando fondo ai risparmi o vendendo un appartamentino per pagare gli avvocati. Erano loro le vere rivoluzionarie, quelle che paravano i colpi, che preservavano, che andavano avanti (A. Negri 2009, 143).

2 For a good history of this movement in Italy, Canada, the United States, and in the international network, see Toupin (2014).

3 Mies (1986, 33) states that the debate on housework was a challenge to the Marxist left, more "to save Marx than to promote women's liberation," and that it contributed little to feminist discourse as a whole.

4 Some members of PO apparently took the issue personally. Toni Negri's daughter, Anna, says her father believed that Mariarosa Dalla Costa "si era inventata le lotte sul salario per il lavoro domestico per contrapporsi politicamente a lui" (had invented the struggle on the wages for housework just to oppose him politically) (A. Negri 2009, 54). Mariarosa Dalla Costa and Toni Negri were both members of the Department of Political Science at the University of Padua in the 1970s.

5 "Questo Lavoro di merda" (This shit job) was an oft-heard slogan (Bianchi and Caminiti 2004, 38). The refusal to work echoed the Mouvement des sacrifiés, an early 1980s Québécois solidarity coalition that demanded not only better work and better wages but also that work not define workers' lives. See Michaud (1987).

6 The hostility of the Italian extra-parliamentary left to the traditional bargaining process may have forced employers to accept specific measures such as the "150 hours" program. This program gave workers educational time during their working hours and was paid for by their employers. The argument was that workers had the same right to knowledge and culture as did their bosses. Working-class women – mainly wives of unionized workers – demanded their own access to knowledge and called for unions to offer courses to respond to their needs. From that moment, waves of working-class housewives filled 150 hours courses. Many courses were taught by feminist activists within a feminist curriculum. The interrelationship between feminism and working-class women, coming from a totally different context and with different history and knowledge, represented another moment of the politics of working from women's experience (Guerra 2005, 60; Melchiori 2006, 132–35). In the early 1980s, some feminists set up the Cooperativa Gervasia Broxon in Milan to fill these needs, followed by the Associazione per una Libera Università delle donne in 1987, which offered a multiplicity of courses to women who were mainly from working-class neighbourhoods. For more information about these organizations, see Melchiori (1987, 2006, 2015).

7 For that occasion, *Memoria* published a double issue (no. 19–20) bearing the title, "Il movimento femminista negli anni '70" (The feminist movement in the 1970s).

8 Guerra (2005, 38) mentions that the LF collective in Rome organized one of the first public demonstrations in 1971, calling for the abrogation of the law criminalizing abortion, and was part of the larger Roman feminist regrouping named Pompeo Magno.

9 Bianchi and Caminiti published a book in 1997 (reprinted in 2004), *Settantasette: la rivoluzione che viene* (Seventy-seven: the coming revolution), which reproduces a number of feminist contributions. *Gli Autonomi* is in three volumes: the one cited here is the second volume.

10 In their second volume published in 2007, Bianchi and Caminiti reproduce Federici's text first published in 1974 but ignore Dalla Costa and James's groundbreaking text, which also argues against the refusal of housework and against the role of the housewife.

11 In this chapter, I refer mainly to LF as the group that initiated the movement in the city of Padua. It is important to know, however, that the collective experienced a major split early on and changed its name to Comitato Triveneto par il salario domestico (Triveneto Committee for wages for housework). See Fraire (2002, 111); Rousseau (2016).

12 The workfare policies implemented since the 1990s in Canada and the United States can be used to illustrate the two opposing feminist strategies. One feminist strategy demands that the work of an individual in the home, who performs mainly activities related to caring for those who are dependent on their presence, be recognized as work and as a contribution to society. See Kittay (1998). The second feminist strategy, on the contrary, reiterates that the best way for women to get out of poverty is to gain their autonomy through security of income and, thus, better access to the job market. The latter strategy opposes staying at home, seeing it as being an imposed, rather than a real, choice. For a critique of these two strategies, see Michaud (2005).

13 According to Maria Mies (1986, 217; emphasis in original), "the vision of a society in *which all time is leisure time* and labour time is reduced to a minimum is for women in many respects a vision of horror, not only because housework and non-wage work have never been included in the labour that is supposed to be reduced by machines, but also because it *will be women* who have to restore to the then idle men a sense of reality, meaning and life."

14 See also a document originally published in 1971 by PO, "Rivoluzione Femminile e lotta proletaria" (Women's revolution and proletarian struggle) in Frabotta (1975).

15 While I was doing my master's research in the 1980s, I wanted to understand why the dream of developing a unitary front between the workers' movement, led by unions, and a coalition of new political subjects responsible for creating a multifaceted urban political front had failed. I used the notion of *hors-travail* to characterize a generation of young women and men either unemployed or underemployed and their critique of the unions' approach to the issue of work. Using the notion of *hors-travail* allowed me, with more or less success, to integrate housework into other political struggles emerging outside the boundaries of paid work (Michaud 1987, 7).

16 It is important to note that not all Marxist work rejected the demand of WfH during the period under study, in particular in English Canada. The first and groundbreaking texts are by Margaret Benston (1969) and Peggy Morton (1971), who opened the debate from which other important Anglo-Canadian research on women's domestic work followed. For a literature review on the housework debate, see Rousseau (2016).

17 The collective was short-lived and most of the anglophone WfH organizing took place in Toronto. The majority of francophone women's groups did not want to form

collectives on this subject at all (Toupin 2014, 22). I discuss the linguistic tension in Montréal in more detail in Chapter 5.

18 Returning to Italy, Dalla Costa described the Montréal conference as a success and stated that WfH was unanimously supported by nine hundred Canadian women (Lotta Femminista 1974).

19 The French version, *Le pouvoir des femmes et la subversion sociale,* was available in 1973. A brief review of the document appeared in *Québécoises deboutte!* in March of the same year.

20 O'Leary and Toupin are referring to the sixth issue of *Québécoises deboutte!* (June 1973), which begins with an article celebrating Mother's Day and demanding a true holiday for mothers and housewives. Mother's Day was enthusiastically celebrated by the Vichy Regime in France during the Second World War. It was surprising for a feminist journal to promote Mother's Day, given its fascist and conservative dimensions. The content of the article is also problematic, making a direct connection between Mother's Day and May 1 celebrations. See Centre des femmes (1983b, 167–71).

21 In a footnote, James (1997, 39) goes deeper into the issue of the socialization of services, arguing that these demands for services are part of "capitalist planning."

22 La maison, le quartier ne sont donc pas des endroits de détente et de liberté annexes à l'usine, où par hasard il y a des femmes qui sont des servantes personnelles des hommes. Au contraire, le quartier est l'autre moitié de l'organisation capitaliste, l'autre secteur de l'exploitation capitaliste, l'autre source cachée de la plus-value. Le point central de cette usine sociale qu'est le quartier, c'est la ménagère qui produit un bien, la force de travail (Centre des femmes 1983c, 191).

23 Feminist leaders of the WfH argued that Black women were not mere appendices of the working class but, rather, an integral component of that class. This point was made during the interview with *Québécoises deboutte!* and reflected the perspective in England and the United States (Centre des femmes 1983c, 193).

24 As an epilogue to Québec's relationship with the WfH, in 1981, the feminist journal *La vie en rose* attempted to revive the debate around wages for housework with "Gagner son ciel ou gagner sa vie? le salaire au travail ménager" (Going to heaven or earning a living? Wages for housework). This special issue essentially reproduced texts from Silvia Federici and the IFC, the leading force behind the New York collective. The journal presented the positions of several women's groups and women's commissions within unions, most of which opposed the WfH. These groups ranged from the most moderate AFÉAS (Association féminine d'éducation et d'action sociale) (Women's Association for Education and Social Action) to extra-parliamentary groups like En Lutte! and the PCO, to women's commissions active within major unions. *LVR*'s own analysis is contained in a single page. See "Gagner son ciel ou gagner sa vie?" (1981).

25 Again, see Giuliani and Lombardi-Diop (2013) on the process of racialization in Italy.

26 Louise Toupin (2014, 389–90n49) gives details of this American collective and its document, *The Autonomy of Black Lesbian Women,* which was presented during an international event organized by the Toronto Wages Due Lesbians collective. In 1996, Toupin was able to consult the text at the Canadian Women's Movement

Archives. The archives have since been reorganized, and, unfortunately, the document seems to have disappeared. Piera Zumaglino (1996, 109) emphasizes the importance of race to the James collective in London and the mobilizing strength that characterized the group regarding this issue.

27 James (1997, 35).

28 Other critiques suggested that LF's political program was a mere replica of the economist demands proposed by the extra-parliamentary left and subordinated to the capitalist system of exploitation (Bicchiere and Roditi 1974, 99). Kathi Weeks (2011, 2) makes the same argument, suggesting that the entire issue of work hardly made it into the field of political theory. She also uses a similar metaphor to Fraire (2002, 111), who stated that the demand for wages acted more as an *immagine provocatoria* (image of provocation) than as a theory.

29 Le implicazioni politiche di un simile discorso ci sembrano però difficilmente accettabili perché sanzionano definitivemente il ruolo della donna nella famiglia e instizionalizzano la sua esclusione dal mondo produttivo maschile. Questo vorrebbe dire riconoscere socialmente alla donna di essere il "negativo" dell'uomo, pagarla per questo compito e non mettere in discussione realmente il patriarcato, inteso come il potere degli uomini, in quanto sesso, di disporre della capacità lavorativa della donna. La proposta politica del salario pecca inoltre di economicismo laddove non dà ragione del fatto che fare la casalingua non è solo un lavoro ma è soprattutto un ruolo, la cui implicazioni a livelli profondi non sono ribaltabili né tanto meno analizzabili soltanto con un più giusto trattamento socio-economico della donna.

30 The first two issues of *Sottosopra* were voluminous compared to later ones, filled with documents sent by LF. Understandably, *Sottosopra* stopped asking women's groups to send materials for publication as it lacked the human resources necessary to fulfill its original mandate. The founders of the Milanese journal acknowledged that this type of reporting – as well as the impossibility of collecting all women's experience – can have a negative impact on the readership and on feminist journalism (Libreria delle donne 2005b, 37).

Chapter 4: Double Activism and Feminist Separatism

1 I use the word "sex," instead of "gender," whenever it is the word used in original documents. I do the same with the word "homosexual" when the words "gay" and "lesbian" are not in the original.

2 "La nostra società, oltre ad essere divisa in classi, presenta anche una situazione castale in cui sono costrette a vivere determinate persone a causa di caratteristiche fisiche ben identificabili come il sesso e il colore. Alla casta si è assegnati fin dalla nascita e non è possibile uscirne con nessun tipo di azione individuale" (Cerchio Spezzato 1970, 127).

3 At the trial, Balcer told the judge: "Si vous ne reconnaissez pas les femmes comme jurés, comment pouvez-vous les reconnaître comme témoins? Moi, en mon âme et conscience je n'ai pas le droit de collaborer à cette discrimination faite aux femmes du Québec" (If you do not recognize women as jury members, how can you accept them as witnesses? I, in my soul and my conscience, do not have the right to participate in this

discrimination against the women of Québec). Lise Balcer spent four months of a six-month sentence in prison for contempt of court. See Péloquin (2007, 37).

4 See the following documents, all of which are found in Fabrotta (1978), concerning leftist groups reluctantly setting up women's commissions and feminist pressure to respond to women's issues: in particular, "Ragioni e torti del femminismo" (Rights and wrongs of feminism) by Adriana Seroni; "Lettera aperta ai compagni del Manifesto a proposito della question femminile" (Open letter to the comrades of the manifesto concerning the women's question) by Luciana Castellina; "Il rapporto tra il movimento della donna e il movimento operaio" (Relationship between the women's movement and the workers' movement) by Avanguardia Operaia; "Le prospettive del movimento delle donne e lo sviluppo di una linea femminista di masse" (Women's movement's perspectives and the development of a mass feminist line) by Maria Teresa Battaglino (1978); "Comunicato della Commissione femminile di Lotta Continua" (Press release from the women's commission of Lotta Continua); and "Le cose buone e le cose cattive e il modo di affrontarle" (The good and the bad things and the way to confront them) by Adriano Sofri.

5 The Unione donne Italiane was created in 1944 by a group of women who, regardless of their political affiliations, decided to join their efforts to end fascism. UDI was a truly national organization with regional groups throughout the country. Several years after the Second World War, the UDI came to be identified with the PCI as several of its leaders and members were PCI members. UDI members often praise it for its achievements regarding the emancipation of Italian women. On the history of UDI, see Ombra (2005). The book features posters organized by themes such as emancipation, the vote, political mobilization, campaigns for peace, paid work, civil rights, welfare, and feminism. See also Guadagni (1984), which analyzes PCI's attitudes towards UDI, and see excerpts from Ergas (1987), and Hellman (1987). For the ways in which UDI dealt with feminism during the 1970s, see two collections of essays edited by Frabotta (1975, 1978), especially documents analyzing UDI's most significant conventions, with Luciana Viviani (1975). The introduction to the second section of Frabotta's 1978 collection is particularly pertinent. Finally, one of my interviewees in Palermo spoke about the division between the North and the South, noting that not all UDI sections followed the national organization's decision to ascribe to the type of feminism evolving in the North. The conference proceedings "I modi e le tematiche del femminismo a Napoli (Modes and themes of feminism in Naples), 1981, dedicated an entire section to the UDI in this southern region.

6 Double activism has another profile in the case of the Movimento di Liberazione delle donne. MLD was federated with the Partito Radicale (Radical party), which promoted free abortion. The group worked in tandem with the PR on issues, including the opening of consultori (feminist health centres) and the practice of obtaining illegal abortions before the adoption of an abortion law by the Italian Parliament.

7 Double activism was also common within the union movement. Several of Lilli and Valentini's (1979) interviewees were members of local, regional, and national unions. See their chapter, "Ma a pagare siamo ancora noi" (We are still the ones who pay the price) (172–81) and the interview with Annamaria Crispino, "Ti costringono ad essere in qualche modo una leader" (They are asking you to be some sort of a leader)

(272–78). A significant experience of feminist organizing among women union members comes from the creation of the Intercategoriale donne di Torino (Women's coalition of Turin), created by activists from different unions in the region. Its main objective was to open a space to hear women's voices concerning their working conditions and demands. The coalition highlighted the need for women to meet outside their respective unions. See Giorda (2007) for detailed information on women union activists, many of whom were involved in feminist struggles, practising autocoscienza at their workplaces. See Ines (1979) for a review of Giorda's book. In many other Italian cities, the desire to meet outside traditional and official union structures was also evident. For further reading, see the section on feminism and the union movement in Borello (1981); Carlini and Pasqua (1979); and Fraire (2002, 142–48).

8 I interviewed a woman who was a member of a small feminist collective in the Sicilian town of Sciacca, where she lives. She said that many members of her collective defended the diversity of political views. They were members of different political parties but none of them claimed to be controlled by a particular party.

9 È il modo di porsi – nei confronti del mondo e di se stesse – di tutte le donne "autocoscienti": che tentino, con un projetto di vita, le difficile strade dell'emancipazione avendo in testa l'utopia della liberazione. Per la sindicalista la vera doppia militanza non è stare contemporaneamente nel sindacato e nel collettivo femminista: ma "come" stare nel sindacato. Per la comunista, non è come conciliare partito e gruppo, ma "come" vivere dentro il partito (Lilli 1979, 27).

10 Cosa vuol dire *doppia militanza?* Innanzitutto prendere parte alla vita di partito (dalla reunione di sezione, all'intervento nel quartiere, nel sindacato, nella scuola, ecc) e prendere parte alla vita del movimento femminista (fatta di piccolo gruppo di autocoscienza, riunioni di collettivo, spesso di intervento nel sociale). Doppie, triple riunioni ogni giorno, lo svuotamento, cioè, di tutto quello nel sul nuovo modo di far politica le donne hanno acquisito. Significa essere militante a tempo pieno, un modello che soffoca e contraddice, schiaccia e stravolge la vita, oltreché la coscienza nuova, delle donne femministe del PdUP. E d'altra parte la doppie militanza per tutta una fase è sembrata essere l'unico modo per guarantire l'autonomia delle compagne e quella del movimento dal pericolo di ricreare da un lato la commissione femminile, il ghetto delle donne, d'all' altro l'avanguardia esterna che va nel movimento a portare la "linea" del partito (Fraire 2002, 125–26).

11 *Differenze* published one short but negative narrative that concluded: "Questa è la doppia militanza, cioè militanza in senso unico per il partito o per l'organizzazione in cui ci si trova a lavorare nella cui ottica noi siamo ancora la 'questione femminile' una tra i tanti problemi della società, e nemmeno tra i più importanti" (This is what double activism is, meaning a double activism going in one direction, for the party or for the organization in which we are currently working and with the same optic we have: the "woman question" is one of many problems in society and not even the most important one) (Cloti 1977, 38).

12 One of the differences between the FLFQ and the CdF was the size of their membership: an average of twenty-five to thirty-nine women filled the FLFQ's regular meetings, with a membership of over sixty women during its height. In contrast, the CdF

worked with a reduced membership and smaller cells in order to better coordinate its activities.

13 The Gramsci women's collective in Rome is an example of a collective that attempted to articulate leftist politics with feminism by proclaiming the need for an autonomous feminist movement, though the collective maintained a classical approach to double activism. See Gruppo Gramsci di Roma (1973); Zumaglino (1996, 185).

14 This is also true of MLD's members. After the '68 Years and the strength of 1970s feminism, several members of UDI began to question the pertinence of their organization and decided to leave. See Libera Cerchia (1981).

15 In Italy, *consultori* (health centres) are known as public institutions that specialize in family planning. From now on, this word is written without italics. During the abortion struggle, Italian activists created and managed their own feminist consultori, providing information on contraception and offering abortions.

16 The homosexual movement during this period focused mostly on lesbian and gay subjectivities. The bisexual question was marginalized or addressed negatively; transsexuality was invisible and intersexuality was missing from the world of possibilities. Queer politics would come later. The theory of sexual difference within feminism negatively affected the development of a genuine queer theory in France as well as in Italy. On this particular issue in France, see S. Bourcier (2018).

17 According to Maria Schiavo (2002, 25), the few lesbians in Fuori! were in many ways captive to the long history of working-class culture and struggles in Turin. She says this explains the group's connections with the extra-parliamentary left.

18 Early feminist literature exploring the politics of sexual difference, like "Rivolta femminile," fell short of declaring lesbians to be part of the feminist project (Schiavo 2002, 35).

19 Muraro and Cigarini were members of Gruppo 4, which authored "Più donne che uomini" (Gruppo 4 1983). In 1975, they founded the Libreria delle donne of Milan. Luisa Muraro with many others created Diotima, a group of feminist philosophers at the University of Verona.

20 Teresa de Lauretis (1990), the translator of the Libreria's *Non credere di avere dei diritti,* as well as Bono and Kemp (1991) translate *affidamento* as "entrustment." Below, I explain why I prefer to translate it as a form of tutelage rather than as entrustment. However, because it is difficult to translate, I leave the term in italics.

21 Note that abortion was still in the criminal code. Like the FLFQ, the CdF came under the microscope of police surveillance. Its office in Montréal was searched twice, and the subscription list of *Québécoises deboutte!* was confiscated. The police were looking for evidence of illegal abortion activities.

22 In the Fondazione Elvira Badaracco Archives I found a series of documents that present the steps in the creation of the feminist journal *Sottosopra* and of the Libreria delle donne of Milan. These documents, "Come e perché è stato fatto questo giornale" (How and why we are making this journal); "La situazione e la nostra politica" (The situation and our politics) (n.d.); "Rapporto analitico e movimento delle donne" (Analytical relations and the women's movement) (1974); "Madre buona e cattiva" (Good and bad mothers) (1974); and a two-page document signed by "Alcuni gruppi di donne di Milano" (Some Milanese women's groups) (1972), nicely

summarize the process of creating a feminist separatist movement. See also the main publication of the Libreria, *Non credere di avere dei diritti* (Libreria delle donne 2005b), which traces the genealogy of feminist separatism in Italy.

23 "original, funny, human, diversified, international and multiracial, that it 'would make visible all struggles, researches and creations made by women, here and elsewhere' and would at last 'provoke necessary debates within feminism itself'" (Guénette (1985b, 5).

24 See the handwritten document "Rapporto analitico e movimento delle donne" (Analytical relations and the women's movement) (1974).

25 See "Madre buona e cattiva" (Good and bad mothers) (1974).

26 "Più donne che uomini," written by the Gruppo 4, was first published in *Sottosopra* in 1983. Representatives of the Libreria delle donne of Milan reproduced the text within which authors analyzed the failure of a decade of feminist practices and the unease with which emancipated women survive within masculine institutions. This text was translated into several languages and was later reprinted in the collective's most famous book, *Non credere di avere dei diritti* (2005). It is worth noting that the Libreria prefers using the word *libertà* (freedom) over *liberazione,* which was the dominant notion within Italian feminism. The Libreria considers that liberation was still too closed to the idea of emancipation. I return to these important documents throughout the book.

27 Two representatives of Libreria told me that the idea of describing the Italian feminist movement as two opposite axes was borrowed from the sociological model and that it was incorrect.

28 The same can be said about the location of lesbianism in Québécois feminism. In 1978, the journal *Les têtes de Pioche* published an exchange of views about the presence of lesbians in feminist collectives. The document crudely reveals the level of anxiety expressed by heterosexuals when facing lesbian sexual subjectivities. See Rioux (1978); Tremblay (1978).

29 Come primo momento [autocoscienza] è importante (benché le donne il piccolo gruppo lo abbiano sempre fatto, al mercato, "in fontana"). Purché sia chiaro che è solo un primo momento: anche perché gli elementi nevrotici circolano solo in quel piccolo, ristretto cerchio: e, se non ci si apre all'esterno, lì rimangono (Lilli and Valentini 1979, 136).

Chapter 5: The Illusion of Unity and Homogeneity

1 It also signified rejecting any claim of the integration of women into public/political institutions.

2 Personal narratives that focus on the tension between lesbianism and feminism appeared in feminist journals such as *La vie en rose, Québécoises deboutte!, Des luttes et des rires, Effe, Bollettino delle donne, Quotidiano donna,* and many others. The American influence on lesbian organizing is notable. See in particular Charlotte Bunch's translated segment of her book, *Not by Degree,* in Bunch (1981). On the importance of the American influence in the analysis of feminism and lesbianism on lesbian subjectivity, see Durocher (1990); Pomeranzi (1984); Zumaglino (1996, 159–65).

3 "I ogni senso del termine, c'è bisogno di una donna più grande di sé" (Libreria delle donne 2005b, 142).
4 Passerini (2005, 182) lists the women who spent a few years abroad and imported consciousness-raising to Italian feminist collectives.
5 Serena Castaldi was a founder of Anabasi in 1970. Its objective was to bring American feminism into Italy by publishing translations and practising consciousness-raising. Carla Lonzi set up the Rivolta femminile collective in Rome the same year (Passerini 2005). She wrote, with others, the *Manifesto Rivolta femminile*. Soon collectives were created in many northern Italian cities.
6 In 1971, the population of Québec was 6,027,765, 80.8% of whom were French-speaking and 14.7% English-speaking. Canada had a total population of 21,650,000. See Statistics Canada, "Population selon la langue officielle parlée à la maison et la géographie, 1971–2016," https://www150.statcan.gc.ca/t1/tbl1/fr/tv.action?pid=1510000501.
7 In May 1971, the United States had a population of about 206,676,000. See US Department of Commerce, "Estimate of the Population in United States to May 1, 1971," in *Current Population Reports: Population Estimates and Projections*, series P-25, no. 462 (June 1971): 1–2, https://www2.census.gov/library/publications/1971/demographics/P25-462.pdf.
8 Here is a series of moments indicative of tensions between the two linguistic communities. In 1970, the FLFQ refused to participate in the organization of an American conference against imperialism in Montréal. In a letter sent to the United States ("Lettre à des féministes américaines," reproduced in O'Leary and Toupin 1982), the FLFQ explained its motives, phrased in Québécois nationalist and anti-Anglo and anti-American imperialist language. Two years later, the CdF did not participate in the Canadian Caravan that marched across the country demanding free abortion on demand. In 1973, the CdF also refused to support the creation of the anglophone feminist group the Montreal Feminist Association, arguing that it was too reformist and opportunist.
9 For instance, the American self-help movement had some impact: *Our Bodies, Ourselves* was published in French in 1984 under the title *Notre corps, nous-mêmes*. Also, the francophone-anglophone divide masks all other divides not just in Québec but also in the rest of Canada. To read more on Canadian feminist nationalisms, see Davia Stasiulis (1999), who offers a complex and sophisticated analysis of how three feminisms – Indigenous, francophone, and anglophone – evolved separately and competitively, and interacted only on rare occasions. See also Green (2009) on Québécois postcolonial thought and its ambiguities.
10 "accettare la competizione con il maschio e dirigere tutti i suoi sforzi per cercare di 'essere uguale al maschio,' con il risultato di diventare 'il negro con la testa da bianco,' discriminato tra bianchi e odiato tra i neri" (Cerchio Spezzato 1970, 127).
11 "An autonomous woman and one who does not have a feminist consciousness is a prospective man, someone potentially unable to understand the most subtle oppressions at work inside of her but capable of using them against someone else" (Brossard 1976, 4).

12 Luisa Passerini (2005, 192) emphasizes this point when she writes that only white feminist influences coming from the United States and Western European countries were felt. There is not a trace of Eastern European women writers in Italian translations of foreign texts. Black feminist writings from the United States were not translated.

13 Bill C-31, passed into law in 1985, was supposed to end the Indian Act's discrimination against women, but it and Bill 3, passed into law in 2010, did not solve the difference in status between men and women. On Indigenous women's struggles that led to Bill C-31 and that partially reinstated their Indigenous status, see Altamirano-Jiménez (2013, 63) and Lawrence (2004). On how Indigenous women reached out to feminist/women's groups in Québec to join their struggles, see Ricci (2017, 2018).

14 Ha impedito che venisse indagata in modo consistente la relazione tra costruzione razziale del Sé e costruzione di genere ... l'intreccio tra norma sessuale e norma razziale pone in luce il nesso tra i meccanismi discorsivi che permettono al soggetto di autodefinirsi in termini di bianchezza e il fenomeno di nazionalizzazione delle donne italiane e della loro progressiva immissione all'interno del corpo simbolico e politico della nazione in difesa della purezza razziale (Giuliani and Lombardi-Diop 2013, 7).

15 The above-mentioned article "Qual'è ora la via da seguire?" (B.L. 1970) is one of the few translated texts that attempted the intersection between race and gender, and it might have pleased Italian activists due to its strong reference to Marxism.

16 The article was originally signed by Christine, who was none other than Christine Delphy. In 1980, Delphy published "Libération des femmes an dix" in *Questions féministes*. Véronique O'Leary (1982, 11), in "Pour ne pas repartir à zéro," commented on this article, noting how difficult it is to transmit feminist experience from one generation of activists to the next.

17 *Le quotidien des femmes* was issued by the French group Psychanalyse et politique.

18 The following list is not inclusive and contains francophone and anglophone feminist journals published by women's groups: *The Other Woman* (1972–76), *Long Time Coming* (1973–76), *Les têtes de Pioche* (1976–79), *Pluri-elles* (1977–79), *Des luttes et des rires de femmes* (1979–81), *La vie en rose* (1980–87), *Communiqu'elles* (1981–91), *Treize* (1984–2001), *Amazones d'hier et lesbiennes d'aujourd'hui* (since 1982). Titles outside the Montréal area include *Les Bulletin du RAIF* (1973–95), *Marie-Géographie* (1983–87). See Dumont and Toupin (2003). For a list of all academic, governmental, scientific, and cultural periodicals and journals between 1778 and 1989, see Fortin (1993).

19 Both encounters took place in France in 1972 in Tranche-sur-Mer and in Vieux-Villez. A third one, in Italy, was organized at Varigotti, where Antoinette Fouque was asked to be more explicit about her views on psychoanalysis (Guerra 2005, 51–52; Schiavo 2002, 87; Zumaglino 1996, 233).

20 According to Christine Delphy (1980, 10–12), the group Psychanalyse et politique judged that women had reached a point beyond revolt and that feminism needed to celebrate its victory against oppression.

21 During my stay in Naples in 2010, I interviewed a representative of the group Nemesiache/Tre Guinee, who vehemently disagreed that Milan was where it began.

22 "La madre prima del padre" si rivelava essere in quel lontano presente, infatti, più che una donna che noi già potessimo chiamare per nome, ancora una madre preedipica, pesante eredità di tutto ciò che volevamo chiamare. Lo penso oggi: allora non le davamo questo attributo, la chiamavamo solo "madre," e sentivamo che era per noi una figura nuova (Schiavo 2002, 88).

23 The word "politique" in the name Psychanalyse et politique was apparently chosen to highlight the political nature of women's liberation through the use of psychoanalysis.

24 Schiavo noticed a difference between the French and Italian words for the practice of psychoanalysis. For the French the chosen word is *analyse* (analysis), while the Italians refer to the *inconscio* (unconscious) (Schiavo 2002, 91).

25 Schiavo (2002, 89) also mentions Melandri's fears of infantilism as the disease of feminism. For more on Melandri's feminist thought, see Melchiori (2015).

26 According to Schiavo (2002, 63), members of Psychologie et politique were for the most part clients of Fouque's own psychoanalytic practice.

27 Bono and Kemp (1991, 9).

28 In 1974, *Sottosopra* published an issue titled "Esperienze dei gruppi femministi in Italia" (Experiencing feminist groups in Italy).

29 "Per sua natura era una pratica politica a termine, non prolungabile oltre il suo frutto che fu di far nascere nelle donne la consapevolezza di essere un sesso altro, non subordinato né assimilabile a quello maschile" (Libreria delle donne 2005b, 39). See also Piera Zumaglino (1996, 36) on the failure to transfer consciousness of oppression to collective action.

30 The authors borrowed the title from the 1933 novel by Ivy Compton-Burnett.

31 "Come se la donna fosse totalmente fuori da questo modello, come se l'essere 'proprietà' o 'parte di' non avesse radici anche nell'inconscio della donna e valenze ambigue, di amore e di violenza, in entrambi."

32 "Astratto, per esempio, è vedere la sessualità vaginale comme atto di colonizzazione, e la clitoride come unico organo 'specificamente,' 'autenticamente' femminile" (Melandri 2000, 29). See also Melandri (1972). For Melandri, the main problem with the theory of sexual difference is that it conceives of women's sexuality in biological terms.

33 See Chapter 3, note 6, for a description of this program.

34 Melandri argues that, due to a major flux of immigration from abroad, the 1980s were the first moment in feminist history that race became an important problem for the movement. I would like to thank Francesca Dall'Acqua, who brought to my attention Melandri's probable lack of recognition of the presence of race as an issue and hence for its absence in her collective writing workshops.

35 Luisa Muraro and Lia Cigarini, two well-known feminist theoreticians of sexual difference, were members of Gruppo 4.

36 *Sottosopra* is often identified with a colour. For instance, *Sottosopra verde* (green) referred to the issue in which the text "Più donne che uomini" appeared in 1983.

37 Non si tratta di qualcosa che ci impedisce dell'esterno. Pensarci e presentarci come vittime di discriminazione antifemminile non significa più l'essenziale della nostra condizione. Rischia ormai di essere una copertura. Si sa che, specialmente quando le condizioni materiali sono più dure, la discriminazione c'è o può ripresentarsi. Ma si tratta di una difficoltà ben riconoscibile, che sappiamo come combattere e che non riesce ad inferiozzare una donna nè a farla sentire inadeguata. Per contro, l'esperienza della propria inadeguatezza contribuisce non poco a rafforzare i residui o i ritorni di discriminazione (Gruppo 4 1983, 1).

38 Che tra donne che si frequentano abbia luogo questo riconoscere un valore e questo fare *affidamento,* crea un precedente di forza; vuol dire avere un riferimento che conferma integralmente l'essere donna, con il più di cui è alla ricerca. Nel riconoscimento della disparità, inoltre, sempre che sia praticabile, trovano una regola, un dinamismo e quindi una fecondità, le elementari emozioni legate all'antico rapporto con la madre. Con il riconoscimento del di più che un altre può essere, quelle antiche emozioni riescono ad esprimersi in positivo liberandosi dall'ambiguità e liberando noi dalla discriminazione (Gruppo 4 1983, 1; emphasis added).

39 The notion of *affidamento* does not exist in the lexicon of Québécois feminism, but it was common to connect more experienced activists with younger ones to ensure that feminist history and collective objectives were not lost when new members joined the group. See O'Leary and Toupin (1982, 171).

40 Bocchetti is the founder of the Virginia Woolf Centre of Rome. Although she expresses some difficulty with the theory of sexual difference, she accepts the practice of *affidamento.* On this last point, see Martucci (2008, 52).

41 Diotima is mentioned by Socrates as the woman who taught him the maieutic (or "Socratic") method of philosophy. See Diotima (1987, 180).

42 The three seminars were "Essere donna pensare filosoficamente" (Think philosophically as a woman) (1985); "Le figure della differenza" (The face of difference) (1986); and "Il pensiero della differenza" (The thought of difference) (1988).

43 Conni Capobianco says that Transizione tried to implement similar experiences elsewhere in the South without success. She said it was her dream to see in Naples a women's collective as notorious as those in Milan (C. Capobianco n.d., 42).

44 Vincenza Perilli (2006) reserves a significant portion of her article to discuss the ways in which the theory of sexual difference treated issues such as race.

45 Teresa de Lauretis's sole negative comment about the book concerns the lack of consideration for lesbianism: this word appears only once in *Non credere di avere dei diritti* and only as a negation of its validity. The Libreria delle donne of Milan seems to have adopted the Psychanalyse et politique position, which denies any revolutionary value to lesbianism (Schiavo 2002). In 2005, the Gruppo Soggettività lesbica (Lesbian group on subjectivity) of Milan critiqued de Lauretis's remarks concerning the ways in which the theory of sexual difference avoids lesbian eroticism and subjectivities (Gruppo di Soggettività lesbica 2005, 161). Nevertheless, de Lauretis denies that the theory of sexual difference is biologically essentialist, implying a "difference of symbolization." She writes: "Seen in this light, the conception of sexual difference as 'originary human difference' proposed by *Sexual Difference* is less an essentialist – biological or metaphysical – view of woman's difference (from man) than a historical

materialist analysis of 'the state of emergency' in which we live as feminists" (de Lauretis 1990, 13).

46 Mangiacapre was a true believer in sexual difference and a separatist, but that was not her only focus. One member of the Nemesiache I interviewed in 2010 argued that sexual difference was invented by Mangiacapre.

47 Rossi-Doria's speech at a conference entitled "Nuova destra e cultura reazionaria negli anni ottanta" (New right and reactionary culture in the 1980s) was reproduced in *Memoria*. See Rossi-Doria (1984). Her text is a response to Noberto Bobbio's genealogy of leftist discourses on equality. Bobbio's response to her is typical of the deafness of the left vis-à-vis feminist demands. Their exchange can be found in *Memoria* 11–12 (2–3) 1984.

Chapter 6: Angel Makers or Troublemakers?

1 Tremate tremate, le streghe sono tornate.

2 See O'Leary and Toupin (1982); Michaud (1995, 56). The Henry Morgentaler clinic in Montréal received some of these referrals before the Comité pour l'avortement libre et gratuit offered the service to women upon demand (D. Lamoureux 1983).

3 Long before this conference took place in 1971, the French periodical *Nouvel Observateur* had published the *Manifeste des 343 salopes* (343 bitches' manifesto). The manifesto denounced the horrible conditions under which women were forced to abort in France and declared its commitment to the struggle for women's right to have an abortion. Many of the 343 names were well-known women – including Simone de Beauvoir, Catherine Deneuve, Marguerite Duras, Agnès Varda, and Monique Wittig – who declared they had had an abortion and had risked their health and lives because of the danger of underground practices. This manifesto is still remembered more than forty-five years later.

4 The Comité de lutte pour l'avortement libre et gratuit (Committee of struggle for free abortion) had published astonishing statistics concerning francophone hospitals, the great majority of which did not have a therapeutic committee responsible for approving women's requests for sterilization and therapeutic abortions. In 1975, of 5,657 abortions performed legally in Québec, 5,418 took place in anglophone hospitals (Michaud 1995).

5 Unlike other women's services groups, which were more numerous and widespread in the province, the Women's Health Centres Network never had more than six centres: Centre de santé des femmes du Quartier (Montréal), Centre de santé des femmes de Québec (Québec City), Centre de santé des femmes de la Mauricie (Trois-Rivières), Clinique des femmes de l'Outaouais (Hull), Centre de santé des femmes de Sherbrooke (Sherbrooke), and Centre de santé des femmes de Lanaudière (Joliette). The latter two centres did not perform abortions: Sherbrooke supposedly because the university hospital provided abortion services that the centre did not want to duplicate, Lanaudière because the pro-life movement was very active and threatening in the region. At the turn of the 1990s, two health centres had ceased to exist (Québec City and Lanaudière), and the Clinique des femmes de l'Outaouais had separated from the network, deciding

to perform abortions only. Among the remaining centres, Montréal and Trois-Rivières were having difficulty balancing their practice of abortion with self-help practices (Michaud 1995).

6 This type of confrontation was equally important during the campaign surrounding the law on divorce, which was not originally a feminist struggle. When the divorce referendum was held, it was with mixed feelings that many feminists took the side of the dissolution of marriage, opposing the PCI. Many women feared that the law would be used by men to justify deserting their families and responsibilities. After seeing the results in favour of the divorce law in 1974, the PCI admitted its mistake in judging working-class families as being too conservative and, thus, not ready for social change. On the PCI's attitude during the divorce debates and referendum, see Gramaglia (1975a).

7 Feminist journals such as *Sottosopra, Effe,* and many others published regularly on issues surrounding women's health, the politics of abortion, and the question raised by the relationship of feminist consultori with public institutions. Many of these articles influenced discussions within the movement, exposing major splits over the abortion struggle. In addition, *Effe* published letters and articles from women talking about their experience of having an abortion abroad or in Italy. In 1975 and 1976, political debates surrounding the adoption of a new law appeared in *Effe,* providing information on what was happening within feminist circles, the best medical method to use for abortions, and the promotion of alternative feminist medicine in opposition to traditional medical practices. *Effe* published book reviews and reported on regional and national activities organized by women's groups and feminist consultori as well as information on reproductive rights in general and on abortion in Italy and abroad.

8 See Frabotta (1978), who reprints an Avanguardia Operaia document that presents this demographic argument in support of abortion.

9 The UDI changed its position in 1972 during its national congress on motherhood. The decriminalization of abortion was on the agenda, and the organization declared its support for the practice in public services. In 1973, the UDI went further in support of self-determination, but the influence of PCI officials still had a strong impact on many feminist consultori. Communist officials played a role when the Policlinico hospital was occupied by feminists from the consultori of San Lorenzo in Rome, an event I look at later in this chapter. See Silvia Tozzi (1979, 1984).

10 There were exceptions: during the campaign surrounding the two referenda on law 194, some associations of Catholic women supported women's self-determination and the law and dissociated from the Roman Catholic Church. See Coordinamento donne cattoliche per la 194 (1981).

11 In Italy, ordinary citizens have the right to submit proposed legislation to Parliament if supported by at least fifty thousand voters. This provision of the Constitution is called "bills of popular initiative."

12 Many groups under the umbrella feminist collective Col di Lana produced documents with the same perspective, some of them in *Sottosopra rosso* published in 1975.

13 See also Collettivo femminista di via Cherubini (1975b).

14 See "Abortito: collettivi a confronto" (1976). It highlights the shortcomings of the proposed law and denounces groups in favour of it, some of whom responded in the same journal (Sassaroli 1977, 19–20).

15 The feminist practice of clandestine abortions began around 1976 in Rome, while the organizing of women's travel to London to receive abortions continued. Calabrò and Grasso (2004, 73) report that the Consultorio di via Scalvini (Milan) was one of the first feminist consultori in Italy – and one that other consultori used as a model.

16 Regardless of political orientation, most feminist groups insisted on acknowledging the meaning and the American origin of the concept of self-help. See Leonelli and Peltonen (1975, 36); Sabatini (1973, 48).

17 The AIED is resolutely secular and radical. See Gruppo femminista per una medicina della donna (1974, 40). It is interesting to note that a similar pamphlet, printed by a group of women at McGill University in 1970, experienced the same success in Québec and was immediately translated into French. See de Sève (1998, 164).

18 The Gruppo claimed it never wanted to become a permanent organization. In 1978, another women's health group opened in Milan, serving women in need of abortion. See Farrington (1978); Percovich (2005, 64).

19 See Tozzi (1984) for a description of Simonetta Tosi's action in the San Lorenzo clinic. In the interview with the feminist journal *Differenze* ("L'occupazione al Policlinico" 1979), Tosi describes the trajectory of the San Lorenzo clinic and the dilemma that emerged over the new law on public consultori as well as all the tensions between the San Lorenzo clinic and the CRAC.

20 In many ways, the feminist practices of the San Lorenzo consultorio mirrored the para-médicale's role instituted in the Clinique des femmes du Quartier in Montréal mentioned earlier. See *Effe* 4, 6 (1976): 20–21; Consultario femminista San Lorenzo (1978).

21 Another collective in Rome, the Gruppo femminista romano per la salute (Roman feminist group for health) was critical of the role of doctors and other health professionals and operated its consultorio without them. See Costa (1978).

22 See how Simonetta Tosi explains the rationale behind the Policlinico occupation (quoted in Tozzi 1978, 1984).

23 News from the South sometimes reached the North. During my field research in Sicilia, I was told about a woman who was sexually assaulted by the doctor to whom she had gone for an abortion. The group Comitato per il consultorio helped the woman to bring a court case against the doctor and the hospital where he worked. The story received national coverage. However, the doctor had connections with the local mafia, which bought all the Sicilian newspapers reporting on the case and completely shut down the story. The group received many threats and had difficulty finding a lawyer. The woman dropped the case.

24 An international call for abortion rights as well as caution against forced abortions similar to those that took place in Seveso appeared in *Des luttes et des rires* 2, 3 (1979): 7.

25 This nuance is important because of the diversity of positions on participation in the public health care system. The majority of women's health centres opposed

collaborating with the state, but this position was possible mainly because of the significant influence of feminists supporting the politics of self-help (Belleau 1985; Michaud 1992, 1995).

26 The three other networks of women's services groups at the time were: L'R des Centres des femmes du Québec (R's of women's centres network), Regroupement des Centres d'aide et de lutte contre les agressions à caractère sexuel (Help centres for women victims of sexual violence), Regroupement des maisons d'hébergement pour les femmes victimes de violence conjugale (Women's shelters for female victims of family violence network). Well known in the 1980s, these networks established a line of communication among groups in order to develop strategies vis-à-vis the Québécois governmental institutions that were their main source of revenue as well as the site where public policies that concerned them were debated and decided.

27 The five points were obtained during an interview conducted during my research on women's health centres in Québec. They can also be found in Belleau (1985, 15–20).

28 See Michaud (1992), comparing the Regroupement's arguments to those put forth by the Regroupement des maisons d'hébergement pour femmes victimes de violence conjugale (Women's shelters for female victims of family violence network) (1990). For a summary of arguments in favour of participation with the health care system, see J. Lamoureux (1994). For similar debates in Australia, see Franzway, Court, and Connell (1989, x).

29 See "Documento del comitato per l'aborto e la contraccezione" (1975): 38.

30 Rossana Rossanda celebrated the adoption of the abortion law as a victory of the feminist movement's extremism (Annunziata 2007, 59).

31 On the origin of CRAC, see Damiani (1978). CRAC was regularly in contact with European feminist activists, exchanging information on the practice of abortion (Percovich 2005, 68–69; Sassaroli and Rossellini 1975, 2).

32 For a good chronology of events and the political context surrounding the adoption of the abortion law in Italy up until the end of 1970s, see "Gli 'obiettivi materiali' del movimento" (On the "material objectives" of the movement), reproduced in Frabotta (1978, 91–97).

Chapter 7: Feminist Approaches to Organizing

1 Le diverse ondate del femminismo erano distinguibili abbastanza nettemente, come passagi dal movimento femminista, al movimento delle donne, al femminismo diffuso: altrove la tipologia non sarebbe state altrettanto riconoscibile, né per la compiutezza dei differenti discorsi ne per sequenzialità (Calabrò and Grasso 2004, 9).

2 Descarries-Bélanger and Roy (1988) propose a typology of the contemporary women's movement along different philosophical lines. *Le mouvement des femmes et ses courants de pensée* (The women's movement and its lines of thought) is an attempt to classify theoretical currents over the previous twenty years of feminism, and it follows two axes: the first concerns the "division sociale des sexes" (social division of the sexes); the second concerns strategies of action (4). From these two axes, the authors delineate all other feminist theoretical trends, placing some currents at the centre – feminism of equality, radical feminism, and what they called

feminism of *fémelléité* – whose definition resembles the theory of sexual difference – while other currents, like lesbian separatism, are relegated to the margins of the women's movement (5). Each of these currents has its own complex ramifications. As an attempt to achieve a scientific classification and to make the movement comprehensible to an audience unfamiliar with it, the exercise leaves one perplexed: many categories were misplaced or not fully understood; others, like feminist anti-racism, were simply missing.

3 This line is attributed to the eighteenth-century French chemist Antoine Lavoisier, although he borrowed the idea from the Greeks.

4 The FLFQ and CdF were not the only collectives critical of other women's groups. Feminist journals like *Les têtes de Pioche* and *Pluri-elles/Des luttes et des rires* opened their pages for critiques on a regular basis.

5 This document can only be found in the complete collection of *Québécoises deboutte!* edited by O'Leary and Toupin (1982, 208–12). It is believed to be one of the last materialist feminist documents that achieved some consensus in the Montréal region. The coalition broke up in 1976 after two years, but the four constitutive groups continued their activities.

6 Micheline de Sève does not really distinguish between the FLFQ and the CdF, which she sees as following identical Marxist-Leninist lines. This is an interpretation that many former members of both collectives have been trying to correct ever since.

7 Nous voulons participer à l'élaboration et à l'organisation du mouvement autonome de libération des femmes, tout en étant solidaires des autres luttes. Nous voulons décloisonner les luttes et les analyses des groupes de femmes, et lier le féminisme au socialisme. Nous voulons contribuer à bâtir des liens avec les groupes de femmes (*Marie-Géographie* 1982, 3).

8 "Le fonctionnement que l'on se donne n'est pas neutre et il influence autant les prises de position que l'action" (*Marie-Géographie* 1982, 7).

9 See Dupont et al. (1979–80). This one-page document announcing the publishing of *LVR*'s first issue in March 1980 was inserted in the journal *Le Temps fou*. *LVR* wanted to provoke some sort of rupture with the type of feminism that had prevailed in Québec throughout the 1970s. See D'amours (1988) and Michaud (2012).

10 On the original mandate, see "Éditorial: Pluri-elles" (1978b).

11 *Bollettino delle donne* in Turin (1978–84) is another journal that resembled *Pluri-elles/Des luttes et des rires*. *Bollettino* evolved within the context of working-class struggles in the city.

12 The article was not signed and made a specific reference to Fachinelli's (1968) "Gruppo chiuso o gruppo aperto?," in which he discusses the decision to open or to close meetings to a larger audience. Fachinelli's discussion, mentioned in Chapter 2, highlights the dis/articulation of psychoanalysis and Marxism.

13 Sono tutti luoghi ed attività che hanno un valore politico ed una agibilità che va al di là della loro difinizione funzionale, dovremmo comprenderli e potenziarli al massimo. Questi luoghi della nostra practica tra donne (Colletivo femminista di via Cherubini 1975a, 2).

14 Un luogo amorfo che vive se qualcuno lo dirige. Cherubini *non viene inteso come luogo di incontro ma come gruppo;* chi parla e ascolta. Il luogo viene sentito gestito da quelle che parlano: sono alcune poche stabili figure storiche del movimento.

Questo si ripete in ogni gruppo del movimento forse perchè all'interno di un gruppo sociale come le donne, dove la parola non è stata mai presa, la presa di parola è importante (Collettivo femminista di via Cherubini 1975a, 3; emphasis in original).

15 "La progettata libreria vuole essere un luogo in cui esso – il nuovo – si raccoglie e si comunica perché divenga ricchezza collettiva." It is interesting to note how those at the origin of the Libreria discussed the difficulty of publishing women's literary works from the past because those authors did not have the theory of sexual difference in mind. The problem was apparently resolved by using the argument that "dietro il prodotto finale ... che richiede certi strumenti e che implica il corpo, e il corpo è caratterizzato sessualmente" (behind the final product ... there are certain instruments that require the body, and the body is sexually characterized) (Libreria delle donne 2005b, 104).

16 "La libreria è un luogo politico perché in esso le donne si frequentano publicamente e liberamente. Lo stare tra donne ... è ... il punto di partenza della nostra politica."

17 On the history of the Casa internazionale delle donne in Rome, see https://www.casainternazionaledelledonne.org/index.php/it/home.

18 Both gatherings were devoted to the dynamic surrounding autocoscienza. All Italian feminist trends were present in Pinarella, and, as usual, they were aligned along only two axes of the movement: one axis considered the limitations of autocoscienza and claimed to use psychoanalysis instead, while the other axis supported the practice because it allowed a direct connection with social struggles (Calabrò and Grasso 2004, 80–81).

19 The women's health centres' network was replaced by the Réseau québécois d'action pour la santé des femmes (Action network for women's health). The three other networks were still active at the time of writing.

20 In 1985, the Ministère des Affaires Sociales (Ministry of social affairs) in Québec published a document stating that women's groups were partners in the implementation of social services, mainly in the area of family violence. The network of Women's Shelters for Victims of Violence against Women was among the first to respond positively to the government call. See Michaud (1992).

21 The FFQ was responsible for the organization of the Forum pour un Québec féminin pluriel. For more information about the FFQ, visit www.ffq.qc.ca.

22 In Québec, feminists had to wait for the Forum pour un Québec féminin pluriel, organized by the FFQ in 1992, to have a first attempt to bring together segments of the Québécois feminist/women's movement, including those that worked on race and/or language. See Guénette (1992); Forum pour Québec féminin pluriel (1994).

23 The PCI transferred several million lira annually to the organization: until 1978, communist leaders intervened directly in UDI affairs, even holding positions of leadership. See Beckwith (1985, 23).

Chapter 8: Capturing Feminist Transgressions through Cultural Productions

1 È dunque comprehensibile che un simile movimento crescesse and si reconosce attraverso gli strumenti della comunicazione culturale, piuttosto che attraverso gli strumento della comunicazione politica. La cultura non è più in strumento di lotta

(come per le generazioni precedenti di rivoluzionari) ma era il terreno stesso della lotta (Balestrini and Moroni 2008, 615).

2 On this issue, it is worth reading the following titles among the vast literature on the subject: Butler (1998) and her criticism of the separation between culture and the social; Marcolini (2012) on the French Situationist movement and how this movement understood the role of art in political protest, and how politics and culture were acting in conjunction with the constant renewal of the critique of society and capitalism. On the same theme, see Zaidah (2013) in the context of producing Palestinian political art.

3 This poem inspired Malcolm Reid's title of his well-known book on the journal *Parti pris – The Shouting Signpainters.* For this book I use the French translation (Reid 2009).

4 Most recently, strikes by Québécois student associations during spring 2012 evolved into the most important mass movement in recent Québec history and provided the occasion for a variety of cultural productions not only among students enrolled in visual arts and design programs but also from those enrolled in other programs as well. Protesters came from all kinds of groups inside and outside universities and colleges. The movement provided the occasion for the production of poetry and other forms of politically engaged literature: numerous publications attempting to make sense of what happened in 2012 appeared in 2013. One of the best books connecting culture, politics, and direct action is the wonderful anthology by Bonenfant, Glinoer, and Lapointe (2013).

5 *Mainmise* (1970–78) is considered to be the journal of the Québécois counterculture that partially filled the gap left by the disappearance of *Parti pris.* Throughout its eight years of publication, the journal translated many articles and documents from other countercultural movements abroad, mainly the United States. In October 1970, the journal translated Carl Wittman's *A Gay Manifesto.* The translation was criticized for its omissions, the erasure of paragraphs containing political analysis, even a whole chapter pertaining to the importance of feminism in the emergence of the gay movement (Michaud 2010, 40; Wilson and Rény 1978, 30). Wilson and Rény argue that *Mainmise* editorials highlight the difficult articulation between politics and the counterculture movement.

6 The most pressing issue at the time was the struggle for abortion. In 1974, the Théâtre des cuisines produced *Nous aurons les enfants que nous voulons* (We will have the children we want). The theatre was clearly identified with the left, in particular the New Left. See Beauchamp and Renaud (1980).

7 This expression resists translation. The way it is written in French means "crazy allies," but the spoken words can be confused with "folles à lier" (women crazy enough to tie up).

8 For a chronology of feminist theatre productions in Québec from 1974 until 1985, see Camerlain (1985).

9 In 1974, the group wrote a series of songs, including "Il canzoniere femminista" (The feminist folk singer) and even produced two albums (Balestrini and Moroni 2008, 97–98; Toupin 2014, 163–64).

10 Maraini (2003, 77–78).

11 From time to time, the Libreria delle donne of Milan continues to publish *Sottosopra,* but issues are very irregular, with gaps of several years. The current generation of *Sottosopra* does not have the same impact as did earlier ones.

12 She gives an overview of the presence of women in leftist and alternative journals and dedicates an entire chapter to the feminist movement and feminist periodicals from the nineteenth century until the mid-twentieth century.

13 Godard (2002, 212).

14 Elsewhere, Godard (2008, 132) is more specific about this third meaning of representation, which "signifies something represented to, addressed to, a reader/viewer/consumer and foregrounds the relation of seer and seen to the economic and political networks which constitute the 'outsider.'"

15 The question of what sort of audiences a journal should target troubled other political movements. Lotta Continua wanted to produce a journal as accessible to workers as to students. The journal aimed at reinventing political practices and found a new political language that would place protagonists of political struggles – their language and their culture – at its heart. The limit of such a goal was that its theoretical language seemed to reach only a restricted circle of knowledgeable readers. Luigi Bobbio argues that Lotta Continua struggled for years over this dilemma, which was never entirely resolved. See Bobbio (1988, 77–78).

16 The content in this section was also obtained from a variety of feminist journals that opposed *Effe.*

17 *Effe* also launched a series of questionnaires and other inquiries to find out what its readership was looking for in a feminist press. During moments of crisis, *Effe* sought the support of its readership, but many unsupportive comments came from those who were readers of *Sottosopra* and *Differenze.* Federica Paoli (2008, 261–64) provides a detailed list of articles published by feminist journals in response to *Effe*'s request to organize a national meeting to discuss the state of the feminist press in Italy. These articles are clear examples of how feminist publications were used as a terrain for exchanging arguments and counter-arguments, feminist theories and counter-theories.

18 Representatives of the other journals present at the meeting were linked to leftist political organizations. They were: *Se ben che siamo donne* (linked to Avanguardia Operaia), *Mezzo cielo* (in connection with the Partito Comunista marxista leninista italiano) and *Quarto mondo* (linked to the Fronte Italiano di liberazione femminile, which did not support feminist separatism). These three journals were very short-lived. The two *Sottosopra* representatives claimed they had been set up, surrounded as they were by representatives of journals linked with the left, and immediately wrote a response published in the next issue of *Effe.* They accused the journal of having organized the event under false pretexts, hiding the fact it was going through a crisis and pretending to be the arbitrator of the discussion ("Continua il dibattito" 1976; "Lettera a *Effe*" 1976). *Effe* sent a response published in *Sottosopra* expressing surprise at the accusation of bad faith but not providing any justification. *Effe* did not add any substantive comment in its own pages. The next editorial incorporated the journal's crisis into the crisis of the movement itself and reaffirmed *Effe* as the terrain of their feminist activism, saying that they were

determined to act as a bridge with women interested in feminism ("Care compagne" 1976).

19 The closure of *La vie en rose* in 1987 did not put an end to feminist journalism and feminist presses. *Amazones d'hier, lesbiennes d'aujourd'hui,* founded in 1982, is one example of a journal that continues to publish regularly.

20 In 1979, when *Pluri-elles* decided to change its name to *Des luttes et des rires* and change its initial mandate, ten women on the original team resigned. In "Un autre son de cloche," they denied having created *Pluri-elles* in order to use it as a feminist avant-garde. See "Dossier-bilan" (1979); Louise et al. (1979, 63).

21 *Differenze* demanded a high degree of human and financial involvement, and, as one woman suggested, the end of the journal was probably contained in the project itself (Migale quoted in Paoli 2011, 138).

22 See "Les femmes et l'information" (1980). The issue also contextualizes the problem of gaining access to information on feminist struggles and provides an overview of Québécois feminist journals. Several short articles mapped the history of feminist journalism in the Western world. The rest of the issue focused on the anglophone feminist press in Canada, the technical process of making a journal, and feminist radio programming in Montréal and Québec City. To participate in the conception of the journal, women's groups had to agree on a common set of principles ("Des groupes d'ici ... " 1978).

23 Nous sommes tannées d'un certain féminisme moralisateur, "ghettoïsant" et pudique, d'un autre qui prône une sororité universelle et qui cherche encore des déesses et des prophètes; de ne parler qu'entre nous et de nous enfermer dans ce que nous avons réussi péniblement à faire connaître comme des "affaires de femmes." Nous sommes féministes mais nous sommes tannées du ton lyrant qu'on s'est forcées d'adopter pour dénoncer les injustices et l'oppression, du rétrécissement en quatre ou cinq revendications d'un mouvement qui aspire à sa liberté; tannées de laisser le pouvoir définir le féminisme, en faire un épouvantail à moineau ou l'unique voie de salut pour l'humanité, en nous abandonnant tout le travail comme d'habitude; tannées d'être au service de tous et de chacun et même des groupes de femmes (Dupont et al. 1979–80, n.p).

24 Similarly good journalism characterized *Le Temps fou.* See Dassas (1983). Véronique Dassas wrote several editorials for *Le Temps fou* lamenting the mediocrity of the Québécois mainstream press.

25 For more about the controversy that followed the publication of this text, see Dandurand (1985) as well as the preface written by Françoise Guénette (1985c).

26 This is the title of the editorial of the issue, "L'amour toujours l'amour" (Love, always love). See "L'amour toujours l'amour" (1982).

27 This section relies on the collection of essays published by Roseanna Dufault and Celita Lamar (2012).

28 Dans mon peuple, dire d'une femme qu'elle est une vache, c'est l'insulte la plus basse, la plus grossière. Utiliser cette expression de mépris suprême pour raconteur l'histoire des femmes, se permettre de transformer les femelles humaines en bêtes grandioses et souveraines qui célèbrent leur beauté dans le ciel étoilé, la nuit, faire de la Voie lactée un véritable chemin constitué d'irruptions de lait des femmes, il y a là une véritable capacité de synthèse et de transformation de multiples éléments, féminins

humains, animales, végétales, cosmiques, qu'il faut qualifier de visionnaire (P. Pelletier 2012, 42–43).

29 In reference to one of Marchessault's titles: "Anaïs dans la queue de la comète," translated as "Anaïs in the Comet's Wake" by Susanne de Lotbinière-Harwood in 1985.

30 *Comme un enfant de la terre* was Marchessault's first novel, published in 1975 and translated by Yvonne M. Klein as *Like a Child of the Earth* in 1988.

31 "Considéré de façon métaphorique, *Comme un enfant de la terre* rejoue chaque phase de la vocation sacrée du chaman au moment du déclin de la civilisation occidentale, tel que le perçoit l'œil clairvoyant de la voyante. Fondamentalement, l'auteur devient le scribe prophétique de son peuple, et de son livre, un guide spirituel pour revivre dans l'espace et dans le temps le voyage chamanique qui rachètera le genre humain de la Chute, qui exorcisera le Christianisme, le Capitalisme et le Colonialisme et qui sera suivi d'une nouvelle ère révolutionnaire, où la femme sera rétablie dans son rôle pré-patriarcale de magnificence cosmique.

Pour la prophète originaire d'Amérique du Nord, la chute va de pair avec l'évangélisation du peuple amérindien et la civilisation du Nouveau monde. Il faut maintenant exorciser le mal inhérent au mythe patriarcal de la Création, imposé par l'oppresseur colonisateur, pour que soit ressuscité l'ordre naturel de l'univers symbolisé par la mère-des-herbes, la Grande-Déesse de la Végétation, et que la vie sur la planète entre dans un cycle de renouveau et de régénération." (Feman Orenstein 2012, 56–57).

32 See Purdy (1991, 270) and his reference to Marchessault's novel, *Des cailloux blancs dans les forêts obscures* (White pebbles in the dark forests).

33 For more about the Inuit understanding of genders and the shifting of boundaries between them, see Saladin d'Anglure (1985, 2006); Roscoe (1998).

34 This section on Mangiacapre's biography and her work comes from the Italian website, Archivio delle memorie delle donne, http://donnedinapoli.coopdedalus.org/1050/lina-mangiacapre/. Other information was found in an interview in *E fu la minigonna* (And the miniskirt was) (1998) as well as interviews in C. Capobianco (n.d.). Finally, I conducted a series of interviews in Naples during the summer of 2010, including one with a representative of the Nemesiache/Tre Ghinee.

35 See the interview in *E fu la minigonna* (1998). In "È nata nel Sud la nuova Strega" (The new witch is born in the south), Mangiacapre accused feminists who advocate for the unconscious of reducing acts of violence to a mere psychological issue (Mangiacapre in C. Capobianco n.d., 83).

36 In an interview, Mangiacapre presented the psico-favola as the first feminist theatrical form ever adopted in Italy and defines it as the theatrical translation of autocoscienza. See *E fu la minigonna* (1998).

37 Ibid.

38 See n.d., "La psicofavola: metodo teatrale e di autocoscienza," as well as the description of the performance on the Nemesiache/Tre Ghinee website, http://www.lenemesiache.it/nemesiache_bio.php.

39 Lina Mangiacapre died suddenly in 2002, but the two groups she created are still active at the time of writing.
40 See C. Capobianco (n.d., 39). Since 2003, the Lina Mangiacapre Award celebrating women's films is presented every year at the International Film Festival in Venice.
41 See *E fu la minigonna* (1998).
42 It is interesting to note that the Nemesiache was equally critical of both feminist journals, *Effe* and *Sottosopra,* for their elitism. See Paoli (2011).
43 One wonders if members of the group were inspired by Shulamith Firestone (1970) regarding the need to free the sexuality of children. The Nemesiache Manifestos are all reproduced in C. Capobianco (n.d.).
44 One participant remembers that the place was filthy and that women imprisoned at the Frullone rarely got outside to breathe fresh air. According to Livia Riccio, the occupation of the Frullone might have provoked the suicide of one of the female health workers. It was also a moment of tension with the PCI, which had control of the site and opposed activists who wanted autonomous management of the space (Riccio in C. Capobianco n.d., 139–40).
45 La donna a Napoli in una resistenza che non a mai fine si unisce in questo momento con l'utopia dei bisogni, in seguito all'evento del terremoto che come fenomeno naturale si è inserito in una serie di fenomeni politici, che dal dopoguerra ad oggi hanno visto tutti i momenti presenti le donne di Napoli a lottare per potere restare in una città, per potere non dovere andare via, non dovere mediare e non dovere morire. A queste lotte oggi, si uniscono tutte le altre lotte, che nostra lotta comme gruppo femminista Napolitano è cominciata sempre su una dose di coscienza di quella che voleva essere una espropriazione storica di una dimensione: quella delle nostre origini. [...] E non solo non volere andare via e non volere accettare la distruzione dei vicoli, l'emarginazione dal centro storico. Affrontare i problemi del territorio, in questo momento, è veramente affrontare insieme, e in modo unito l'utopia dei bisogni e il bisogno del utopia (C. Capobianco n.d., 54–57).
46 During my stay in Naples, I discovered the wonderful trilogy of Ermanno Rea (2009) which is the story of the city revealed through a series of personal narratives. The geopolitical context of the end of the Second World War and bad political decisions at the municipal level are presented as being responsible for the city's gradual political and economic decline.

Chapter 9: Who Should Write Our History?

1 "History should not be made by historians in universities but by those who lived it" (Raymonde, quoted in O'Leary and Toupin 1983, 368).
2 The history of the feminist/women's movement is not merely the recollection of events of the era. Among the three areas of feminist research listed by Yasmine Ergas (1986), only one segment concerns the field of women's history. Her study is sociological, although it can also be viewed as a contribution to the history of a movement she knows well.
3 These remarks can be found in O'Leary and Toupin (1982, 1983), in Péloquin (2007); and in Dumont and Toupin (2003). Neither Véronique O'Leary nor Louise Toupin were established academics at the time they completed the anthology. After the

publication, Toupin began researching and teaching at the Institut de recherche d'études feministes, Université du Québec à Montréal, while O'Leary pursued an artistic career in the theatre.

4 When referring to the fragmentation of a political movement, Scott's ideas parallel Gramsci's notes in a section of his 11th Notebook, "Appunti per una introduzione e un avviamento allo studio della filosofia e della storia della cultura" (Notes for the introduction and the beginning of the study of philosophy and of the history of culture), where he wrote: "Occurre dunque spiegare come avviene che in ogni tempo coesistano molti sistemi e correnti di filosofia, come nascono, come si diffondono, perché nella diffusione seguono certe line di frattura e certe direzioni ecc." (Therefore, it is necessary to explain how it happens, in any period of time, the coexistence of several systems and philosophical currents, how they arise, how they disperse, why during the diffusion, they follow certain lines of fracture and certain directions, etc.) (Gramsci 1975, 1379).

5 Groppi and Pelaja also underline the approach adopted by *Memoria,* which is to avoid taking any methodological or analytical direction. Created in 1981, *Memoria* was the first feminist journal on women's history to work from an interdisciplinary perspective. See Mantini (2000).

6 From a personal conversation with Danielle Cooper. See Cooper (2016).

7 See also Michel Cordillot (2009, 111). Cordillot tells the story of how his grandfather, during the McCarthy era, decided to burn the files he had inherited from his own father, a key protagonist in the francophone socialist movement in the United States at the turn of the twentieth century. It was a great loss.

8 This maxim is often attributed to Antonio Gramsci, but, according to Joseph A. Buttigieg (2011, 429), Gramsci is said to have borrowed the quote from Romain Roland. No one has been able to find these words in Roland's work. Buttigieg suggests they might appear during an interview that Roland gave.

9 See, for instance, Rowbotham (1996) and Briskin (1999).

10 In many aspects, the anthology corrects oversights and misinterpretations of previous attempts at Québécois feminist history, like Collectif Clio (1982 [second ed. 1992]), and other historical interpretations based on Diane Lamoureux's work (Dumont and Toupin 2003, 462).

11 The subsection on marginalized women is particularly heterogeneous and eclectic. It includes themes such as Indigenous women, immigrant women from Italy and Haiti, women victims of crimes of honour, and Christian feminists.

12 One could argue quite accurately that all three periods were much more diversified in terms of ideological and political trends. I am focusing on the third, in accordance with Dumont and Toupin's time frame.

13 The first edition of the first volume came out in 1973. The introduction to both volumes is co-signed by Giuseppina Ciuffreda.

14 In the second volume, there are some articles from the Collettivo di via Cherubini (via Cherubini collective) related to the abortion struggle, reprinted from *Sottosopra,* but little reference to the feminist ideological trend these texts represent.

15 Scott (2011, 82–83) makes the same argument.

16 Bono and Kemp (1991, 7).

References

"Aborto: collettivi a confronto." 1976. *Effe* 4 (12): 18–19.

Alcuni donne di Turino. 1975. "La perdita del nostro corpo." *Sottosopra rosso* (February): 39–42.

Alcuni gruppi di donne di Milano. 1972. Fondazione Elvira Badaracco. Milan: 2 pp.

Altamirano-Jiménez, Isabel. 2013. *Indigenous Encounters with Neoliberalism: Place, Women, and the Environment in Canada and Mexico*. Vancouver: UBC Press.

Amazones d'hier, lesbiennes d'aujourd'hui. 1987. "Lesbianisme radical." *RFR/DRF:* 15 (4): 5–7.

Ambrosino, Sylvana. 1978. "Anche a Sciacca un movimento femminile." 2 pp.

Andrew, Caroline. 1984. "Women and the Welfare State." *Canadian Journal of Political Science* 17 (4): 667–84. https://doi.org/10.1017/s0008423900052537.

Anna, Emmanuela, Paola, and Rossella. 1977. "Commissione femminista 'Donne e politica' nell' occupazione dell'Università di Roma." *Ombre Rosse* 20: 49–52.

Annunziata, Lucia. 2007. *1977: l'ultima foto di famiglia*. Turino: Einaudi.

Austin, David. 2007. "All Roads Led to Montreal: Black Power, the Caribbean, and the Black Radical Tradition in Canada." *Journal of African History* 92 (4): 516–39. https://doi.org/10.1086/jaahv92n4p516.

"Autogestione." 1975. *Effe* 3 (1): 2–3.

Baeri, Emma. 2002. "Corpi della memoria: un percorso politico e metodologico negli archivi del femminismo." *Genesis* 1, 2: 216–25.

–. 2005. "Violenza, conflitto, disarmo: pratiche e riletture femministe." In *Il femminismo degli anni settanta*, ed. Teresa Bertilotti and Anna Scattigno, 119–68. Rome: Viella.

Balestrini, Nanni, and Primo Moroni. 2008 [1988]. *L'orda d'oro, 1968–1977: la grande ondata revoluzionaria e creativa politica ed esistenziale*. Milan: Feltrinelli.

Bannerji, Himani. 2000. *The Dark Side of the Nation: Essays on Multiculturalism, Nationalism and Gender*. Toronto: Canadian Scholars' Press.

–. 2001. "Pygmalion Nation: Towards a Critique of Subaltern Studies and the 'Resolution of the Women's Question.'" In *Of Property and Propriety: The Role of Gender and Class in Imperialism and Nationalism*, ed. Himani Bannerji, Shahrzad Mojab, and Judith Whitehead, 34–84. Toronto: University of Toronto Press.

Battaglino, Maria Teresa. 1978. "Le prospettive del movimento delle donne e lo svoluppo di una linea femminista di masse." In *La politica del femminismo: il movimento femminista, l'Unione delle donne italiane, le forze politiche di sinistra di fronte al femminismo nei documenti, 1973–1976*, ed. Biancamaria Frabotta, 240–44. Rome: Savelli.

Beauchamp, Hélène, and Judith Renaud. 1980. "Justement! Oui, encore! Entretien avec le Théâtre des cuisines." *Revue de théâtre Jeu* 16 (3): 97–115.

Beaudry, Lucille. 1983. "Militantisme et dissidence des femmes dans les organisations révolutionnaires au Québec (1976–1982)." *Groupe Interdisciplinaire pour l'Enseignement et la Recherche des Femmes (GIERF)* 1: 48–79.

–. 1990. "Le Marxisme au Québec: une hégémonie intellectuelle en mutation (1960–1980)." In *Un siècle de Marxisme*, ed. Lucille Beaudry, Christian Deblock, and Jean-Jacques Gislain, 259–79. Sillery: Les Presses de l'Université du Québec.

Beaulieu, Elsa. 2010. "Theorizing Feminist and Social Movement Practice in Space." In *Solidarities beyond Borders*, ed. Pascale Dufour, Dominique Masson, and Dominique Caouette, 56–85. Vancouver: UBC Press.

Beckwith, Karen. 1985. "Feminism and Leftist Politics in Italy: The Case of UDI-PCI Relations." *Western European Politics* 8 (4): 19–37. https://doi.org/10.1080/01402388508424552.

Bellavitis, Anna. 1990. "L'histoire des femmes en Italie: bilan de quinze années de débats." *Les Cahiers du Centre de Recherches Historiques* 5. https://doi-org.ezproxy.library.yorku.ca/10.4000/ccrh.2891.

Belleau, Josée. 1985. "Le Regroupement des centres de santé pour les femmes et la non-participation." In *Compte-rendu de la journée de réflexion organisée par Relais-femmes*, 15–20. Montréal: Relais-femmes.

Benston, Margaret. 1969. "The Political Economy of Women's Liberation." *Monthly Review* 21 (4): 13–27. https://doi.org/10.14452/mr-021-04-1969-08_2.

Bentaous, Taryn McQuain. 2012. "La maternité symbolique et la création littéraire dans l'univers au féminin de Jovette Marchessault." In *De l'invisible au visible: l'imaginaire de Jovette Marchessault*, ed. Roseanna Dufault and Celita Lamar, 111–26. Montréal: Les éditions du remue-ménage.

Berardi, Franco (Bifo). 2004 [1997]. "Pour en finir avec le jugement de Dieu." In *Settantasette: la rivoluzione che viene*, ed. Sergio Bianchi and Lanfranco Caminiti, 171–80. Rome: DeriveApprodi.

–. 2007 [2006]. "Genesi e significato del termine autonomìa." In *Gli autonomi: le storie, le lotte, le teorie*, ed. Sergio Bianchi and Lanfranco Caminiti, 40–54. Rome: DeriveApprodi.

Bergeron, Marie-Andrée. 2011a. "De *Québécoises deboutte!* à *Jesuisfeministe.com:* croisements politiques et éditoriaux dans la presse des féministes radicales au Québec." *Mémoires du livre/Studies in Book Culture* 3 (1). https://doi.org/10.7202/1007571ar.

–. 2011b. "*La vie en rose* (1980–87): construction rhétorique d'un leadership." *Globe* 14 (2): 105–20. https://doi.org/10.7202/1008784ar.

Bertilotti, Teresa. 2004. "Un oggetto di studio interessante e 'un imprescibile' teorico di fonti, transmissione della memoria e storia del movimento femminista." *Genesis* 3, 1: 220–29.

Bertilotti, Teresa, and Anna Scattigno. 2005. "Introduzione." In *Il femminismo degli anni settanta,* ed. Teresa Bertilotti and Anna Scattigno, vii–xviii. Rome: Viella.

Betta, Emmanuel, and Enrica Capussotti. 2004. "'Il buono, il brutto, il cattivo': l'epica dei movimenti tra storia e memoria." *Genesis* 13, 1: 113–23.

Bianchi, Sergio, and Lanfranco Caminiti. 2004 [1997]. *Settantasette: la rivoluzione che viene.* Rome: DeriveApprodi.

–, eds. 2007a. *Gli autonomi: le storie, le lotte, le teorie.* Rome: DeriveApprodi.

–. 2007b. "Avvertanze alla lettura." In *Gli autonomi: le storie, le lotte, le teorie,* ed. Sergio Bianchi and Lanfranco Caminiti, 5–7. Rome: DeriveApprodi.

Bicchiere, Cristina, and Giulia Roditi. 1974. "Note del quarto anno." *Sottosopra,* 97–102.

B.L. 1970. *Qual'è ora la via da seguire?* Fondazione Elvira Badaracco. Milan. 7 pp.

Blais, Marie-Claire. 2012. "Retour à 'Comme une enfant de la terre' (livre I)." In *De l'invisible au visible: l'imaginaire de Jovette Marchessault,* ed. Roseanna Dufault and Celita Lamar, 27–33. Montréal: Les éditions du remue-ménage.

Bobbio, Luigi. 1988. *Storia di Lotta Continua.* Milan: Feltrinelli.

Bocchetti, Alessandra. 1987. "Per sé/per me." *Sottosopra,* 2–3.

Boccia, Maria Luisa. 1981. "Da un dialogo sulla diversità." *Memoria* 2: 36–48.

–. 1983. "Dentro e fuori le istituzioni: le intelletuali tra professionalità e Politica." *Memoria* 9 (3): 36–49.

Boccia, Valeria. 1987. "Il filo del discorso." *Memoria* 19–20 (1–2): 85–108.

Bollettino del Comitato per il salario al lavoro domestico di Trieste. 2007 [1975]. "Donne all'attacco." In *Gli autonomi: le storie, le lotte, le teorie,* ed. Sergio Bianchi and Lanfranco Caminiti, 143–44. Rome: DeriveApprodi.

Bolognese, Lucia. 1977. "Consultori: a che punto siamo." *Effe* 5 (6): 22–28.

Bonenfant, Maude, Anthony Glinoer, and Martine-Emmanuelle Lapointe. 2013. *Le printemps québécois: une anthologie.* Montréal: Écosociété.

Bono, Paola, and Sandra Kemp. 1991. "Introduction: Coming from the South." In *Italian Feminist Thought,* ed. Paola Bono and Sandra Kemp, 1–28. London: Blackwell.

Borduas, Paul-Émile. 1987. *Écrits I,* critical edition by André-G. Bourassa, Jean Fisette, and Gilles Lapointe. Montréal: Les presses de l'Université de Montréal.

Borello, Giovanna. 1981. "Donna, scuola e sindacato." In *I modi e le tematiche del femminismo a Napoli.* Atti del Convegno, 41–43. Naples: Comune di Napoli, Centro Studi, Condizione della donna.

Bourcier, Marie-Hélène. 2013. "Wittig la politique." In *Monique Wittig, La pensée straight,* 23–35. Paris: Amsterdam.

Bourcier, Sam. 2018. *Queer zones : la trilogie.* Paris: Éditions Amsterdam.

Bourque, Gilles. 1967. "UGEQ." *Parti Pris* 5 (2–3): 51–52.

Bracciali, Ludovica. 1976. "Seveso veleno nell'utero." *Effe* 4 (9–10): 27–28.

Bradbury, Bettina. 2011. *Wife to Widow: Lives, Laws, and Politics in Nineteenth-Century Montreal.* Vancouver: UBC Press.

Braghetti, Anna Laura, and Paola Tavella. 2008 [2003]. *Il prigioniero.* Milan: Feltrinelli.

Braidotti, Rosi. 1986. "Les italiennes toujours." *Les Cahiers du Grif* 34: 149–53.

Bravo, Anna. 2004. "Noi e la violenza. Trent'anni per pensarci." *Genesis* 3, 1: 17–56.

Bravo, Anna, Daniela Del Boca, and Lucetta Scaraffia. 1977. "Gli angeli del personale: ancora sul movimento femminista." *Quaderni Piacentini* (April): 73–87.

Briskin, Linda. 1999. "Mapping Women's Organizing in Sweden and Canada: Some Thematic Considerations." In *Women's Organizing and Public Policy in Canada and Sweden*, ed. Linda Briskin and Mona Eliason, 3–47. Montreal and Kingston: McGill-Queen's University Press.

Brodie, Janine, Shelley A.M Gavigan, and Jane Jenson. 1992. *The Politics of Abortion*. Toronto: Oxford University Press.

Brossard, Nicole. 1976. "Féminisme ou lutte spécifique des femmes." *Les têtes de Pioche* (March): 4.

Brunsdon, Charlotte. 1996. "A Thief in the Night: Stories of Feminism in the 1970s at CCCS." In *Stuart Hall. Critical Dialogue in Cultural Studies*, ed. David Morley and Kuan-Hsing Chen, 276–86. London and New York: Routledge.

Bunch, Charlotte. 1981. "Una teoria per sopravvivere." *Bollettino delle donne* 6: 2–3.

Burgoyne, Lynda. 1991. "Biographie et théâtre chez Jovette Marchessault: du mentir-vrai." *Cahier de théâtre Jeu* 60 (September): 111–20.

Busatta, Sandra, Laura Staffieri, and Laura Lanzi. 1973. "La società per mogli." *Quaderni di Lotta Femminista*, speciale Il personale è politico, Tommaso Musolini editore 2: 15–44.

Butler, Judith. 1998. "Merely Cultural." *New Left Review* I/227 (January–February): 33–44.

Buttigieg, Joseph A. 2011. "Notes on Notebook 6, 1930–32." In *Antonio Gramsci Prison Notebooks*, ed. and trans. Joseph A. Buttigieg, 385–485. Vol. 3. New York: Columbia University Press.

Calabrò, Anna Rita, and Laura Grasso. 2004 [1985]. *Dal Movimento femminista al femminismo diffuso: storie e percorsi a Milano dagli anni 60 agli anni 80*. Milan: Fondazione Elvira Badaracco – FrancoAngeli.

Camerlain, Lorraine. 1985. "En de multiples scènes." *Canadian Theatre Review* 43 (Summer): 73–90.

Caminiti, Lanfranco. 2004 [1997]. "Settantasette: introduzione alla prima edizione." In *Settantasette: la rivoluzione che viene*, ed. Sergio Bianchi and Lanfranco Caminiti, 45–67. Rome: DeriveApprodi.

Capobianco, Conni (Nausicaa). n.d. *Interpreti e protagoniste del movimento femminista napolitano, 1970–1990*. Naples: Cornu Copia.

Capobianco, Laura. 1993. "Femminismo: 'eredita senza testamento.'" Interview in *Gli anni '70 e Napoli*, ed. Lucia Mastrodomenico, 51–56. Naples: Magistra Edizioni per lo Specchio di Alice.

Capobianco, Laura, and Cristina Minneci. 1981. "Le matrice del femminismo a Napoli (1968–1973)." *I modi e le tematiche del femminismo a Napoli*. Atti del Convegno a Napoli, 8–22 May, 1980, 11–17. Naples: Comune di Napoli, Centro Studi Condizione della Donna.

Cardon, Dominique, and Fabien Granjon. 2010. *Mediaactivists*. Paris: Les Presses de Sciences Po.

"Care compagne." 1976. *Effe* 4 (3–4): 2.

Carlini, Paola, and Giuseppina Ciuffreda. 1979. "Perchè?," *Effe* 7 (1): 2–3.

Carlini, Paola, and Marielle Pasqua. 1979. "Sindacato: dietro l'apparato donna." *Effe* 7 (1): 17–18.

Castellano, Lucio. 2007 [1980]. "Il rifuto del lavoro." In *Gli autonomi: le storie, le lotte, le teorie*, ed. Sergio Bianchi and Lanfranco Caminiti, 11–25. Rome: DeriveApprodi.

Centre des femmes. 1983a [1973]. "Pour un mouvement de femmes mais lequel?" In *Québécoises deboutte!*, ed. Véronique O'Leary and Louise Toupin. Collection complète, tome 2, 94–96. Montréal: Les éditions du remue-ménage.

–. 1983b [1973]. "Pour une vraie fête des mères et des ménagères." In *Québécoises deboutte!*, ed. Véronique O'Leary and Louise Toupin. Collection complète, tome 2, 167–71. Montréal: Les éditions du remue-ménage.

–. 1983c [1973]. "Rencontre avec deux féministes marxistes." In *Québécoises deboutte!*, ed. Véronique O'Leary and Louise Toupin. Collection complète, tome 2, 109–203. Montréal: Les éditions du remue-ménage.

–. 1983d [1973]. "Sur notre condition: un salaire à la ménagère?" In *Québécoises deboutte!*, ed. Véronique O'Leary and Louise Toupin. Collection complète, tome 2, 132–35. Montréal: Les éditions du remue-ménage.

Cerchio Spezzato. 1970. "Non c'è rivoluzione senza liberazione della donna." Document reprinted in *Donne è bello*, ed. Anabasi, 126–28.

"C'est quoi Pluri-elles." 1977. *Pluri-elles* 1 (3): 10.

Chakrabarty, Dipesh. 2002. "A Small History of Subaltern Studies." In *Habitations of Modernity: Essays in the Wake of Subaltern Studies*, 3–19. Chicago: University of Chicago Press.

Chamberland, Line. 1996. "Le lesbianisme comme fait social." In *Mémoires lesbiennes*. Montréal: Les éditions du remue-ménage.

Chamberland, Paul. 1964. *L'afficheur hurle*, poème. Montréal: Éditions Parti pris.

Chambers, Ian. 2008. *Mediterranean Crossings: The Politics of the Interrupted Modernity*. Durham, NC: Duke University Press.

Charpentier, Louise, René Durocher, Christian Laville, and Paul-André Linteau. 1990. *Nouvelle histoire du Québec et du Canada*, 2nd ed. Montréal: Centre éducatif et culturel inc.

Chianese, Gloria. 1981. "Riflessione femminista. Storia e scienze sociali. Alcune osservazioni introduttive." *I modi e le tematiche del femminismo a Napoli*. Atti del Convegno a Napoli. 8–22 May, 1980, 63–69. Naples: Comune di Napoli, Centro Studi Condizione della Donna.

Cigarini, Lia. 1987. "Sulla reppresentanza politica femminile, sull'arte di polemizzare tra donne e sulla rivoluzione scientifica in corso." *Sottosopra*, 1–2.

Cigarini, L., D. Pellegrini, and E. Rasi. 1969. "Il maschile come valore: al di là dell'emancipazione." *Il Manifesto*, September: 62–66.

Cirillo, Lidia. 2003. *La luna severa maestra: il contributo del femminismo ai movimenti sociali e alla costruzione dell'alternative*. Milan: Il dito et la luna.

Ciuffreda, Giuseppina, and Biancamaria Frabotta. 1975 [1973]. "Introduzione." In *Femminismo e lotta di classe in Italia, 1970–1973*, ed. Biancamaria Frabotta, 7–16. Rome: Savelli.

Ciuffreda, Giuseppina, and Stefania Raspini. 1999. "Il femminismo questo sconosciuto." *Effe* 7 (2): 29–31.

C.L. 1980. "Le référendum, l'avenir et nous." *Le Temps fou* (March–May): 6–8.

Cleveland, John. 1983. "The Political Is Personal: Why Women in the Canadian Marxist Group IN STRUGGLE Changed from Opposing to Supporting the

Feminist Ideology of the Autonomous Women's Movement." MA thesis, Simon Fraser University.
–. 2004. "New Left, Not New Liberal: 1960s Movements in English Canada and Québec." *CRSA/RCSA* 41 (1): 67–84. https://doi.org/10.1111/j.1755-618x.2004.tb02170.x.
Cloti. 1977. "Doppia militanza." *Differenze* 4 (4): 37–38.
Code, Lorraine. 2000. *Encyclopedia of Feminist Theory*. New York: Routledge.
Collectif Clio. 1982. *L'histoire des femmes au Québec*, 1st ed. Montréal: Quinze.
Collettivo di via Lombroso. n.d. "Come siamo nate: il Collettivo di via Lombroso e i rapporti con 'Psychanalyse et politique.'" *Bollettino delle donne* 3: 19–20.
Collettivo femminista Comunista di Via Pomponazzi. 1975. "Femminismo oggi: esperienza di un gruppo." *Effe* 3 (5): 23–32.
Collettivo femminista di Bologna. 1974. "Vogliamo meno figli." *Effe* 2 (7–8): 74–75.
Collettivo femminista di Milano. 1973. "A proposito dell'aborto." *Sottosopra* (February): 93.
Collettivo femminista di via Cherubini. 1975a. *I Luoghi delle femministe e la pratica del movimento*. Milan: Fondazione Elvira Badaracco, 4 pp.
–. 1975b. "Perchè non participiamo alle manifestazioni." *Effe* 3 (1): 35.
Collettivo femminista "Santa Croce." 1975. "Noi non vogliamo più abortire." *Sottosopra rosso:* 44–46.
Collettivo femminista Trentino. 1975. "L'aborto: documento da Trento." *Effe* 3 (1): 34.
Colombo, Daniela, and Giuseppina Giuffreda. 1978. "Informazione/le vocci diverse." *Effe* 6 (7–8): 3–8.
Colotti, Geraldina, Elettre Deiana, Manuela Fraire, Paola Massi, and Marina Pivetta. 2004 [1997]. "Dissonanze." Discussion organizata da Marina Campanale, in *Settantasette: la rivoluzione che viene*, ed. Sergio Bianchi and Lanfranco Caminiti, 219–37. Rome: DeriveApprodi.
Comitato Triveneto per il salario al lavoro domestico. 1976. "Femminismo e cattolicesimo." *Effe* 4 (2): 2–11.
Commissione femminile di Lotta Continua. 1978 [1975]. "Comunicato della Commissione femminile di Lotta Continua." In *La politica del femminismo: il movimento femminista, l'Unione delle donne italiane, le forze politiche di sinistra di fronte al femminismo nei documenti, 1973–1976*, ed. Biancamaria Frabotta, 233–46. Rome: Savelli.
Constantini, Silvia. 1979. "Aborto anno primo." *Effe* 7 (6): 27.
Constantini, Silvia, and Sandra Sassaroli. 1976. "Incontro del CRAC con le donne del sud." *Effe* 4 (3–4): 35–36.
Constantino, Emilio. 2004 [1997]. "Agli ex 'militanti du professione.'" In *Settantasette: la rivoluzione che viene*, ed. Sergio Bianchi and Lanfranco Caminiti, 246–52. Rome: DeriveApprodi.
Consultario femminista San Lorenzo. 1978. "Ancora polemiche." *Effe* (May): 30–33.
"Continua il dibattito sulla stampa femminista." 1976. *Effe* 4 (2): 32.
"Convegno donna ante società." 1978. *Effe* 6 (4): 31–32.
"Convegno Donna – Arte – Società: all'ombra del totem fallico." 1978. *Effe* 6 (2): 9–13.
Conway, Janet. 2010. "Troubling Transnational Feminism(s) at the World Social Forum." In *Solidarities beyond Borders*, ed. Pascale Dufour, Dominique Masson, and Dominique Caouette, 149–72. Vancouver: UBC Press.

Cooper, Danielle. 2016. "Personal Touches, Public Legacies: An Ethnography of LGBT Libraries and Archives." PhD diss., York University.

Coordinamento donne cattoliche per la 194. 1981. "In nome della libertà e dell'amore, voteremo no." *Mille e une donna: periodico meridionale autogestito di cultura e attualittà femminista* 4 (6–7): 17–18.

Cordillot, Michel. 2009. *Révolutionnaires du Nouveau Monde: une brève histoire du mouvement socialiste francophone aux États-Unis, 1885–1922*, Montréal: Lux éditeur.

Costa, Stephania. 1978. "Le recerche fatte dalle donne e le implicazioni politiche del self-help." *Differenze* 6 (6–7): 14–15.

CRAC. 1975. "Vogliamo consultori autogestiti." *Effe* 3 (11): 7–8.

Crispino, Annamaria. 1979. "Ti costringono ad essere in qualche modo una leader." In *Care compagne: il femminismo nel PCI e nelle organizzioni di massa*, ed. Laura Lilli and Chiara Valentini, 272–78. Rome: Editori Riuniti.

–. 1981a. "Introduzione." *I modi e le tematiche del femminismo a Napoli*. Atti del Convegno a Napoli: 8–22 May, 1980, 5–7. Naples: Comune di Napoli, Centro Studi Condizione della Donna.

–. 1981b. "Le parole del femminismo." *I modi e le tematiche del femminismo a Napoli*. Atti del Convegno a Napoli. 8–22 May, 1980, 20–26. Naples: Comune di Napoli, Centro Studi Condizione della Donna.

Cyr, François, Jean Lalande, and Richard Poulin. 1982. "Heurs et Malheurs d'En Lutte! Genèse et trajectoire." *Les cahiers du socialisme* 10–11: 263–86.

Dalla Costa, Mariarosa. n.d. "The Door to the Garden: Feminism and Operaismo." 5 pp. https://libcom.org/library/the-door-to-the-garden-feminism-and-operaismo-mariarosa-dalla-costa.

Dalla Costa, Mariarosa, and Selma James. 1997 [1972]. "Women and the Subversion of Community." In *Materialist Feminism: A Reader in Class, Difference, and Women's Lives*, ed. Rosemary Hennessy and Chris Ingraham, 40–53. New York: Routledge.

Damiani, Christiana. 1978. "Aborto: leggie e pratica." *Differenze* 6 (6–7): 28–31.

D'Amours, Martine. 1988. "De quoi *La vie en rose* est-elle morte?," *La Gazette des femmes* 10 (3): 20–22.

Dandurand, Anne. 1985. "Histoire de Q." *La vie en rose* (special summer edition) 28 (July–August): 34–35.

Dassas, Véronique. 1982. "Orthodoxie féministe: la majorité a des problèmes." *Le Temps fou* 19 (February–March): 24–27.

–. 1983. "Plus que 35,000." *Le Temps fou* 31 (September): 2–3.

Davis, Kathy. 2008. "Intersectionality as a Buzz Word." *Feminist Theory* 9 (1): 67–85. https://doi.org/10.1177/1464700108086364.

Day, Richard J.F. 2005. *Gramsci Is Dead: Anarchist Currents in the Newest Social Movements*. London/Toronto: Pluto Press/Between the Lines.

de Lauretis, Teresa. 1990. "The Practice of Sexual Difference and Feminist Thought in Italy: An Introductory Essay." In *Women's Milan Bookstore, Sexual Difference: A Theory of Social-Symbolic Practice*, 1–21. Bloomington: Indiana University Press.

de Sève, Micheline. 1998. "Féminisme et nationalisme au Québec, une alliance inattendue." *International Journal of Canadian Studies/Revue internationale d'études canadiennes* 17 (Spring): 157–75.

–. 2005. "La chute du mur de Berlin et l'ébranlement de la gauche chilienne." *Politique et sociétés* 24 (2): 87–107. https://doi.org/10.7202/012692ar.

Delphy, Christine. 1972 [1970]. "L'ennemi principal." *Partisans: Libération des femmes. Année zéro*, special issue, 113–37.
–. 1980. "Nouvelles du M.L.F: libération des femmes an dix." *Nouvelles Questions Féministes* 7: 3–13.
DEMAU. 1966a. *Documento per un'apertura dibattito*. Milan: Fondazione Elvira Badaracco, 3 pp.
–. 1966b. *Manifesto programmatico del gruppo DEMAU*. Milan: Fondazione Elvira Badaracco, 3 pp.
–. 1970. *Schema di ipotesi della ricerca sulla procreazione*. Milan: Fondazione Elvira Badaracco, 2 pp.
"Des groupes d'ici ... *Pluri-elles* a grandi." 1978. *Des luttes et des rires* 2, 1 (October–November): 42–44.
Des Ormeaux, Odette. 1979. "Femmes autochtones: solidarité et discrimination." *Des luttes et des rires* 3 (1): 18–20.
Des Rivières, Marie-Josée. 1995. "*La vie en rose*, 1980–1987: un magazine féministe haut en couleur." *Recherches féministes* 8 (2): 127–36. https://doi.org/10.7202/057849ar.
Descarries-Bélanger, Francine, and Shirley Roy. 1988. *Le mouvement des femmes et ses courants de pensée: essai de typologie*. CRIAW papers/Les documents de l'ICREF. Ottawa: Institut Canadien de recherches sur les femmes/Canadian Research Institute for the Advancement of Women, 40 pp.
Désy, Marielle, Marc Ferland, Benoît Lévesque, and Yves Vaillancourt. 1980. *La conjoncture au Québec au début des années 80: les enjeux pour le mouvement ouvrier et populaire*. Rimouski: La librairie socialiste de l'Est du Québec.
Dhruvarajan, Vanaja, and Jill Vickers. 2002. *Gender, Race and Nation: A Global Perspective*. Toronto: University of Toronto Press.
Di Lello, Lucianna. 1975. "L'aborto: non berlinghiamo." *Effe* 3 (1): 33.
Diotima. 1987. *Il pensiero della differenza sessuale*. Milan: La Tartaruga edizioni.
"Documento del comitato per l'aborto e la contraception." 1975. *Effe* 3 (5): 38.
Donne e politica. 1978. "Documento." *Effe* 6 (6): 39–41.
Donolo, Carlo. 1968. "La politica ridefinita: note sul movimento studentesco." *Quaderni Piacentini* 35: 93–125.
–. 1976. "Oltre il '68: la società italiana tra mutamento e tranzizione." *Quaderni Piacentini* 60–61: 3–38.
Dossier de lutte pour l'avortement et la contraception libre. 1975. *Dossier spécial sur l'avortement et la contraception libres et gratuits*. Collaboration, Claire Brassard. 46 pp.
"Dossier: femmes immigrantes." 1978. *Des luttes et des rires* 2 (1): 12–41.
"Dossier-bilan." 1979. *Des luttes et des rires* 3 (1): 21–28.
Dubois, Sophie. 2017. *Refus Global: histoire d'une réception partielle*. Montréal: Les presses de l'Université de Montréal.
Dûchaine, Vivien. 1986–87. "Les femmes haïtiennes au Québec." *RFR/DRF* 15 (4): 10–12.
Dufault, Roseanna. 2012. "L'essentiel de Jovette Marchessault: les 'Terribles vivantes' de Dorothy Todd Hénaut." In *De l'invisible au visible: l'imaginaire de Jovette Marchessault*, ed. Roseanna Dufault and Celita Lamar, 75–88. Montréal: Les éditions du remue-ménage.
Dufault, Roseanna, and Celita Lamar. 2012. *De l'invisible au visible: l'imaginaire de Jovette Marchessault*. Montréal: Les éditions du remue-ménage.

Dumont, Micheline. 1998. "L'histoire nationale peut-elle intégrer la réflexion féministe sur l'histoire?" In *À propos de l'histoire nationale*, ed. Robert Comeau and Bernard Dionne, 19–36. Québec: Septentrion.

Dumont, Micheline, and Louise Toupin. 2003. *La pensée féministe au Québec*. Montréal: Les éditions du remue-ménage.

Dupont, Sylvie, Ariane Emond, Lise Moisan, and Francine Pelletier. 1979–80. "Faire La vie en rose." *Le Temps fou* (December–February), n.p.

Dupuis-Déri, Francis. 2008. *Québec en mouvements: idées et pratiques militantes contemporaines*. Montréal: Lux.

Durocher, Constance. 1990. "L'hétérosexualité: sexualité ou système social." *RFR/DRF* 19 (3–4): 18–22.

"Éditorial." 1976. *Les Têtes de Pioche* (March): 2.

"Éditorial: Aimons-nous les hommes?" 1982. *La vie en rose* (June–August): 4–5.

"Éditorial: Enfin un 8 mars unitaire ... ou presque." 1978. *Pluri-elles* 1 (4): 3–4.

"Éditorial: *Pluri-elles*, un an après des changements s'amorcent." 1978. *Pluri-elles* 1 (6): 3–5.

"Éditorial: Pourquoi *Pluri-elles* maintenant?" 1977. *Pluri-elles*. 1 (1): 2.

E fu la minigonna: protagonisti e interpreti del '68 a Napoli. 1998. ed. Nadia Nappo. Naples: Biblioteca Nazionale di Napoli.

Ellena, Liliana. 2005. "Spazi e culture politiche nel femminismo torinese: un percorso tra memoria e ricerca storica degli anni Noventa ad oggi." In *Il femminismo degli anni settanta*, ed. Teresa Bertilotti and Anna Scattigno, 225–44. Rome: Viella.

Emilia. 1981. "Lesbismo – Se hai buona memoria ... la mia lotta è anche la tua." Del M.F.R. di via Pompeo Magno, *Quotidiano Donna* 4 (14): 12.

Epstein, Barbara. 2001. "What Happened to the Women's Movement?" *Monthly Review* 53 (1): 1. https://doi.org/10.14452/mr-053-01-2001-05_1.

Ergas, Yasmine. 1976. "Aborti con orrore." *Effe* 4 (9–10): 28–30.

–. 1981. "Femminismo e giovani." *Inquiesta* 54: 44–51.

–. 1982. "Biografie femministe: la militanza fra cultura e politica negli anni '70 in Italia." *Memoria* 4: 88–100.

–. 1986. *Nelle maglie della politica: femminismo, istituzioni, e politiche sociali nell'Italia degli anni '70*. Milan: FrancoAngeli.

–. 1987. "Tra sesso e genere." *Memoria* 19–20 (1–2): 11–18.

Ergas, Yasmine, and Sandra Sassaroli. 1976. "CRAC: il punto sull'aborto." *Effe* 4 (11): 37–38.

Fachinelli, Elvio. 1968. "Gruppo chiuso o gruppo aperto? Frammento di un'analisi di gruppo." *Quaderni Piacentini* 36: 107–24.

Falquet, Jules. 2005. "Trois questions aux mouvements sociaux 'progressites': apports de la théorie féministe à l'analyse des mouvements sociaux." *Nouvelles questions féministes* 24 (3): 18–35. https://doi.org/10.3917/nqf.243.0018.

Fanon, Frantz. 1952. *Peau noire, masques blancs*. Paris: Éditions du Seuil.

Farrington, Doris. 1978. "La politica dei consultori gestiti dalle donne." *Differenze* 6 (6–7): 17–20.

Federici, Silvia. 2007 [1974]. "Il Salario contro il lavoro domestico." In *Gli autonomi: le storie, le lotte, le teorie*, ed. Sergio Bianchi and Lanfranco Caminiti, 123–30. Rome: DeriveApprodi.

Feman Orenstein, Gloria. 2012 [1978]. "Jovette Marchessault ou la quête extatique de la nouvelle chaman féministe." In *De l'invisible au visible: l'imaginaire de Jovette*

Marchessault, ed. Roseanna Dufault and Celita Lamar, 55–73. Montréal: Les éditions du remue-ménage.
"Femminismo oggi: esperienza di gruppo." 1975. *Effe* 3 (5): 23–32.
Fillieule, Olivier, Lilian Mathieu, and Patricia Roux. 2007. "Introduction." *Politix* 2 (78): 7–12. https://doi.org/10.3917/pox.078.0007.
Fillieule, Olivier, and Patricia Roux. 2009. *Le sexe du militantisme*. Paris: Presses de Sciences Po.
Firestone, Shulamith. 1970. *The Dialectic of Sex and Feminism and Ecology*. Toronto: Bantam.
Foletti, Lara. 1975. "Aborto: solo la donna puo decidere." *Effe* 3 (1): 16.
Fondazione Elvira Badaracco. 2003. *Archivi del Femminismo: "Conservare, Progettara, Comunicare."* Milan: Fondazione Elvira Badaracco.
Fortin, Andrée. 1993. *Passage de la modernité: les intellectuels québécois et leurs revues*. Québec: Presses de l'Université Laval.
Forum pour un Québec féminin pluriel. 1994. *Pour changer le monde*. Montréal: Les éditions Écosociété.
Frabotta, Biancamaria. 1975 [1973]. *Femminismo e lotta di classe in Italia: analisi, documenti e prospettive*. Rome: Savelli.
–. 1978. *La politica del femminismo: il movimento femminista, l'Unione delle donne italiane, le forze politiche di sinistra di fronte al femminismo nei documenti, 1973–1976*. Rome: Savelli.
Fraire, Manuela. 1977. "Il nostro movimento e il loro." *Quaderni Piacentini* 64: 43–51.
–. 1979. "Femminismo: politica dell'emancipazione o emancipazione della politica." *Effe* 7 (10–12): 28–29.
–. 2002 [1978]. *Lessico politico delle donne: teorie del femminismo*. Milan: Fondazione Elvira Badaracco/FrancoAngeli.
Fraire, Manuela, Mariella Gramaglia, Margherita Ripetto, and Giglia Tedesco. 1977. "Movimento e instituzioni." *DWF (Donnawomanfemme)* 4: 5–45.
Francescato, Donata. 1977. "Consultori: val la pena di participare." *Effe* 5 (6): 29–33.
Francescato, Grazia. 1975. "No al compromesso sul nostro corpo. No al compromesso sull'aborto." *Effe* 3 (11): 9–10.
–. 1976. "Contraddizioni della doppia militanza." *Effe* 4 (6): 12–13.
Franzinetti, Vicky. 1987. "Il senso dell'autogestione." *Memoria* 19–20: 181–87.
Franzway, Suzanne, Dianne Court, and R.W. Connell. 1989. *Staking a Claim: Feminism, Bureaucracy and the State*. Cambridge: Polity Press.
Front de libération des femmes du Québec. 1982 [1970]. "Lettre à des féministes américaines." In *Québécoises deboutte!* Collection complète, ed. Véronique O'Leary and Louise Toupin, 79–80. Montréal: Les éditions du remue-ménage.
Gaboriau, Linda. 1985. "A Luminous Wake in the Space." *Canadian Theatre Review* 43 (Summer): 91–99.
"Gagner son ciel ou gagner sa vie?" 1981. *La vie en rose* (March–May): 13–25.
Gagnon, François-Marc. 1998. *Chronique du mouvement automatiste québécois, 1941–1954*. Montréal: Lanctôt Éditeur.
Giorda, Nicoletta. 2007. *Fare la differenza: l'esperienza dell'Intercategoriale donne di Torino, 1975–1986*. Turin: Edizioni Angolo Manzoni.
Giuliani, Gaia, and Cristina Lombardi-Diop. 2013. *Bianco e nero: storia dell'identità razziale degli Italiani*. Milan: Mondadori.

Glynn, Ruth. 2009. "Writing the Terrorist Self: The Unspeakable Alterity of Italy's Female Perpetrators." *Feminist Review* 92: 1–18. https://doi.org/10.1057/fr.2009.6.

Gobetti, Daniele, Carlotta Graffigna, and Giulia Tappi. 1979. "Torino: cosa rimane delle lotte delle donne?" *Effe* 7 (6): 28–29.

Godard, Barbara. 2002. "Feminist Periodicals and the Production of Cultural Value: The Canadian Context." *Women's Studies International Forum* 25 (2): 209–23. https://doi.org/10.1016/s0277-5395(02)00231-5.

–. 2008. "The Politics of Representation: Some Native Canadian Women Writers." In *Canadian Literature at the Crossroads of Language and Culture*, ed. Smaro Kamboureli, 109–59. Edmonton: NeWest Press.

Gramaglia, Mariella. 1975a. "Divorzio, PCI, liberazione della donna." In *Femminismo e lotta di classe: analisi, documenti e prospettive*, ed. Biancamaria Frabotta, 193–99. Rome: Savelli.

–. 1975b. "Introduzione." In *La rivoluzione più lunga: saggi sulla condizione della donna nella società a capitalismo avanzato*, ed. Mariella Gramaglia, 5–21. Rome: Savelli.

–. 1987. "Affinità e conflitto con la nuova sinistra." *Memoria* 19–20 (1–2): 19–37.

Gramsci, Antonio. 1975. *Quaderni del carcere*, ed. Valentino Gerratana, Edizione critica dell'Istituto Gramsci. Turin: Einaudi.

"Grande è il disordine nella testa dei compagni la situazione è dunque preoccupante." 1977. *Operaie della casa*. Numero speciale/documento. 24 pp.

Grandi, Aldo. 2003. *La generazione degli anni perduti: Storie di Potere Operaio*. Turin: Einaudi.

Green, Mary Jane. 2009. "Locating Québec on the Postcolonial Map." In *Postcolonial Thought in the French-Speaking World*, ed. Charles Forsdick and David Murphy, 248–58. Liverpool: Liverpool University Press.

Groppi, Angela, and Margherita Pelaja. 1983. "L'io diviso delle storiche." *Memoria* 9 (3): 7–19.

Grossberg, Lawrence, Cary Nelson, and Paula A. Treichler. 1992. *Cultural Studies*. London: Routledge.

Gruppo 4. 1983. "Più donne che uomini." *Sottosopra verde*, special issue, Milan: 1–4.

Gruppo di compagne del centro romano del *Il Manifesto*. 1975. "Documento." In *Femminismo e lotta di classe: analisi, documenti e prospettive*, ed. Biancamaria Frabotta, 227–48. Rome: Savelli.

Gruppo di Soggettività Lesbica. 2005. *Cocktail d'amore: 700 e più modi di essere lesbica*. Milan: Libera Università delle Donne.

Gruppo femminista per la salute delle donne di Roma. 1977. "Parliamo della nostra salute." *Effe* 5 (9): 16–19.

Gruppo femminista per una medicina della donna. 1974. "Anti concezionali: della parte della donna: perché abbiamo deciso si scrivere questo libretto?" *Sottosopra*, 39–42.

Gruppo Femminista per una medicina delle donne di Milano. 1976. "Seveso: la scelta non esiste." *Effe* 4 (9–10): 38–39.

Gruppo Gramsci di Roma. 1973. "Perché si cerca di organizzarsi interno al problema donna." In *Femminismo e lotta di classe in Italia: analisi, documenti e prospettive*, ed. Biancamaria Frabotta, 222–26. Rome: Savelli.

Guadagni, Anna Maria. 1984. "Nuova face dell'UDI." *Memoria* 13 (4): 13–30.

Guay, Lorraine. 1998. "Les différents courants de l'économie sociale." *Des pratiques novatrices en économie sociale,* Actes du colloque, Économie communautaire de Francheville: 7–37.

Guberman, Nancy, Jocelyne Lamoureux, Jennifer Breeman, Danielle Fournier, and Lise Gervais. 2004. *Le défi des pratiques démocratiques dans les groupes de femmes.* Montréal: Éd. Saint-Martin.

Guénette, Françoise. 1985a. "Débat pour un journal." *La vie en rose* 28: 15.

–. 1985b. "La gloire aller-retour." *La vie en rose* 24: 4–5.

–. 1985c. "Histoire de Q ... prologue." *La vie en rose. Tenter l'érotisme,* special summer edition (July–August): 32–33, 36–37.

–. 1992. "Un Québec féminin pluriel: l'année de tous les défis." *Gazette des femmes,* 1 September. http://www.gazettedesfemmes.ca/5455/un-quebec-feminin-pluriel-lannee-de-tous-les-defis/.

Guerra, Elda. 2004. "Femminismo/femminismi: appunti per una storia da scrivere." *Genesis* 3, 1: 87–111.

–. 2005. "Una nuova soggettività: femminismo e femminismi nel passaggio degli anni settanta." In *Il femminismo degli anni settanta,* ed. Teresa Bertilotti and Anna Scattigno, 25–67. Rome: Viella.

Guha, Ranajit. 2000. "On Some Aspects of the History of Colonial India." In *Mapping Subaltern Studies and the Postcolonial,* ed. Vinayak Chaturvedi, 1–7. London: Verso.

Hall, Stuart. 1996 [1992]. "Cultural Studies and Its Theoretical Legacies." In *Stuart Hall: Critical Dialogue in Cultural Studies,* ed. David Morley and Kuan-Hsing Chen, 262–75. London: Routledge.

Hanisch, Carol. 1970. "The Personal Is Political." In *Notes from the Second Year: Women's Liberation; Major Writings of the Radical Feminists,* ed. Shulamith Firestone and Ann Koedt, 76–77. New York: New York Radical Women.

Hellman, Judith Adler. 1987. *Journeys among Women: Feminism in Five Italian Cities.* New York/Cambridge: Oxford University Press/Polity Press.

Hill Collins, Patricia, and Sirma Bilge. 2016. *Intersectionality.* Cambridge: Polity Press.

Horguelin, Christophe. 2010. "Postface." In *Manifeste d'octobre 1970: Front de libération du Québec,* 27–40. Montréal: Lux.

Hull, Gloria T., Patricia Bell Scott, and Patricia Smith. 1982. *All the Women Are White, All the Blacks Are Men, But Some of Us Are Brave.* New York: The Feminist Press.

"Il Corpo politico: In che modo è stata colpita la donna nei fatti di Firenze." 1975. *Sottosopra* (February): 3–27.

Ines. 1979. "Un utile strumento do conoscenza e riflessione." *Bollettino donne di Torino* 5: 13.

Ingargiola, Lilliana, and Marinella Cucchi. 1987. "Dialogo sul movimento di Liberazione della donna." *Memoria* 19–20: 49–65.

Jacquemart, Alban. 2013. "L'engagement féministe des hommes, entre contestation et reproduction du genre." *Cahiers du genre* 2 (55): 49–63. https://doi.org/10.3917/cdge.055.0049.

James, Selma. 1997. "Introduction to *The Power of Women and the Subversion of Community.*" In *Materialist Feminism: A Reader in Class, Difference, and Women's Lives,* ed. Rosemary Hennessy and Chris Ingraham, 33–39. New York: Routledge.

–. 2012a [1974]. "Sex, Race and Class." Reprinted in *Sex, Race and Class: The Perspective of Winning – A Selection of Writings, 1952–2011*, 92–101. Oakland, CA: PM Press.

–. 2012b [1972]. "Women, the Unions and Work, or What Is Not to Be Done." Reprinted in *Sex, Race and Class: The Perspective of Winning – A Selection of Writings, 1952–2011*, 60–75. Oakland, CA: PM Press.

Jean, Michèle. 1979. "Éditorial." *Les têtes de Pioche* 3 (7): 2.

Jenson, Jane. 1992. "Getting to Morgentaler: From One Representation to Another." In *The Politics of Abortion*, ed. Janine Brodie, Shelley Gavigan, and Jane Jenson, 15–56. Toronto: Oxford University Press.

Jessica, Ines, and Marcella. 1983. "Nuovi antichi lavori." *Bollettino delle donne* 2 (2): 6–7.

Jèwell, Keala, and Maricla Tagliaferri. 1976. "Femminismo USA, un tentativo di analisi." *Effe* 4 (1): 8–10.

Jezo-Vannier, Steven. 2013. *Contre-culture(s): des Anonymous à Promethée*. Marseille: Éditions les mots et le reste.

Kaplan, Caren, Norma Alarcón, and Minoo Moallem. 1999. *Between Woman and Nation: Nationalisms, Transnational Feminisms, and the State*. Durham, NC: Duke University Press.

Keucheyan, Razmig. 2010. *Hémisphère Gauche: une cartographie des nouvelles pensées*. Montréal: Lux.

Kinsman, Gary, and Patrizia Gentile. 2010. *The Canadian War on Queers: National Security as Sexual Regulation*. Vancouver: UBC Press.

Kittay, Eva Feder. 1998. "Welfare Dependency, and a Public Ethic of Care." In *Whose Welfare*, ed. Gwendlyn Mink, 189–213. Ithaca, NY: Cornell University Press.

K.J. 1972 [1970]. "Les militantes." *Partisans: Libération des femmes, Année zéro* 54–55: 90–100.

Kostash, Myrna. 1992 [1977]. *All of Baba's Children*. Edmonton: NeWest Press.

"La diversità che c'è tra di noi." 1976. *Effe* 4 (1): 3–6.

"La 'nuova strategia.'" 1977. *Operaie della casa*. Numero speciale/documento. 23 pp.

"La situazione e la nostra politica." n.d. Milan: Fondazione Elvira Badaracco. 6 pp.

Labelle-Hogue, Simon-Pier. 2013. "La contre-culture québécoise par la méthode, lieux de distinction." In *Contre-culture*, ed. Christophe Bourseillier et Olivier Penot-Lacassagne, 62–74. Paris: Éditions du CNRS.

Lacelle, Nicole. 1988. *Entretiens avec Madeleine Parent et Léa Robak*. Montréal: Les éditions du remue-ménage.

Laforce, Hélène, and Francine Saillant. 1993. "Le jeu des règles." In *Avortement: pratiques, enjeux, contrôle social*, ed. Diane Lamoureux, 17–47. Montréal: Les éditions du remue-ménage.

Lamar, Celita. 2012. "Jovette Marchessault: jalons d'un parcours exceptionnel." In *De l'invisible au visible: l'imaginaire de Jovette Marchessault*, ed. Roseanna Dufault and Celita Lamar, 17–24. Montréal: Les éditions du remue-ménage.

Lamontagne, Christian. 1978. "Une crise idéologique contemporaine." *Le Temps fou* 1 (1): 45–53.

"L'amour toujours l'amour." 1982. *La vie en rose* (June–August): 25–44.

Lamoureux, Diane. 1983. "La lutte pour le droit à l'avortement (1969–1981)." *Revue d'histoire de l'Amérique française* 37 (1): 81–90. https://doi.org/10.7202/304126ar.

–. 1986. *Fragments et collages: essai sur le féminisme québécois des années 70*, Montréal: Les éditions du remue-ménage.
–. 1987. "Nationalism and Feminism in Québec: An Impossible Attraction." In *Feminism and Political Economy: Women's Work, Women's Struggles*, ed. Heather Jon Maroney and Meg Luxton, 51–68. Toronto: Methuen.
–. 1989. *Citoyennes? Femmes, droit de vote et démocratie*. Montréal: Les éditions du remue-ménage.
–. 1993. "Une victoire à la Pyrrhus? La lutte pour le droit à l'avortement." In *Avortement: pratiques, enjeux, contrôle social*, ed. Diane Lamoureux, 171–98. Montréal: Les éditions du remue-ménage.
–. 2001. *L'amère patrie: féminisme et nationalisme dans le Québec contemporain*. Montréal: Les éditions du remue-ménage.
Lamoureux, Jocelyne. 1994. *Le partenariat à l'épreuve*. Montréal: Éditions Saint-Martin.
Lanctôt, Louise. 1981. *Une sorcière comme les autres*. Montréal: Québec Amérique.
Larose, Karim. 2013. "Terra incognita" (interview by Jean-Philippe Warren). *Liberté: art et politique* 299 (Spring):14–18.
Laura. 1978. "Fuori-donna polemico." *Effe* 6 (5): 40.
Laurin, Nicole. 2005. "Génèse de la sociologie marxiste au Québec." *Sociologie et sociétés* 37 (2): 183–207. https://doi.org/10.7202/012917ar.
Laurin-Frenette, Nicole, and Jean-François Léonard. 1980. "Par-delà l'écran référendaire." In *L'impasse: enjeux et perspectives de l'après-référendum*," ed. Nicole Laurin-Frenette et Jean-François Léonard, 13–23. Montréal: Nouvelle optique.
Lawrence, Bonita. 2004. *"Real" Indians and Others: Mixed-Blood Urban Native Peoples and Indigenous Nationhood*. Vancouver: UBC Press.
Lazzarato, Maurizio. 2004 [1997]. "La generazione dell '77 nel Veneto orientale." In *Settantasette: la rivoluzione che viene*, ed. Sergio Bianchi and Lanfranco Caminiti, 273–81. Rome: DeriveApprodi.
"Le journal, pourquoi." 1982 [1971]. *Québécoises deboutte!* 1 (9): 2–3.
Lea, Giorgia, Maria, Zulma, Virginia, Franca, Leonella, and *Sottosopra Rosso*. 1975. "Intransigenza rivoluzionaria o separazione?" Fondazione Elvira Badaracco. 2 pp.
Leonelli, Leslie E. 1975. "Il costo sociale dell'aborto." *Effe* 3 (1): 17.
Leonelli, Leslie, and Pirkko Peltonen. 1975. "Self-Help: le streghe sono tornate." *Effe* 3 (5): 36–39.
"Les femmes et l'information: une lutte constante, un besoin fondamental." 1980. *Des luttes et des rires* 3 (5): 21–51.
Lesage, Marc. 1986. *Les vagabonds du rêve: vers une société de marginaux*. Montréal: Boréal.
Lessard, Diane. 1989. "Le militantisme politique des femmes de l'extrême-gauche québécoise entre 1972 et 1982." PhD diss., Université de Montréal.
"Lettera a *Effe*." 1976. By Giordana and Elena, letter followed by a response from some women comrades of *Effe*. *Sottosopra*: 80–81.
Lévesque, Andrée. 1973. "The Canadian Left in Quebec during the Great Depression: The Communist Party of Canada and the Co-operative Commonwealth Federation in Quebec, 1929–1939." PhD diss., Duke University.
–. 1984. *Virage à gauche interdit: les communistes, les socialistes et leurs ennemis, 1929–1939*. Montréal: Boréal.

–. 1999. *L'Époque de Jeanne Corbin, 1906–1944*. Montréal: Les éditions du remue-ménage.

Libera Cerchia. 1981. "Percorso del'autonomia." *I modi e le tematiche del femminismo a Napoli*. Atti del Convegno a Napoli. 8–22 May, 1980, 47–52. Naples: Comune di Napoli, Studi Centro ondizione della Donna.

"Liberare la vita dal lavoro." 2007 [1975]. In *Gli autonomi: le storie, le lotte, le teorie*, ed. Sergio Bianchi and Lanfranco Caminiti, 174–78. Rome: DeriveApprodi.

Libraro, Gabriella, Chiara Mercogliano, and Teresa Tommaselli. 1981. "Trace dell'identità-donna nella storia della familia." In *I modi e le tematiche del femminismo a Napoli*. Atti del Convegno a Napoli. 8–22 May, 1980, 70–73. Naples: Comune di Napoli, Centro Studi Condizione della donna.

Libreria delle donne. 2005a. *Noi, utopia della donna di ieri, memoria della donna di domani 1965–2005: cronologia, fotografie e documenti sui percorsi delle donne a Milano*. Fotomontaggio. Milan: DonnaMostra.

–. 2005b [1987]. *Non credere di avere dei diritti: la generazione della libertà femminile nell'idea e nelle vicende di un gruppo di donne*. Turin: Rosenberg and Sellier.

Lilli, Laura. 1979. "La doppia militanza come esistanza." In *Cara compagne: il femminismo nel PCI e nelle organizzazioni di massa*, ed. Lilli and Valentini, 9–31. Rome: Editore Riuniti.

Lilli, Laura, and Chiara Valentini. 1979. *Cara compagne: il femminismo nel PCI e nelle organizzazioni di massa*. Rome: Editore Riuniti.

"L'occupazione al Policlinico." 1979. Interview with Simonetta Tosi. *Differenze* 10: 42–46.

Lonzi, Carla. 1970a. "Manifesto di Rivolta femminile." *Rivolta femminile* 1–3: 11–18.

–. 1970b. "Sputiamo su Hegel." *Rivolta femminile* 1–3: 19–61.

–. 1978. "Io dico io." La presenza dell uomo nel femminismo. *Rivolta femminile* 9: 7–9.

Lotta Femminista. 1973. "Convegno di Londra." *Sottosopra* 1: 5–7.

–. 1974. "8–9–10 a Mestre: comitato per il salario alla casalinga." *Sottosopra* 2: 119–31.

Lotta Femminista and Collettivo Internazionale Femminista. 1972. "Alla Redazione del *Manifesto*." Quaderni di Lotta Femminista. Tommaso Musolini Editore 1: 18–21.

Louise, Céline, Wendy, Gail, Marie-Josée, Carole, Cécile, Nicole, Chris, and Danièle. 1979. "Un autre son de cloche ..." *Des luttes et des rires* 3 (2): 63.

Mac an Ghaill, Mártín, and Chris Haywood. 2007. *Gender, Culture and Society: Contemporary Femininities and Masculinities*. London: Palgrave Macmillan.

"Madre buona e cattiva." 1974. Milan: Fondazione Elvira Badaracco. 14 pp.

Magaraggia, Sveva, and Mariagrazia Leone. 2010. "Gender and Women's Studies in Italy: Looking Back to Look Forward." *European Journal of Women's Studies* 17 (4): 425–29. https://doi.org/10.1177/1350506810377407.

Major, Robert. 2013 [1979]. *Parti pris: idéologies et littérature*. Montréal: Éditions nota bene.

Mangiacapre, Lina. 1979. "Follia come poesia: riprendiamoci il corpo mare." *Documenti della III e IV Rassegna del cinema femminista*. Sorrento: 9–11.

–. 1998. "Intervista." In *E fu la minigonna: protagoniste e interpreti del '68 a Napoli*, ed. Nadia Nappo, n.p. Naples: Biblioteca Nazionale.

–. n.d. "La psicofavola: metodo teatrale e di autocoscienza." http://www.lenemesiache.it/nemesiache_bio.php.
Mantini, Silvia. 2000. "Women's History in Italy: Cultural Itineraries and New Proposals in Current Historiography." *Journal of Women's History* 12 (2): 170–98. https://doi.org/10.1353/jowh.2000.0041.
Maraini, Dacia. 2003. "Interview of Dacia Maraini by Branko Gorjup." *Love Letters*. Toronto: Guernica.
Marchessault, Jovette. 1981. "Fait d'hiver." *La vie en rose* (December–February 1981–82): 39–40.
–. 2012. "Le chemin où j'avance." In *De l'invisible au visible: l'imaginaire de Jovette Marchessault*, ed. Roseanna Dufault and Celita Lamar, 11. Montréal: Les éditions du remue-ménage.
Marcolini, Patrick. 2012. *Le mouvement situationiste: une histoire intellectuelle*. Montreuil: L'Échappée.
Marie-Géographie. 1982. "D'un 8 mars à l'autre ... : dossier." Québec: *Marie-Géographie – écrits rebelles féministes et socialistes*. 18 pp.
Martin, Agathe. 1976. "Le silence des femmes et la censure politique." *Les têtes de Pioche* (October), 6.
Martucci, Chiara. 2008. *Libreria delle donne di Milano*. Milan: FrancoAngeli.
Masi, Paola. 1984. "Come vive un'istituzione: il Centro culturale Virginia Woolf." *Memoria* 13: 57–62.
Masson, Dominique. 1998. "With and Despite the State: Doing Women's Movement Politics in Local Service Groups in the 1980s in Québec." PhD diss., Carleton University.
Mazzuca, Floriana. 1981. "Il movimento femminista e le questioni di informazioni." In *I modi e le tematiche del femminismo a Napoli*, 103–11. Atti del Convegno, Naples: Comune di Napoli, Centro di Studi, Condizione della donna.
McAndrew, Michael. 1965. "Le syndicalisme étudiant québécois." *Parti Pris* 2 (6): 19–28.
McKay, Ian. 2005. *Rebels, Reds, Radicals: Rethinking Canada's Left History*. Toronto: Between the Lines.
Melandri, Lea. 1972. "Picolo pene, escolta." *Erba voglio* 2 (7): 14–21.
–. 1977. *L'infamia originaria: facciamola finite col cuore e la politica*, Milan: Edizioni L'erba voglio.
–. 2000. *Una visceralità indicibile: la pratica dell'inconscio nel movimento delle donne degli anni settenta*. Fondazione Elvira Badaracco. Milan: FrancoAngeli.
–. 2002. "Gli oggetti seppellitti negli archivi delle donne." *Genesis: Società italiana delle storiche* 1 (2): 205–12.
–. 2003. "Letture d'archivio." *Archivi del femminismo: conservare, progettare, communicare*, 39–46. Milan: Fondazione Elvira Badaracco.
–. 2005. "La 'protesta estrema' del femminismo." In *Il femminismo degli anni settanta*, ed. Teresa Bertilotti e Anna Scattigno, 81–98. Rome: Viella.
Melchiori, Paola. 1987. "Verifica d'identità, materiali, esperienze, reflessioni sul fare cultura tra donne." Milan: Utopià.
–. 2006. "The 'Free University of Women': Reflections on the Conditions for a Feminist Politics of Knowledge." *Advances in Gender Research* 10: 131–50. https://doi.org/10.1016/s1529-2126(06)10006-5.

–. 2015. “Psychoanalysis in Early Italian Feminism: The Contributions of the Practice of the Unconscious.” In *Contemporary Italian Philosophy*, ed. Antonio Calcagno, 75–98. Albany, NY: SUNY Press.

Menapace, Lidia. 1975. “L’autogestione è il nostro obiettivo.” *Effe* 3 (8): 10.

Meringolo, Patrizia. 1978. “L’autocoscienza come ricerca del movimento.” *DWF (Donnawomanfemme)* 9: 123–34.

Michaud, Jacinthe. 1987. “L’état des rapports entre le mouvement syndical et les groupes de base issus des nouveaux mouvements sociaux.” MA thesis, Laval University.

–. 1992. “The Welfare State and the Problem of Counter-Hegemonic Responses within the Women’s Movement.” In *Organizing Dissent: Contemporary Social Movements in Theory and in Practice*, 1st ed., ed. William K. Carroll, 200–14. Toronto: Garamond Press.

–. 1995. “Angel Makers or Trouble Makers? The Health Centres Movement in Québec and the Conditions of Formation of a Feminist Counter-Hegemony on Health.” PhD diss., University of Toronto, 1995.

–. 1996. “Le mouvement féministe sur la santé des femmes: forces et limites de sa formation discursive et des conditions d’émergence du côté de l’espace public.” In *Femmes francophones et pluralisme en milieu minoritaire, Actes du Colloque du Réseau des chercheures de l’Ontario français*, ed. Dyane Adam, 73–88. Ottawa: University of Ottawa Press.

–. 1997a. “Le mouvement des centres de santé: grandeur et misère de la participation et stratégies politiques de transformation du discours de l’État.” *Nouvelles pratiques sociales* 10 (1): 97–110. https://doi.org/10.7202/301389ar.

–. 1997b. “On Counter-hegemonic Formation in the Women’s Movement and the Difficult Integration of Collective Identity.” In *Organizing Dissent: Contemporary Social Movements in Theory and in Practice*, 2nd ed., ed. William K. Carroll, 197–212. Toronto: Garamond Press.

–. 1998. “Auto-santé et avortement: difficile cohabitation de la lutte politique et de la politique des services.” *Atlantis* 22 (2): 62–73.

–. 2000. “The Restructuring of the Health Care System in Québec: Its Impact on the Women’s Health Movement.” *Studies in Political Economy* 61: 31–48. https://doi.org/10.1080/19187033.2000.11675252.

–. 2005. *Conscience subalterne, conscience identitaire: la voix des femmes assistées au sein des organisations féministes et communautaires.* Ottawa: University of Ottawa Press.

–. 2006. “Is Social Economy for Women better than Workfare? The Case of Home Care Services in Québec and Ontario.” *RFR/DRF* 31 (3–4): 43–65.

–. 2007. “Teaching Women’s Organizing and the Women’s Movement: The Question of Arts and Culture within Feminism.” *RFR/DRF* 32 (3–4): 29–43.

–. 2008. “Nationalism, Marxism, Tiers-Mondism and Counter-Culturalism: Towards a Discursive Genealogy of Québec Feminism during the ’70s and ’80s.” Paper presented at the International Congress, Women’s World, Universidad Complutense, Madrid, Spain, July.

–. 2009. “La représentation des besoins et l’obstacle de la double loyauté dans la recherche féministe.” *Canadian Review of Social Policy* 62 (Spring): 72–88.

–. 2010. “La reconnaissance des apports théoriques du féminisme dans la presse alternative de gauche: le cas du *Temps fou*.” *Politique et sociétés* 29 (2): 29–45. https://doi.org/10.7202/045154ar.

–. 2012. "Au *Temps fou* de *La vie en rose*: deux visions féministes des rapports amoureux et du changement social." *Canadian Woman Studies/Les cahiers de la femme* 29 (3): 160–73.

–. 2013. "The Politics Representation and the Problem of Loyalties within Feminist Research: Revisiting the Position/Location of the 'Native Informant' in Gayatri Spivak." *Studies in Political Economy* 91: 159–84. https://doi.org/10.1080/19187033.2013.11674986.

–. 2016. "Synergy between Feminism and the Left: Two Moments in the Genealogy of Feminism as a Political Movement." In *A World to Win: Contemporary Social Movements and Counter-Hegemony*, ed. William Carroll and Kanchan Sarker, 342–55. Winnipeg: ARP Books.

Mies, Maria. 1986. *Patriarchy and Accumulation on a World Scale: Women in the International Division of Labour*. London: Zed Books.

Miles, Angela. 1992. "Le féminisme, la nouvelle gauche et la politique post-industrielle." In *Les formes modernes de la démocratie*, ed. Gérard Boismenu, Pierre Hamel, and Georges Labica, 225–43. Paris/ Montréal: L'Haramattan/ Presses de l'Université de Montréal.

Mills, Sean. 2004. "Québécoises Deboutte! Le Front de libération des femmes du Québec, le Centre des femmes et le nationalisme." *Mens* 4 (2): 183–210. https://doi.org/10.7202/1024596ar.

–. 2010. *The Empire Within: Postcolonial Thought and Political Activism in Sixties Montreal*. Montreal and Kingston: McGill-Queen's University Press.

Milot, Pierre. 1982. "Généalogie du discours Marxiste-léniniste au Québec, 1972–1982." *Les Cahiers du socialisme* 10–11: 181–207.

Miron, Gaston. 1998 [1970]. *L'homme rapaillé*. Montréal: Typo.

MLD (Movimento di liberazione delle donne). 1975. "Congressi a confronto MLD." *Effe* 3 (3): 36.

–. n.d. "Piattaforma dei principi del Movimento di Liberazione della donna (MLD)." Fondazione Elvira Badaracco. 8 pp.

Moallem, Minoo. 2005. *Between Warrior Brother and Veiled Sister: Islamic Fundamentalism and the Politics of Patriarchy in Iran*. Berkeley: University of California Press.

Mohanty, Chandra Talpade. 1988. "Under Western Eyes: Feminist Scholarship and Colonial Discourses." In *Feminist Postcolonial Theory: A Reader*, ed. Reina Lewis and Sara Mills, 49–74. New York: Routledge.

Monti, Adriana. 1980. *Scuola senza fine*. Short film, Milan.

Moraga, Cherrie, and Gloria Anzaldúa. 1981. *This Bridge Called My Back*. New York: SUNY Press.

Moretti, Mario. 2004 [1997]. "Con quell movimento abbiamo interagito pocchissimo." Interview by Carla Mosca and Rossana Rossanda, in *Settantasette: la rivoluzione che viene*, ed. Sergio Bianchi and Lanfranco Caminiti, 404–6. Rome: DeriveApprodi.

–. 2007. *Brigate Rosse: una storia italiana*. Interviews with Carla Mosca and Rossana Rossanda. Milan: Mondadori.

Morley, David, and Kuan-Hsing Chen. 1996. *Stuart Hall: Critical Dialogue in Cultural Studies*, ed. David Morley and Kuan-Hsing Chen, 262–75. London: Routledge.

Morton, Peggy. 1971. "A Woman's Work Is Never Done." In *From Feminism to Liberation*, ed. Edith Hoshino Altbach, 211–27. Cambridge: Schenkman Publishing.

Motapanyane, Maki. 2009. "The Politics of Feminism in South Africa: Gender Consciousness and Political Agency in the Twentieth Century." PhD diss., York University.

Movimento Femminista Romano. 1975. "Aborto a Londra." *Effe* 3 (1): 18.

Muraro, Luisa. 1985. "Il pensiero della differenza sessuale." Interviewed in *Donne e politica* 4 (July–August): n.p.

–. 1991. *L'ordine symbolico della madre*. Rome: Editori Riuniti.

Murphey, Timothy S. 2012. *Antonio Negri*. Cambridge: Polity Press.

Nancy and Danièle. 1980. "Indiennes! Oui ou non?" *Des luttes et des rires:* 26.

Napikoski, Linda. 2017. "Feminist Consciousness-Raising Groups." https://www.thoughtco.com/feminist-consciousness-raising-groups-3528954.

Negri, Anna. 2009. *Con un piede impigliato nella storia*. Milan: Feltrinelli.

Negri, Toni. 2004 [1997]. "Quell'intelligente moltitudine." In *Settantasette: la rivoluzione che viene*, ed. Sergio Bianchi and Lanfranco Caminiti, 89–100. Rome: DeriveApprodi.

Nolli, Maria Luisa. 1981. "Il movimento delle donne e il rapporto con le istituzioni." *I modi e le tematiche del femminismo a Napoli*. Atti del Convegno. Naples, 8–21 May, 1980, 56–60.

O'Leary, Véronique. 1982. "Pour ne pas repartir à zéro." Preface in *Québécoises deboutte!*, ed. Véronique O'Leary and Louise Toupin 1: 7–20.

–. 1987. "Conception féministe de la santé." In *Mémoire d'un forum de femmes: questions pratiques en éducation, en santé et sur le pouvoir*. Montréal: Centrale de l'enseignement du Québec.

O'Leary, Véronique, and Louise Toupin. 1982. *Québécoises Deboutte!* Vol. 1. Montréal: Les éditions du remue-ménage.

–. 1983. *Québécoises deboutte!* Vol. 2. Montréal: Les éditions du remue-ménage.

Ombra, Marisa. 2005. *Donne Manifeste: l'UDI attraverso i suoi manifesti, 1944–2004*. Milan: Il Saggiatore.

Paoli, Federica. 2008. "La controinformazione femminista nelle pagine di 'Effe.'" *Genesis: rivista della Società Italiana delle Storiche* 7 (1–2): 247–78.

–. 2010. "Diversità fantastiche: periodici del femminismo Romano nei primi anni ottanta." *Zapruder* 21 (January–April): 24–40.

–. 2011. *Pratiche di scrittura femminismo: la rivista "Differenze" 1976–1982*. Milan: Fondazione Elvira Badaracco, FrancoAngeli.

Paolucci, Gabriella. 1987. "Progettara al presente." *Memoria* 19–20 (1–2): 125–33.

–. 1991. "Amiche: figure dell'amicizia femminile e femminismo." *Memoria* 32 (2): 56–66.

Partisans. 1972 [1970]. "Libération des femmes: année zéro." Paris: François Maspéro, éditeur.

Passerini, Luisa. 2005. "Corpi e corpo collettivo: rapporti internazionali del primo femminismo radicale italiano." In *Il femminismo degli anni settanta*, ed. Teresa Bertilotti and Anna Scattigno, 181–96. Rome: Viella.

Pelletier, Francine. 1980. "Vu de la première rangée." *La vie en rose* (September–November): 30–32.

–. 1985. "La mort de l'indépendance." *La vie en rose* (February): 5, 19.

Pelletier, Pol. 2012. "Jovette Marchessault visionnaire." In *De l'invisible au visible: l'imaginaire de Jovette Marchessault*, ed. Roseanna Dufault and Celita Lamar, 39–44. Montréal: Les éditions du remue-ménage.

Péloquin, Marjolaine. 2007. *En prison pour la cause des femmes: la conquête du banc des jurés*. Montréal: Les éditions du remue-ménage.

Percovich, Luciana. 2005. *La coscienza nel corpo: donne, salute e medicina negli anni settanta*. Milan: Fondazione Elvira Badaracco, FrancoAngeli.

Percovich, Luciana, Franca Petronio, and Cesarina Damiani. 1994. *Donne del nord, donne del sud: verso una politica della relazione tra diversità, solidarità e conflitto*. Associazione per una Libera Università delle donne. Milan: FrancoAngeli.

Perilli, Vincenza. 2006. "'Sexe' et 'race' dans les féminismes italiens." *Les Cahiers du CEDREF* 14: 105–43. https://doi.org/10.4000/cedref.420.

Pesante, Luisa. 1977. "Il tempo della parola." *Quaderni Piacentini* 64: 35–41.

Pesanti, Rosangela. 2002. "Gli archivi dell'UDI e una storia da racontare." *Genesis* 1, 2: 212–16.

Petricola, Elena. 2005. "Parole da cercare: alcune reflessioni sul rapporto tra femminismo e movimenti politici degli anni settanta." In *Il femminismo degli anni settanta*, ed. Terese Bertilotti and Anna Scattigno, 199–224. Rome: Viela.

Phillips, Ruth B. 2011. "APEC at the Museum of Anthropology: The Politics of Site and the Poetics of Sight Bite." In *Imagining Resistance: Visual Culture and Activism in Canada*, ed. J. Keri Cronin and Kirsty Robertson, 171–91. Waterloo, ON: Wilfrid Laurier Press.

Piccirillo, Agnese. 1996. "La presa di coscienza." In *Femminismi a Torino*, ed. Piera Zumigliano, 349–80. Milan: FrancoAngeli.

Pifano, Danielle. 2004 [1997]. "L'Autonomia operaia romana." In *Settantasette: la rivoluzione che viene*, ed. Sergio Bianchi and Lanfranco Caminiti, 369–77. Rome: DeriveApprodi.

Piperno, Franco. 2004 [1997]. "La parabola del'77: dal 'lavoro astratto' al 'general intellect.'" In *Settantasette: la rivoluzione che viene*, ed. Sergio Bianchi and Lanfranco Caminiti, 101–28. Rome: DeriveApprodi.

Pomeranzi, Bianca Maria. 1984. "Differenza lesbica e lesbofemminismo." *Memoria* 13 (4): 72–78.

Pompei, Giuliana. 1975 [1972]. "Casa, Scuola, Fabbrica, Quartiere: Salario per il lavoro domestico." In *Femminismo e lotta di classe in Italia: analisi, documenti e prospettive*, ed. Biancamaria Frabotta, 113–26. Rome: Savelli.

Potvin, Claudine. 1991. "Entrevue avec Jovette Marchessault." *Voix et images* 16 (2 [47]) (Winter): 218–29. https://doi.org/10.7202/200895ar.

–. 2012. "L'inscription du visuel dans l'écriture: le 'voyage magnifique' de Jovette." In *De l'invisible au visible: l'imaginaire de Jovette Marchessault*, ed. Roseanna Dufault and Celita Lamar, 247–62. Montréal: Les éditions du remue-ménage.

Pravadelli, Véronica. 2010. "Women and Gender Studies, Italian Style." *European Journal of Women's Studies* 17 (1): 61–67. https://doi.org/10.1177/1350506809350863.

Purdy, Anthony. 1991. "Des cailloux blancs pour les forêts obscures." *Voix et images* 16 (2 [47]): 262–71. https://doi.org/10.7202/200899ar.

Ramondino, Fabrizia. 1993. "L'uomo? Un apprendista stregone." Interview in *Gli anni '70 e Napoli*, ed. Lucia Mastrodomenico, 88–93. Naples: Magistra Edizioni per le Specchio di Alice.

"Rapporto analitico e movimento delle donne." 1974. Milan: Fondazione Elvira Badaracco. 13 pp.

Raymond, Carole. 1980. "Le spectacle de la récupération." *La vie en rose* 1 (1): 10–11.

Rea, Ermanno. 2009. *Rosso Napoli: trilogia dei ritorni e degli addii*. Milan: BUR.

Rebick, Judy. 2005. *Ten Thousand Roses: The Making of a Feminist Revolution.* Toronto: Penguin, Canada.

Reid, Malcolm. 2009 [1972]. *Notre parti est pris: un jeune reporter chez les écrivains révolutionnaires du Québec, 1963–1970.* Trans. Héloïse Duhaine. Québec: Presses de l'Université Laval.

Reiter, Ester. 2016. *A Future without Hate or Need: The Promise of the Jewish Left in Canada.* Toronto: Between the Lines.

Remiddi, Laura. 1974. "Aborto: cosa significa per noi il progetto legge 'Fortuna.'" *Effe* 2 (10–11): 44–46.

Renaud, Thérèse. 2004. *Un passé recomposé.* Éditions Nota Bene.

Reyes, Alvaro. 2007. "Huey Newton e la nascita dell'autonomia." In *Gli autonomi: le storie, le lotte, le teorie,* ed. Sergio Bianchi and Lanfranco Caminiti, 454–76. vol. 2. Rome: DeriveApprodi.

Ricci, Amanda. 2017. "Contesting the Nation(s): Haitian and Mohawk Women's Activism in Montreal." In *Women's Activism and "Second Wave" Feminism,* ed. Barbara Molony and Jennifer Nelson, 273–94. London: Bloomsbury.

–. 2018. "Bâtir une communauté citoyenne: le militantisme chez les femmes autochtones pendant les années 1960 à 1990." *Recherches amérindiennes au Québec* 46 (1): 75–85. https://doi.org/10.7202/1038936ar.

Ricouart, Janine. 2012. "La question des origines dans le triptyque autobiographique de Jovette Marchessault." In *De l'invisible au visible: l'imaginaire de Jovette Marchessault,* ed. Roseanna Dufault and Celita Lamar, 91–109. Montréal: Les éditions du remue-ménage.

Rioux, Eliette. 1978. "Une minoritaire qui en a assez." *Les têtes de Pioche* 2–3 (February): 9.

Ripetto, Margherita. 1981. "Movimento di emancipazione e organizzazioni femminili cattoliche: spunti per un'analisi. " *DWF (Donnawomanfemme)* 16 (Spring): 40–53.

Risoldi, Chiara. 1983. "Il disagio della civiltà e l'agio delle donne." *Rinascita* (March): 26–27.

Roscoe, Will. 1998. *Changing Ones: Third and Fourth Genders in Native North America.* New York: St. Martin's Griffin.

Rossanda, Rossana. 1979. "Tre domande a Rossana Rossanda." *Differenze:* 23–26.

–. 1983. "Il tempo di esistere." *Orsaminore* 10 (March): 11–17.

–. 2004 [1997]. "Idee e non idee del '77." In *Settantasette: la rivoluzione che viene,* ed. Sergio Bianchi and Lanfranco Caminiti, 154–58. Rome: DeriveApprodi.

–. 2005. *La ragazza del secolo scorso.* Turin: Einaudi.

Rossi-Doria, Anna. 1978. "Conservazione e rottura nel movimento delle donne." *Ombre Rosse* 25: 12–16.

–. 1979. "Alcuni interrogativi, oggi." *Differenze* (special issue): 27–29.

–. 1981. "Rapporto tra storia e storia della donna." *I modi e le tematiche del femminismo a Napoli.* Atti del Convegno a Napoli, 8–22 May, 1980, 89–94. Naples: Comune di Napoli, Centro Studi Condizione della Donna.

–. 1984. "Nuova destra e movimento delle donne." *Memoria* 11–12 (2–3): 152–62.

–. 2005. "Ipotesi per una storia che verrà." In *Il femminismo degli anni settanta,* ed. Teresa Bertilotti and Anna Scattigno, 1–23. Rome: Viella.

–. 2007. *Dare forma al silenzio: scritti di storia politica delle donne.* Rome: Viella.

Rousseau, Christina. 2016. "Housework and Social Subversion: Wages, Housework and Feminist Activism in 1970s Italy and Canada." PhD diss., York University.

Roux, Patricia, Céline Perrin, Gaël Pannatier, and Valéry Cossy. 2005. "Le militantisme n'échappe pas au patriarcat." *Nouvelles questions féministes* 24 (3): 4–16. https://doi.org/10.3917/nqf.243.0004.

Rowbotham, Sheila. 1981. "The Women's Movement and Organizing for Socialism." In *Beyond the Fragments: Feminism and the Making of Socialism*, ed. Sheila Rowbotham, Lynne Segal, and Hilary Wainwright, 21–155. Boston: Alyson Publications.

–. 1996. "Mapping the Women's Movement." In *Mapping the Women's Movement*, ed. Monica Threlfall and Sheila Rowbotham, 1–16. London: Verso.

Rutter, Itala T.C. 1990. "Feminist Theory as Practice: Italian Feminism and the Work of Teresa de Lauretis and Dacia Maraini." *Women's Studies International Forum* 13 (6): 565–75. https://doi.org/10.1016/0277-5395(90)90051-x.

Sabatini, Alma. 1973. "Self-Help Clinic." *Effe* 1 (2): 48–49.

–. 1974. "Il piccolo gruppo: struttura di base del movimento femminista." *Effe* 2 (1): 1–2.

Said, Edward. 1993. *Culture and Imperialism*. New York: Vintage.

Saint-Jean, Armande. 1978. "Lettre ouverte à toutes mes sœurs *Têtes de Pioche*." *Les Têtes de Pioche* 3 (3): 2.

–. 1980. "Préface." In *Les Têtes de Pioche*. Collection complète, 5–10. Montréal: Les éditions du remue-ménage.

Saladin D'Anglure, Bernard. 1985. "Du projet PAR.AD.I au sexe des anges: notes et débats autour d'un troisième sexe." *Anthropologie et sociétés* 9 (3): 139–76. https://doi.org/10.7202/006293ar.

–. 2006. "The Inuit 'Third Gender.'" In *Aboriginality and Governance: A Multidisciplinary Perspective*, ed. Gordon Christie, 167–78. Penticton, BC: Theytus Books.

Sangster, Joan. 2010. "Radical Ruptures: Feminism, Labor, and the Left in the Long Sixties in Canada." *American Review of Canadian Studies* 40 (1): 1–21. https://doi.org/10.1080/02722010903536920.

–. 2011. "Looking Backwards: Re-Assessing Women and the Canadian Left." In *Through Feminist Eyes: Essays on Canadian Women's History*, 81–93. Edmonton: Athabasca University.

Sansfaçon, Jean-Robert. 1982. "Écologie: les paradoxes de la survie." *Le Temps fou* (June–August), 22–27.

Saraceno, Chiara. 2003. "Changes in Italian Families from the Sixties to the Present." In *Women's Work, the Family, and Social Policy*, ed. Daniela Del Boca and Margherita Repetto-Alaia, 1–32. New York: Peter Lang.

Sarrazin, Hélène. 1985. "Femmes terroristes: des sorcières comme les autres." *La vie en rose* 30 (October): 28–32.

Sartre, Jean-Paul, Michel Foucault, Felix Guattari, Gilles Deleuze, Roland Barthes, F. Wahl, Philippe Solers, D. Roche, P. Gavi, Maria-Antonietta Macciocchi, and C. Guillerme. 2004 [1977]. "L'apello degli intellettuali francese." In *Settantasette: la rivoluzione che viene*, ed. Sergio Bianchi and Lanfranco Caminiti, 238–50. Rome: DeriveApprodi.

Sassaroli, Sandra. 1977. "La posizione del CRAC." *Effe* (March): 19–20.

Sassaroli, Sandra, and Isabella Rossellini. 1975. "Commento sulla legge-truffa." *Effe* 3 (11): 2.

Schiavo, Maria. 2002. *Movimento a più voci: il femminismo degli anni Settanta attraverso il racconto di una protagonista*. Milan: Fondazione Elvira Badaracco FrancoAngeli.

Scott, Joan Wallach. 2011. *The Fantasy of Feminist History*. Durham, NC: Duke University Press.
"Secondo noi." 1976. *Differenze* 1: 3–6.
Segreteria dei collettivi politici di Milano. 2007 [1976]. "Agire collettivo e autonomo nella fase attuale." In *Gli autonomi: le storie, le lotte, le teorie*, ed. Sergio Bianchi and Lanfranco Caminiti, 185–95. Rome: DeriveApprodi.
Senatore, Giovanna. 1981. "Donne e salute." *I modo e le tematiche del femminismo a Napoli*. Atti del Convegno, Naples, 8–21 May, 1980: 38–40.
Seroni, Adriana. 1978. "Ragioni e torti del femminismo." In *La politica del femminismo: il movimento femminista, l'Unione delle donne italiane, le forze politiche di sinistra di fronte al femminismo nei documenti (1973–1976)*, ed. Biancamaria Frabotta, 216–26. Rome: Savelli.
Ship, Susan, Judith. 1991. "Au-delà de la solidarité féminine." *Revue québécoise de science politique* 19: 5–36. https://doi.org/10.7202/040680ar.
Signorelli, Amalia. n.d. "Prefazione." In *Interpreti e protagoniste del movimento femminista napolitano, 1970–1990*, ed. Conni Capobianco (Nausicaa), 1–5. Naples: Cornu Copia.
Simon, Sherry. 2004. "Malcolm Reid et la traversée de la ville." *Anthropologie et sociétés* 28 (3): 91–102. https://doi.org/10.7202/011284ar.
Smart, Patricia. 1998. *Les femmes du Refus Global*. Montréal: Boréal.
Smith, Andrea. 2005. *Conquest: Sexual Violence and American Indian Genocide*. Cambridge: South End Press.
Sofri, Adriano. 1978 [1975]. "Le cose buone, le cose cattive e il modo di affrontarle." In *La politica del femminismo: il movimento femminista, l'Unione delle donne italiane, le forze politiche di sinistra di fronte al femminismo nei documenti, 1973–1976*, ed. Biancamaria Frabotta, 246–56. Rome: Savelli.
Sottosopra. 1973. "Come e perché è stato fatto questo giornale: esperienze dei gruppi femministi in Italia." 1.
Spagnoletti, Rosalba. 1971. *I movimenti femministi in Italia*. Rome: Edizioni Samonà e Savelli.
Spivak, Gayatri Chakravorty. 1988a. "Can the Subaltern Speak?" In *Marxism and the Interpretation of Culture*, ed. Cary Nelson and Lawrence Grossberg, 271–313. Urbana: University of Illinois Press.
–. 1988b. "Subaltern Studies: Deconstructing Historiography." In *In Other Worlds: Essays in Cultural Politics*, 197–221. New York: Routledge.
–. 2012. "Interview with Gayatri Shakravorty Spivak." In *The Postcolonial Gramsci*, ed. Neelam Srivastava and Baidik Bhattacharya, 221–32. New York: Routledge.
Staderini, Michi. 1979a. "Ambiguità." *Differenze* (special issue): 16–17.
–. 1979b. "Parliamo di revoluzione." *Differenze* (special issue): 34–36.
Stasiulis, Davia K. 1999. "Relational Positionalities of Nationalisms, Racisms, and Feminisms." In *Between Women and the Nation: Nationalism, Transnational Feminism, and the State*, ed. Caren Kaplan, Norma Alarcón, and Minoo Moallem, 182–218. Durham, NC: Duke University Press.
St-Denis, Vera. 2007. "Feminism Is for Everybody: Aboriginal Women, Feminism and Diversity." In *Making Space for Indigenous Feminism*, ed. Joyce Green, 33–52. Halifax: Fernwood.
"Strutture e tipi di lavoro del gruppo." 1980. *Differenze* 11: 4–10.
Surprenant, Marie-Ève, and Mylène Biguaouette. 2013. *Les femmes changent la lutte au cœur du printemps québécois*. Montréal: Les éditions du remue-ménage.

Tagliaferri, Maricla. 1977. "La nostra informazione." *Effe* 5 (6): 13–18.

Takai, Yukari. 2008. *Gendered Passages: French-Canadian Migration to Lowell, Massachusetts, 1990–1920*. New York: Peter Lang.

Tani, Ilari. 2005. "Oltre il grido e il silenzio: la parola nei manifesti dell'UDI." In *Donne Manifeste: l'UDI attraverso i suoi manifesti 1944–2004*, ed. Marisa Ombra, 23–29. Milan: Il Saggiatore.

Tatafiore, Roberta. 1979. "Uno sguardo 'fuori' la lotta armata." *Differenze* (special issue): 9–10.

Tavola rotunda. 2004 [1997]. "Dissonanze," with the participation of Geraldina Colotti, Elettra Deiana, Manuela Fraire, Paola Masi, and Marina Pivette. In *Settantasette: la rivoluzione che viene*, ed. Sergio Bianchi and Lanfranco Caminiti, 219–37. Rome: DeriveApprodi.

Taylor, Judith. 1998. "Feminist Tactics and Friendly Fire in the Irish Women's Movement." *Gender and Society* 12 (6): 674–91. https://doi.org/10.1177/089124398012006005.

"Tenter l'érotisme." 1985. *La vie en rose* (July–August): 16–39.

Toupin, Louise. 2014. *Le salaire au travail ménager: chronique d'une lutte féministe internationale, 1972–1977*. Montréal: Les éditions du remue-ménage.

Tozzi, Silvia. 1978. "Aborto si discute ancora." *Effe* (May): 34–35.

–. 1979. "Riflettendo un anno doppo." *Differenze* 10 (November): 46–47.

–. 1984. "Il movimento delle donne, la salute, la scienza: l'esperienza di Simonetta Tosi." *Memoria* 11–12 (2–3): 128–44.

–. 1987. "Molecolare, creativita, materiale: la vicenda dei gruppi per la salute." *Memoria* 19–20 (1–2): 153–80.

Tremblay, Louise-Isabelle. 1978. "Réunion frustrante." *Les têtes de Pioche* 2–3 (February): 8.

Trimberger, Ellen Kay. 1979. "Women in the Old and New Left: The Evolution of a Politics of Personal Life." *Feminist Studies* 5 (3): 431–50. https://doi.org/10.2307/3177504.

Turcotte, Louise. 2013. "La révolution d'un point de vue." In *Monique Wittig: la pensée straight*, 17–22. Paris: Amsterdam.

Turone Lantin, Danielle. 1975. "Aborto: solo la donna può decidere." *Effe* 3 (1): 15.

Un groupe de femmes. 1972. "Introduction à l'édition de 1972." *Partisans* 5–7. Paris: François Maspéro.

Un groupe de femmes de Montréal. 1971. *Manifeste des femmes québécoises*. Montréal: L'étincelle.

Vallières, Pierre. 1994 [1968]. *Nègres blancs d'Amérique*. Montréal: Typo.

Vergerau-Dewey, Pascale S. 2012. "Passé recomposé, matriarcat jouissif et 'filliation' chez Jovette Marchessault." In *De l'invisible au visible: l'imaginaire de Jovette Marchessault*, ed. Roseanna Dufault and Celita Lamar, 127–53. Montréal: Les éditions du remue-ménage.

"Viaggio attraverso un'esperienza." 1976. *Differenze* 2: 3–7.

Virdis, Marina. 1978. "Il convegno sulla spiaggia." *Effe* 6 (4): 33–34.

–. 1979. "Una università tutta per se." *Effe* 7 (2): 28.

Viviani, Luciana (dell'Esecutivo Nazionale UDI). 1975. "La donna e la maternita nell'ambito delle reforme: convegno dell'Unione delle donne Italiane." In *Femminismo e lotta di classe in Italia: analisi, documenti e prospettive*, ed. Biancamaria Frabotta, 89–100. Rome: Savelli.

Warren, Jean-Philippe. 2007. *Ils voulaient changer le monde: le militantisme Marxiste-léniniste au Québec*. Montréal: VLB éditeurs.

–. 2008. *Une douce anarchie: les années 68 au Québec*. Montréal: Boréal.

Weeks, Kathi. 2011. *The Problem with Work: Feminism, Marxism, Antiwork Politics and the Postwork Imaginary*. Durham, NC: Duke University Press.

Wilson, Mark, and Conrad Rény. 1978. "Il me semble qu'on s'est déjà vu quelque part ... " *Le Temps fou* (June–August): 25–35.

Winter, Bronwyn. 2000. "Who Counts (or Doesn't Count) What as Feminist Theory? An Exercise in Dictionary Use." *Feminist Theory* 1 (1): 105–11. https://doi.org/10.1177/14647000022229092.

Zancan, Marina. 2003. "Conservare, progettare, comunicare." In *Archivi del femminismo. Conservare, progettare, comunicare,* 9–20. Milan: Fondazione Elvira Badaracco.

Ziadah, Rafeef. 2013. "Art for Palestine: 'Renarrating' History and the Present." In *Organize! Building from the Local for Global Justice*, ed. Aziz Choudry, Jill Hanley, and Eric Shragge, 111–22. Oakland, CA: PM Press.

Zuffa, Gracia. 1987. "Le doppie militanze: donna comunista, donna femminista." *Memoria* 19–20 (1–2): 38–48.

Zumaglino, Piera. 1996. *Femminismi a Torino*. Milan: FrancoAngeli.

Index